Verónica Rivera Pelayo

DESIGN AND APPLICATION OF QUANTIFIED SELF APPROACHES FOR REFLECTIVE LEARNING IN THE WORKPLACE

Design and Application of Quantified Self Approaches for Reflective Learning in the Workplace

by
Verónica Rivera Pelayo

KIT Scientific Publishing

Dissertation, genehmigt von der Fakultät für Wirtschaftswissenschaften des Karlsruher Instituts für Technologie (KIT), 2015

Tag der mündlichen Prüfung: 2. Februar 2015
Referenten: Prof. Dr. Rudi Studer, Univ.-Prof. Dr. Stefanie Lindstaedt

Impressum

KIT Scientific Publishing

Karlsruher Institut für Technologie (KIT)
KIT Scientific Publishing
Straße am Forum 2
D-76131 Karlsruhe

KIT Scientific Publishing is a registered trademark of Karlsruhe Institute of Technology. Reprint using the book cover is not allowed.

www.ksp.kit.edu

Print on Demand 2015

ISBN 978-3-7315-0406-1
DOI 10.5445/KSP/1000047818

To my love Jan & my family — mamá, papá y hermana

Abstract

Learning by reflection has been identified as one of the core processes for improving work performance. However, theories of reflective learning are of a cognitive or sociological nature and do not sufficiently consider the use of technologies to enhance reflective learning processes. The aim of this thesis is to investigate if and how Quantified Self approaches can aid reflective learning at the workplace. Quantified Self (QS) is a collaboration of users and tool makers who share an interest in self-knowledge through self-tracking, resulting in a variety of tools to collect personally relevant information. These are rather experimental approaches and currently there is no unifying framework that clusters and connects these many emergent tools with the goals and benefits of their use.

From a theoretical perspective, this thesis contributes with an integrated model that provides a framework for technical support of reflective learning, derived from unifying reflective learning theory with a conceptual framework of Quantified Self tools. To instantiate our approach, mobile and web-based applications have been iteratively designed and developed following a design-based research methodology.

Within the first use case of the empirical validation, we introduce and evaluate mood self-tracking in distinct work scenarios of the telecommunications and IT sector. The second use case explores the impact of reflection on trading behavior by integrating mood self-tracking in experimental asset markets. In the third use case, an application to track feedback from audiences enables reflective learning support for lecturers and public speakers. These applications have been evaluated in thirteen studies that demonstrate the support of reflective learning and measure the impact on work performance. The results of these user studies lead to the validation of the holistic approach through a body of empirical application-oriented insights. This thesis provides a novel approach for reflective learning support by transferring and adapting practices from the Quantified Self to workplace settings.

Acknowledgments

I would like to express my profound gratitude to Prof. Dr. **Rudi Studer** for his constant support, unconditional supervision and useful feedback throughout this research work. For me it was an honor to have him as my *Doktorvater* and be part of his excellent team. I am deeply thankful to him for giving me the freedom to be creative in my research in an innovative field, yet being always present with his advice and mentorship. I am also proud of having Univ.-Prof. Dr. **Stefanie Lindstaedt** as my co-advisor. I would like to thank her for her generosity and hospitality, for sharing with me her extensive experience and knowledge, and for her valuable time and comments before, during and after my stay in Graz. It was a pleasure having the advice of these two great scientists and leaders. I would also like to thank Prof. Dr. **Thomas Setzer** and Prof. Dr. **Oliver Stein** for taking the time to review my thesis, giving their feedback from the point of view of their research fields, and serving on my committee.

I would like to give my deepest gratitude and thanks to **Valentin Zacharias**, who supervised my work, guided me during the whole journey and offered me encouragement. Thanks for introducing me to the Quantified Self; it has not only contributed to my innovative research, but also changed my life. This thesis would not have been possible without him and his invaluable support. I am particularly grateful to **Lars Müller** for being such a great fellow adventurer in MIRROR and for his valuable contribution to my research. Special thanks go to **Simone Braun** who was not only an unconditional colleague and friend but also a role model from whom I could learn so much. Had it not been for her, I would have not embarked on this exciting experiential academic journey I undertook. Thanks to **Andreas Schmidt** and **Christine Kunzmann** for their supporting advice and constant encouragement. I will never have enough words to thank all of them the inspiring discussions, valuable feedback as well as great help on my journey to accomplish this thesis and to become a good researcher.

I thank all my colleagues and students at FZI Forschungszentrum Informatik and all the people I worked with in MIRROR for their feedback, help and collaboration in the realization of this work. Special thanks to **Philipp Astor** and **Achim Hendriks** for their support and great joint work with the MoodMarket as well as to **Angela Fessl** for our joint work with the MoodMap App. I am particularly grateful to **Athanasios Mazarakis** for so many constructive discussions, his valuable advice and significant help. I also want to thank **Heike Döhmer**, **Mercè Müller-Gorchs**, **Basil Ell**, **Julia Hoxha**, **Markus Ewald**, and **Christian Reichelt** for their friendship and contribution to my daily work and life.

I thank all the students that contributed to this research. I hope you have learned from working with me as much as I learned working along with you. Particularly, I would like to thank **Inra Kühn** for her valuable input and unconditional help, as well as **Johannes Munk**, **Emanuel Lacić**, **Tomislav Đuričić**, and **Leif Becker** for their support and great joint work.

I also thank **Karlsruhe House of Young Scientists** which financially supported my stay in Graz and the **European Commission** for funding the MIRROR Project. Thanks to all collaborating organizations (especially to my close collaborators **Ellen Leenarts**, **Hans Dirkzwager**, **Andrew Patterson**, **Marco Parigi** and **Michele Biolè**) and anonymous participants in my studies.

Thanks to all the people who have influenced my life and career. My immense thank to **Jan Gutzeit** for always believing in me and accompanying me in good and bad times. I am so lucky and grateful to have Jan in my life. I would like to express my deepest and most sincere appreciation to my parents **Mª Carmen** and **José Antonio** and sister **Noemí**: *gracias mamá, papá y hermana, por vuestro amor incondicional y por apoyarme en cada uno de mis días. Gracias por haberme transmitido todos esos valores que hacen de mí la persona que soy hoy y por ayudarme a llegar hasta aquí y seguir adelante. Espero que estéis orgullosos de mí.* Thank you very much to my whole **family** and my **friends**, who have supported me from a distance and encouraged me to overcome every difficulty

For those whom I may have left out, you may be the last but you are certainly not the least. I greatly appreciate all your invaluable contributions.

This would not have been possible without you. Thank you!

Contents

II Implementation and Empirical Validation

III Conclusions

Appendix

List of Figures

List of Tables

"Learning is experience. Everything else is just information."

(Albert Einstein)

1. Introduction

The challenge of lifelong learning involves learning new marketable skills as well as personal development of individuals in their many roles as family members, citizens and workers [Passarelli and Kolb, 2012]. Formal learning is insufficient to lead this development and efficiently support the constant adaptations required in today's dynamic and fast-paced workplaces. Therefore, learning mainly takes place in the form of informal processes, which involve reflection on what has been experienced and observed [Kolb, 1984]. For instance, a call taker in a call center dealing with a challenging customer will only be able to succeed if she applies her knowledge resulting from previous experiences and similar situations. However, despite the widespread acknowledgment of the importance of reflective learning, it has mainly been considered on a theoretical level and the question of how to use technology to support it in the workplace is still open.

1.1. Motivation and Problem Statement

Learning by reflection has been identified as one of the core processes for improving work performance [Eraut and Hirsh, 2007]. According to Boud et al. [1985], learning by reflection (or *reflective learning*) offers the chance of learning by returning to and evaluating past work and personal experiences in order to improve future experiences and promote continuous learning.

Theories of reflective learning are currently of a cognitive or sociological nature and do not sufficiently consider the use of technologies to enhance reflective learning processes. Although there is a wide range of facilitating techniques for reflective learning especially in formal education (e.g. [Sugerman et al., 2000; Brockbank and McGill, 2007]) and several approaches have shown initiatives to support reflective learning through technology in different settings [Strampel and Oliver, 2007; Fleck, 2009; Krogstie et al., 2013], we lack an unifying framework that describes the role of technology in the reflective process and guides the design of tracking applications for reflection support at work.

Recent advances in technology offer a plethora of possibilities for this technical support. Sensor technologies are being improved, mobile technologies and devices are becoming more widespread, and the Internet provides ubiquitous access to information. This growth of technological solutions has driven the emergence of a community called the Quantified Self (QS)[1], a collaboration of users and tool makers who share an interest in self-knowledge through self-tracking, with the principle *"self-knowledge through numbers."* This interest results in a variety of tools to collect personally relevant information with the purpose of gaining self-knowledge about one's behaviors, habits and thoughts. This personal behavior tracking includes basic activities like sleeping, eating or exercising, as well as factors influencing behavior like emotions or mood, and context information like location, pollution or weather. The Quantified Self movement investigates not only the gathering of data but also what to do with the new tracking capabilities, the form of the gathered data, the risks that it can entail, and the possible goals that are to be achieved. Hence, Q-Selfers offer us a useful perspective from which to re-examine the current design of self-tracking technologies and ways to improve them [Choe et al., 2014].

One of the success factors of the QS is the approach to make vaguely defined aspects of our lives measurable; for instance, our mood or the quality of our sleep. Therefore, QS approaches offer a rich source of data that has not been available for learning processes before. Their tracking initiatives offer a wide potential for awareness augmentation, quantification of abstract measures and analysis of data that were not possible to perform until now or not considered to be of relevance for learning processes. Approaches like emotional awareness provided; e.g., by self-tracking, or enrichment of data provided; e.g., by annotation, can broadly support learners' experiences and shed light on the process of personal learning and improvement. However, these are rather experimental approaches and currently there is no unifying framework that clusters and connects these many emergent tools with the goals and benefits of their use. Recent research work has concentrated on understanding the motivation behind the QS community [Gimpel et al., 2013; Rooksby et al., 2014] and identifying main challenges and pitfalls from their experiences [Choe et al., 2014], but there is no elaborated theory behind it that helps us understand, systematize and transfer their approaches.

Taking into account these two strands, we can conclude that QS approaches are pragmatic with experimentation being their main drive, whereas reflective learning is driven by theories that are evolving since the nineteenth century. On the one hand, reflective learning provides strong contributions towards understanding the underlying mental process, but often refers to pen and paper diaries to provide support and do not consider the major changes that happened in workplace environments during the last decades. On the other hand, the novel approaches used by the Quantified Self have the potential to support reflective learning by guiding the capturing of the right data not only in daily life but also

[1] `http://quantifiedself.com`

at the workplace. In order to achieve this, the introduction of self-tracking in a work environment has to account for the unique requirements and challenges that professionals face in each work domain. Since this gap and the challenges that arise have not been investigated yet, our objective is to bring these two strands together and show how QS approaches can support reflective learning processes at the workplace.

1.2. Research Questions

This thesis aims at investigating if and how Quantified Self approaches can aid learning. To this end, we have identified four sub-problems and derived the corresponding following research questions (RQ):

- RQ1: *How can Quantified Self principles and tools support reflective learning at work?*
- RQ2: *Can self-reporting QS applications capture and quantify data about our daily work activities as basis for the support of reflective learning?*
- RQ3: *What different data visualizations and motivation techniques foster learning processes by facilitating making sense of the data?*
- RQ4: *Can learning based on data from own personal and work life improve the learner's work?*

The first research question tackles the general approach of how Quantified Self can support reflective learning based on an analysis of both strands. Research questions two and three refer to the design of reflective learning support with concrete approaches in selected work domains. With the final research question we strive to investigate the improvements at personal and professional level that can be achieved.

1.3. Research Approach

The first step of this thesis is to show how Quantified Self approaches can support reflective learning processes. In order to achieve this, we develop a theoretical framework based on the analysis of both strands; i.e., reflective learning theories and the Quantified Self, including their methods and tools.

Based on this theoretical framework, we build on design-based research to instantiate QS approaches by developing and evaluating prototyping applications. Wang and Hannafin [2005] define design-based research as *"a systematic but flexible methodology aimed to improve educational practices through iterative analysis, design, development, and implementation, based on collaboration among researchers and practitioners in real-world settings and leading to contextually-sensitive design principles and theories."* Following this methodology, the development of our prototypes is based on an iterative cycle with the following phases: definition of collaborative requirements, design of prototypes, evaluation and subsequent redesign. In this design-based approach, we use participatory design methods by involving users in the design process and thus enhancing the quality of the resulting system [Bødker et al., 2000]. Following Muller et al. [1997], participatory design allows *"the ultimate users of the software make effective contributions that reflect their own perspectives and needs, somewhere in the design and development life cycle of the software."* This ensures that not only the quality of the software design and its development are improved, but it adheres to the end users' needs and therefore increases the acceptance of the applications.

Our research questions two to four are investigated through three use cases following the approach explained below:

1. **Identification of a work context and its requirements.**
   Through the analysis of different work contexts, we aim at identifying which requirements must be met, as well as which processes and tasks could be improved. In this analysis, we pay special attention to which data are available and which data could be made available. The instantiation of reflective processes is analyzed, too, in order to identify at which stage of the reflective process an application will offer support.

2. **Iterative development of an application.**
   Once the context is selected and the data to be captured is defined, a first prototype of the application is developed. During the development, several design choices are implemented regarding capturing methods, data formats, user interface, data analysis and overall impact on the user. The main goal is having a first prototype which can be evaluated in the real context where it will be finally deployed. This allows us to receive feedback directly from the end users (participatory development) and iteratively improve the prototype. Each of these evaluations can tackle several criteria; e.g. user acceptance, user interface or technical aspects. In this iterative process we distinguish between design studies and formative evaluations. The main goal of a design study is to inform the design of the developed app. Diagnostic techniques are used to provide qualitative feedback which is then used to guide the software development of the next app version. Users may not be from the target group or the app would not be integrated in their real work environment. In formative evaluations, the application is integrated in a real work environment and evaluated with

target users. Therefore, they contribute to investigate the aspects addressed by our research questions two and three.

3. **Summative evaluation.**
   The application is evaluated at larger scale and in a real world context, with the goal of answering our fourth research question. The main goal is to measure the impact of reflective learning and analyze any existing barriers. In order to prove the impact of reflective learning, Key Performance Indicators and other metrics are analyzed.

Finally, the empirical application-oriented insights gained from the conducted studies lead to the validation and extension of the developed integrated model. Figure 1.1 illustrates the research approach described above.

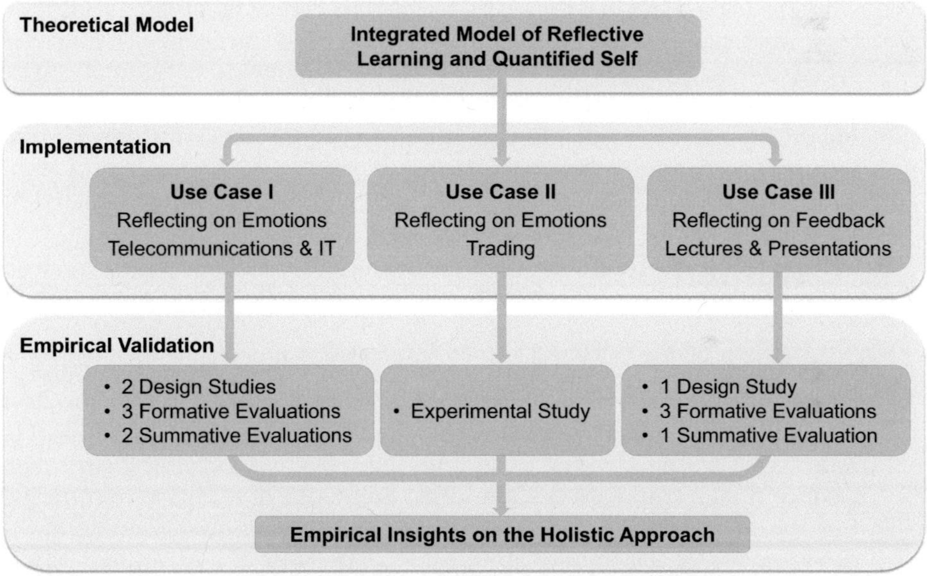

Figure 1.1.: Research approach and contributions

We have empirically investigated the design and application of Quantified Self approaches to support reflective learning in three work domains. These work contexts were selected because reflective practice is seen as promising but it has not been integrated in their work processes yet. The three selected work scenarios encompass:

- **Telecommunications and IT sector:** Professionals working in consultancy services, software development and call centers face highly demanding reoccurring situations with their customers. Being aware of how their emotions influence their everyday tasks, the communication with customers as well as their colleagues has the potential to improve their work performance. Within this use case, we introduce and evaluate mood self-tracking in several work scenarios of the telecommunications and IT sector.
- **Experimental trading:** Financial decisions of traders and investors can be affected by their emotional states. Therefore, learning approaches to increase emotional awareness and regulation have the potential to improve financial decision performance. To address these issues, we investigate the integration of mood self-tracking in experimental asset markets.
- **Lectures and presentations:** When addressing an audience, professionals who participate in talks may benefit from receiving feedback about their presentation skills and performance. Comparing the speaker's own perspective with how it is perceived by the participants is a potential source for reflection triggering. Our research in this use case addresses reflecting on captured feedback in presentations, which are daily activities for lecturers, researchers and consultants.

1.4. Contributions

The investigation of the outlined research questions has led to the following three main contributions of this thesis:

a. An integrated model that constitutes a framework for technical support of reflective learning, derived from unifying reflective learning theory with a conceptual framework of Quantified Self tools. In addition to ordering this strand of research, this framework provides an understanding of the design space for this kind of applications. Therefore, the Integrated Model of Reflective Learning and Quantified Self (IMRLQS) is the basis for the development of this thesis by categorizing and defining which dimensions can be supported by QS applications.

b. The instantiation of our approach through three self-reporting applications. These prototyping applications allow the quantification and gathering of data in three different use cases: (i) mood tracking in the telecommunications and IT sector, (ii) mood tracking in trading, and (iii) capturing of feedback in lectures and professional presentations. These are novel applications that have adopted QS techniques and adapted them in order to be successfully integrated in real workplace settings.

c. A framework of empirical application-oriented insights gained from thirteen user studies. The results of the conducted design studies and evaluations lead to the validation of the holistic approach of applying Quantified Self approaches to support reflective learning at work. The resulting insights provide best practices and pitfalls from a socio-technical perspective and thereby inform the future design of this type of applications.

1.5. Thesis Structure

This thesis is structured in three parts. In the first chapters of Part I, we provide the theoretical and pragmatic background that establishes the foundation of our approach. In Chapter 2, we introduce the theories of reflective learning (Section 2.1) and describe the Quantified Self community (Section 2.2). Chapter 3 presents the Integrated Model of Reflective Learning and Quantified Self (IMRLQS), which constitutes the unification of these two strands on a theoretical level.

The second part of this thesis (Part II) describes the design, implementation and evaluation of several QS approaches in selected work scenarios. Chapter 4 details the conception of the MoodMap App and the seven user studies conducted during the design and implementation process. The investigation of mood self-tracking in trading and the description of the conducted MoodMarket experiment are detailed in Chapter 5. Chapter 6 presents the design and development of the Live Interest Meter (LIM) before giving an overview of the five studies that have provided insights on the capturing of feedback for reflective learning. At the end of this part, gained empirical and application-oriented insights are discussed and illustrated in Chapter 7.

The final Part III concludes the thesis by summarizing our contributions and giving an outlook on future work in Chapter 8.

1.6. Publications

Parts of this thesis' contents have been published and/or presented in several venues. In order to adhere to the common framework of this thesis, published contents haven been updated and extended. The European Integrated Project MIRROR[2] has been serving as background of this research work. Consequently, user studies conducted in this thesis and core contents have been published

[2] http://www.mirror-project.eu

within the context of the MIRROR Project. In the following, we detail the publications of the author that have already been peer-reviewed and relate them to the main achieved contributions.

The Integrated Model of Reflective Learning and Quantified Self (IMRLQS) as the first framework that considers the unification of these two strands has been published in the following venues:

- V. Rivera-Pelayo, V. Zacharias, L. Müller, and S. Braun. Applying Quantified Self Approaches to Support Reflective Learning. In *Proceedings of the 2nd International Conference on Learning Analytics and Knowledge*, LAK '12, pages 111–114, New York, NY, USA, 2012a. ACM. ISBN 978-1-4503-1111-3. doi: 10.1145/2330601.2330631
- V. Rivera-Pelayo, V. Zacharias, L. Müller, and S. Braun. A Framework for Applying Quantified Self Approaches to Support Reflective Learning. In I. Arnedillo Sánchez and P. Isaías, editors, *Proceedings of the IADIS International Conference Mobile Learning 2012, 11-13 March 2012, Berlin, Germany*, pages 123–131, 2012b. ISBN 978-972-8939-66-3.
- V. Rivera-Pelayo. Applying Quantified Self Approaches to Support Reflective Learning, September 2012. URL `https://www.academia.edu/7608381`. Doctoral Consortium Track at MobileHCI 2012, 21-24 September 2012, San Francisco, USA
- L. Müller, M. Divitini, S. Mora, V. Rivera-Pelayo, and W. Stork. Context Becomes Content: Sensor Data for Computer-Supported Reflective Learning. *IEEE Transactions on Learning Technologies*, 8(1):111–123, January 2015. ISSN 1939-1382. doi: 10.1109/TLT.2014.2377732

The design and development of the MoodMap App, along with the insights gained on mood tracking to support reflective learning have been published in:

- S. Mora, V. Rivera-Pelayo, and L. Müller. Supporting Mood Awareness in Collaborative Settings. In *Proceedings of the 7th International Conference on Collaborative Computing: Networking, Applications and Worksharing (CollaborateCom '11)*, pages 268–277, October 2011
- A. Fessl, V. Rivera-Pelayo, V. Pammer, and S. Braun. Mood Tracking in Virtual Meetings. In A. Ravenscroft, S. Lindstaedt, C. Delgado-Kloos, and D. Hernández-Leo, editors, *21st Century Learning for 21st Century Skills*, volume 7563 of *Lecture Notes in Computer Science*, pages 377–382. Springer Berlin Heidelberg, 2012. ISBN 978-3-642-33262-3. doi: 10.1007/978-3-642-33263-0_30

- V. Rivera-Pelayo and M. Kohaupt. Comparing Objective and Subjective Methods to Support Reflective Learning: an Experiment on the Influence on Affective Aspects. In T. Holocher-Ertl, C. Kunzmann, L. Müller, V. Rivera-Pelayo, A. P. Schmidt, and C. Wolf, editors, *Motivational and Affective Aspects in Technology Enhanced Learning (MATEL) : Proceedings of the MATEL Workshop 2013-2014*, volume 26. KIT, Karlsruhe, 2015. URL `http://nbn-resolving.org/urn:nbn:de:swb:90-480487`
- A. Fessl, G. Wesiak, V. Rivera-Pelayo, S. Feyertag, and V. Pammer. In-App Reflection Guidance for Workplace Learning. In *Design for Teaching and Learning in a networked World - Proceedings of the 10th European Conference on Technology Enhanced Learning (EC-TEL '15)*. September 2015. To appear
- V. Rivera-Pelayo, A. Fessl, L. Müller, and V. Pammer. Introducing Mood Self-Tracking at Work: Empirical Insights from Call Centers. Manuscript submitted for publication, in prep

The experimental study with the MoodMarket conducted to investigate mood tracking in trading was included in:

- V. Rivera-Pelayo, P. J. Astor, A. Hendriks, and M. T. P. Adam. Investigating Reflective Learning in Trading: Mood Self-tracking in Financial Decision Making. Working paper, Karlsruhe Institute of Technology (KIT), 2015

We have described the conception of the Live Interest Meter (LIM) and its usage to investigate the capturing of feedback for reflective learning support in the following articles:

- V. Rivera-Pelayo, J. Munk, V. Zacharias, and S. Braun. Live Interest Meter: Learning from Quantified Feedback in Mass Lectures. In *Proceedings of the Third International Conference on Learning Analytics and Knowledge*, LAK '13, pages 23–27, New York, NY, USA, April 2013a. ACM. ISBN 978-1-4503-1785-6. doi: 10.1145/2460296.2460302
- V. Rivera-Pelayo, E. Lacić, V. Zacharias, and R. Studer. LIM App: Reflecting on Audience Feedback for Improving Presentation Skills. In D. Hernández-Leo, T. Ley, R. Klamma, and A. Harrer, editors, *Scaling up Learning for Sustained Impact - Proceedings of the 8th European Conference on Technology Enhanced Learning (EC-TEL '13)*, volume 8095 of *Lecture Notes in Computer Science*, pages 514–519. Springer Berlin Heidelberg, September 2013b. ISBN 978-3-642-40813-7. doi: 10.1007/978-3-642-40814-4_48
- B. S. Morschheuser, V. Rivera-Pelayo, A. Mazarakis, and V. Zacharias. Gamifying Quantified Self Approaches for Learning: an Experiment with the Live Interest Meter. In *Learning and Diversity in the Cities of the Future. Proceedings of the 4th International Conference on Personal Learning Environments, PLE Conference '13*, pages 66–78. Logos Verlag Berlin, 2014a.

ISBN 978-3-8325-3811-8. URL http://www.logos-verlag.de/cgi-bin/buch/isbn/3811

- B. S. Morschheuser, V. Rivera-Pelayo, A. Mazarakis, and V. Zacharias. Interaction and Reflection with Quantified Self and Gamification: an Experimental Study. *Journal of Literacy and Technology*, 15(2):136–156, 2014b. URL http://www.literacyandtechnology.org/volume-15-number-2-june-2014.html

Additionally, the following exploratory and ethnographic studies have contributed to our understanding of the requirements for the support of reflective learning in workplace settings.

- A. Fessl, V. Rivera-Pelayo, L. Müller, V. Pammer, and S. Lindstaedt. Motivation and user acceptance of using physiological data to support individual reflection. In *2nd International Workshop on Motivational and Affective Aspects in Technology Enhanced Learning (MATEL '11)*, 2011. URL http://ceur-ws.org/Vol-957/matel11_submission_5.pdf
- L. Müller, V. Rivera-Pelayo, C. Kunzmann, and A. Schmidt. From Stress Awareness to Coping Strategies of Medical Staff: Supporting Reflection on Physiological Data. In A. A. Salah and B. Lepri, editors, *Human Behavior Understanding*, volume 7065 of *Lecture Notes in Computer Science*, pages 93–103. Springer Berlin Heidelberg, 2011b. ISBN 978-3-642-25445-1. doi: 10.1007/978-3-642-25446-8_11
- A. Schmidt, C. Kunzmann, S. Braun, T. Holocher-Ertl, U. Cress, A. Mazarakis, L. Müller, and V. Rivera-Pelayo, editors. *Proceedings of the 2nd and 3rd International Workshops on Motivational and Affective Aspects*, volume 957 of *CEUR Workshop Proceedings*, MATEL 2011 and 2012, Palermo, Italy, Sep 20, 2011 and Saarbrücken, Germany, Sep 18, 2012, 2012. CEUR-WS.org. URL http://ceur-ws.org/Vol-957/. ISSN 1613-0073
- L. Müller, V. Rivera-Pelayo, and S. Heuer. Persuasion and reflective learning: closing the feedback loop. In *Persuasive Technology. Design for Health and Safety*, pages 133–144. Springer, 2012
- T. Holocher-Ertl, C. Kunzmann, L. Müller, V. Rivera-Pelayo, and A. P. Schmidt. Motivational and Affective Aspects in Technology Enhanced Learning: Topics, Results and Research Route. In D. Hernández-Leo, T. Ley, R. Klamma, and A. Harrer, editors, *Scaling up Learning for Sustained Impact - Proceedings of the 8th European Conference on Technology Enhanced Learning (EC-TEL '13)*, volume 8095 of *Lecture Notes in Computer Science*, pages 460–465. Springer Berlin Heidelberg, 2013. ISBN 978-3-642-40813-7. doi: 10.1007/978-3-642-40814-4_39

Part I.

Theoretical Model

Overview

The goal of this part is to introduce the theoretical and pragmatic background of our work (Chapter 2), which is the basis of our theoretical model. The theoretical model presented in Chapter 3 consists in the unification of theories from reflective learning and approaches from the Quantified Self.

Reflective learning has been identified as a core process for improving work performance [Eraut and Hirsh, 2007; Høyrup, 2004]. Despite the existence of substantial theoretical work, diverse theories of reflective learning provide different definitions of and views on the role of reflection. In addition, none of these theories sufficiently considers the use of technologies to enhance reflective learning processes. We present a review of existing reflective learning theories and motivate the **theoretical background** of our model (Section 2.1).

On the pragmatic side, new kinds of lifelogging approaches pursued by a community known as Quantified Self (QS)[3]are becoming increasingly popular. Quantified Self is a collaboration of users and tool makers who share an interest in self-knowledge through self-tracking with the principle "self-knowledge through numbers." This interest results in a variety of tools to collect personally relevant information for self-reflection and self-monitoring, with the purpose of gaining knowledge about one's own behaviors, habits and thoughts. As part of the **pragmatic background**, we present a review of the approach followed by the Quantified Self and describe a survey of tools found in this community (Section 2.2).

The QS community and their tools are relevant for research on reflective learning at work because they aim at stimulating reflection, a core process for improving work performance [Eraut and Hirsh, 2007; Høyrup, 2004]. Similar data tracking processes take place in organizations such as call centers, which define and track Key Performance Indicators (KPIs) to facilitate reflection on work processes [Colombino et al., 2014]. While reflection is often understood as a cognitive process which enables an individual to learn, it can also be understood as a social process, that enables teams or organizations to learn [Høyrup, 2004]. In organizational settings, collaborative reflection enables the "collaborative re-design of work" [Prilla et al., 2013] by transforming work experiences into

[3] `http://quantifiedself.com`

applicable lessons learned. Self-tracking technology therefore has the potential to support reflection and awareness (i) as enabling technology for individual or collaborative self-tracking, (ii) by facilitating awareness via suitable data representations and (iii) supporting the interactive exploration and analysis of data within reflection sessions [Krogstie et al., 2012].

In an approach to join these two streams, we present a **model** that shows how QS approaches can support the process of learning by reflection and informs the design of new QS tools for informal learning purposes (Chapter 3). The starting point for the design of the framework was the survey of several QS tools, which allowed the analysis of the characteristics these tools may have in common. In order to establish the connection with reflective learning, the gathering of data by these tools is a relevant process to support the re-calling of experiences that form the basis for reflective learning. Finally, we instantiate our model for two applications known from the Quantified Self Community for exemplary purposes.

This model aims at outlining the possible design space and its implications for learning. This informs the subsequent design, implementation and evaluation of applications for reflective learning, which were deployed and validated in different workplace scenarios (Part II).

2. Background

2.1. Reflective Learning at Work

Decades of research on reflective learning have highlighted different aspects of reflective learning, leading to multiple theories [Dewey, 1938; Kolb, 1984; Boud et al., 1985; Schön, 1987]. Hence, it is difficult to define a shared understanding about reflection. In the following some of the most important approaches are briefly summarized. A more detailed description and discussion of existing approaches can be found in Moon [1999].

Nearly all research on reflective learning refers back to the idea of experiential learning by Dewey [1938]. According to Dewey, we learn by comparing our expectations to what we experience. Our expectations form a continuity that is built on former experiences. We learn by adapting this continuity in interaction with the environment or as Dewey puts it: *"Continuity and interaction in their active union with each other provide the measure to educative significance and value of the experience."* Dewey's work is mainly concerned with the benefits of reflective thinking for learning. Emotional aspects are rather neglected.

Boud et al. [1985] explicitly sheds light on these affective aspects and describes reflection as a cyclic process. According to Boud, attending to feelings is a major aspect of the reflection process.

Kolb [1984] also describes experiential learning in the form of a cyclic process; the so-called Kolb Cycle. Reflective observation is one of its four components. This implies that reflection is a process that is not only involved in reinterpreting existing experiences but also in the initial perception and interpretation of the raw experience. This cultivation of the capacity to reflect in action (while doing something) and on action (after having done it) has become an important feature of professional training programs in many disciplines [Schön, 1987].

One example building on this approach of reflective practice is presented by Daudelin, who defines reflection as *"the process of stepping back from an experience to ponder, carefully and persistently, its meaning to the self through the development of inferences; learning is the creation of meaning from past or current events that serves as a guide for future behavior"* [Daudelin, 1996]. Her approach is tailored to her work on reflective practice in the domain of management support.

In summary, there is a vast body of research, but this research does not take into consideration the possibilities provided by technology; i.e., these theories do not consider the major changes in the workplace in the last decades, including advances in technology to support learning processes (e.g., social media, mobile devices, data availability, etc.). Even later work like Moon [1999] and Daudelin [1996] use only traditional instruments like learning journals and structured interviews. Therefore, we were looking for a theory that provides insights into the cognitive processes and can be a basis for the integration of technology into the reflection process. We chose the model introduced by Boud et al. [1985] as theory behind our framework because it considers the complete cognitive process, including affective aspects, but does not define the concrete activities around this process or a specific domain.

2.1.1. Reflective Learning by Boud et al.

In the model by Boud et al., reflective learning refers to *"those intellectual and affective activities in which individuals engage to explore their experiences in order to lead to new understandings and appreciations"* [Boud et al., 1985]. Therefore, the reflective process is based on the experiences of the learner, which are considered as *"the total response of a person to a situation, including behavior, ideas and feelings."* The process described by Boud et al. consists of three stages, in which the learner re-evaluates past experiences by attending to its various aspects, and thereby producing outcomes. The defined outcomes can be cognitive, affective or behavioral. The reflection process and its context, experiences and outcomes, are depicted in Figure 2.1.

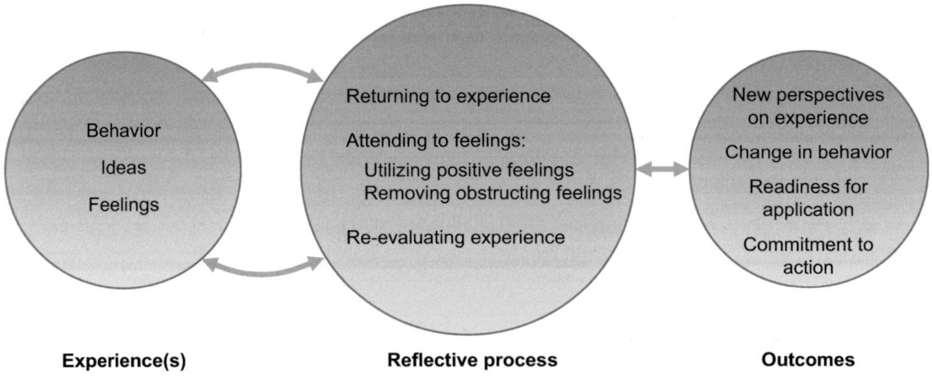

Figure 2.1.: The reflection process in context by Boud et al. [1985]

A detailed look at the stages of the reflection process in this model provides insights into the involved cognitive processes and opportunities for support. The learner starts by returning to an experience and thereby recalls details about an event or incident. Boud et al. suggest being as objective as possible during this stage and *"refrain from making judgments."* However, recollected events are most probably connected to emotions. These should not lead to judgments but the learner should be aware of them after the first stage. When constructing the description of the experience, *"acknowledging feelings, whether experienced as positive or negative, can enable us to enter into the second and third phases of reflection more easily"* [Boud et al., 1985]. In the second stage, these feelings are evaluated. Positive feeling should be utilized to support the reflective process. Negative feelings that obstruct the process *"need to be discharged or transformed."* Articulating these feelings either by writing or talking about them is advised as helpful. While it might be tempting to jump over this second step, this might lead to wrong assumptions because experiences are still blurred by negative feelings or premature judgments. In the final third stage, the experiences are re-examined by associating them to the existing knowledge and integrating them in an appropriate fashion in the conceptual framework of the learner. The whole process might repeat these three stages several times and by doing so skip stages, but these three stages are part of the desired process to produce outcomes.

The outcomes are mainly intangible, like the experiences and the reflection process itself. For instance, a new perspective becomes only apparent by articulating it or by a behavioral change. There might be outcomes that lack the commitment to action and remain hidden in the first place. However, these changes in the cognitive framework of a learner will influence the behavior in the long term.

A critical point is the start of the reflection process that leads to the initial return to an experience. Boud et al. do not explicitly define the beginning of the reflection process because *"most events which precipitate reflection arise out of normal occurrences of one's life."* However, the provided examples can be easily linked to cognitive dissonance theory [Festinger, 1957]. Cognitive dissonance theory describes how a mismatch between attitudes and behavior could lead to rethinking attitudes and experiences. This mismatch is perceived as psychological discomfort (dissonance) and motivates a reconsideration of existing attitudes. These type of dissonances triggers the reflective process. This dissonance might be due to an external event or agent (external trigger/incident) or might develop from one's own thinking (internal trigger/inner need to reflect). The environment could trigger a reflective process by creating an awareness of a discrepancy that leads to a dissonance in the cognitive system of the learner. Examples for such discrepancies are knowledge gaps, unfulfilled expectations or positive surprises like improvements in productivity or well-being.

2.2. Quantified Self

On the pragmatic side, we consider a new kind of lifelogging approaches coming from the recently emerged Quantified Self[1] (QS) community that promotes *"self-knowledge through numbers."* Lifelogging is the process of tracking personal data generated by our own behavioral activities. Personal data like sleep, exercise, food, mood, location, alertness, productivity, and even spiritual well-being may be collected and measured to be part of this log. Their lifelogging experiments and their tools have the intention of gaining knowledge about their own behaviors, habits and thoughts by collecting relevant information related to them. The starting point of the QS initiative is not a set of scientific theories; it is based on empirical self-experimentation. Apart from Quantified Self, all these approaches and tools can also be found under a variety of names including personal informatics, living by numbers, self-surveillance, self-tracking and personal analytics [Li et al., 2010].

2.2.1. The Quantified Self Community

Quantified Self (QS) has emerged as a community pursuing different lifelogging approaches. QS is a collaboration of users and developers who share an interest in self-knowledge through self-tracking. They are a diverse group of *"life hackers, data analysts, computer scientists, early adopters, health enthusiasts, productivity gurus, and patients"* [Choe et al., 2014]. The experiments that they perform and the tools they use have the intention of gaining knowledge about their own behaviors, habits and thoughts by collecting relevant information related to them. Tools used to track data about themselves range from pen and paper to user-developed tracking applications or commercially available tools.

This community of self-trackers was born with the eagerness to experimentally know more about human life. They were motivated by the potential experiments that they observed around: *"People experiencing some change in their lives, going on or off a diet, kicking an old habit, making a vow or a promise, going on vacation, switching from incandescent to fluorescent lighting, getting into a fight. These were potential experiments, not real experiments, because typically no data was collected and no hypotheses are formed. But with the abundance of self-tracking tools now on offer, everyday changes can become the material of careful study"* [Wolf, 2009]. Its starting point was the creation of the *quantifiedself.com* blog by Gary Wolf and Kevin Kelly in 2007. Their initiative was extended in 2008 with a regular Meetup to discuss and share their practices with personal data tracking.

[1] `http://quantifiedself.com`

One of the pioneering projects in lifelogging was MyLifeBits [Gemmell et al., 2006], which was inspired by Vannevar Bush's article *"As We May Think"* [Bush, 1945]. In this project, Gordon Bell captured a lifetime's worth of articles, books, cards, CDs, letters, memos, papers, photos, pictures, presentations, home movies, videotaped lectures, and voice recordings and stored them digitally. Afterwards, since the QS community was founded, we have seen a wide variety of approaches where people track; e.g., more than 40 different categories of information about the own health, the power usage of a thatched cottage or Vitamin D consumption [Brophy-Warren, 2008].

Although the main purpose of the QS community is to know how they are affected by diverse factors, these self-trackers not only use the captured data for themselves, but they make their data available and report about the insights that they gain.

Blogs, Meetups and QS Conferences

Since its creation, the blog entries posted in the QS community have served as the main platform for the sharing of self-tracking practices. Both videos from their meetups as well as traditional blog articles are used as content for these entries. As of November 10, 2014, over 300 video posts in their QS post and 700 "Show&Tell" videos in the QS online video blog[2] have been posted. Participants also share their practices, experiences, mistakes and lessons learned in regular QS meetups and annual conferences. In their QS meetups they promote a specific type of format called "Show & Tell", conceived to explain firsthand experiences with self-tracking and help with the narrative. This format organizes the talk by answering the Three Prime Questions [Wolf, 2011]:

1. What did you do?
2. How did you do it?
3. What did you learn?

By answering these three questions, speakers talk about (1) their basic approaches including problems, motivations and goals, (2) the tools and methods that they used, and (3) the insights and outcomes gained from the data and tracking process.

Recently, the videos originated from these meetups and conferences (and posted in the QS blog) have been of interest to HCI research and were used to analyze what motivates them to keep tracking data, what tools they use, what insights they gain, and what challenges they face [Choe et al., 2014].

[2] `http://vimeo.com/groups/quantifiedself`

2.2.2. The Quantified Self Approaches

Besides all these personal experiments, plenty of tools are already available, which facilitate the tracking of different aspects of our lives. Numerous applications and tools were found during the survey that we conducted. Therefore, therefore the following review contains only the most important and significant approaches to our current research work.

Projects

MylifeBits[3] is a project of Microsoft Research based on a lifelong storage of everything. It is the fulfillment of Vannevar Bushs 1945 Memex vision including full-text search, text annotations, audio annotations, and hyperlinks. There are two parts of MyLifeBits: an experiment in lifetime storage, and a software research effort [Bell and Gemmell, 2010]. In his experiment, Gordon Bell has captured a lifetime's worth of articles, books, cards, CDs, letters, memos, papers, photos, pictures, presentations, home movies, videotaped lectures, and voice recordings and stored them digitally. According to Gemmell et al. [2006], Bell is now paperless, and is beginning to capture phone calls, IM transcripts, television, and radio. The developed MyLifeBits software leverages SQL servers to support hyperlinks, annotations, reports, saved queries, pivoting, clustering, and fast search [Gemmell et al., 2006].

SenseCam [Hodges et al., 2006] is a wearable digital camera that takes photographs passively. SenseCam contains different electronic sensors (light sensors, an infrared detector, a temperature sensor and accelerometers) whose measurements are used to automatically trigger photographs to be taken. Originally, the main goal of SenseCam was to provide an aid for people with memory loss. However, it has been used in a variety of settings[4]. For instance, it has been used to automatically generate images from landmarks, to capture a person's environment in order to analyze the amount of exercise people take, to enable teachers to reflect on logs about their days, or to study how office workers work simultaneously on different tasks.

The **SenseWear Armband** developed by Bodymedia was motivated by the lack of an easy-to-use, reliable and cost efficient way to accurately assess metabolic physical activity and energy expenditure by consumers, clinicians and researchers [Andre et al., 2006]. It allows users to track energy expenditure, physical activity durations and levels, and lifestyle information. The SenseWear Armband has

[3] `http://research.microsoft.com/en-us/projects/mylifebits/`

[4] `http://research.microsoft.com/en-us/um/cambridge/projects/sensecam/applications.htm`

been validated in several in the field studies in the field and in numerous clinical and scientific studies and patient programs.

Another example of projects associated with the QS community is **Mappiness**[5]. This research project aims at gaining insights about how people's happiness is affected by their local environment; e.g., pollution, noise, location, or people around. Users enter how they feel by rating several moods (happy, relaxed, awake, etc.) within a certain scale (not at all–extremely). Users receive feedback about their mood and the factors that affect it. Aggregated values of users from the UK and London are also visualized in their online platform.

Tools

Below, we review some of the tools found in the Quantified Self community. This is not an exhaustive list, but it gives the reader a good perception of the kind of tools they are dealing with.

Web-based and Desktop Applications

- daytum[6]: a platform consisting of a web-based application and a complementary iPhone App to collect, categorize and communicate users' personal and everyday data in form of items count; e.g., number of beverages taken or films watched.
- mycrocosm [7]: web service that uses the visualization of statistics to share chunks of personal information and allows users to track several aspects of their daily lives ranging from hours of everyday sleep to what color clothes a person wears.
- moodscope[8]: web-based application to measure user's mood through a card game, track its evolution on a graph and share the scores with friends, hoping to receive support from them.
- Dagaz[9]: Dagaz is an application to train meditation level through a game experience. The application makes use of mandala shapes, generated by the user's mind. Mandala shapes are symmetrical shapes used in many cultures and almost every religion.

[5] http://www.mappiness.org.uk
[6] http://daytum.com
[7] http://mycro.media.mit.edu
[8] http://www.moodscope.com
[9] http://store.neurosky.com/products/dagaz

- Microsoft HealthVault[10]: online personal health-record service that is compatible with a growing number of home health monitors. Data from these devices can be uploaded directly into a patient's HealthVault record, where users can then create a handy graph of their blood pressure, weight, blood sugar, or other data, and share it with their doctors or family.
- Yawnlog[11]: a website that lets users track how much sleep they are getting, note how good the sleep was, record their dreams and compare all of that information with their friends.
- Time Sink[12]: activity tracking application that logs user activity on a Mac laptop or computer by keeping track of windows and programs used.

Physiological or Environmental Sensors

- Nike+[13]: tracking of running activity. It includes measurement of physical constants (calories, heart beats), time, distances, goals to achieve and challenges to fulfill with other users.
- Fitbit[14]: sensor that tracks a person's movement to produce a record of steps taken, calories burned, and sleep quality. Data are uploaded to the Web so that users can monitor their activity and compare it with that of their friends.
- Philips DirectLife[15]: the Activity Monitor tracks your body motion every time you move up, down, forwards, backwards and sideways. By measuring the acceleration of these movements, it calculates how much energy you used to make them. With DirectLife, a program is offered to increase your activity levels and they provide you a personal coach who can help you stay motivated.
- SenseCam[16]: wearable camera with a wide-angle lens that periodically takes photos without user intervention.
- SenseWear[17]: physical activity monitor to track movement. It has an accelerometer to measure motion and steps, a galvanic skin response monitor

[10] http://www.healthvault.com
[11] http://yawnlog.com
[12] http://manytricks.com/timesink
[13] http://www.nikeplus.com
[14] http://www.fitbit.com
[15] http://www.directlife.philips.com
[16] http://research.microsoft.com/en-us/um/cambridge/projects/sensecam
[17] http://sensewear.bodymedia.com/

to measure the electrical conductivity of the skin, skin temperature, and heat flux—the amount of heat dissipating from the body.

- MIO[18]: watches and bands to track different physiological measures.

Mobile Applications

- Sleep Cycle[19]: Sleep Cycle is an iPhone app that allows users to track their sleep. It creates a nightly record of users' sleep by analyzing the measurements from the device accelerometer.
- Trixie Tracker[20]: application conceived to keep tracking of a baby's life; e.g., naps taken or bottles fed. Its goal is to discover patterns and detect sleep schedules.
- oneLog[21]: application for iPhone that allows tracking of any sort of information or activity.
- My Tracks[22]: application that uses GPS position to track several parameters (path, speed, elevation) while the user walks, runs, or does any other outdoors activity. Data are available live, announcements notify users about their progress, and annotation features are provided.
- Memolane[23]: this application collects and connects content from other sites such as Facebook or Twitter. Its goal is to create an easy way of exploring past social network content.

Table 2.1 shows a categorization of the reviewed applications and tools. The categorization is made according to their topic/field of application (columns) and the composition of the tool (rows).

[18] http://www.mioglobal.com
[19] http://www.sleepcycle.com/
[20] http://www.trixietracker.com
[21] http://itunes.apple.com/za/app/onelog/id327834312?mt=8
[22] http://mytracks.appspot.com
[23] Not available. Shut down in February 2013

Table 2.1.: Categorization of a set of reviewed Quantified Self tools

	Private Life Loggers	**Health and Sport Trackers**	**General Activity Trackers**
App/Website	Memolane MyLifeBits Time Sink	Sleep Cycle Microsoft HealthVault	Tixie Traker YawnLog OneLog moodscope mappiness
Device		MIO BodyCare Telcare Vitality's GlowCaps	SenseCam
Device + App/Web		Nike+ Fitbit Philips DirectLife Cogito MedApps BodyMedia	Affectiva

The reviewed apps are only a representative set of applications that are being developed and used in the QS community. On their QS blog[24] a list of more than 500 available tools and apps can be found. It must also be taken into consideration that the survey conducted as basis for the model was completed in 2012. Since then, new tools and applications have proliferated, especially in the context of health and sport tracking. These new tools are not included in the presented survey in order to be consistent with the background that served as basis for the created model.

[24] `http://quantifiedself.com/guide/tools`

3. Unification of Reflective Learning and the Quantified Self

In the previous chapters, reflective learning and Quantified Self were introduced and defined for the purpose of our work. We now present an Integrated Model of Reflective Learning and Quantified Self (IMRLQS) that combines these research strands into a model for the technical support for reflective learning; centered around the model of Boud et al. [1985].

3.1. Integrated Model of Reflective Learning and Quantified Self

In the IMRLQS model, three main support dimensions are identified, namely: tracking cues, triggering, and recalling and revisiting experiences (see Figure 3.1):

1. Tracking cues: capturing and keeping track of certain data as basis for the whole reflective learning process.
2. Triggering: fostering the initiation of reflective processes in the learner, based on the gathered data and the analysis performed on it.
3. Recalling and revisiting experiences: supporting learners in recalling and revisiting past experiences through the enrichment and presentation of data in order to make sense of past experiences.

Figure 3.1 shows these three dimensions in relation to the reflective learning model of Boud et al., presented in the previous subsection. Firstly, *tracking cues* is directly related to tracking of behavior, ideas and feelings, which are the source of the reflective process on the one hand and are related to the measurement of outcomes on the other (e.g., new perspectives or change in behavior). These are continuously integrated with the original cues in order to feed future iterative reflection processes. Secondly, *triggering* is related to the start of the reflective process. Finally, *recalling and revisiting experiences* enriches the process of returning to and evaluating experiences, as well as that of attending to feelings.

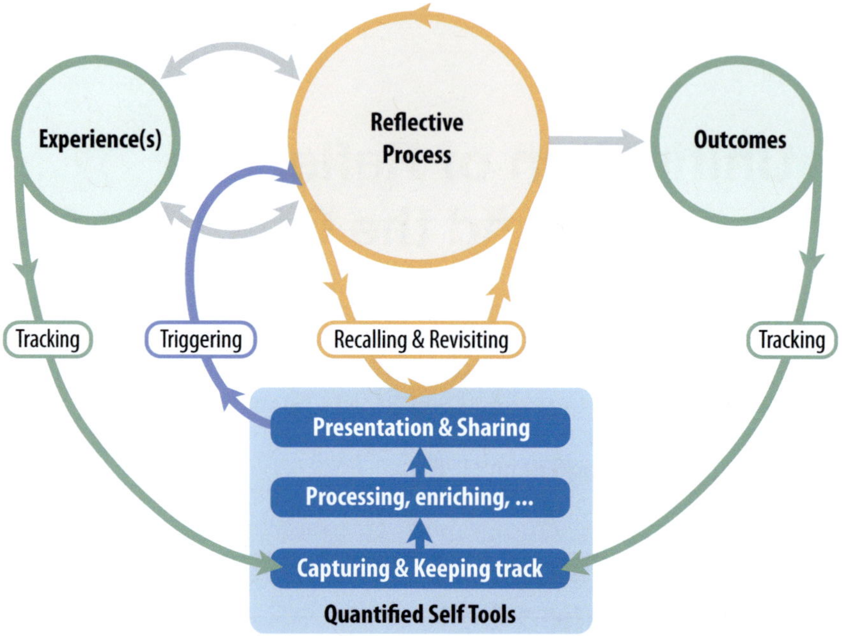

Figure 3.1.: Integrated Model of Reflective Learning and Quantified Self (IMRLQS): Role of the three QS potentials in the reflective learning process.

In the following, we further differentiate the support dimensions based on how these can be instantiated by Quantified Self tools. Table 3.1 shows a summarized overview of the relationship of the three defined support dimensions with the different aspects of reflection in learning and the identified QS characteristics.

3.2. Tracking Cues

Tracking means the observation of a person and his or her context in order to aid the reflective process. Tracking strives to quantify (aspects of) a person's life in order to enable some objectivity in understanding it. Tracking facilitates reflective learning by collecting data on experiences and outcomes that can then be used as objective basis in reflection and triggering. We further characterize tracking by the means that are used, the object that is tracked, and the goal that is being strived for.

Table 3.1.: The dimensions of QS, their characteristics and how they relate to the different aspects of reflection in learning.

QS Support Dimension	QS Characteristics	Reflective Learning Aspects
Tracking	Tracking means Tracked aspects Purposes	Experience (information about behavior, ideas and feelings) and outcomes (results from the reflective process)
Triggering	Active Passive	Initiation of the reflective process
Recalling & Revisiting	Contextualization Data fusion Data analysis Visualization	Reflective process

3.2.1. Tracking Means

Two main ways for tracking exist: self reporting through often specialized software and hardware sensors that directly track behavior.

- **Software Sensors.** Software sensors are applications (desktop-based, web-based or mobile-based) that aid the user in capturing experiences. Software sensors are particularly important for experiences that cannot (currently) be directly measured (such as feelings and/or ideas) and are often much simpler, more flexible and cheaper to produce than hardware sensors. Software sensors are currently used in a broad variety of QS applications.
  Daytum[1] is one example of a QS application that relies exclusively on software sensors. It consists of a web application for desktop computers and mobile devices as well as an iPhone app (Twitter and SMS can also be used for data input). The application enables users to track any number of arbitrary things about their lives, to categorize them and to view infographics based on this data. Another example is the more specialized Trixie Tracker[2] that supports parents in tracking data about their child and their interaction with it (such as diaper changes, naps and bottles fed).

- **Hardware Sensors.** Hardware sensors are devices that automatically capture data that can be used to deduce experiences or collect contextual information. Common categories of sensors are: environmental sensors

[1] http://daytum.com
[2] http://www.trixietracker.com

(e.g., light sensors, thermometers or microphone) and physiological sensors (accelerometers, heart rate sensors, sphygmomanometers, etc.). One example is the application Sleep Cycle[3] that makes use of an iPhone's acceleration sensor to track sleep states in order to help people better understand their sleep. Another well known application is Nike+[4], an application built around an accelerometer that is attached to a shoe. The goal of the application is to measure and track the distance of a walk or run.

3.2.2. Tracked Aspects

The tracked aspects for a QS application can be very broad—as, for example, in "Total Capture" applications like the SenseCam project[5], which attempts to use a camera to track all aspects of daily life. However, research so far has found little evidence of such systems being effective in serving as a digital memory or supporting reflection processes [Sellen and Whittaker, 2010]. Situation specific tracking applications—as, for example, the above mentioned Trixie Tracker[6]—concentrate on only a small class of experiences (in this case some experiences related to child-rearing).

The tracked aspects found in Quantified Self applications can be classified in the following four categories:

- **Emotional aspects.** Emotional aspects such as mood, stress, interest, anxiety, etc.
- **Private and work data.** Data from work processes and our lives such as photos, the browser's history, digital documents, music, or use of a particular software etc.
- **Physiological data.** Physical indicators and biological signals that describe a person's state of health. The main approaches comprise the measurement of physical activity (for applications focusing on sport) and factors indicating health and sickness (e.g., glucose level).
- **General activity.** Data about a user's general activity, such as the number of cigarettes, cups of coffee, hours spent in a certain activity or number of times that something is done.

[3] http://www.sleepcycle.com/
[4] http://www.nikeplus.com
[5] http://research.microsoft.com/en-us/um/cambridge/projects/sensecam
[6] http://www.trixietracker.com

3.2.3. Purposes

Another important classification dimension is that of the purpose of a QS application, the goal which the user tries to achieve by using this application. This purpose drives and guides which measures are tracked and which means are appropriate.

Within their framework, Li et al. [2011] have identified six different purposes or questions people have in mind when tracking data. These are to get to know (1) their current status for determining if goals are met or if correction in behavior is needed, (2) the history of their data for determining trends and progress making, (3) (new) goals worth pursuing, (4) discrepancies between their set goal(s) and current behavior either to correct or maintain it, (5) the context that may influence their current status, and (6) long-term influencing factors in order to monitor trends.

Seen within the reflective learning model, the purpose is the outcome that the user tries to achieve. An example of a goal would be mood improvement in the Moodscope application that encourages users to track and share their mood. For the already mentioned Daytum application the purpose is a general self-improvement, as the user is largely free to determine what he or she wants to track.

3.3. Triggering

Within the reflective learning process, triggers are responsible for starting the actual reflection process. The role of triggers is to raise awareness and detect discrepancy. We differentiate between *active* and *passive* triggering.

3.3.1. Active Triggering

Active triggering consists of the tool sending a notification or catching the attention of the user explicitly. In order to support active triggering, an application must perform data analysis to detect experiences that are suitable for initiating reflection. Such an experience or situation may be a mismatch between users' goals and their current achieved level, a comparison to a global threshold or other persons, or a deviation from personal patterns. An example for active triggering are alerts on RescueTime[7]: the user can specify goals such as expending a maximum amount of time on 'distracting' web sites or being a minimum

[7] `http://www.rescuetime.com`

number of hours doing productive work per day. The system alerts the user with a notification when the goal has been achieved or the certain amount of time has passed by.

3.3.2. Passive Triggering

A system supporting only passive triggering does not identify experiences suitable for fostering reflection or it does not actively contact the user. This kind of system mainly displays the collected data in a suitable way. It relies on the user to be triggered by something outside of the system or on the user regularly visiting the site and then detecting something that starts a reflection process. Daytum (described above) is one application that relies purely on passive triggering.

3.4. Recalling and Revisiting Experiences

Different aspects affect the recalling and revisiting of past experiences, when analyzing the benefits that QS approaches could offer. Enrichment and presentation of the data may facilitate the revisiting of the data to analyze past experiences and reflect on them, and therefore enhance the learning process of the user.

Support of Quantified Self applications can exist along multiple dimensions: Contextualization, Data Fusion, Data Analysis, and Visualization.

3.4.1. Contextualizing

The data being tracked can be enriched with other context data. This contextualization of the data with other sources of information may be performed by the same tool or result from the interaction between tools (e.g., two mobile applications or a sensor with a desktop application). An example for the contextualization for reflection is Garmin Connect[8]. With the right hardware, this application can track heart rate, bicycle speed, cadence, altitude and location and display this in the context of a map—thereby facilitating a better understanding of fitness data.

Adapting the context definition from Dey [2001], we define context within this model as: *"any information that can be used to characterize the situation of a tracked entity and that can aid the reflection process."* For the types of context that

[8] `http://connect.garmin.com`

can be of relevance, we have to go beyond usual classifications of context in computer science (e.g., location, identity, activity and time [Dey and Abowd, 1999]) since these focus on the context of a concrete interaction with a context-aware application. For this model we need to consider as context everything that can aid the understanding of sequences of (data about) experiences and outcomes. Based on a review of existing Quantified Self applications we have identified the following classes of context:

- **Social context.** Data can be augmented with information about the social context of the user. This can be a comparison to Facebook friends or a comparison to all users. This helps to compare own performance/measures with the others. Sharing in a social context provides additional data to others in expectation to retrieve more data in exchange and ultimately see one's own experiences in relation to others' experiences. It can also support the active processing of difficulties; e.g., by talking about problems and finding peers with similar problems. Sharing is a way of communicating with others and retrieving additional feedback on one's own data. An aggregation of data over multiple users may provide new perspectives on experiences and offer new abstraction levels. Such an aggregation can be useful for individual reflection but also at a collaborative level; e.g., reviewing team performance over one month [Müller et al., 2011a].
- **Spatial Context.** The location in terms of city, street or even the room. As context information, this data can aid reflection by helping the user to understand the relation between a place and his behavior—such as understanding the effects of high altitude on his or her heart rate, the calming effect of visits to specific places or the identification of the places where most time is lost in traffic.
- **Historical context.** Historical data is an additional type of context data that can aid in the reflection process. Comparing current values to historic ones allows seeing upward or downward trends or to identify deviations from a historic norm that may indicate a problem. Historic data may also help to identify the difference between periodic fluctuations (such as variations in weight or fitness according to the seasons) and other deviations from the norm that may indicate progress or a problem.
- **Item Metadata.** Any metadata available about the things a user interacts with—such as the information that a particular website's user is accessing is not work related but rather distracting, or the information that a food someone ate contains a large amount of sugar.
- **Context From Other Datasets.** In addition, there are numerous datasets (e.g., weather or work schedule) that can also be used in contextualizing.

3.4.2. Data Fusion: Objective, Self, Peer and Group Assessment

One important aid to the reflection process can be the fusion and comparison of objective (i.e., measured by sensors), self (i.e., self-reported data from the user), peer and group assessment (reported data from others about a user). There may be differences and discrepancies between these views that can foster reflection, can help to bridge the gap from subjective to objective experiences and in this way yield new insights and lead to learning. This relates to stage two of the reflection process—attending to feelings. Negative impressions can be discharged by comparing the individual perspective to objective measurements. Aggregation of subjective articulations over time or over different users can result in a more objective view (see also [Müller et al., 2011c]).

3.4.3. Data Analysis: Aggregation, Averages, etc.

Different forms of data processing help to present the user useful measurements (e.g., number of cups of tea per day/week, average mood of my colleagues, etc.). In Müller et al. [2011a], three types of aggregation are suggested: mathematically; e.g., into averages and correlations, graphically; e.g., in charts and plots, or formally; e.g., by relation networks or tag clouds. The selected type of aggregation depends on the kind and amount of available data as well as on the purpose of the aggregation. For instance, graphs and plots require quantitative data and can show trends or help to identify high level patterns. Aggregation in tag clouds may need large amounts of data to become valuable but can be applied to semi or unstructured data like texts. Further, it might be desirable to hide the source of the underlying data through aggregation and in this way create anonymity and privacy.

3.4.4. Visualization

Presentation and visualization that are attractive and intuitive for the users should be chosen which, at the same time, foster the analysis of the data for reflective learning purposes and being otherwise one of the major barriers (see [Li et al., 2010]).

This first version of the Integrated Model of Reflective Learning and Quantified Self was created in 2012. A summarized version was initially published in [Rivera-Pelayo et al., 2012a] and its complete version was published in [Rivera-Pelayo et al., 2012b].

3.5. Exemplary Applications

In order to illustrate the application of the IMRLQS model, we present two QS tools and how they are classified. These two exemplary applications have been chosen with the intention of covering several of the main presented points: having one hardware sensor and one software sensor; dealing with data about physical activity and data related to emotions; and finally having a goal-oriented approach and an approach with an unclear general goal.

3.5.1. Philips DirectLife

Philips DirectLife[9] is an activity monitor that tracks the body motion of the user and converts it into calories burned. By measuring the acceleration of movement, it calculates how much energy the user used to make them. DirectLife is based on a motion sensor together with a website. In this personalized website, the user can upload the data from the sensor, review how active he or she has been and monitor his or her progress against the personal plan. In addition, an activity program is offered to increase activity levels and a personal coach is provided, with the role of keeping the user motivated.

- **Tracking.** DirectLife consists of an accelerometer; i.e., a sensor that can measure a person's body motion. Therefore, the tracking of the user activity is done through a physiological sensor [3.2.1]. In this case, the measurement and tracking of the activity is based on the physiological data provided by the sensor and therefore this tool supports the tracking of health and sport related measures [3.2.2]. The main motivations for users to use this system include staying active, being healthier or losing weight [3.2.3]. With DirectLife, goals are set based on the current activity levels of the user. Some example goals that the user can explicitly choose are being healthy, fit, active or sporty; and the difference between them is the level of activity and caloric targets.
- **Triggering.** Although DirectLife performs analysis on the data, namely aggregation of data, average calculation, goal comparison and social ranking, we would identify it as a passive triggering tool [3.3.2]. With this system, the data are shown to the user in order to take a decision by him or herself and the tool does not explicitly arise the attention of the user to certain discrepancies or particularities of the data. The function of triggering the user to change her behavior and being more active might be in this case attributed to the personal coach (which is actually a person and not the tool itself).

[9] `http://www.directlife.philips.com`

- **Recalling and Revisiting.** In DirectLife, the main factor used to contextualize the data is time; i.e., it allows the user to see the data according to a certain day, week or month [3.4.1, historical context]. Users can see their history, their daily average activity, their weekly activity and their personal plan [3.4.3]. Moreover, they are ranked among other participants based on their age and gender and they can compare themselves and feel more motivated with this social comparison [3.4.1, social context]. The burned calories calculated according to the body motion of the user is an objective measure [3.4.2], as it is not the perception of the user, but the data provided by the sensor. DirectLife provides the user with different bar graphics which show the data in a daily, weekly, monthly and yearly basis [3.4.4]. Users can also see their progress in their website by comparing their activity with the ongoing target.

3.5.2. Moodscope

Moodscope consists of a web-based application that allows users to track their mood through a card game, see their mood evolution on a graph and share their scores with friends. The purpose of this sharing is the support that the user can receive from his or her friends, when they are aware of the user's emotional state. According to the website of this tool, *"measuring your own mood is a daily must-do, just like cleaning your teeth or washing your face."*

- **Tracking.** Moodscope is based on a web application [3.2.1] that supports the capturing and tracking of emotional aspects, concretely a person's mood [3.2.2]. The measurement of the mood is done through a card game based on a psychological mood questionnaire called PANAS [Watson et al., 1988]. Users can choose among twenty double-sided cards every day. They can do it once a day and it is suggested to do it best at the same time each day. Having chosen a card, the user receives a score, which is a percentage between 0 (sad) and 100 (happy). The reason to choose this card game is the fact that cards engage the more thoughtful and reflective side of the human brain [Moodscope]. The general goal that any user of Moodscope may have is being happier and thereby feeling better [3.2.3], which is a rather undefined, unspecific and unclear goal.
- **Triggering.** Moodscope follows the particular phenomenon called "The Hawthorne Effect" with the theory that when we believe that we are being observed, our behavior can change for the better. Therefore, Moodscope sends an email with the user's daily score and a progress graph to the people that act as a user's "buddy." These buddies are chosen by the users themselves and may be friends, colleagues or relatives. This sharing of the data acts as a motivation for users and affects the progress of their

emotions, but it is not a trigger itself. This tool may then support a kind of passive triggering, when showing users the evolution of their mood [3.3.2].

- **Recalling and Revisiting.** The mood data tracked in Moodscope can be contextualized through comments made in the progress graph [3.4.1, historical context]. Apart from presenting the evolution of the user's mood in a line graph [3.4.4], this tool does not apply any other data analysis [3.4.3]. As explained before, users can share their moods with the people that they choose as buddies and these receive a daily email with their mood status and progress. In this case, although data are shared, there is no comparison established with the mood of anyone else [3.4.1, social context]. Due to the fact that the capturing of data is user-driven and chosen by themselves with a card, we can say that Moodscope deals with subjective data of the user [3.4.2].

3.6. Related Work

Overall the proposed combination of reflective learning and QS applications in this thesis materializes the vision of learning analytics for a particular model of learning and a specific class of support tools. In the following, we present a review of related theoretical and application-oriented approaches found in the literature.

3.6.1. The Quantified Self and Personal Informatics

Recent studies have explored the motivation behind the Quantified Self. Gimpel et al. [2013] conducted a survey to understand the underlying motivations of self-triggered health monitoring in the QS community focused on patient-driven approaches and the implications for healthcare information systems. They show that self-tracking is a voluntary activity driven by both intrinsic and extrinsic motivations [Gimpel et al., 2013] that requires time and effort to first collect the data, then review and reflect on the data subsequently. In [Choe et al., 2014], main challenges as well as pitfalls are identified and analyzed using the experiences of QS members. They report that their *"ultimate goal is to reflect upon one's data, extract meaningful insights, and make positive changes, which are the hardest part of QS"* [Choe et al., 2014]. Rooksby et al. [2014] investigate what *"people are making of personal trackers for themselves"* and report an interview study with current users. These studies provide valuable insights about personal tracker users, but we lack empirical evidence whether these insights also apply in a work setting.

Previous research in self-tracking has predominantly focused on improving physical activity, sustainable living, health, and well-being [Isaacs et al., 2013; Li et al., 2011; Morris et al., 2010; Froehlich et al., 2009]. Additionally, applications typically target individuals rather than teams. Issues under investigation are often tracking effort [Li et al., 2011] and support for behavior change [Isaacs et al., 2013]. While social features are common in QS tools (e.g. sharing activity levels in minutes or distance run), Rooksby et al. [2014] argue that these features are not necessarily put to use, but users rather share data to announce their achievements to friends or to compete with other users. Hence, sharing typically serves to increase user motivation via competition or peer recognition [Maitland et al., 2006] rather than to support team and communication processes, as it is necessary in work settings.

In the study of Li et al. [2010], the authors surveyed and interviewed people who track and reflect on personally relevant information. Based on this, they derived a five-stage model of personal informatics systems. The stages comprise preparation, collection, integration, reflection, and action. The model focuses especially on barriers in each stage. In comparison to our framework, Li et al. [2010] address how to design personal informatics systems from a technical perspective, whereas we focus on how to use such systems especially for reflective learning. This aspect is missing in their work. Reflection is only considered as short- and long-term reflection. Nevertheless, we may extend the model by Li et al. [2010] and provide a more detailed view with the QS characteristics of our framework; for instance, regarding the collection of information with our tracking means and tracking objects.

Within their framework, Li et al. [2011] have identified six different purposes or questions people have in mind when tracking data (see also Section 3.2.3). These are to get to know (1) their current status for determining if goals are met or correction in behavior is needed, (2) the history of their data for determining trends and progress making, (3) (new) goals worth pursuing, (4) discrepancies between their set goal(s) and current behavior either to correct or maintain it, (5) the context that may influence their current status, and (6) long-term influencing factors in order to monitor trends. They further identified two different phases of reflection, maintenance and discovery, related to the questions and provide suggestions on how to support these with technology. However, these insights are disconnected from their model.

Self-tracking has been also investigated from the perspective of human-computer interaction systems. However, these research works have focused on approaches related to well-being, sport, mental health, or multiple types of disease [McDuff et al., 2012; Sengers et al., 2005; Isaacs et al., 2013; Consolvo et al., 2009a; Rachuri et al., 2010; Tollmar et al., 2012]. There are few related works that deal with structuring QS approaches towards the purpose of reflection, but this is mainly from an HCI design perspective. Fleck and Fitzpatrick [2010] provide a literature review and framework on reflection together with guiding questions for designing for reflection. Their framework identifies purposes, conditions and levels of reflection. They suggest uses of technology to support these different levels of reflection: technology for revisiting, technology for prompting explanation, technology to see more and technology for transformation.

3.6.2. Computer-Supported Reflective Learning

In Technology-Enhanced Learning (TEL), reflection has played a significant role, but the main focus has been formal learning in the classroom [Strampel and Oliver, 2007; Krogstie, 2009]. This has been reflected by the recent emergence of Learning Analytics (LA), a research area that draws from multiple disciplines such as educational science, information and computer science, sociology, psychology, statistics and educational data mining [Shum and Ferguson, 2012]. A review of the development of analytics in educational settings is provided by Ferguson [2012], including its origins and drivers, development and challenges of this young research area.

MIRROR[10] is one of the few projects that have investigated the support of informal learning in workplace settings. The work presented in this thesis was conducted as part of this project, which aimed at providing technological support for learning by reflection and observation. Within the MIRROR project, a model for Computer-Supported Reflective Learning in the workplace was created [Krogstie et al., 2012, 2013]. The CSRL model describes the reflection process as a cycle and presents the possible support categories. The four stages of this reflection cycle are depicted in Figure 3.2.

The "Plan and do work" stage refers to doing everyday work, planning and monitoring any activity. When a trigger occurs, the next stage "Initiate reflection" is where the reflection cycle starts, having as input the data generated in the previous stage. The frame resulting from the reflection initiation leads to the "Conduct reflection" session stage. Finally, "Apply outcome" is the stage in which reflection outcomes resulting from the reflection session are used to create changes or feed further reflection. As a complement to this model, the transitions between different levels inside of an organization and how to facilitate these transitions through design are discussed in [Prilla et al., 2012]. They present three levels: individual, collaborative and organizational.

[10] `http://www.mirror-project.eu`

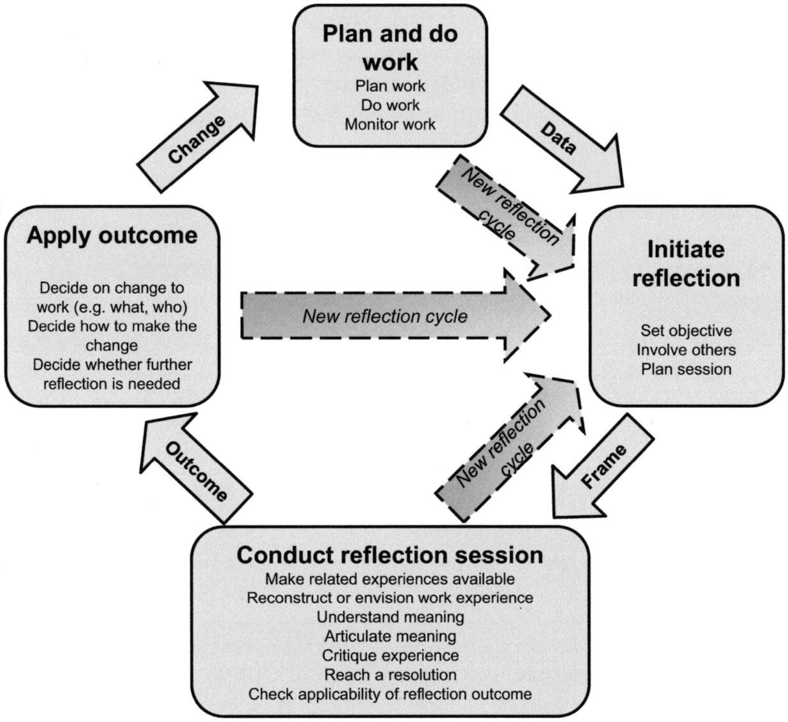

Figure 3.2.: Model of Computer-Supported Reflective Learning (CSRL)—Reflection cycle diagram by Krogstie et al. [2013]

The four stages of the CSRL model outline the main points in the process in which technology can facilitate reflection. Whereas the CSRL model aims at describing the support of technology from a general procedural perspective, our IMRLQS model provides an understanding of the design space for the specific case of QS applications and offers a systematized review on how this technological support can be realized.

Besides our work on supporting reflective learning with QS approaches, there are other applications that have been developed within the MIRROR Project. These applications include a broad variety of tools and systems, ranging from serious games and creativity applications to sensor-based systems and other automatic approaches.

A subset of these MIRROR applications is most closely related to our work. The KnowSelf App [Pammer and Bratic, 2013] logs activity data created by automatic activity tracking on a PC and its main goal is to support knowledge workers with time management. At a theoretical level, this application aligns well with our theoretical model presented in Chapter 3. However, the use cases investigated in this thesis address distinct work settings. Another example is the TalkReflection app [Prilla, 2014], which allows employees to take notes on difficult talks. Unlike our applications, the TalkReflection app especially aims at supporting collaborative reflection (by providing annotation and sharing features) and its target work contexts have been public administration, care homes and hospitals.

Also as part of MIRROR, and therefore sharing similar goals with this thesis, the work by Müller [2014] investigated the design and use of sensor based applications to support reflective learning. The work presented in [Müller et al., 2012] aims at joining persuasive technology (i.e., technology intentionally designed to change attitudes and behavior of users [Fogg, 2003]) and reflective learning theories to facilitate that both approaches learn from each other. By using approaches like psychophysiological sensing [Müller et al., 2011b] and proximity measurement [Müller, 2013], his work focuses on the use of hardware sensors to turn context into learning content. His work also differs to ours in the targeted work settings, as it has been conducted in the healthcare domain, aiming to support nurses, physicians, and care staff.

Finally, Fleck and Fitzpatrick [2009] investigated how to support collaborative reflective practices of school teachers and university tutors as part of their professional development. In their studies, tutors wore a SenseCam [Hodges et al., 2006] to automatically capture images during lessons, which were discussed afterwards with their mentors. Their results show that the use of the SenseCam and its images supported the returning to their experiences as defined by Boud et al. [1985], prompted discussion of thoughts, created a sharing of background context, allowed participants to identify patterns, and supported reflective discussions in a social context.

This review shows several initiatives to support reflective learning through technology in different settings, but we lacked a unifying framework that describes how technology can support users in the stages of the reflective process. This gap has been fulfilled with the Integrated Model of Reflective Learning and Quantified Self presented in this Part I of the thesis. This model has guided the implementation of the prototypes that have been investigated in the remaining of this thesis.

Part II.

Implementation and Empirical Validation

Overview

In this part, we present three use cases which serve to investigate the application of Quantified Self approaches to support reflective learning in different work settings. For each use case, we present our contributions to the technical implementation (prototype), as well as to the empirical validation of our work (studies and evaluations).

We conducted several studies following the design science research principles of iterative cycles of design, implementation, evaluation and redesign. Each of the evaluations fed back into the design and development of the application used as well as into the refinement of the theoretical model. The studies further show the feasibility and usefulness of our approach and the developed applications. The validation of our holistic approach was conducted through a total of thirteen studies with more than 600 participants involved.

Our **first use case** (Chapter 4) is related to the telecommunications and IT sector. We aim at supporting knowledge workers in their daily work activities; e.g., virtual meetings or customer calls. In our approach to applying QS approaches to support learning by reflection, we propose an application that allows tracking, sharing and visualizing one's mood and emotions. The application, whose design process is explained in detail, received the name of MoodMap App (Section 4.2). In this context, the main goal is the improvement of the employees' performance by increasing emotional awareness and re-evaluating their daily work experiences as well as the impact of their emotions on it. Additionally, the impact on communication and coaching practices was investigated in the conducted studies.

We conducted seven studies with the MoodMap App. The first design study let us explore tools and methods that can collect information about the mood of employees (Section 4.4). Following that, the first prototype of the MoodMap App (Section 4.2.2) was developed and evaluated in a study involving users participating in virtual meetings (Section 4.5). The results of this evaluation together with a design study with end users (Section 4.6) informed the further development of the application towards the second prototype (Section 4.2.3). Subsequently, we conducted two formative evaluations in a telecommunications company, but in two different work contexts. The evaluation in Section 4.7 describes the usage of the application in the virtual meetings of one team and the evaluation in Section 4.8 details its usage in one team of a call center. The results from this last evaluation led to the third prototype of the MoodMap App, which we describe in Section 4.2.4. Finally, the MoodMap App was evaluated in two summative studies. The first summative evaluation was conducted in the United Kingdom with four teams in two different telecommunications call centers (Section 4.9). The second summative evaluation was conducted in Italy, involving the whole staff team of a small software company (Section 4.10).

Our **second use case** (Chapter 5) aims at measuring the impact of reflection on work performance by investigating mood tracking in a controlled environment. To achieve this, we designed the MoodMarket (presented in Section 5.2), a prototype that integrates mood tracking in an experimental trading platform. The MoodMarket was evaluated in an experiment consisting of an asset market, which is described in Section 5.3.

In our **third use case** (Chapter 6), we investigate the support of reflective learning in lectures and conferences, which are one of the main activities in several professional fields, like teaching, research and business. In this context, the typical scenario involves a presenter who is addressing an audience. In order to successfully address this audience, the presenter needs certain skills as well as previous preparation. In such scenarios, there is a great potential to improve professional skills and presenter's performance, by reflecting on data captured during the event.

To address these issues, we developed the Live Interest Meter App (LIM App), which allows users to track and visualize feedback from the audience to support reflective learning. With the first prototype detailed in Section 6.2.2 and the subsequent tests and evaluations (Sections 6.4 and 6.5), we investigated how to realize the technical support for reflection on captured feedback, including aspects such as which data the end users are interested in or how to present and visualize the necessary information. Subsequently, we developed the second prototype of the LIM App (described in Section 6.2.3) and conducted an evaluation with it in three lectures at university level (Section 6.6). Section 6.7 contains a study to explore the use of the LIM App with speakers from different work settings (lectures, research and business). Finally, the summative evaluation of the LIM App (Section 6.8), conducted during a whole semester in a German university, allowed us to investigate the learning outcomes and improvements at work derived from reflection on tracked feedback.

4. Use Case I: Reflecting on Emotions in the Telecommunications and IT Sector

As Boud et al. [1985] identify in their model, emotions play an important role in the reflection process. Positive as well as negative feelings can lead to a re-evaluation of past experiences and in the end to a change of behavior. This need for addressing emotional aspects in reflective learning motivated the design and development of a tool to support reflection on emotions. From a professional perspective, the telecommunications and IT sector was identified as one of the work environments where emotions significantly affect work performance. Emotional awareness enables users to become aware of the emotional state of their collaborators and act accordingly to achieve better results in their joint work [García et al., 1999]. This key mechanism also predicts the potential benefits of self-tracking of mood. We concretely identified three work settings: virtual meetings and teleconferences where non-verbal communication is missing, call centers where there is a constant relationship with customers, and a company dealing with software-technology development and cloud services in the emergency domain. In the following, we specify the requirements and challenges we found in each of them.

4.1. Work Context, Requirements and Challenges

The goal of developing a tool to support reflection on emotions and work is to provide users an easy and integrated means to track their mood during work. The application should facilitate awareness of their moods and insights on how their moods influence their daily work tasks. Explicit awareness and a deeper understanding of their attitude to work, confidence as well as skills should be achieved, by reflecting on their own mood development and on the development of their team's mood. The mood of team colleagues should contribute to detect discrepancies and consequently acquire new knowledge.

4.1.1. British Telecom – FWS Department

British Telecom (BT) is a large European telecommunications company, serving customers in more than 170 countries. Most employees work from home as teleworkers. Teams are dispersed all over the country, and they are managed virtually. One of its departments is called Flexible Working Services (FWS) and its 13 employees are based mainly in the UK and the Netherlands. They are responsible for product support, and therefore work in contact with several products at BT. This team has been working together for a long time, and they depend on virtual meetings for their communication and collaborative work. The team BT Learning Solutions (LS) is part of this FWS department and has 4 members. The task of this team is to deal with requirements for web-based learning and e-Learning.

The members of this department participate in weekly (FWS, excluding BT Learning Solutions) and monthly 'all hands' FWS conference calls. Especially in challenging situations, which may take place in such virtual conference calls or that are discussed in them, emotions play a very important role in team communication. These emotions are relevant for reconstructing and reflecting on experiences from work and learning from them to achieve improvements in their daily work. Therefore, the needs to improve the team non-verbal communication, as well as supporting reflective learning at individual and team level were identified by some members of the teams.

In each of the FWS monthly meetings, the manager of the team explains what is going on in the organization and which changes or news they have, which may affect the FWS team. The FWS team has also a weekly call on Wednesdays, where they mainly present and discuss the state of their work. They also have a weekly call on Fridays where they explain what they like to do in their free time and what their plans for the weekend are. The employees have several professional backgrounds, including product managers, business development managers and business consultants. Their work brings them into contact with several technological solutions, especially in the area of technology-enhanced learning and learning solutions in a professional context.

The following storyboard illustrates well the needs at BT and how they could benefit from a mood tracking tool[1]: *"BT has an extensive IT infrastructure. This implies that solutions for reflective learning need to integrate closely with current technologies and practices of using them. BT already has in place advanced, often computer-supported, processes of managing competence development and training, which means that employees' awareness of the usefulness of new elements of learning support is strong. Meetings at BT are often virtual and rooms for collocated meetings are*

[1] We produced this storyboard for British Telecom (BT) in the framework of the MIRROR Project (refer to Krogstie [2011] for a detailed description of the storyboard including personas).

generally rented upon need (e.g., 'war rooms' used in the preparation of a client offer). We address the potential to improve virtual meetings by supporting social awareness and reflection. In this story, the manager of a team is running a virtual team meeting. The team members are dispersed and they cannot have a collocated meeting. They have to run the meeting as a phone conference. The communication in the meeting is audio based. To get some non-verbal feedback in such meetings, a mood self-tracking app has been introduced. The team manager can use the app to prompt the participants for their moods at particular points in time; e.g., before and after the meeting. Moods can be shared anonymously if desired, and real time mood visualizations can be used to show the range and average mood of the meeting participants."

The major goals in this setting are (i) to capture the participants' mood, (ii) to share and become aware of the mood of the team, (iii) to trigger the participants to reflect about significant mood changes or relevant situations, and (iv) to show them a clear benefit, both at individual and team level.

4.1.2. British Telecom – Telecommunications Call Centers

British Telecom (BT) has call centers all over the world offering their services to their customers. In Scotland, there are two call centers situated in Dundee and in Alness, which are responsible for incoming product support and information inquiries from business and consumer customers. BT employs more than 1,000 people in its Dundee center in a range of functions from directory inquiries to residential and business broadband services. They handle an average of 27,000 calls from all over the UK every day—almost 10 million calls over a year[2].

Roles and processes in the investigated call centers align well with the characteristics of emotional labor [Jaarsveld and Poster, 2013]: contact with the public, manipulation of customers' emotional state, and control of employer organization via supervision and training. The employees have different roles: call takers, managers and coaches. Work is organized in teams of 10 to 20 call takers that are led by one manager. Furthermore, each team has one or two coaches, who support the call takers of the team. Coaches are part of a so-called coaching team and they usually work with more than one team of call takers.

Call takers are responsible for taking calls and solving any issues directly with the customers in an efficient, professional and friendly way. They need to have excellent listening, problem solving and communication skills as they face demanding situations on a daily basis. The resolution of queries first time is one of their priorities in order to provide an efficient service and reduce subsequent contact of the customers. Call takers work individually in an open plan office

[2] This information has been obtained from BT News Releases (2012).

and have individual callback queues. A specialized software program guides them through each call. Internal web applications are used to get necessary information (e.g., customer information). Instant messaging is used for internal communication and a desktop application is available for taking notes on calls. Breaks are done individually when there is time between calls and therefore it is difficult to synchronize one call taker's breaks with others'. Thus, collaboration among call takers is in most cases limited to few meetings where management communicates organizational matters.

Team managers coordinate work within a call center team, review and ensure that call takers perform against targets, supervise their coaching, and train them to achieve the agreed personal objectives. Managers see it as challenging to be aware of the call takers' ongoing difficulties. On the one hand, managers cannot always be available for the call takers, when an issue or problem occurs during a call. On the other hand, it is not always possible for managers to talk to each of his or her call takers during a working day.

Coaches support and train call takers for their work. They conduct weekly coaching sessions of 30 minutes with each call taker, which focus on individual work performance and possible improvements. Coaches ensure that the call takers have the skills, knowledge, and behaviors to deal with any aspect of a call and resolve queries first time. The company's specific Key Performance Indicators (KPI) and call recordings serve as basis for the coaching sessions.

Although the articulation of mood and emotions at work is often seen as unprofessional [Mentis et al., 2013], the problems and communication patterns of customers affect call takers' moods, whilst call takers have to continue communicating in a friendly and professional manner towards customers. Accordingly, work in call centers is considered emotional labor [Jaarsveld and Poster, 2013]. Furthermore, previous research [Jaarsveld and Poster, 2013; Colombino et al., 2014] has shown that call centers are challenging work environments due to their fast paced work. In this environment, reflection may be considered a liability rather than a benefit, because it distracts from the next call. Additionally, the work of call takers is based on individual working routines, while they are part of big teams at the same time. Work performance is crucial in settings such as call centers, where periodic performance data are the key output for the service provider, and the measured performance of the call center is quite literally the aggregated performance of all its agents [Colombino et al., 2014]. Although many aspects of employees performance are monitored and while being an emotional labor job [Jaarsveld and Poster, 2013], mood as indicator of performance has not been considered yet. This offered us more potential to achieve positive improvements in both individual performance and team working atmosphere.

Together with call takers, managers and coaches, we explored the potential benefits of mood self-tracking and the integration into work processes. We identified the following possibilities to embed mood self-tracking: (i) mood is captured before and after calls by call takers, (ii) mood is reviewed during the coaching sessions, and captured during and after coaching sessions, and (iii) managers review mood as part of their routine work process.

4.1.3. Regola – Software Solutions Department

Regola is an Italian company which is leading the development of software-technology and cloud services in the emergency domain, including ICT systems for emergency centers and volunteering associations. The company is located in Turin and has 35 employees organized in five departments. Each of the departments has four to sixteen staff members and is led by a manager, and one of the managers is responsible for two departments.

The different departments include development, production, service desk, sales and management. Therefore, there are several teams and profiles according to their competences; e.g., system technicians, developers, project managers, call takers from service desks, sales consultants and marketing staff.

The Administrative department consists of four staff members. Their daily tasks include controlling, finance, accounting, secretarial activities, personnel management, and trademarks registration. Potential situations, which were identified as more stressful or emotional, encompass the rectification of errors, meeting deadlines, contacting morose or non-paying customers, and obtaining financial resources. Moreover, in order to fulfill these tasks they have to collect the necessary information from other areas of the company, which usually leads to stress and conflicts.

The department of Sales and Marketing consists of one sales director and three staff members. Their daily work tasks are scouting, managing offers, attending conferences/exhibitions/fairs, preparing events, social management, evaluating new projects and opportunities, assisting clients and partners, documenting objectives as well as managing accounts and contacts (B2B). Possible stressful or emotional situations arise from simultaneous requests and ongoing activities, impending deadlines of offers or commercial opportunities, complaints or difficult relationships with clients and competitors. Further challenging tasks for them encompass the introduction of several different projects to potential clients, packaging and communicating to recipients all the latest innovations from the production area, as well as handling periodic or yearly contracts.

The Support and Service Desk department consists of one operational director and six staff members. The employees are software skilled operators, application specialists, system technicians and network security specialists. They provide first, second and third level support and assistance to clients. Their work is mainly conducted via telephone or internet, remote connections and eventually on-site actions to investigate and solve critical issues, according to predefined Service Level Agreements (SLA). Several stressful and emotional situations identified by the Regola staff include: crashes of emergency centers or a critical problems in the global infrastructure, tasks registered with a high priority (e.g., typically blocking issues in their software applications), and remote support and assistance of users (perceived as highly stressful if the user speaks another language). Occasionally, they have a 24 hour turnover to eventually support and fix critical issues occurring in emergency centers. This creates additional burden given that it is out of their normal working routine and usually an employee is on his or her own.

The Production department has a chief technical officer (CTO) and five project managers. The major tasks of the CTO are planning the global activities, designing global projects, choosing the right technologies and organizing coordination meetings. The CTO receives input from each project and keeps control of the global design of the projects in terms of integration and technology. He also handles the requests from the sales department. Project managers deal with team management and organize the corresponding meetings. They are also responsible for the requirements engineering processes. Stressful and emotional situations occur with respect to hard deadlines, investigation of new technologies, documentation of requirements analysis, discussions with customers, checking of the development progress, and the debate of issues with the developers.

The Development department is led by the CTO of the previous team and has 16 developers. Their main tasks are new developments, bug fixing, and testing of their software. Stressful situations might occur when they have to meet project deadlines, provide urgent bug fixes, or use new technologies they are not profficient with.

In conclusion, employees at Regola often face stressful and emotional situations, as they are not only dealing with the challenges of traditional software development but also with the difficulties of the emergency domain. From an organizational perspective, new regulations are being created in Italy that consider stress levels and emotional overload at work a major problem and therefore it is mandatory to take actions to reduce them. Therefore, Regola was aiming at (i) creating awareness that the organization is caring about their staff, (ii) raising awareness on the importance of individuals for managers, and (iii) improving self-awareness about employees' own mood development and stress levels. As a result they want to understand how they can improve the mood of their employees, how such mood influences their work, and how to identify and change particular issues that arise in the different departments.

4.2. MoodMap App

The MoodMap App (MMA) is a web application which allows users to track, share, and visualize moods and annotations. It provides the user with the possibility to capture and contextualize his or her mood during a working day or within specific situations like meetings. The analysis of the captured moods, on an individual as well as collaborative level, aims at initiating and guiding the reflective learning process. In collaborative settings, the MoodMap App allows seeing the mood of others in an anonymized way, which in the end could also be a starting point for reflective learning.

Intuitively, one would say that by using self-reported tracking we are able to capture individuals' emotions rather than moods. Nonetheless, the most extended term concretely in research and generally in the society is "mood tracking." In our research with self-reported mood capturing, we cannot differentiate if a user tracks a mood or an emotion, as they will not be able to specify it and they simply state if they are, e.g., feeling happy, angry or sad. However, this fact does not affect our research because our consideration is based on how a person is feeling (is he or she happy? or angry?) and not on the differentiation if it is an emotion or a mood. Russell [2003], who did extensive research on emotion and cognition, also downplays the relevance of terminology to a pragmatic level: *"At the heart of emotion, mood, and any other emotionally charged event are states experienced as simply feeling good or bad, energized or enervated."*

The mood representation within the MoodMap App (called mood map) is based on the Circumplex Model of Affect by Russell [1980]. This model distinguishes between valence (negative to positive feeling) and arousal (low to high energy). Each mood can be understood as a linear combination of these two dimensions, or as varying degrees of both valence and arousal (see Figure 4.1). The mood map has as background a gradient of colors, which are associated with the main moods placed in each of the quadrants of the map. This representation is based on Itten's color system [Itten, 1971], which was adjusted to fit Russell's Circumplex Model of Affect (see [Ståhl et al., 2005]). This mood representation was chosen because it offers a simplified way of assessing mood (based on two numerical components) but it does not limit users by offering only a set of discrete mood variables (as it is the case in, e.g., taxonomies or smileys).

The MoodMap App allows users to select a mood on the colored bi-dimensional map, by indicating how pleasant/unpleasant and activated/deactivated they feel. The wording of the user interface was adapted to facilitate the understanding by end users. Both axis are numerically represented in the range [0,1]. The mood can be entered by clicking in the mood map and therefore mood capturing is made through a user-initiated mechanism. The aggregation of moods at group level is done through the mathematical calculation of the mood average, which is computed by averaging the valence and arousal components separately as defined in Equation 4.1.

$$MoodAVG = \left[\frac{1}{n} \sum_{i=1}^{n} V_{latest_i}, \frac{1}{n} \sum_{i=1}^{n} A_{latest_i} \right] \tag{4.1}$$

where:

n is the number of users in the group
V_{latest_i} is the valence level of the last present-day mood of user i
A_{latest_i} is the arousal level of the last present-day mood of user i

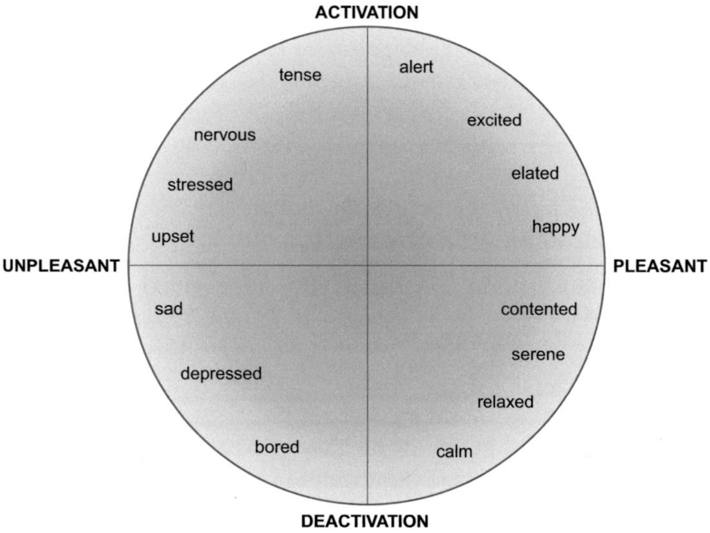

Figure 4.1.: Circumplex Model of Affect by Russell [1980]

4.2.1. MoodMap App: IMRLQS Support Dimensions

According to our Integrated Model of Reflective Learning and Quantified Self (presented in Chapter 3), the MoodMap App offers support for the dimensions shown in Table 4.1.

Table 4.1.: Dimensions of the IMRLQS that are supported by the MoodMap App

Support Dimension	Characterization	MoodMap App
Tracking	Tracking means	Software sensor (web-based application)
	Tracked aspects	Emotional (mood), activity (work task)
	Purposes	Raise emotional awareness, improve communication and work performance
Triggering	Active	Emails with reports, user prompts
	Passive	Live mood visualizations, mood reports
Recalling & Revisiting	Contextualization	Social context (sharing and comparing moods) and historical context
	Data fusion	Subjective data (self) and group data
	Data analysis	Mathematical and graphic aggregation
	Visualization	Daily and weekly timelines showing mood trends and annotations, visualizations for comparing self- and group values, smileys to represent single values, visualization to show overall amount of captured data

We conducted a first exploratory study with formative aspects to evaluate the potential of a mood tracking tool in a project meeting (Section 4.4). The first prototype of the MoodMap App (version 1.0, see Section 4.2.2) was evaluated at British Telecom (BT)within the Learning Solutions department. A team with 12 participants used the app in weekly virtual team meetings, in order to overcome the lack of non-verbal communication during such meetings (for further details refer to Section 4.5).

After this evaluation study, we received crucial insights concerning the further development of the MoodMap App. The results showed especially that the participants did not perceive enough benefits for themselves, and could not yet identify how the MoodMap App could help them during their daily work and support reflective learning. We gathered qualitative as well as quantitative feedback that inspired and motivated the development for the second prototype.

Together with members from the same organization (BT), we conducted a design workshop in order to define the next necessary features that would improve the reflection support capabilities of the MoodMap App. The workshop development and its results are described in detail in Section 4.6.

The development of the second prototype (see Section 4.2.3) focused on the guidance of the reflective process. This guidance included features to support reflection during the day, when moods are captured, as well as at the end of certain events (e.g., after a meeting). The designed features to guide reflection encompass (1) user prompts, (2) richer contextualization, (3) meeting reports as well as (4) a reflection journal and (5) direct feedback via emails. This second prototype was evaluated in a formative user study at British Telecom Flexible Working Services (see Section 4.7).

In summer 2013, we conducted a second formative evaluation with the second prototype of the MoodMap App (2.0). The study was conducted at a British Telecom call center (see Section 4.8). The evaluation results guided the development of the third prototype of the MoodMap App (see Section 4.2.4). The main changes in the MoodMap App 3.0 included the adaptation of the moods' contextualization to the working processes, the inclusion of teams and user roles in the application, as well as the design of new views to offer insights on individual team members.

Table 4.2 shows an overview of the developed prototypes and the main added or modified features in each prototype.

Table 4.2.: Overview of the MoodMap App prototypes

Prototype Version	Release Date	Added/Modified Features
MoodMap App 1.0	January 2012	Capturing mood and moodlist Personal Views (Timelines) Collaborative Views (Compare Me and Collaborate) Simple MoodMap Meetings
MoodMap App 2.0	June 2013	Timeline View Meeting configuration Meeting reports Contextualization of moods User prompts Email functionality
MoodMap App 3.0	November 2014	Team capabilities Adapted contextualization Team Views

4.2.2. MoodMap App 1.0

In the following, we describe the interface and the features of the first prototype of the MoodMap App.

Capturing Mood

In the MoodMap App, a two-dimensional color-coded visualization called 'mood map' is used to represent moods. This visualization is used directly for mood capturing and is preserved in all representations of captured mood as well. As detailed above, this representation is based on the Circumplex Model of Affect by Russell [1980]. It must be noticed that the use of a scientific or psychological terminology was avoided. Therefore, in the MoodMap App valence is called *feeling* whereas arousal is named *energy*. Users can express how they feel by clicking at the appropriate area of the mood map (Figure 4.2).

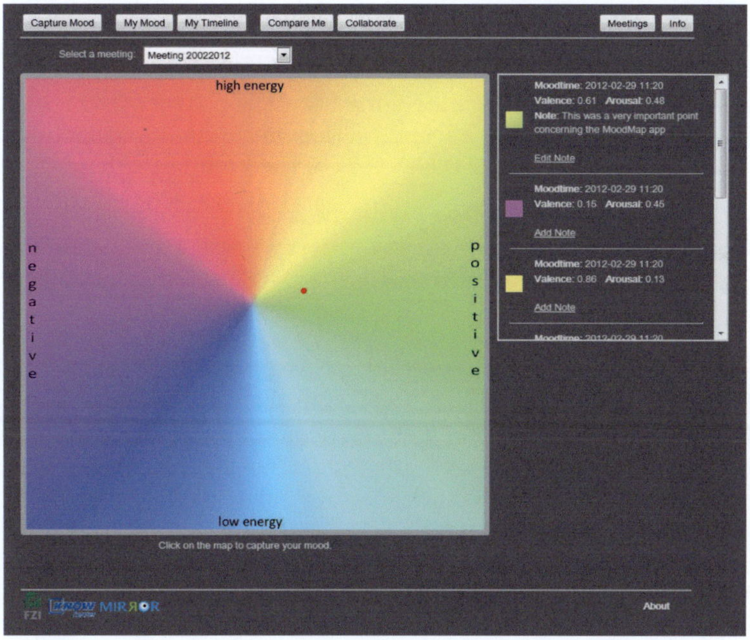

Figure 4.2.: Capturing Mood View: Users track their own mood in the two-dimensional color-coded mood map (left) and review it in the moodlist (right).

As soon as the user expresses a mood within the MoodMap App, it appears in the moodlist (see Figure 4.2 to the right). The moodlist is a list of the moods and their attached notes that have been captured during the day or during a certain meeting. This feature was inspired by the well-known lists of posts from numerous social networks like Twitter[3]. An entry in the moodlist has a timestamp and shows the color of the captured mood. Notes can be added to any mood in this moodlist; e.g., to comment on the mood or add any appreciation.

Personal Views

Users can review their personal mood data on a timeline, which is part of the *My Timeline* View (see Figure 4.3). Two timeline visualizations are available: (a) the *Energy Timeline* (Figure 4.3, left), with a vertical axis that indicates the arousal level and colored smileys that represent the valence level, and (b) the *Feeling Timeline* (Figure 4.3, right), with a vertical axis that indicates the valence level, while the arousal level is coded by the color and dimension of a circle.

Collaborative Views

Besides the individual visualizations, the MoodMap App provides two views at collaborative level: *Compare Me* and *Collaborate*. These visualizations contain anonymized information about the moods of the group members.

Users can compare their own mood with the mood of other colleagues or team members using the *Compare Me* visualization (Figure 4.4 to the left). In order to facilitate this comparison, both valence and arousal values are represented separately through bars. The vertical bars represent the range of values (from 0 at the bottom to 1 at the top of the bar). The bar on the left shows the user's valence levels (from good to bad) whereas the bar on the right shows his or her arousal levels (from low to high energy). On each bar, the blue arrow on the left represents the individual user's value, whereas the black arrow on the right shows the average value. The average values for both consist of the average computed over all latest entries from all users, calculated separately for valence and arousal values (see Equation 4.1). In case the user is in a meeting, the average mood considers all participants in the meeting. By moving the mouse over the arrows, the user will get more information about the current number of participants.

[3] `http://twitter.com/`

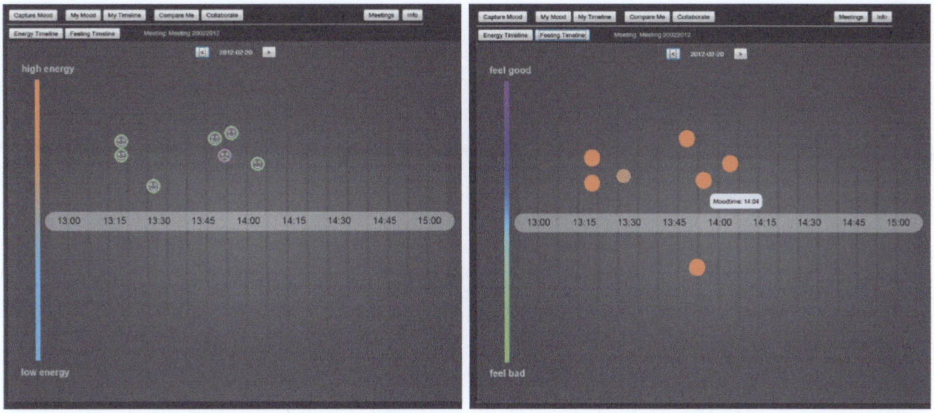

Figure 4.3.: Personal Timelines showing the same moods with different visualizations.

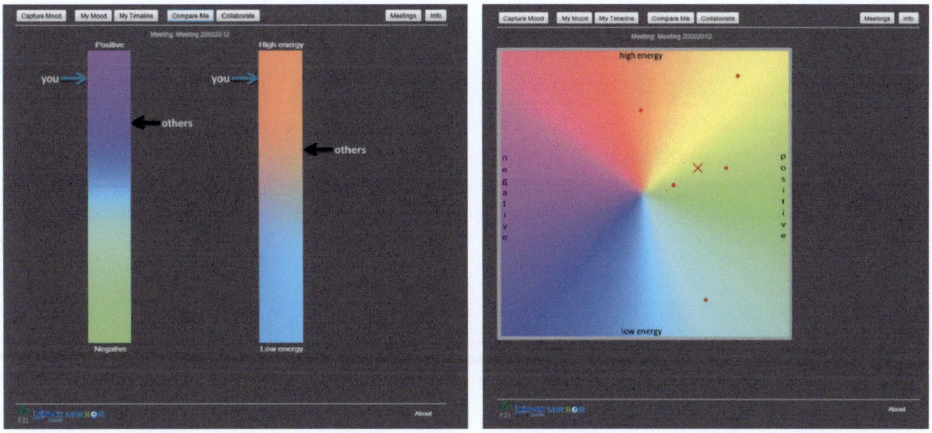

Figure 4.4.: With *Compare Me* (left) users can compare their own valence and arousal levels with the averages of the team members. With *Collaborate* (right) users see the average mood (cross) and distribution of individual moods (single dots) in the mood map.

In the *Collaborate* View (see Figure 4.4 on the right), a large red cross placed on the mood map shows the average of the latest mood entries of all users. By clicking this cross, the distribution of the anonymous individual entries (small red dots) is shown. With this view, users can get an overall impression of the team's mood, besides seeing in a more precise way, if all participants have similar moods.

MoodMap Meetings

Every user has the possibility to create a meeting which is visible for all users in the application. A meeting is defined by a title and a brief description.

Before capturing a mood, the user can select a meeting to which the moods will be attached (see Figure 4.2). When clicking on the drop-down menu, all available meetings are presented in a list. By clicking on one title, the meeting is selected, and all further captured moods are automatically assigned to this meeting. If no meeting is selected, the mood is stored associated to the current day. All other visualizations like *My Timeline*, *Compare Me*, and *Collaborate* will also show the information of the currently selected meeting.

4.2.3. MoodMap App 2.0

One of the changes made in the MoodMap App 2.0 was the adaptation of the mood map and its colors to faithfully follow the Itten's color system [Itten, 1971]. This adjustment was done following the work of Ståhl et al. [2005], who adjusted this color system to fit Russell's Circumplex Model of Affect [Russell, 1980]. This improved the user interface of the application by relying on foundations for the description and expression of emotions [Ståhl et al., 2005]. All visualizations containing the mood map or derived visualizations were slightly changed according to this new color scheme. As an illustrative example, Figure 4.5 shows how this color coding affected the collaborative views.

In this second prototype, several features to guide reflection were introduced. These features include user prompts, richer contextualization, meeting reports containing a reflection journal, and direct feedback via emails. User prompts are implemented to motivate users to insert their moods or being more active in using the MoodMap App during a meeting. These prompts should also make users aware of significant mood changes in their own mood as well as crucial deviations from the average team meeting mood. They encourage users to reflect about their mood development directly during the usage of the MoodMap App. Providing a field for inserting the current meeting topics in a contextualization field should facilitate the recall of the past meeting.

Two different types of meeting reports have also been implemented to motivate users to reflect on the meeting when it is over. These reports provide general information about the meeting, as well as information about the average mood development of all participants during the meeting, which offer deeper information for reflection. The possibility of comparing one's own mood to the average team mood provides further input to reflect about the individual mood development during a meeting. The available reflection journal is intended to store the individual insights and reflection outcomes in relation to the meeting. In case a user prefers to reflect about the meeting later on and wants to be reminded, feedback functionality via email was also integrated. The content of these emails depends on the individual user settings, which allow defining what kind of information will be sent to him or her, along with a direct link to the meeting report in the MoodMap App.

With the development of the meeting reports, the MoodMap App can support the two types of reflection defined by Schön [1984]. On the one hand, reflection-in-action, which takes place while doing work, is supported by the different live visualizations, both individual and collaborative ones. On the other hand, the new implemented reports are designed to support reflection-on-action; i.e., in retrospective by analyzing reactions to any situation and exploring the reasons and consequences afterwards.

Timeline View

The *Timeline* View (see Figure 4.6) was simplified to allow users to see their moods in a single timeline. In this prototype, each mood point is split into its two dimensions: valence and arousal. The blue line in the figure represents the valence, whereas the red line shows the arousal. The value of the y-axis goes from 0 to 1 representing the state from very low to very high valence and arousal values. The x-axis represents the time. If a mood point has an attached note, it will be shown when the mouse moves over the point in the timeline. If context information was added in the *Capture Mood* View, it is shown to the bottom part of the timeline. By moving the mouse over the context symbol, the context information is displayed. If numerous mood points are shown in the timeline within a short time span (e.g., a minute), the user can zoom in by selecting the according points in the timeline visualization (holding the mouse while selecting the fragment of the timeline that should be zoomed).

MoodMap Meeting Configuration

The most relevant added feature in this second prototype was the administration of meetings in the application. In order to fit the usage in virtual meetings, the configuration of meetings as well as reports on the gathered data were needed. Users can define several parameters when creating a meeting; e.g., name, meeting place and time. They can also select participants and a moderator for the meeting (per default the current user is set as moderator). The moderator as well as the participants can be invited to the meeting via email.

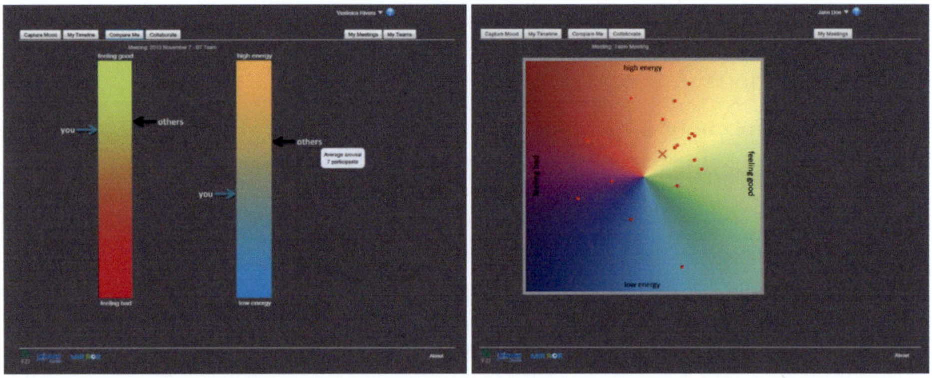

Figure 4.5.: Example of adapted color scheme in the collaborative views of MoodMap App 2.0: Compare Me (left) and Collaborate (right)

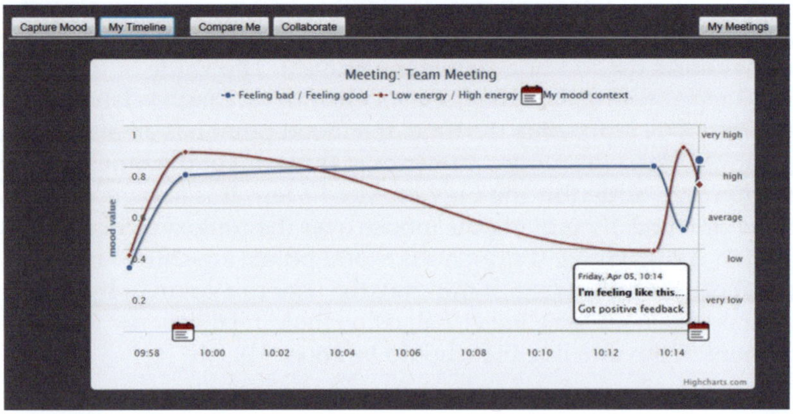

Figure 4.6.: Timeline View: Users track their own mood and visualize it in a timeline

MoodMap Meeting Reports

When a meeting is over, the user can visit two types of reports. The *Meeting Reports* and the *Meetings & Me Report*, which are both accessible via the *My Meetings* tab. The *Meeting Report* provides information about a past meeting and the captured moods of the participants, whereas the *Meetings & Me* offers a comparison of the user's personal mood during the meeting and that of his or her colleagues (team mood).

Users can see reports about all the meetings they have participated in. On the left side of the report (see Figure 4.7), general information on the meeting is available, including the meeting date, duration, moderator, type, place and number of participants. The *Meeting Mood News* visualizes relevant mood changes, which were detected during the meeting. These changes refer to significant individual mood changes, but also to remarkable deviations of the individual mood from the average team mood. The small picture of the mood map in the upper right corner shows the number of mood points that were entered by the participants in each quadrant during the whole meeting. The timeline including the individual context information shows the average team mood development over the meeting time. Using this information, users can reflect about the whole meeting; e.g., bringing together the meeting mood news with the average mood on the timeline, or seeing the mood distribution of the whole meeting might lead to personal insights or thoughts. These thoughts could then be inserted into the reflection journal, which gathers all the insights that the user gained by exploring the data.

The *Meetings & Me* tab gives access to meeting reports with information about what happened during the meeting in relation to the user's individual mood. Through the select box with all the meetings a user has ever participated in, the user can select which report is visualized. In each report (see Figure 4.8), the *Meeting Mood News* is shown, analogous to the previous *Meeting Reports*. Additionally, two timelines with the corresponding context information are visible. The first timeline represents the valence level, where the individual valence development and the average collaborative valence development are represented in two separated lines (light and dark blue respectively). The second timeline covers the arousal values, showing the individual (light red), as well as the average arousal (dark red) levels of the team, separately. These visualizations facilitate the direct comparison of the individual to the average collaborative mood development. Reflecting on the data and associating them with the *Meeting Mood News* might lead to new insights. These insights can also be stored in the reflection journal, which the user can revisit later.

Figure 4.7.: Meeting Report: Summary and analysis of captured moods and notes during a meeting or a working shift

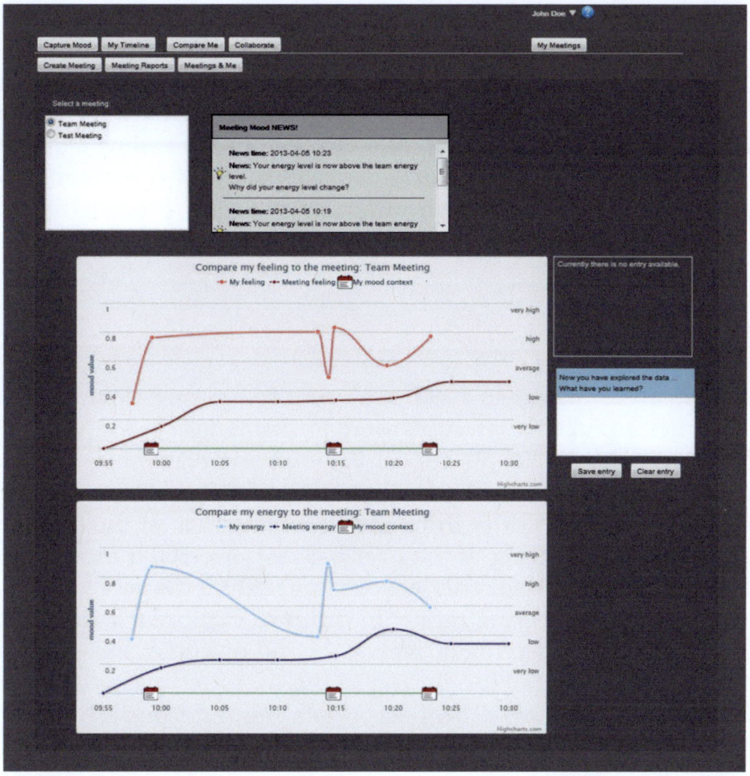

Figure 4.8.: Meetings & Me Report: Analysis and comparison of one own's mood and the average mood of the team

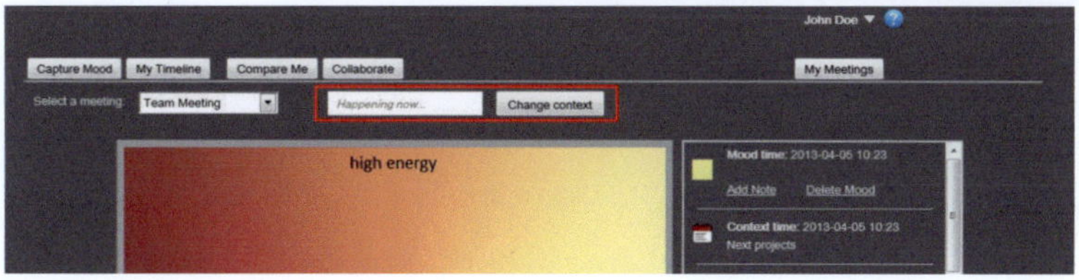

Figure 4.9.: Contextualization of moods: Text field to enter the current situation

Contextualization of Moods

For a better contextualization of the captured moods; i.e., to add information about the situation in which the current mood emerged, a context input field is available (see Figure 4.9). The added context is also added to the moodlist in order to follow the mood development and the corresponding context. This feature aimed at facilitating a subsequent reflective learning process, by providing further information about the user when a certain mood was captured.

User Prompts

User prompts were added to motivate users to capture data and to trigger reflection. Different types of prompts were implemented in the MoodMap App (see Figure 4.10). These prompts appear if something relevant or significant has happened during a meeting. The first type of prompts aims at increasing data capturing. They appear under different circumstances: at the beginning of a meeting, during the meeting, if the user has not inserted a mood for a while, and at the end of the meeting. This last prompt enables the user to jump straight to the corresponding meeting report in order to explore the data and reflect on it directly when the meeting is over. A second option in this prompt allows the user to receive an email (according to the users setting) with information about the meeting. This email will serve as a reminder for the user to reflect about the meeting at a later time (see further details in Section 4.2.3). The second type of prompt is used as guidance for the user to reflect on his or her mood directly during the meeting. Significant mood changes may trigger a reflective process, but also discrepancies with the collaborative mood could lead to new insights. The changes on the individual level encompass significant increments or decrements of the valence or arousal levels from one mood to the next one. Comparing the user's mood to the average team mood makes the user aware of significant deviations with respect to the mood of his or her colleagues. In both cases, the user is asked for the reason of that change or deviation; e.g., why the arousal level raised, or why his or her mood is much better than the average team mood.

Email Functionality

In the user settings there is the possibility to configure the email options. There are three available email settings: (1) *Send me email reports containing only the information about the meeting (name, date, etc.)*: emails will only consist of general information about the meeting; e.g., the name of the meeting, the date of the meeting or the number of participants. Additionally, a link will be available to go directly to the "Meeting Report" section in the MoodMap App. An example of this email is depicted in Figure 4.11. (2) *Send me email reports with information about the meeting and my moods*: emails will encompass, besides general meeting information, also information about the individual mood development during the meeting. This email will contain a link to the corresponding meeting within the MoodMap App too. (3) *Don't send me any email reports*: when selecting this option, the current user will not receive any emails of the MoodMap application containing reports about the meetings.

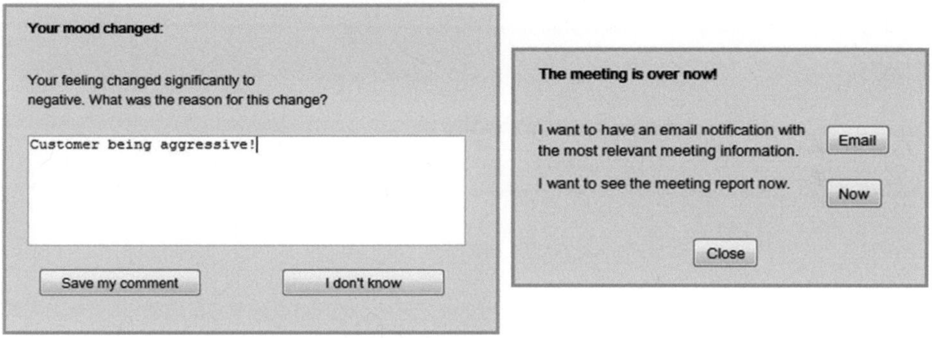

Figure 4.10.: Examples of prompts: increasing awareness of significant mood changes (left) and pointing out to available data reports after a meeting (right)

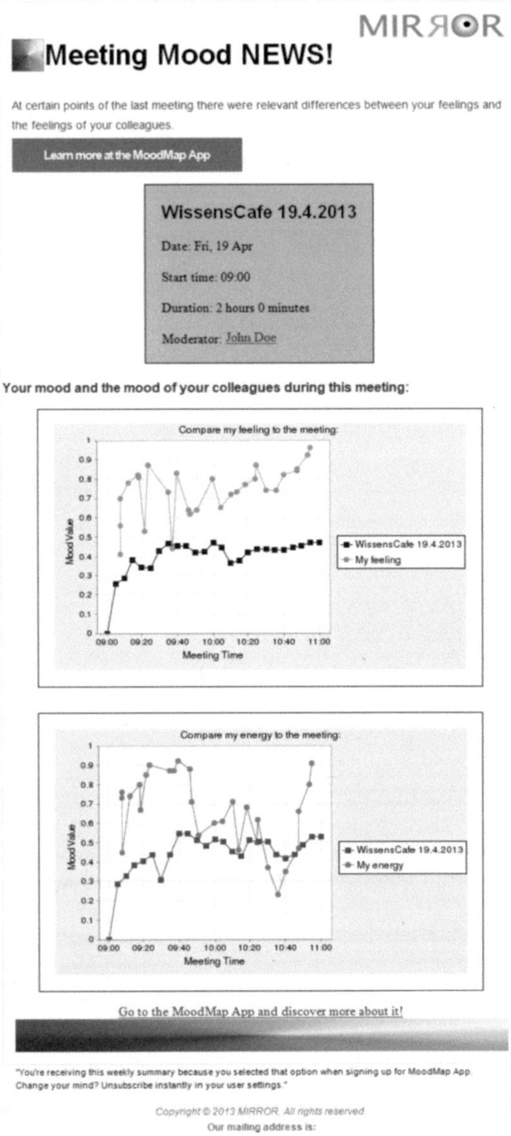

Figure 4.11.: Email containing information about a meeting and the participants' moods

4.2.4. MoodMap App 3.0

In this third prototype, the features that remained (i.e., Capture View, Personal Views, Collaborative Views and Meeting Reports) were slightly adapted to the new user interface but no changes were produced. Therefore, we will not describe them again, but show how they visually looked like in this third and last prototype.

The MoodMap App 3.0 underwent three major modifications. Firstly, team capabilities were added to the application, allowing the aggregation of users in teams and the automatic generation of working shifts. Secondly, pre-defined context types were implemented and users were asked to select one of them every time they captured a mood. Finally, three new team visualizations only accessible for managers and coaches were added. These visualizations give said managers and coaches further insights about the moods of each single employee of his or her team and serve as triggers to reflect upon the mood development of their team members as well that of the whole team. All these changes also required adding user management and distinguish the different types of users in the MoodMap App; i.e., managers, coaches and staff (call takers, software developers, etc.).

Team Capabilities

One of the most important structural changes in the application was the support for teams. The app users have to subscribe to previously configured teams and their moods are automatically aggregated in the corresponding team and shift, depending on the time when the mood was captured. The selection of the team is done when registering in the application and is subsequently configurable through the user's settings. They must also specify their role in the team; e.g., call taker, coach or manager. Users are automatically redirected to their teams' shift when entering the MoodMap App. This reduces the efforts to capture moods during the daily work and allows a faster classification of the moods.

Adapted Contextualization

In order to add information about the situation in which the current mood emerged, users are asked to select a pre-defined context (i.e., after a call, after a coaching session, after a break, others) and add a free-text note (e.g., why he or she is feeling like this) immediately after capturing a mood. For each inserted mood a pop-up appears, asking explicitly for the corresponding context (see Figure 4.12). The context is added to the moodlist which allows following the mood development and the associated context. This feature aims at guiding contextualization and, as a consequence, facilitating a subsequent reflective learning process.

As part of this adaptation, each inserted mood is also represented in the form of a smiley in the bottom right corner of the app. This smiley appears after the user has captured a mood and entered the corresponding context. The size of the smiley represents the arousal level; i.e., the bigger the smiley the higher the arousal value is. The expression of the smiley represents the valence level; i.e., the more a smiley smiles, the better the valence of the individual is, whereas a sad smiley represents a negative valence of the user. The color of the smiley corresponds to the color of the point that the user clicked in the mood map.

Team Views

If the user is a manager or a coach, further visualizations with non-aggregated moods of the team members are available. Each manager or coach can only see the moods of members in his or her own team(s). Other users in the app (e.g., call takers) are not able to see these visualizations. There are three team visualizations available: *Team Day*, *Daily Timeline* and *Weekly Timeline*. These views give the manager the possibility to gain more insights about the mood of each individual team member and at the same time get an impression of the team as a whole. Figure 4.13 shows a screenshot of the *Team Day* visualization with the current mood of each team member in the form of a smiley (the codification of the smiley was previously explained in Section 4.2.4). Additionally, the color of the smiley is the same as the corresponding point in the mood map. When clicking on a smiley, the timeline is opened representing the arousal and valence development of the selected user of the corresponding day (see bottom part of Figure 4.13). The visualization *Daily Timeline* is shown in Figure 4.14, with all single mood points of each user on the timeline and the average development of the team moods (continuous line). This view gives the manager a possibility to see how the single mood points have developed during the whole day according to the arousal and the valence levels of the whole team.

The third Team View *Weekly Timeline* (Figure 4.15) shows the mood development of each single team member during the whole week. The timeline is interactive, allowing the user to select which values should be visualized. By clicking on the *Feeling* and *Energy* of each team member in the legend, the arousal and valence levels of each person can be added or removed of the timeline as required. When clicking on the *Hide all* button, all individual arousal and valence lines are removed and only the average arousal and valence lines of the whole team are displayed.

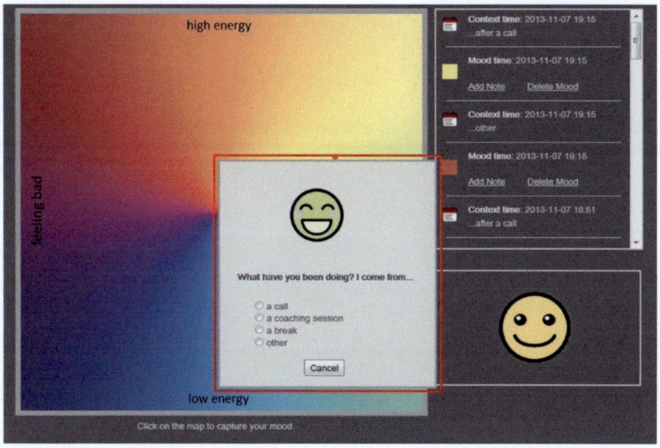

Figure 4.12.: Compulsory context for each inserted mood

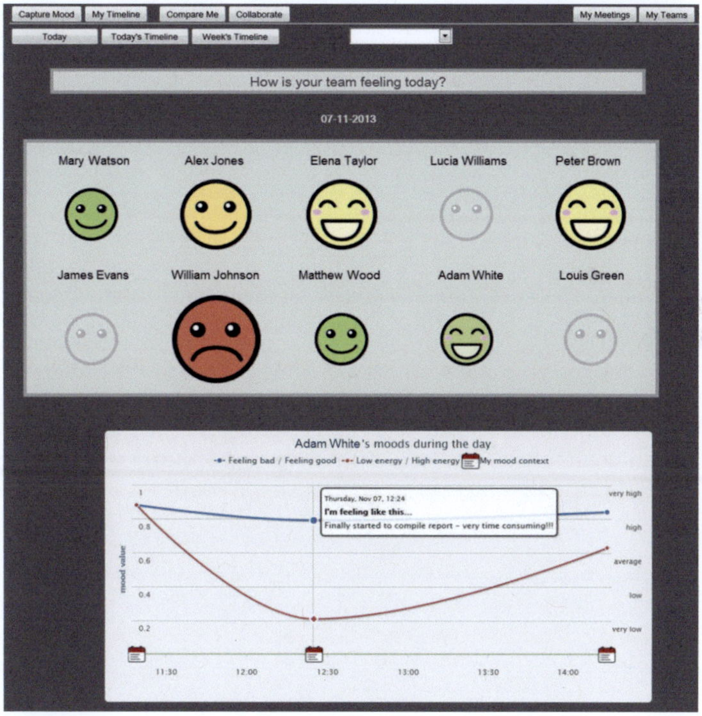

Figure 4.13.: Smileys View: Smileys visualization with today's average mood of each individual team member. When selecting a smiley, the moods and notes of the selected user are shown in the timeline below.

Figure 4.14.: Daily Timeline: Development of the moods of all team members (single points) and average team mood (lines). Moods are divided in their two components: The upper timeline shows valence values (feeling) and the lower timeline shows arousal values (energy) of each mood. The small dialog with the name of the user and the context appears when hovering over a certain mood point.

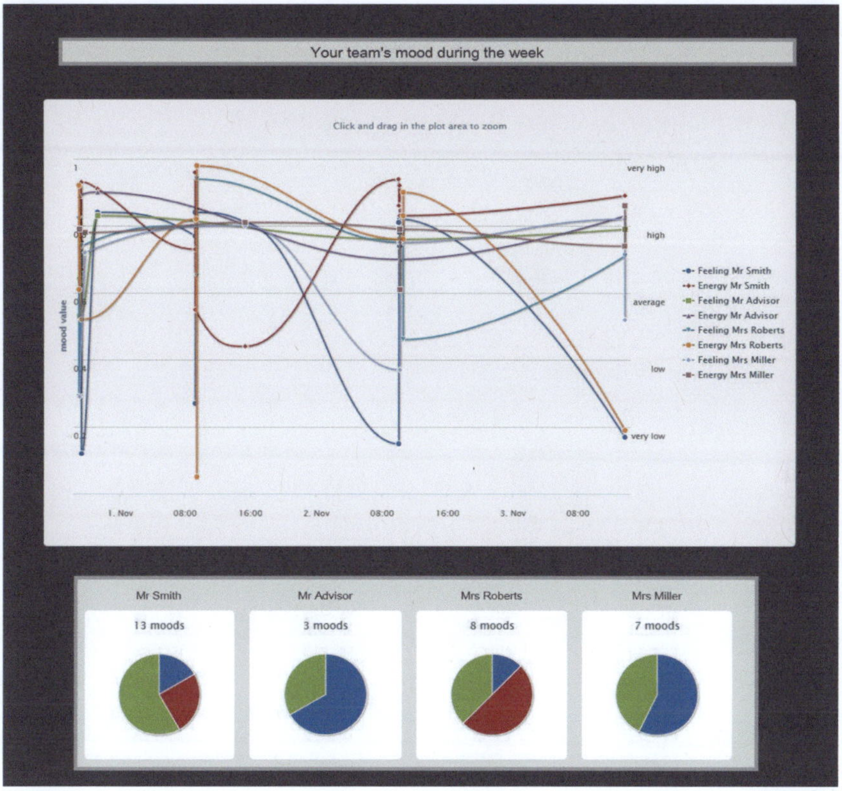

Figure 4.15.: Weekly Timeline: Mood development of each single team member during the whole week (top) and interactive charts with distribution of types of mood contexts for each team member (bottom). Available context types were: after a call (blue), after a break (green), after a coaching session (red), and other (purple).

Below the timeline visualization, a pie chart visualization per team member is shown. Each pie chart represents the total number of captured moods and the percentage of moods that were attached to each type of context, according to the options available in the contextualization of moods (see Figure 4.12).

4.2.5. Implementation

The MoodMap App is a web-based application built with a three-tier architecture. An overview of the architecture is shown in Figure 4.16.

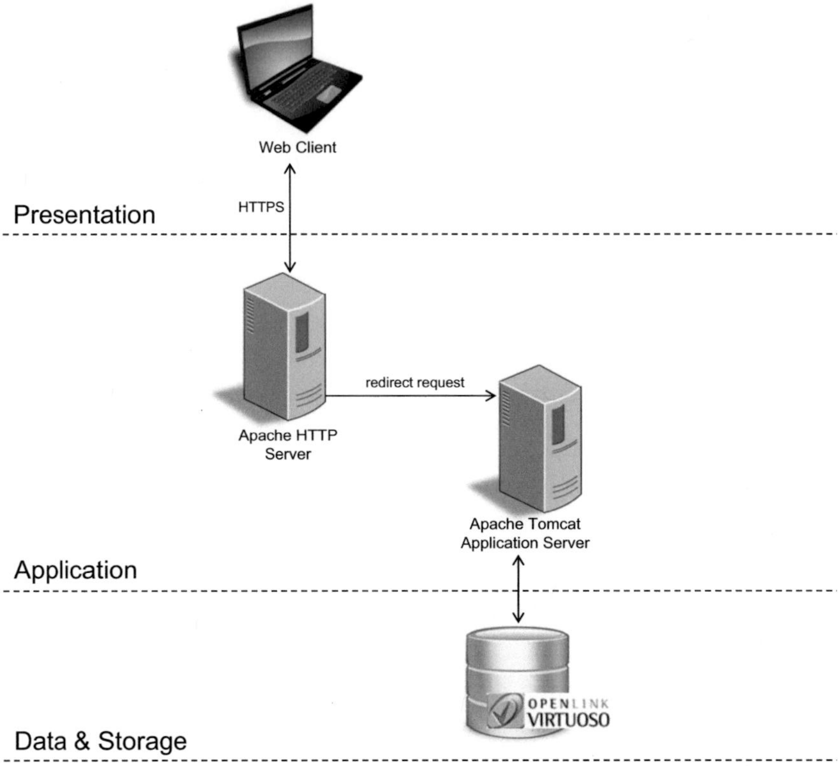

Figure 4.16.: MoodMap App Architecture

Presentation

The MoodMap App Interface defines the GUI that allows users to interact with the application. The MoodMap App client is an AJAX[4] web application implemented in Java. The Google Web Toolkit is responsible for the compilation of the Java code into a deployable Web application based on JavaScript and CSS. From a developers' point of view, this facilitates the process of building a Web application, as Java code is commonly employed and many compatible libraries

[4] Asynchronous JavaScript And XML [Garrett, 2005]

already exist. The Web application is hosted by Apache Tomcat[5]. Client and server communicate via HTTP requests.

Application

The MoodMap App server takes care of data management. Therefore, it provides the necessary services as well as the database. Each service provides methods which carry out a specific task. Each task communicates with the database to read and write data.

Data and Storage

Users, moods and other data are stored as RDF data in a triple store. The triple store used to manage the MoodMap App data is Virtuoso[6], which is an open source database engine. Virtuoso provides data management based on the RDF and SPARQL query language standard. In addition to the capabilities of any other relational database, Virtuoso has additional benefits; e.g., the reuse of existing vocabulary (SIOC, FOAF) when designing the MoodMap App data model or the easy installation and maintenance.

All classes and properties listed in this section which do not have a prefix use the MoodMap App Schema prefix (`http://moodmap.org/2012/schema#`). In the following, we give further details about the classes of the MoodMap App Schema.

- **User:** Users are part of the graph with the IRI: `http://moodmap.org/2012/namedgraph/user`. Users are identified uniquely by a username, which is part of the IRI. The data of a user is divided in two classes. The first class (foaf:Person[7]) saves the name and account of the user. The second class (sioc:UserAccount[8]) is used for the email and configuration of the account in the application. The triples contained for each Mood in the ontology are detailed in Table 4.3.
- **Meeting:** All Meetings are saved as part of the Meeting Graph (`http://moodmap.org/2012/namedgraph/meetings`). The data of a Meeting is divided in several concepts, whose root is the Meeting itself. The triples contained for each Meeting in the ontology are detailed in Table 4.3. Meetings are identified by a unique ID consisting of a 128-Bit random

[5] `http://tomcat.apache.org/download-70.cgi`
[6] `http://virtuoso.openlinksw.com/dataspace/doc/dav/wiki/Main/`
[7] foaf: `http://xmlns.com/foaf/0.1/#`
[8] sioc: `http://rdfs.org/sioc/ns#`

number (UUID, Immutable Universally Unique Identifier). The type and place of the Meeting is defined in the MoodMap Schema.

- **Mood, Context and User Prompt:** Moods are grouped in Graphs according to the date when they are created. This structure facilitates the search and retrieval of moods because the use cases we are dealing with are focused on certain days (e.g., all moods of a user in a certain day). Contexts and User Prompts are also grouped following the same principle in the corresponding graphs. Moods, Context and User Prompts are always linked to a user of the MoodMap App, and optionally to a Meeting. The triples saved for each of these elements in the ontology are detailed in Table 4.4.
- **Reflection Entry and Journal:** A Reflection Entry is an annotation of a user done in a mood report. A report can contain more than one Entry from a certain user and they compose the Reflection Journal. All Reflection Entries are grouped in a graph. Table 4.4 shows the triples saved for each Entry in the ontology.

Table 4.3.: Triples of the MoodMap App ontology for Users and Meetings

Element	Subject	Predicate	Object
User	foaf:Person (User IRI)	foaf:firstname	rdfs:Literal
	foaf:Person (User IRI)	foaf:lastname	rdfs:Literal
	foaf:Person (User IRI)	foaf:account	sioc:UserAccount (BN)
	sioc:UserAccount (BN)	foaf:AccountName	rdfs:Literal
	sioc:UserAccount (BN)	sioc:email	rdfs:Literal
	sioc:UserAccount (BN)	has_email_settings	xsd:string
	sioc:UserAccount (BN)	has_sharing_settings	xsd:string
	sioc:UserAccount (BN)	has_password	xsd:string
	sioc:UserAccount (BN)	sioc:account_of	foaf:Person (User IRI)
Meeting	Meeting (BN)	rdf:type	Meeting
	Meeting (BN)	time:hasBeginning	time:Instant
	Meeting (BN)	time:hasEnd	time:Instant
	Meeting (BN)	of_type	type_of_meeting
	Meeting (BN)	at_place	place_of_meeting
	Meeting (BN)	rdfs:label	rdfs:Literal
	Meeting (BN)	has_id	xsd:integer
	Meeting (BN)	has_creator	sioc:UserAccount
	Meeting (BN)	sioc:has_moderator	sioc:UserAccount
	Meeting (BN)	sioc:has_usergroup	sioc:UserGroup
	Meeting (BN)	do_notify_moderator	xsd:boolean
	Meeting (BN)	do_invite_participants	xsd:boolean
	Meeting (BN)	allow_coolaborative_views	xsd:boolean
	Meeting (BN)	allow_reflection_amplifiers	xsd:boolean
	sioc:UserGroup (BN)	sioc:has_member	sioc:UserAccount
	time:Instant (BN)	time:inXSDDateTime	xsd:dateTime

*BN indicates Blank Node

Table 4.4.: Triples of the MoodMap App ontology for Moods, Contexts, Reflection Entries, and User prompts

Element	Subject	Predicate	Object
Mood	Mood (BN)	rdf:type	Mood
	Mood (BN)	time:inXSDDateTime	time:Instant (BN)
	Mood (BN)	is_mood_of	foaf:Person (User IRI)
	foaf:Person (User IRI)	has_mood	Mood (BN)
	Mood (BN)	has_energy	xsd:double
	Mood (BN)	has_feel	xsd:double
	Mood (BN)	aroused_at	Meeting (BN)
	Mood (BN)	rdfs:label	xsd:string
	Meeting (BN)	aroused	Mood (BN)
Context	Context (BN)	rdf:type	Context
	Context (BN)	time:inXSDDateTime	time:Instant (BN)
	Context (BN)	has_creator	foaf:Person (User IRI)
	Context (BN)	is_context_of	Meeting (BN)
	Context (BN)	rdfs:label	xsd:string
	Meeting (BN)	has_context	Context (BN)
	foaf:Person (User IRI)	creator_of	Context (BN)
Reflection Entry	ReflectionEntry (BN)	rdf:type	ReflectionEntry
	ReflectionEntry (BN)	time:inXSDDateTime	time:Instant (BN)
	ReflectionEntry (BN)	has_creator	foaf:Person (User IRI)
	ReflectionEntry (BN)	is_entry_of	Meeting (BN)
	ReflectionEntry (BN)	rdfs:label	xsd:string
	Meeting (BN)	has_reflection_entry	ReflectionEntry (BN)
	foaf:Person (User IRI)	creator_of	ReflectionEntry (BN)
User prompt	User prompt (BN)	rdf:type	Amplifier
	User prompt (BN)	time:inXSDDateTime	time:Instant (BN)
	User prompt (BN)	has_creator	foaf:Person (User IRI)
	User prompt (BN)	is_amplifier_of	Meeting (BN)
	User prompt (BN)	rdfs:label	xsd:string
	Meeting (BN)	has_amplifier	User prompt (BN)
	foaf:Person (User IRI)	creator_of	User prompt (BN)

*BN indicates Blank Node

4.3. Evaluation Approach

Table 4.5 summarizes the studies and evaluations conducted with the MoodMap App in chronological order. In the following sections, we describe the procedure and the results of each evaluation.

During our research, seven studies were conducted with the MoodMap App enrolling a total of 193 participants.

Table 4.5.: Overview of the MoodMap App evaluations

Type of Evaluation	Organization/ Setting	App Version	Participants	Start–End
Design Study	Project Meeting	0.5	32 researchers	10-05-2011 12-05-2011
Formative	BT (FWS*)	1.0	12 product managers and consultants	13-02-2012 12-03-2012
Design Study	BT (FWS)	1.0	9 product managers and consultants	15-10-2012
Formative	BT (FWS)	2.0	12 product managers and consultants	24-05-2013 24-08-2013
Formative	BT Dundee	2.0	2 managers 10 coaches 10 call takers	13-06-2013 16-08-2013
Summative	BT Dundee BT Alness	3.0	4 managers 2 coaches 65 call takers	20-11-2013 20-12-2013
Summative	Regola	3.0	35 employees from different departments	12-02-2014 31-03-2014

*FWS: Flexible Working Services

4.4. Design Study I: European Project Meeting

The goal of this first design study was to identify tools and methods that can collect information about the mood of employees. Mood capturing needs minimal involvement of the employee and could be used to support the reflection process. Stating the current mood with a single click needs much less time than writing a diary. Additionally, this data can be anonymously collected and aggregated for teams or organizations. This aggregated data could be used as feedback to reward employees for stating their mood. Besides, the use of different visualizations can motivate the user and stimulate reflection.

Considering these hypotheses, the following three main aspects were researched in this design study:

- How to motivate employees to capture and share their mood?
- Does mood data indicate critical events?
- Does mood data support reflection?

In this design study, an early prototype of the MoodMap App (which we will just call Mood App) was used, which only included a capturing interface (Mood Map) and one visualization (Mood Bars)—see Figures 4.17, 4.18 and 4.19. Additionally, other applications participated in the study, but we will concentrate on the parts of the study that only involve the MoodMap App. This study was performed in collaboration with the Norwegian University of Science and Technology (NTNU), in the context of the EU project MIRROR. For further details about this design study, we refer to its publication in [Mora et al., 2011].

4.4.1. Procedure

In this design study, we developed several applications that allow the capturing and visualization of users' moods. The Mood App consisted of a web application that tried to leverage the curiosity of the employee to motivate the data collection. The individual user was rewarded with information of his or her mood in comparison to others. Other applications involved in the study used a slightly different approach and focused more on the hedonistic value of their application and the capturing of additional data. Therefore, multiple visualizations and a mobile application that combined moods with pictures and additional notes were also used.

All the applications were integrated and evaluated in a project meeting of the EU MIRROR Project, which took place in Karlsruhe, from May 10 to May 12, 2011. This project meeting provided a unique test environment because all participants shared a common work context and were in a real work situation without focusing on this experiment, but on the work that they had to do. Therefore, the time constraints and cognitive efforts to use the mood capturing tools matched a user at work. Moreover, this meeting was a well documented event and therefore offered rich available reference data.

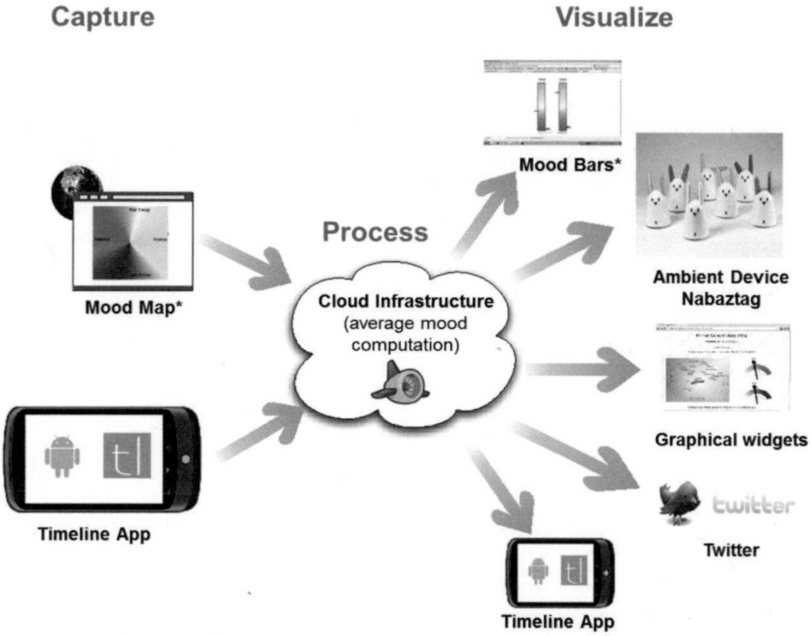

Figure 4.17.: Interfaces used for mood capturing, processing and visualization. Prototypes that served for the development of the MoodMap App (Mood Map and Mood Bars) are marked with an asterisk (*).

At the beginning of the project meeting, the experiment was shortly presented and additional mobile devices were given to volunteers. During the meeting, participants could state their mood with the different tools and see the changes of the average through the different visualizations. Figure 4.17 shows the schematic representation of the architecture, with the four different mood visualizations, as well as the two input interfaces described in the following sections.

All entered mood data and the means of capturing (used tool) were stored for later analysis. Additional data that was captured using the mobile devices was stored as well. The meeting agenda, the meeting protocol and additional notes served as a reference to analyze the captured data. Some sessions had more intense discussions that should be visible in the data. Additionally, participants were asked during breaks for feedback on their experience with the system.

All the mood entries provided by the Mood App and the TimeLine App (one of the involved apps from partners) were stored in a cloud-based architecture which calculated the average mood of the latest 10 mood entries (captured by any user). The system also provided interfaces for fetching the current mood average. This functionality was exploited to provide multiple visualizations of that data.

Capturing moods

The Mood App allowed users to introduce their moods in a two-dimensional map (see Figure 4.18 to the left) and afterwards directly compare them with the average mood of the other users (see Section 4.4.1 and Figure 4.19).

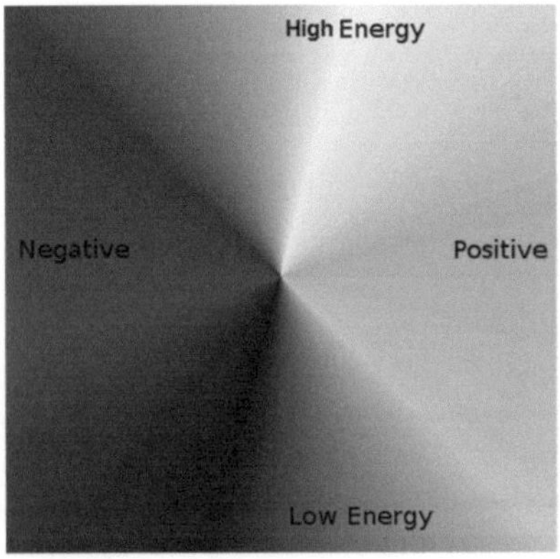

Quadrant	X and Y values	Representation
Top Right	x(0,5-1,0), y(0,5-1.0)	- happy
Top Left	x(0,0-0,5), y(0,5-1.0)	- nervous
Bottom Right	x(0,5-1,0), y(0,0-0,5)	- calm
Bottom Left	x(0,5-1,0), y(0,0-0,5)	- sad

Figure 4.18.: Two-dimensional Mood Map to introduce the user's mood (left). Table showing the mapping from a quadrant in the Mood Map to the representation as a smiley in the Timeline App (right).

It was developed as a web-based application and may therefore be used from any browser. The current average is calculated with the last ten entered moods due to the anonymous entered data. It must be noticed that this was a preliminary version of the MoodMap App with no user management and therefore this calculation is different to the average mood described in the Equation 4.1. With this mood feedback and the possibility to compare the own mood with the rest of users, it was intended to motivate users to capture data. Here, users were not just giving input for the system, but receiving a personalized response and being able to derive a benefit for themselves. This benefit of comparing themselves with the other users could lead to regularly introducing their mood and therefore capturing more data about themselves.

The mobile Timeline Application running on Android devices adopted the same mood model. Due to the limited dimensions of the display, it might be difficult and confusing to show the mood in the time line through a mood map or through the corresponding color of the mood. We therefore decided to use emoticons. The mood map is divided into four quadrants, representing four different mood statuses and mapping those to four different emoticons that the user could choose from in the Timeline Application to set the mood (see table in Figure 4.18 to the right).

Visualizing moods

To explore different ways of visualizing moods, we developed four prototypes of media for visualization:

- Local: Mood Bars
- Ambient: Nabaztag (ambient device in the form of a rabbit)
- Ambient: Public display with graphical widgets
- Social: Twitter

Each of these visualizations (Figure 4.19) fitted best a determined context. The local Mood Bars visualization allowed seeing the average in the same application display and the ambient device Nabaztag could provide non-disruptive information during a meeting, whereas a public display was the best media to provide information in a corridor or in a public hall. Figure 4.19 shows the three visualization prototypes used in this study.

The Mood Bars' web interface showed the visualization of the compared moods through two colored bars: the first bar for valence and the second bar for arousal. The vertical bars represented the range of values, numerically comprised between 0 (bottom) and 1 (top). The blue arrows showed the values introduced by the user, whereas the black arrows showed the average mood. A "Back to Mood Map" button placed at the bottom of the site allowed the user to go back to the mood map (initial state of the application) and introduce new mood values when desired (see Figure 4.19 to the left).

Large public displays are useful to show information such as charts and images that can be seen from a distance. The prototype used in this study showed the average mood on a mood map and the valence and arousal component via graphical gauge widgets (see Figure 4.19 to the right). Data were updated every

15 seconds. This visualization allowed several people to meet in front of it in a shared space and might trigger collaborative reflection.

The average mood was also tweeted on the microblogging service Twitter[9] every 15 minutes. Our first prototype only showed valence and arousal values by float numbers ranging between 0 (minimum) and 1 (maximum). A (non-human) twitter user was created and it is possible for other twitter users to leave comments on average mood statuses.

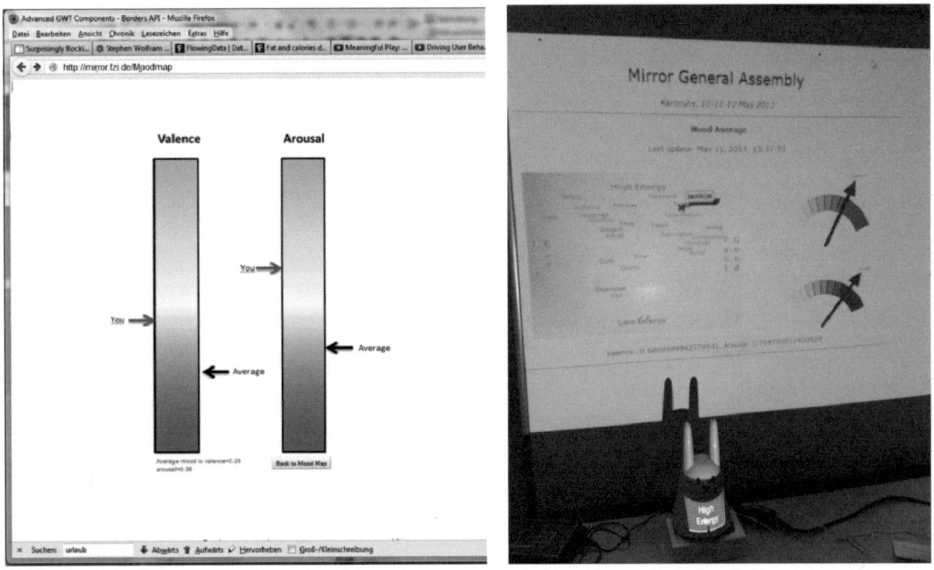

Figure 4.19.: Ambient display and ambient device Nabaztag (right); Mood Bars visualization in the web application (left)

4.4.2. Results

Attendees extensively used the apps throughout the 3-days meeting. They entered their moods using two available interfaces and they showed a general interest in the evolution of the average mood in relation to the events taking place at the moment.

[9] https://twitter.com/

Acceptance of the Applications

The integration of the aforementioned prototypes achieved a good reliability. Hundreds of moods were shared during the meetings, and low usage peaks were recorded during heated discussions, as users were engaged in the discussion. The ambient visualizations provoked both technical and ethical discussions. Most of the speakers who shared the stage checked, at least once, the outcome of their talks against the rabbit, in order to assess whether the audience were actually paying attention to the speech or were bored/tired. While during the meeting sessions the mood map web-interface was the most used, during breaks and informal meetings the smartphone-based interface was the most utilized.

Data gathered

During the three days, more than 1,100 mood entries were captured. The meeting was observed to shed light on the relation between captured mood data and work context. Figure 4.20 shows the average arousal and valence during the first day of the meeting.

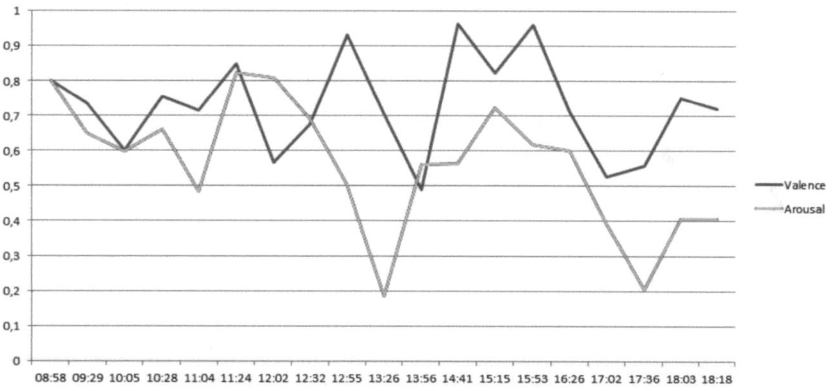

Figure 4.20.: Average mood (valence and arousal) during the first day of the meeting

The arousal line in Figure 4.20 shows how the arousal goes down towards the lunch break and the end of the meeting. At these points, participants entered their mood to achieve a desired reaction of the presenter or the moderation; e.g., having a break, ending a discussion or closing the day. Later, they pointed at the projected mood or complained over the delay of the displayed mood. By analyzing the meeting protocol, other trends could be identified too:

- When a heated discussion took place the average arousal increased.
- The valence decreased if the discussion was not evolving satisfactory.
- When the meeting was reaching the end of the last session the valence level decreased till reaching very low values ("sad/unpleasant").

Participants actively referred to the displayed average mood several times during the second day. Presenters started their presentations with sentences like "I hope I can keep this arousal level" or ended a presentation with sentences like "Look at the Nabazmood, low arousal, we should have a break!" While these statements always had a mocking tone, the result was the desired break.

The log data shows that during the meeting the online web application was preferred. The mobile MoodTimeline was used mainly during breaks and during a lab visit in the afternoon. During the lab visit, additionally pictures were taken using the mobile application. On the second day, some unexpected behavior was observed. Single participants tried to manipulate the mood values by spamming the system with mood statements. They later explained that they wanted to see the Nabazmood to move its ears into a certain position. This spamming was possible because the average value was computed from the last ten values without considering which user had entered them. By adding user management and considering the last mood of each user, this spamming could be avoided in the future.

Feedback from Users

Informal feedback was collected by short interviews during breaks and by analyzing posted messages in the MoodTimeline. The results concerned the idea to capture moods, the design of the apps, and the relation between aggregated mood values and the meeting. Statements on the mood capturing and deployed applications were in general very positive; the visualization using the Nabazmood rabbit was especially appreciated, since most discussions evolved around the two ambient visualizations. When asked about the different user interfaces, participants highlighted the suitability of the different interfaces according to their mobility. They pointed out that a mobile application like the MoodTimeline was much more helpful and more used when they were mobile and that a web-based application like the Mood App was more suitable when attending the different presentations at the meeting room. Participants could see relations between the aggregated mood data and the work process, in this case the meeting. For instance, two participants sent the following two messages:

P1: *"Does the discussion of the project reports affect the mood of the group?"*
P2: *"For sure it did!"*

One participant even considered introducing an automatic alarm:
P3: *"There should be an automatic break alarm when energy gets below a specific level."*

Other participants tried to interpret the data:
P4: *"Low arousal in the group now. Do people need lunch? Good valence though :-)"*

Furthermore, participants discussed the displayed mood with each other and drew conclusions on the relation between current topics and reaction of the group. The MoodTimeline served as a source of tracking reference data too; i.e., information about what is happening and that can be directly connected to the available moods to offer richer context information. In this direction, users introduced comments like *"Storyboards, finding the relationships with the user studies"* or *"Clustering cards with suggested reflection activities."*

The integration of two different abstractions for the mood input, the mood map and the emoticons, was evaluated positively. The users could understand it intuitively and appreciated the integration of different interfaces that allowed a richer collaborative collecting of moods.

4.4.3. Discussion

The high amount of mood entries and the positive feedback of users indicated a high user acceptance. Users were willing to capture and share their moods. While we expected the playful user interface or the curiosity of the users to be most important, the possible influence on the meeting turned out to be the biggest motivator for them. The relation between the average mood and the meeting was visible from the captured mood data and was confirmed by participant's feedback. However, our implementation of the mood average had several flaws that were exploited during the test and that will be addressed in future prototypes further in this thesis.

The applications created awareness of the average mood during the meeting; however, due to the user-centered nature of our mood tracking interfaces, awareness was only made of moods of active users while we did not have any information from users who did not send moods. We conclude that the system, besides keeping mood entries anonymous, should highlight the level of involvement of users in building awareness and the distribution of moods-entries over the crowd; this can be considered as an index of plausibility of the awareness. The complete involvement of the crowd could only be achieved by relying on approaches like sensor-based systems where users have a passive role and data from all of them is being gathered automatically. However, the freedom to decide which data should be tracked would be limited.

Providing different levels of abstraction in the input mechanism (mood map and emoticons), despite allowing tracking interfaces to be context-aware, adds bias during the aggregation phase. Fine-grained moods as those provided on a two-dimensional space by the Mood App were aggregated with low-grained and discrete moods represented by emoticons on the Timeline app. The trade-off between system accuracy and freedom, allowing the users to choose the interface that best fits an ongoing context, should be decided according to the usage scenario.

Other than when speakers actively reminded the crowd to share moods, users were not asked to submit moods on a regular basis. Observations showed that people engaged in heated discussion tend to not send mood entries, leaving the aggregated mood to be influenced by users who are not part of the discussion.

Observations showed that some users manipulated the system by spamming mood entries. Interviewed users admitted to behaving in that manner in order to play with the Nabazmood rabbit. A future implementation should only consider the last mood statement of each individual user. This would require user management techniques. According to their behavior, two groups of users were identified:

- Users who referred to the system and discussed the average mood with others, thus supporting a collaborative reflection process.
- Users who were interested in influencing meetings by "voting" with their mood entries, in order to support coordination of collaborative work.

While both groups contributed to provide mood awareness, this led to the question, whether the captured mood really reflected the average mood of the group or was it considerably influenced by this "voting". Nonetheless, this does not impede the data from being used for reflection. Additionally, the mentioned user management would contribute to mitigate this bias. Given the amount of data and the relation between meeting and average mood, it could be used for later reflection. However, the evaluation was limited to three days in a prepared environment that visualized the average mood in different forms and further reflection sections on the data were not organized.

We presented a design study on mood awareness in collaborative environments attending to the design dimensions necessary to provide mood awareness and the influence of this awareness on the participants. We have seen that mood tracking provides an alternative channel for participants in a meeting to anonymously communicate their opinion and mood. Our results show that there is a strong relation between the context or activity taking place and the mood of the participants. Besides, we have presented several cases where mood awareness had an influence on the participants' behavior.

The approach used in this first study aimed at minimizing the barriers for potential users. As a result, the developed system does not have a user management technique. A future solution should offer user management to prevent mood spamming. New users could use the system for a number of requests without registration to keep the barriers low. If the user likes the system and wants to send more mood requests, the user would have to register.

This first design study was also used to awaken the interest of potential organizations and to start discussions on how mood affects work performance. With this, a basis for subsequent studies was set. The prototypes Mood App and Mood Bars were refined and included in the first prototype of the MoodMap App (see Section 4.2).

4.5. Formative Evaluation I: British Telecommunications Company

A first field study with the first prototype of the MoodMap App took place in a large British telecommunications company. This study was conducted in 2012. The results of this study contributed to the development of the second prototype of the MoodMap App as well as to the understanding of the support of reflective learning in the context of a big telecommunications company. For further details about this formative evaluation, the reader can refer to its publication [Fessl et al., 2011].

The MoodMap App was motivated by the need of addressing emotional aspects in reflective learning at work. In the evaluation scenario reported in this section, the MoodMap App was deployed within a spatially distributed team at the Learning Solutions Department of British Telecom (BT). The app was used in four consecutive virtual team meetings, which took place once a week during the period. In these meetings, team members inform about their current tasks and synchronize their work. The MoodMap App was used to capture the mood development during the meeting on an individual as well as on a team level.

The purpose of this evaluation was to undertake a first formative evaluation with the MoodMap App in a work context at BT, concretely in virtual team meetings. In such a setting, the integration in the users' established working practices as well as a high need for privacy and anonymization of the data become important requirements. Besides, it is necessary to investigate users' attitudes towards mood tracking and sharing, since participants may be differently motivated and interested. Additionally, there must be a clearly perceived benefit for users to continue using a mood tracking application at work. Thus, we proposed combining individual aspects of mood self-awareness with collaborative aspects of mood sharing and awareness of others' mood. Through this combination, not only new possibilities for mood assessment were offered, but users may create new perspectives about shared experiences too, as a basic prerequisite to promote reflective learning.

4.5.1. Procedure

The MoodMap App was evaluated in four meetings (which were scheduled every Monday) starting on February 13, 2012 and ending on March 12, 2012 (notice that no meeting took place on March 5). No installation was needed and the app was accessed through the Internet browsers that participants had already available in their work environments.

We designed the user study to answer the following research questions:

- RQ1: *Are participants interested in tracking their own mood and that of others?*
- RQ2: *Do participants appreciate the usability and features of the MoodMap App as it is implemented?*
- RQ3: *What benefits do participants perceive from the use of MoodMap App?*

The first two questions stem from the realization that, in such a team setting, not all participants will be similarly interested in mood tracking and motivated to use the MoodMap App. With the last question we want to verify our hypotheses that mood tracking and sharing (i) raises mood self-awareness and thus facilitate reflective learning from work experiences and (ii) raise awareness of others' mood and thus improve their team communication.

Before the evaluation period, the MoodMap App was briefly introduced to the participants, showing them the different features and explaining the general purpose of the app. In each of the meetings, the app was mapped to the following scenario: (1) Enter the MoodMap App and log in, (2) select the corresponding meeting, (3) add a mood at the beginning, during and in the end of the meeting, (4) add notes, and (5) have a look at the different views within the MoodMap App (individual and collaborative views). After each of the four meetings, the participants were invited to have a look at the past meeting again, think about their mood development during the meeting and fill in a short questionnaire. When the last meeting had taken place, the participants were asked to answer a final questionnaire. Some of the participants also agreed to be interviewed a week after the last meeting.

Participants

The team participating in the evaluation was composed of 12 participants. We gathered demographic data from 10 participants, who answered the pre-questionnaire. These 10 participants consisted of 6 men and 4 women. Participants in the evaluation were between 30 and 59 years old, with 20% of them aged between 30 and 39, 60% between 40 and 49 and 20% between 50 and 59. The team was composed of 4 consultants, 2 developers, 2 engineers and 2 managers. Regarding their work schedule, 7 participants work full-time and 3 part-time. On average, participants had spent 6.00 ($SD = 3.20$) years in their current position, ranging from participants with 2 years in that position and to a maximum of 13 years. The average number of years in a similar position (e.g., at another company) was 4.70 ($SD = 4.57$).

Evaluation Tools

Several tools were used to evaluate the use of the MoodMap App. We used a short questionnaire which was distributed after each meeting. It consisted of six questions about the atmosphere of the meeting, the participant's role in the meeting, the current mood and what insights they gained during the meeting. At the end of the meeting series, the team members were asked to fill in the final questionnaire. The final questionnaire consisted of 23 questions concerning general interest in mood tracking and other aspects regarding the MoodMap App. Precisely, (a) attitude towards the app, (b) how difficult it was to use it, (c) how useful the app was and how participants actually used it, (d) perceived benefits of using the MoodMap App, and (e) participants' ideas/feature requests for future versions that would increase the app's usefulness. The majority of the questions were based on a 5-point Likert scale of agreement and some of them were open questions.

Finally, interviews with some participants were also conducted online. Each interview lasted a maximum of 30 minutes. We addressed in the interviews the main points of the long questionnaire, but adapted the different issues to more open questions, which allowed participants to give more elaborated feedback.

4.5.2. Results

Table 4.6 offers an overview of the data collected during the evaluation, including short questionnaires (Sh-q), final questionnaire and interviews (Intw).

Table 4.6.: Overview of the collected data: questionnaire and interviews

N	Sh-q. 1*	Sh-q. 2*	Sh-q. 3*	Sh-q. 4*	Final quest.	Intw.
12	10 / 12	9 / 11	6 / 7	9 / 11	10**	6

*No. of filled in short questionnaires / no. of participants in the meeting

**4 of these participants also participated in an interview

Reaction and Usage

We analyzed the data captured by the participants directly through the usage of the MoodMap App. All moods captured by users during the four meetings were analyzed by meeting, in order to compare the four meetings to each other, taking into account valence and arousal values (in a range from 0 to 1). Table 4.7 shows the overall statistics of each meeting.

Table 4.7.: Overview of virtual meetings using the MoodMap App

Meeting	No. of Users	Avg. Mood/User	Avg. Valence	Avg. Arousal	Start Time	End Time
Meeting 1	12	21	0.65	0.61	13:32:47	14:06:02
Meeting 2	11	4	0.68	0.61	13:22:13	14:07:59
Meeting 3	7	9	0.68	0.62	13:22:34	14:02:56
Meeting 4	11	4	0.68	0.67	13:27:04	14:14:17

The number of participants of each meeting lay between 7 (meeting 3) and 12 (meeting 1) people. The average number of moods captured by the participants during a meeting was between 21 and 4 moods per user. Especially the high value in *meeting 1* refers to the trying out of the MoodMap App. The average team valence is very stable during all four meetings, the arousal (energy level) increases smoothly.

Figure 4.21 shows the evolution of the average mood in each meeting.

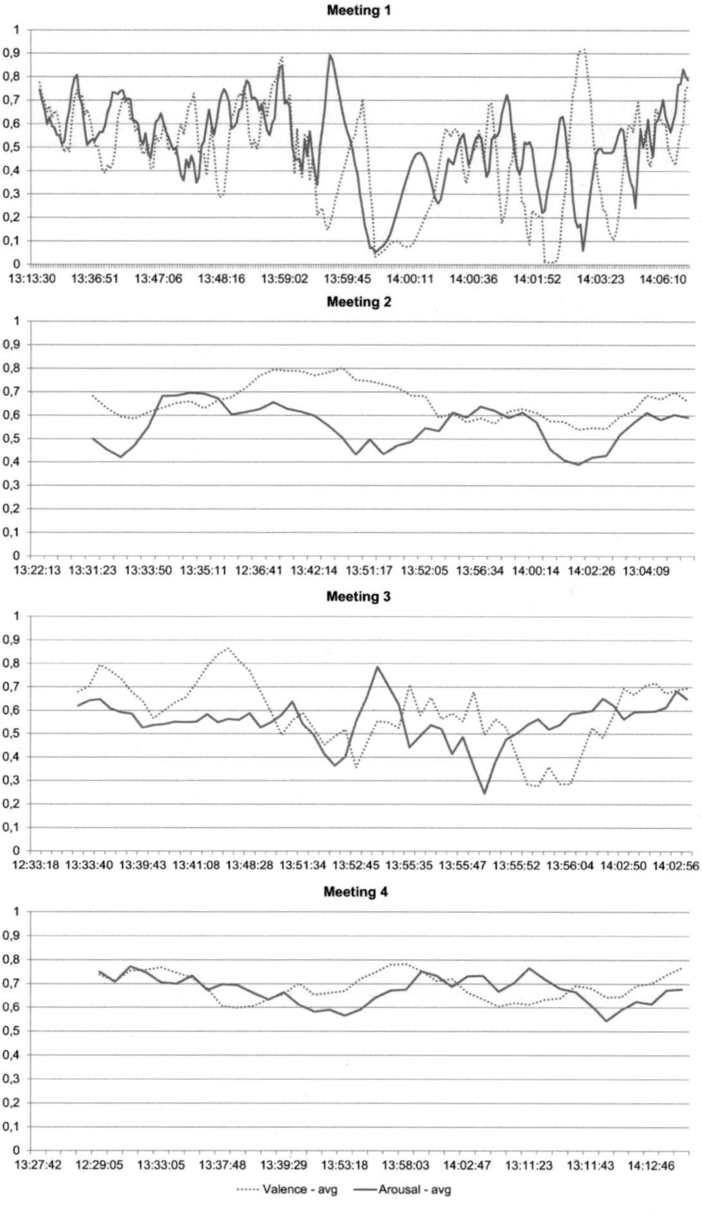

Figure 4.21.: The x-axes represent the time of the meeting. The y-axes represent the average values of valence (blue dash line) and arousal (red solid line), both normalized to values 0 and 1.

In *Meeting 1*, we can see that the average values of valence and arousal change rapidly and this may reveal excitement and nervousness among participants. Due to the fact that it was the first meeting using the MoodMap App, we suspect that the participants were playing with the application, which was confirmed by a participant *"... I think at some point during the meeting I just clicked around a bit, ..., it was more trying the application on a technical level than testing it regards to content."* In *Meeting 2*, the participants seem to get used to the MoodMap App, as the values follow a more rational tendency. Most of the time valence is high (indicating positive feelings) and arousal values are middle (indicating an average level of energy). In *Meeting 3*, the graphic is showing several changes in valence and arousal values. As this was the meeting with fewest participants, each mood point has a higher influence on the average values, creating more sudden changes in the average calculation. In *Meeting 4*, the average of valence and arousal stayed slightly stable, being valence positive (values between 0.87 and 0.43) and arousal also quite high (values between 0.77 and 0.91). This could be interpreted as, on the one hand, that participants are getting used to the application and know how to express their current mood or, on the other hand, that they have not already seen any benefit or insights for themselves, as some of the participants stated, and just used it without any deeper interest.

Taking into consideration that the first meeting was used to become familiar with the MoodMap App, the overall analysis shows us that in the current team setting, valence and arousal are very stable over all meetings. Unfortunately, we have no information about the topics discussed in the team meetings.

RQ1: Are participants interested in tracking their own mood and that of others?

In the long questionnaires, the participants were asked about their interest in tracking and reviewing their own mood, as well as the mood of others. The answers show that the participants have widely diverging views on this matter. On the one hand, the majority of the participants agreed or was neutral with respect to their interest in capturing their own mood and the mood of their colleagues (see Figure 4.22). Some participants stated that they really liked the application and found it interesting and useful to capture their moods, especially their individual mood awareness was mentioned explicitly *"... it made me aware of my mood and if there was a shift in my mood...."* Some statements from the participants confirmed that they were more interested in the mood captured by their colleagues and to compare themselves with others; e.g., *"I find it okay—it was nice to see that you can compare your mood with others attendees in the meeting...."*

On the other hand, we had statements declaring the opposite. Some participants mentioned that they were not very interested in capturing their own mood,

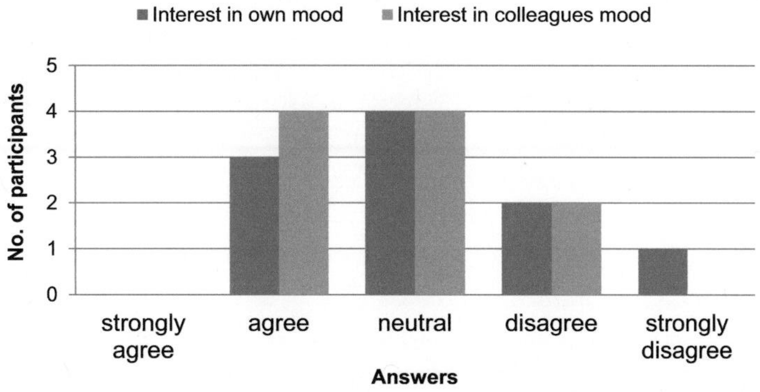

Figure 4.22.: Results on interest in one's own mood and in colleagues' mood

because they know how they feel: *"...you know what your mood was during the meeting and for me it was not that valuable."* For some participants, having only their mood expressed in valence and arousal was not enough to contextualize and understand their moods: *"What other people put in there, well, it's interesting, but it does not say anything for me personally."*

RQ2: Do participants appreciate the usability and features of the MoodMap App as it is implemented?

Most of our participants liked the look and feel of the MoodMap App, especially the mood representation in a two-dimensional map of valence and arousal (see Figure 4.23). Regarding the aspects of liking the MoodMap App or having fun using it, the opinions were rather neutral among the participants (using the MoodMap App is fun: 20% agree, 70% neutral, 10% disagree; like using the MoodMap App: 10% agree, 70% neutral, 20% disagree). There was consensus that the MoodMap App was very easy to use, no user guide was necessary, and the interface was kept simple as stated by one participant: *"I like the simple interface."* Interestingly, this simplicity led to more critical thinking about the meaning of such an application, which one participant expressed as: *"But at the same time, because you see at a glance that it is so simple, you could think 'What does it do for me?'."*

Regarding potential improvements, the participants stated, for instance, that the application should give direct feedback or make it more fun or more attractive with, e.g., flash animations. Although most of the participants found the capturing method easy to use (easy to state my mood: 10% strongly agree, 50% agree, 0% neutral, 30% disagree, 10% strongly disagree), it was interesting to see that for one participant the bi-dimensional representation of the mood was very difficult to understand. This participant had problems in associating a mood to the corresponding color and would prefer smileys, icons or text-based mood expression techniques, as mentioned in the following sentence: "*The current Diagram is abstract with colors, for me it would be easier to have things like smileys or icons to use it or textual decisions as well....*"

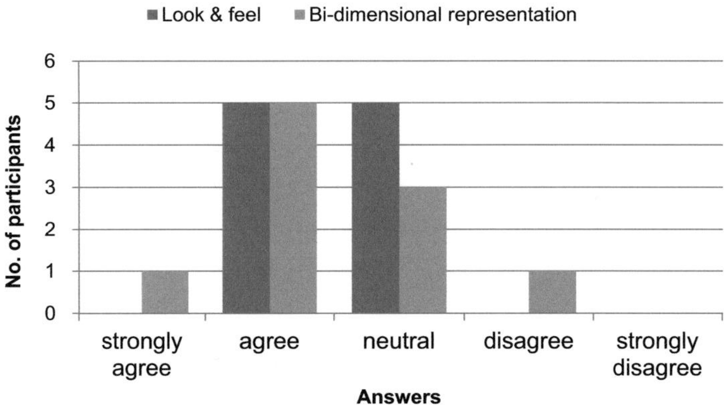

Figure 4.23.: Results on liking of the look & feel and liking of the bi-dimensional representation of the MoodMap App

RQ3: What benefits do participants perceive from the use of MoodMap App?

Regarding the perceived benefits, the evaluation of the MoodMap App shows mixed results and different opinions. Several participants already identified some benefits, became aware of their mood, and saw some influences on it during the meeting. For example, one participant stated that "*an interesting subject influences your mood in a positive way*" or that "*a lack of activity slowly brings the energy level down.*" One participant got insights about her energy level when capturing her mood during the meeting: "*my energy level was more related to my general energy level of today than related to the meeting. Energy influences the way I feel positive.*" The possibility of comparing the mood of oneself with the team's mood was emphasized and seen as benefit: "*my mood was slightly different as compared to other members of the group.*" The awareness concerning the team's mood was especially raised; e.g., in "*I think it helps to develop the emotional intelligence of the team.*" The comparison itself was seen as the most obvious benefit to the majority of the participants. These reflections the participants already made, especially related to the team comparison, is a positive feedback regarding the usefulness of the MoodMap App for reflective learning.

On the other hand, there also were participants who did not perceive any benefits. They mainly argued that the evaluation period was too short and, especially at the beginning of the study, there were some technical issues and some features were missing like *"it is difficult to gain insights when you can't see a timeline across all participants."* Still one participant admitted that he had to clearly see the benefits of the application beforehand, in order to feel motivated using it (*"Because I'm struggling with the benefits I'm not really motivated to use the tool."*). Despite this fact, they saw great potential for the MoodMap App and made suggestions for improvement. They suggested using the MoodMap App over a longer period of time, to see how the mood of the participants evolves. Further, mood trend analysis could be used to find out why the mood is going down during a meeting or to find out if a weekly virtual team meeting is necessary. Getting more feedback about the evolution of their moods from meeting to meeting would be also appreciated. Some participants stated that this information would be very useful to reflect on the work experiences, not only from their individual point of view, but from the perspective of the whole team too (e.g., establishing collaborative debriefing meetings). Feedback given directly after a meeting could provide information about one's own mood in comparison to the team, or striking mood changes.

4.5.3. Discussion and Outlook

The results of our study show quite diverging opinions. People's reactions to mood tracking and sharing in virtual meetings ranged from being very interested to not being able to deal with such an application. Some people perceived the MoodMap App as easy to use, while some perceived its interface as too abstract. The benefits of tracking and sharing mood were not directly recognizable for all the users. This point definitely needed discussion and further investigation—both technically by improving the MoodMap App and conceptually by establishing a more precise relationship between awareness of own and others' mood and work-related benefits. An added challenge in this discussion is to distinguish between benefits gained from using the MoodMap App *during* virtual meetings and benefits gained from answering the (short) questionnaires *after* the virtual meeting.

Analyzing the study results from the perspective of reflective learning, we conclude that most of the participants agreed that the collaborative views had major potential to trigger reflection. Unfortunately, the team did not reflect together on the past meetings neither alone nor in a subsequent meeting, which could have led to more benefits or insights. Reviewing the individual moods; e.g., on the timeline, was not seen as very useful to re-experience the meeting. Comparing one's own mood with the average mood of others in, e.g., the timeline as well as comparing all collaborative moods of the four meetings on the other hand was seen as useful.

The participants saw further potential to reflect especially on critical topics, which might occur during a meeting when the mood changes significantly. Similarly, the participants saw a high potential for additional context information. For instance, integrating more information from other applications (*"I think the best way to reflect is when you receive new input from outside and this is quite simple input..."*) or a better contextualization, like replaying the recorded meeting in comparison to the moods.

Based on these results and insights, we identified the following issues, which needed further investigation:

- more contextualization in order to give a meaning to the data and use it for learning purposes
- support the step from awareness to reflection
- more feedback and visualizations from the app
- explore the influence of teams and groups with the app.

Therefore, we were able to identify important needs of the users and summarized them in four important design challenges, which were necessary to make the MoodMap App a reflective learning tool. These challenges encompassed (i) giving employees a clear benefit for themselves, (ii) providing more contextualization when revisiting a day or meeting, (iii) providing reflection guidance, and (iv) implementing more collaborative visualizations. Based on these challenges, we made a mock-up based design workshop (see Section 4.6) on how user needs could be converted into features for the MoodMap App and how they could be implemented in a meaningful way.

4.6. Design Study II: British Telecommunications Company

In order to further investigate the design challenges identified in the first formative evaluation of the MoodMap App (see Section 4.5) and implement them in the application, we conducted a one-day workshop along with British Telecom. The main challenge was to figure out how the MoodMap App has to be enriched and improved, so that it could fulfill the following goals: (i) users should see a clear benefit for themselves and the motivation for users to reflect on their mood development should be achieved, (ii) provide user guidance for reflection and more feedback to support reflection, (iii) offer more contextualization of the mood data to remind people about past meetings, and (iv) capture the learning outcomes.

4.6.1. Procedure

Taking the results from the first formative evaluation (see Section 4.5) into account, we prepared a one-day design workshop at the same telecommunications company. This workshop was conducted in the framework of the EU project MIRROR, in collaboration with Know-Center Graz.

This workshop was attended by three participants (apart from the two researchers conducting this study): two members of the telecommunications company (BT) and the quality manager of the project within which the MoodMap App is developed (MIRROR Project). Additionally, for one session during the workshop, six end users of the MoodMap App were also participating.

The workshop was divided into several sections, where different mock-ups were created and discussed (see examples in Figure 4.24). These sections were:

- **Goal session:** This session was conducted to detect, on the one hand, possible scenarios where the MoodMap App could be used in, including different types of meetings, and in which departments of the company the application could be used. On the other hand, we wanted to define, which prerequisites have to be fulfilled to make the MoodMap App a successful application to support reflective learning.
- **Brain Sketching Session (part 1):** With this session, we wanted the participants to draw on paper-based MoodMap App empty mock-ups (i.e., mock-ups with solely the layout of the MoodMap App, but leaving free space inside the layout which they could use), how the application could be enhanced to overcome the current weaknesses and to improve the application. Having drawn a sketch on a sheet of paper, it was put into the middle of the table. Other participants could take this sheet and add his or her ideas or comments to the already drawn sketch. At the end of this session, the results were summarized.
- **Brain Sketching Session (part 2):** In this session, we presented our participants several mock-ups, which the developers had created in advance of the workshop (see Figure 4.24). These mock-ups and the proposed features on them were discussed and brought up in line with the results of the previous session. Afterwards, the results were summarized and prepared for the next session.

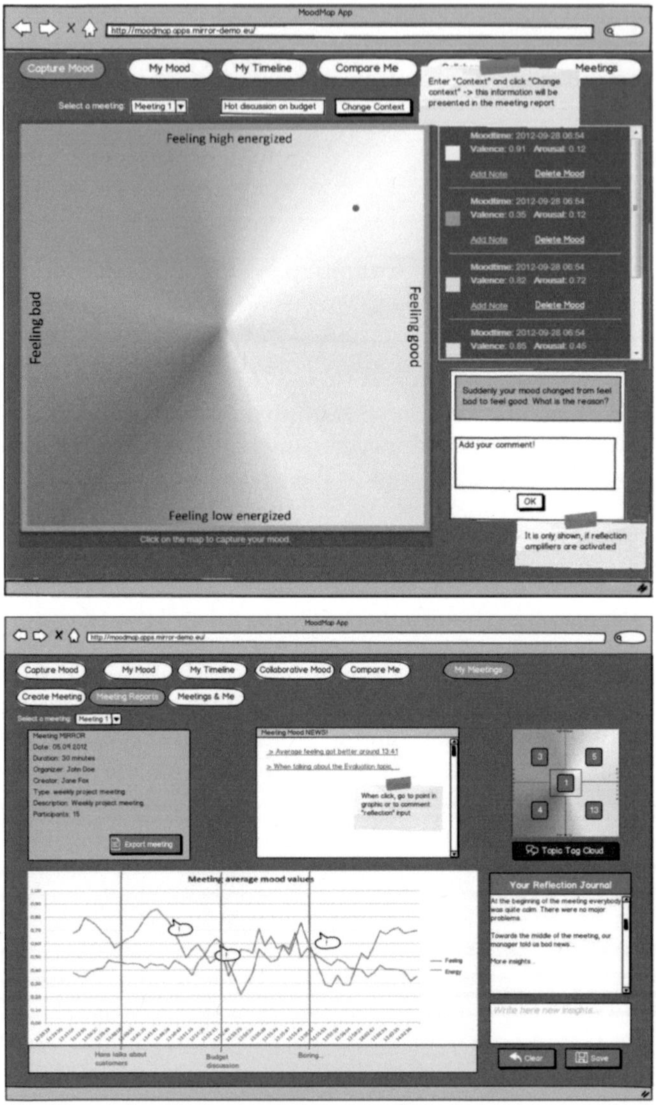

Figure 4.24.: Examples of the mock-ups used in the design workshop

- **Feedback round:** We invited to this session six of the participants, who had participated in the first evaluation of the MoodMap App, to discuss the new features developed in the brain sketching sessions. Additionally, they were asked to bring in their own ideas on how to improve the MoodMap App and how learning from mood data could be achieved.
- **Wrap-up session:** In the last session, we summarized the whole results, prioritized the features, which should be implemented in the next MoodMap App version, and defined a rough development timeline.

After the workshop, the application developers updated the mock-ups according to the workshop discussions and a feature implementation list was provided, including their defined prioritization. After the agreement of all partners to these documents, the implementation phase started.

4.6.2. Results

Condensing the results of the first evaluation and the design workshop, we extracted the following major design components which would improve the learning support of the MoodMap App. Following Schön [1987], we can divide these components in design elements that support "reflection-in-action" (which occurs during an on-going activity) or "reflection-on-action" (which takes place after the completed action).

"Reflection-in-action" Components

The "reflection-in-action" components are features that should make people aware of some significant mood changes during the ongoing meeting, to provide a more accurate guidance of the reflective process.

- **User prompts for capturing:** User prompts for capturing are used to motivate the users of the MoodMap App to capture their moods or to use the application in general. For example, prompts in the form of textual feedback are shown at the beginning of a meeting to suggest inserting his or her mood, or if the user has not switched from one visualization to another for a while, they are invited to have a look at them.
- **User prompts for reflecting:** User prompts for reflecting aim at making users aware of significant mood changes, which may trigger a reflective learning process. They are shown in relevant situations related to the moods; e.g., the user's mood has significantly changed from bad to good (or vice versa) or the user's mood deviates significantly from the team

mood. The user prompts contain corresponding questions to make the users reflect on their current mood change and motivate them to track these thoughts into the MoodMap App.

"Reflection-on-action" Components

The "Reflection-on-action" components are features that should enhance the reflection of the participants outside of the meetings by re-evaluating their mood development. They comprise the following features:

- **Contextualization:** It is important to give the users an easy means of inserting context during a meeting. This context could be a word or a short phrase, just a hint, which represents what is currently ongoing in the meeting. Displaying this context information when revisiting mood trends of a past meeting on a timeline would help users remember a situation or a significant discussion during the meeting.
- **Mood Reports:** At the end of a meeting a report about it is created, which aims at providing a better user guidance for reflection and more feedback to support it. It contains general information about the meeting; e.g., number of participants or meeting name. The average team mood development of the whole team during the meeting is also visualized on a timeline including the context, which was inserted by the user. Most important are what we have dubbed "Reflection News", which refer to significant mood changes that have occurred during the meeting, and pose related questions to the meeting situation. After viewing the report, the users are asked to insert the gained insights into the reflection journal. Additionally, if the user configures it, they will receive, at the end of a meeting, an email with some information regarding this report. This email includes an invitation to visit the complete report in the MoodMap App and therefore supporting the user to take some time to reflect.
- **Reflection Journal:** The reflection journal stores all insights, thoughts or learning outcomes of the MoodMap App user. Using this journal consequently; e.g., after all meetings, could lead to an important collection of reflection outcomes and might also trigger reflective learning; e.g., when going through the entries again to detect either changes of own behavior over time or detect significant patterns concerning a meeting.

4.6.3. Discussion

After this design workshop, the implementation of the second prototype of the MoodMap App started, incorporating all the elements described above. This prototype is described in detail in Section 4.2.3.

Taking into account the lessons learned in the first evaluation and the design workshop, the following issues should be addressed in subsequent studies:

- Did the new guidance offered by the app increase the benefits of tracking mood data?
- Did the new contextualization and visualizations improve the recalling of past experiences?
- What is the impact of tracking emotions following a self-reported approach for reflective learning at work?
- Did the general learners motivation to use the MoodMap App increase?

4.7. Formative Evaluation II: British Telecommunications Company

The use of the MoodMap App was initially suggested by the some of the participants, who noticed that the communication in their virtual meetings was not optimal. After the user study carried on with the first prototype of the MoodMap App, many other members of the team identified the potential that the app has to improve their work, especially if they use it for a longer period of time. This user study was done with BT Learning Solutions, which originally consisted of 9 members and all participated in the first formative evaluation of the MoodMap App (see Section 4.5). Additionally, their manager expressed his interest in having more information about what is happening in the team and how they are personally feeling.

The second prototype of the MoodMap App was used in monthly virtual team meetings to enhance the non-verbal communication within the locally spread teams. In this setting, the MoodMap App should give the individual the possibility to reflect on his or her own mood during the meeting. With the help of some guidance offered by the app, the participant should be activated to re-evaluate his or her mood or mood changes and to learn from this critical reflective thinking about the meeting topic or his or her own behavior during the meeting. Additionally, it should give participants (and/or the team leader) the possibility to think about the team's mood, if there might be some problems or if everything runs smoothly within the team. According to these results and the insights gained after reflecting on them, possible actions could be taken.

After redesigning and reimplementing the MoodMap App according to the results obtained in the first study, it was expected that the users recognize a clear benefit for themselves and for their own work as well as for their team. With the implementation of the new features in the second prototype (see Sections 4.5 and 4.2.2 for details), we expected that the users are triggered to reflect on relevant situations from their daily work (e.g., a virtual meeting) and capture their learning outcomes.

4.7.1. Procedure

During the evaluation period, from May 24, 2013 until August 24, 2013, team members used the MoodMap App in their weekly and monthly calls. There were 6 meetings planned for the evaluation. Unfortunately, 3 of these meetings were canceled and the MoodMap App was used only in the first 3 meetings. For this reason, we concentrated on identifying barriers for adoption and reasons for the low usage. No outcomes regarding learning or behavior change could be assessed.

Participants

Participants were part of the BT Flexible Working Services (FWS) department and were based mainly in the UK and the Netherlands. They were responsible for product support; working in contact with several products at BT. This team had already been working together for a long time, but depended on virtual meetings for communication and coordination of their work (see Section 4.1.1 for details about participants' profiles).

The team participating in the evaluation was composed of 12 members. We gathered demographic data from 10 participants, who answered the pre-questionnaire. The team was formed by product/business managers (40%), directors (20%), administrators/helpdesk (20%) and consultants (20%). These 10 participants consisted of 5 men and 5 women. Participants in the evaluation were between 40 and 59 years old, with 60% of them aged between 40 and 49, and 40% between 50 and 59. Regarding their work schedule, 8 participants work full-time and 2 part-time. The participants had spent on average 6.90 ($SD = 4.15$) years in their current position, ranging from participants with 1 year in that position and to a maximum of 15 years. The average number of years in a similar position was 7.00 ($SD = 5.32$) and the average years that the participants were in this team was 7.88 (4.52).

4.7.2. Results

Table 4.8 gives an overview of the data gathered through questionnaires and interviews for all participants during the whole evaluation.

Table 4.8.: Overview of the types of gathered data from participants during the evaluation

Data available	No. participants
Complete data*	9
Pre- and post-questionnaires	1
Post-questionnaire and interview	1
Only post-questionnaire	1
Total participants	12

*Complete data means: pre-questionnaire, post-questionnaire and interview

The post-questionnaire was answered by all the participants ($N = 12$). The questionnaire focused on identifying which were the concrete barriers for adoption and which were the main reasons for the low usage of the app. Table 4.9 shows the average scores of participants to the various investigated barriers. Results showed that many issues may be the cause for ceasing usage of the app, but no single one of them was outstanding, as most of the average answers were in the range 2.50–3.50. In a 5-point Likert scale, these results are too neutral to allow taking clear conclusions about it. Therefore, we decided to conduct the subsequent interviews in order to gain more insights about the evaluation.

With the aim of weighing potential barriers for the users, we asked participants to select which of the following reasons were decisive to stop using the MoodMap App in their personal case (see Table 4.10). Participants could select a maximum of 5 reasons. Results showed that, besides distraction with the app and not wanting to share their emotions, the lack of benefits and expectations were the most mentioned reasons.

Based on the results from the post-questionnaire, there was the need to look deeper into their answers and try to derive new insights for the future. Therefore, we conducted interviews with 10 of the participants. In the interviews, we addressed several topics including meaningful situations to use the application, feedback on the usage of the MoodMap App, insights about the decision to stop using the MoodMap App, and which benefits they would expect. In the following, we summarize the most relevant topics and the answers of the participants.

Table 4.9.: Barriers for usage and adoption: Results from the questions included in the post-questionnaire (answered on a 5-point Likert scale)

Question	Answer
I did not have time to use the MoodMap App during the meetings.	$M = 2.50$ ($SD = 0.90$)
I did not have time to use the MoodMap App out of the meetings.	$M = 3.33$ ($SD = 1.15$)
I did not see an advantage in using the MoodMap App.	$M = 3.25$ ($SD = 1.29$)
I was not motivated to use the MoodMap App.	$M = 3.58$ ($SD = 0.90$)
I could find out how the MoodMap App worked by myself.	$M = 3.42$ ($SD = 0.79$)
I am satisfied with the MoodMap App.	$M = 2.92$ ($SD = 0.79$)
I think that the MoodMap App is useful for professional work.	$M = 2.58$ ($SD = 1.31$)
I think that the MoodMap App can be used to complement professional work.	$M = 2.92$ ($SD = 1.00$)
I often reflect on the way we work in our organization.	$M = 3.25$ ($SD = 0.97$)
I do not think it is beneficial for me to reflect on my work.	$M = 2.17$ ($SD = 0.83$)
I do not think it is beneficial for me to reflect on my feelings during work.	$M = 2.58$ ($SD = 0.90$)

To the question *"How does your mood influence your work?"*, the indicated number of participants mentioned the following aspects: motivation and enthusiasm (3x), work results or performance (3x), ability to get distracted (2x), way of dealing with other people (2x), and no influence at all (3x).

Only for 60% of the participants the mood of their colleagues was important and meaningful. This result differs from other conducted evaluations, where interest on others' moods was usually mentioned as motivation to use the MoodMap App. 80% of the participants admitted that the app was easy to use and had no problems with it. One participant mentioned that the app did not work for him or her, whereas another one had problems remembering his or her login details.

We asked them again about the main reasons to stop using the application, besides the fact that so many meetings were canceled. Participants argued that the app was not useful in their context—small conservative team and with few meetings—(3x), that they did not see any additional benefit from the usage (3x), and that they did not get into the habit of using it (2x). However, some participants also recognized some benefits: help to detect problems in the team (2x), awareness sparking reflection (1x), get feedback from silent people (1x), and finally comparing personal with others' mood (2x).

Table 4.10.: Reasons for no usage: Number of votes of each reason included in the post-questionnaire

Reason	No. votes
I would prefer to use the app with people I don't know that well.	0
I do not think that reflecting on our work can be supported by the app.	0
I prefer to keep my emotions and my work separated.	1
I did not understand how to use the app.	1
I did not think that our team work would be improved by using the app.	1
I did not like the look & feel of the app.	2
It takes too long to get interesting feedback from the app.	2
I did not want the researchers to use data on my emotions.	3
The cognitive load to use the app was too high during the meetings.	3
Other team members didn't use it, either.	3
I did not want to share my emotions, even if it was anonymously.	4
I was more distracted because of the app.	4
There was not need to improve the meetings.	4
I do not see a concrete goal that drives the use of the app.	4
I know my colleagues very well and don't need an app to see their emotions.	5
I did not think that our meetings would be improved by using the app.	5
I did not see any benefit in using app.	6

Final remarks from the interviewees revealed further insights about the evaluation and their experience:

"If we would do it again, I would really try to start with a half-day workshop to agree objectives with the team. It has to be clearer from the start [...]. It was a one-way communication and we underestimated it; we need to engage them more, set our objectives, clarify how to get to them with the app and then start using it, if there is a commitment."

"I think that when you have problems in a team you can detect it, and find out what the problem is. We do not have that many problems in our team."

And also some critical opinions, which nonetheless suggested further possibilities for the future:

"So these would be the things I would need to make it more useful: it needs to be simpler to access, it needs to be less intrusive (e.g., by including it in our software) and it needs to make sure that the data is compatible and, in the end, it needs to provide some form of value, some form of output or insight that I wouldn't get without using it."

"Personally I cannot see the need to use that sort of app. I could see the benefit maybe in other environments like call centers perhaps, where you can measure the mood in a room as a whole, the mood of the center population having the mood across 100 people."

4.7.3. Discussion

The majority of the participants mentioned that the small size of the group, the lack of motivation, and the many canceled meetings led to the ceasing of the app usage. The few who had the motivation to use it unfortunately lost it due to the colleagues not using the app, as well as the difficulties to identify clear benefits.

We know from previous research that benefits are difficult to see in such a short period [Müller et al., 2011c]. Although we tried to balance this with short-term benefits, the approach in this team was not successful. In this evaluation, we struggled with the fact that users wanted clear benefits and needed achievable objectives. These objectives cannot be defined by us, as researchers, and it was a challenge to show to participants how reflection can lead to improvements at work, although these improvements are usually unknown at the beginning. These results suggested that closer work with managers and other people from the organization was necessary to define clear goals for their employees, as well as to introduce users to reflective practices from the concrete perspective of their work setting.

With this evaluation, the results did not inform the development of the application and its support for learning, but it served to gain further insights on barriers that exist for reflective learning and dealing with emotions, especially from a business and work perspective.

4.8. Formative Evaluation III: British Telecommunications Call Centers

We attended a two-day workshop where the planned usage and evaluation of the MoodMap App was welcomed by the visited BT call center staff members, including managers and call takers. Following, a formative evaluation was conducted to derive changes and improvements necessary in the MoodMap App in order to be used at the call center.

This study aimed at eliciting required changes for the MoodMap App to obtain acceptance by call takers and management and to embed it into their existing work processes.

4.8.1. Procedure

A formative evaluation of the MoodMap App was planned within two teams of the visited call center with a total of 22 participants. The goal of this study was to introduce the app in the identified use cases, investigate the potential of the gathered mood data, and evaluate if the app needs changes to improve reflective learning support. The evaluation was conducted between June 13, 2013 and August 16, 2013.

Managers introduced the app to their teams and organized weekly meetings to discuss usage and potential of the app. Furthermore, they committed to using the collected information as a basis for their work. The concrete procedure of the evaluation was as follows:

- June 13–18: there were several meetings with the second and first level management to arrange the evaluation and do minor technical adaptations.
- June 19–20: the MoodMap App was presented in a workshop to the participants of the evaluation. Their managers did the presentation.
- July 21–31: period of app usage. Several meetings with management were conducted to follow the evaluation.
- August 1–7: call takers answered the distributed questionnaire.
- August 8–16: the results of the questionnaire were analyzed and finally presented to the managers involved in the evaluation.

Participants

The study was conducted with two teams, comprised of 2 managers, 10 coaches and 10 call takers. We obtained demographic data from 17 participants (1 manager, 9 coaches and 7 call takers). These 17 participants consisted of 13 men and 4 women. Participants in the evaluation were between 20 and 59 years old, with 53% of them aged between 20 and 29, 29% between 30 and 39, 12% between 40 and 49, and 6% between 50 and 59. The participants had on average 2.82 (SD = 2.55) years in their current position, ranging from participants with less than one year in that position and to a maximum of 10 years. The average number of years in their current team was 2.14 (SD = 1.60).

Evaluation Tools

At the beginning of the study, a pre-questionnaire was used to obtain demographic data of the participants at the beginning of the study. After using the application, a post-questionnaire was distributed to collect quantitative data of all team members. At the end of the study, interviews with some participants were conducted. During the whole evaluation period, weekly meetings were conducted with the manager of the call center in order to follow the progress.

4.8.2. Results

Post-questionnaires

We asked the 10 call takers why they had been using the MoodMap App. Out of these call takers, 7 used the application because they were asked to. However, they also made comments on their reasons to use it; e.g., "it was simple and easy to use; I could easily fill it in between calls" and "I did try using the mood map. Even though it did not take very long to use it, it was difficult to remember to use it on a daily basis. It was a good idea but it's just way too busy here to remember anything extra, along with the 4 different things we need to do after every call."

When asking about their motivations to use the MoodMap App, the answers of the participants could be divided in three categories:

(a) Related to the app and mood tracking

- *"It is interesting to see how your mood changes throughout the day and how it compares to other people's"*
- *"To give feedback on what affects my mood"*
- *"Interested in the results"*
- *"If we had [...] a reminder to use the app I would have used it much more"*

(b) Related to the work practice

- *"If we had the time [...] I would have used it much more"*
- *"To give feedback at certain situations which happen throughout the day"*
- *"If the data collected was looked at and used to get things improved to raise moods to feel one is being productive or cared about"*

- *"Discussing the information I have entered in the app during coaching sessions"*

(c) Related to the job itself (and manager)

- *"Being told I must use it"*
- *"I was told I had to, as part of my job"*
- *"Manager requesting us to use it"*

Among the things that participants liked about the MoodMap App, they mentioned it was easy to use (4x) and liked how the app collated all the information (1x), it allowed comparing moods with others (2x), and it helped to vent problems (1x) and see patterns (1x). On the contrary, they did not like that there was hardly any time to use the app (1x), that no structure was given when to enter moods (1x), felt like a burden (1x), other things are more pressing (1x), and the colors were hard to state the mood (1x).

Finally, the meetings with the management revealed that knowing the feelings of their teams could help managers to identify problems and directly help the appropriate person. Therefore, we asked call takers their opinion about this issue. 70% of the participants stated that they had no problems with sharing their non-anonymized moods and mentioned that *"I feel that it is important for my manager to know how his or her team mates are feeling"* or *"So they understand what affect our moods."* 20% of the participants preferred not to share their moods, but they did not specify the reasons for it. Finally, 10% was unsure about this, stating that *"I'm not really sure where I stand on this. In theory, there would be no problem with that, but in reality that's not really how things work."*

Summarizing the results, the participants saw potential in using the MoodMap App, as illustrated by the words of one call taker: *"The whole thing was a good idea. It seems morale is pretty poor in this place at the moment, so something like this is a good step towards actually caring about the staff here and getting to the bottom of when or why people feel bad."*

They did not mention any major problems with the app itself and they did not have technical problems. However, there were several barriers which did not allow continuing the usage of the MoodMap App: there was not much time to use the app, and time pressure during and between calls and a clear benefit for their work was still a challenge. Regarding sharing their data, most of the participants had no problems with it and even mentioned some benefits that would derive from this change.

Management Meetings

The results of the post-questionnaires were discussed with the managers in order to define which the requirements to fulfill are, as well as the changes that needed to be done in the application. The key results of this formative study, both at design and process level, were the following:

- Being a standalone system was seen as a barrier, so the app should be integrated in their call center systems.
- Call takers did not see a clear benefit if the data gathered is not used in work processes. Some comments of the participants stated how this could be achieved: "If data collected was looked at and used to get things improved to raise moods to feel one is being productive or cared about" or "discussing the information I have entered in the app during coaching sessions."
- Visualizing not anonymized data to managers and coaches would offer a big benefit as they could better identify the upcoming issues and moods of their team members. Call takers did not have concerns with sharing not anonymized data with managers and coaches.
- The integration of automatic management of teams and shifts in the app would reduce the current usage efforts.
- The app would benefit from a clearer connection between the mood data and the tasks of their work processes.

According to the results, the MoodMap App was further designed and developed. The following changes which lead to the third prototype of the MoodMap App (see Section 4.2.4) were made:

1. A better process integration was implemented by making the connection between mood entries and work processes mandatory. Mood entries must be contextualized (mood context and personal notes), in order to support re-construction of work experiences surrounding the referenced mood. After capturing a mood, a dialog box showed four single choice options to contextualize the mood entry. The list of available mood contexts was adapted to the call center setting and included *after a call*, *after a coaching session*, *after a break* and *other*. Immediately after the contextualization, a personal note had to be entered. In the case of calls, a specific field for the call reference was available in order to provide a direct link to each processed call.
2. To achieve an easier data capturing, a direct link to the MoodMap App was placed into the user interface of the call center software. Furthermore,

team management was implemented and users could automatically enter a session with their team members and managers to share data upon login. As a result, no team sessions had to be manually created and the required number of clicks to start capturing mood was reduced from 3 to 1.

3. In order to make data analysis easier for managers and coaches, three new visualizations based on non-anonymized data were added:

   - Smileys View: Managers and coaches are shown the current average mood of every team member (including themselves). If the manager clicks on a smiley, a daily timeline of the team member's mood including context and notes appears.

   - Daily Team View: Managers also see aggregated information on a daily timeline per team. This visualization shows each single mood point captured by the whole team and the average team mood development, depicted in two timelines on a daily basis (one timeline for valence and one for arousal).

   - Weekly Team View: Managers also see aggregated information on a weekly timeline. This third visualization shows the mood development of all single team members' according to their valence and arousal values. The interactive timeline allows selecting and comparing the average mood development of the team to each single user, or between selected users.

These changes were backed by adapting managerial work processes. Managers and coaches committed to using these visualizations in their routine supervisory work processes and to acting on captured mood data. Coaches also committed to using them in their coaching sessions, where data from the call center was already used as basis of the meetings with the call takers.

4.8.3. Discussion

The results of this formative evaluation, especially the changes related to process integration and anonymization of the data, will be analyzed in detail in future studies, in order to evaluate if their impact brings the desired outcomes. Managers and call takers demanded together to remove anonymization of data to simplify analysis and remove barriers on communication. Generalizing this attitude towards privacy should be carefully considered; call takers are used to being monitored during their work but this cannot be generalized for other professionals. Nevertheless, it was necessary to explicitly consider this issue and evaluate which were the benefits of this change.

With these changes in the MoodMap App, it was possible to conduct a summative evaluation (see Section 4.9) which not only considers acceptance and usability issues, but also allows us to analyze the impact of the app on learning and work performance.

4.9. Summative Evaluation I: British Telecommunications Call Centers

The use of the MoodMap App was initially identified by the managers of the call center, who were willing to be aware of how their advisors (call takers) feel at work. The managers and coaches in the center were also introducing a new model of coaching, in order to allow employees to take more decisions regarding their learning process at work. Until that moment, the model they had followed had been quite passive from the employees' side. This change was a decisive aspect that pointed towards the necessity of supporting learning by reflection. With this, a new culture is being created in order to encourage employees to take their own decisions and take into account how they feel and what they need for themselves and in order to improve their work performance. Aligned with this new learning perspective, a strategy for the introduction of the app was established. The operational online team that started the evaluation of the MoodMap App is a team with very high customer satisfaction scores. Therefore, the expectation is that they are positive and energetic at work, and that it would be easy for them to integrate the MoodMap App without interfering with their daily work. If the introduction of the app in their daily practices is successful, this team will contribute to scaling up the use of the MoodMap App in the center and facilitate the participation of other teams in the evaluation.

The goal of this summative evaluation was to study the impact of mood self-tracking on individuals as well as on work patterns in call center teams. Through the usage of the MoodMap App we analyzed the acceptance of the tool, the support for reflection, the impact on work performance and the effects on team collaboration and communication. The evaluation took place in the context of the EU project MIRROR, in collaboration with Know-Center Graz. The study reported herein is included for publishing in other form in Rivera-Pelayo et al. [in prep.].

4.9.1. Procedure

The MoodMap App was used by BT employees belonging to all three roles; i.e., call takers, managers and coaches. The call takers were asked to fill in their individual moods after a call, after a coaching session, after a break or whenever they thought their mood was relevant for them or had changed in a significant way. Additionally, they were compulsory asked to insert a note to each of the captured moods.

We asked coaches to use the inserted moods to better support the call takers during their work and to improve and/or adapt the coaching sessions to the call takers' needs.

Managers could follow the mood development of each single call taker to directly contact them if necessary. They also kept an eye on the mood development of the whole team in order to arrange one-on-one meetings (i.e., a meeting between a manager and a single call taker) or huddles (whole team meetings) to discuss arising issues and improve the whole team spirit. Additionally, managers and coaches were also asked to capture their moods and use the MoodMap App themselves with the goal of reflecting on their own mood development and how they were influenced by their emotions.

The summative evaluation of the MoodMap App started on November 20, 2013 and lasted until December 20, 2013. The MoodMap App was introduced by the responsible project manager of BT to six different teams (encompassing 103 participants) and four of these teams were selected to pursue with the evaluation.

Participants

A total of 67 employees participated in this evaluation, belonging to four distinct teams from two different call centers, namely Team inactive_1 (from the call center in Dundee), Team inactive_2 (Dundee), Team active_1 (Alness), Team active_2 (from the call center in Alness). Teams active_1 and active_2, belonging to the same call center, captured more than twice as many moods as teams inactive_1 and inactive_2 (for further details on app usage refer to Section 4.9.2). Consequently, the teams were labeled "active" and "inactive" respectively. This terminology is used consistently in the remainder of this section. With this differentiation, we also analyze the reasons and implications for the different behavior in the teams.

The demographic questionnaires were filled by 43 participants; thus the information of the demographic data is referring only to this 64% of the participants. These 43 participants consisted of 26 men and 17 women. Participants in the evaluation were between 20 and 59 years old, with 56% of them aged between 20 and 29, 26% between 30 and 39, 14% between 40 and 49 and 5% between 50 and 59. The participants had on average 3.47 ($SD = 3.66$) years in their current position, ranging from participants with less than one year in that position and to a maximum of 15 years. The average number of years in their current team was 1.76 (*SD* = 2.28) and the average years in a similar position were 5.21 (*SD* = 4.32). Due to the fact that not all participants have filled in both questionnaires, Table 4.13 gives a summary of the amount of answers we received from each team. In the sections where it is referred to the evaluation of both question-naires, only the answers of those users who have filled in the pre- as well as the post-questionnaire will be considered ($N = 26$).

The adapted MoodMap App was used by managers, coaches and call takers in the described call centers within 4 teams over 4 weeks. Participants could access the web application at any time of the day and capture their moods through the whole shift. When users captured a mood, they selected a predefined context (after a call, after a break, after a coaching session or others) and entered a note to describe the current situation. All users were asked to use the different visualizations in order to reflect on on their and the teams moods. Managers and coaches were obliged additionally to use the Team Views to track the mood development of each call taker and their team as a whole.

Evaluation Tools

Within this evaluation, we aimed at assessing relevant indicators for reflective learning and their impact for individuals and teams as well as the organization as a whole. To achieve this, we used the summative evaluation toolbox developed in the framework of the MIRROR Project [Knipfer et al., 2012]. This evaluation toolbox is based on a modification of the Kirkpatrick model [Kirkpatrick and Kirkpatrick, 2006] and defines four levels: reaction and usage, learning, behavior, and work outcomes. A detailed description of the whole toolbox can be found in Knipfer et al. [2012].

During this introduction phase the team members were asked to fill in a pre-questionnaire including their consent form. Regarding the application usage, all types of participants (call takers, coaches and managers) of the trial were asked to insert their moods during all days during the evaluation period. They were also asked to reflect on their inserted moods and notes individually. The coaches and managers were additionally instructed to use the team visualizations in order to reflect about the mood development of their teams and take actions if necessary. At the end of the trial, they were requested to fill in a post-questionnaire.

Table 4.11 provides an overview of used evaluation tools and the data gathered with them. Pre- and post-questionnaires measured agreement with questions on a 5-point Likert scale (from 1 = strongly disagree to 5 = strongly agree). A print version of the online questionnaires (pre- and post-) can be found in the Appendix A. We used log data for descriptive statistics about app usage, and interviews to gain rich information about our research questions, including anecdotal examples. It is important to note that KPIs and interviews are only available for the active teams, as there were restrictions from one of the call centers.

Table 4.11.: Evaluation tools used in the summative evaluation

Tool	Evaluation Stage	Content
pre-questionnaire	start of evaluation	consent form, demographic data, expectations regarding the app, reflection scale
post-questionnaire	end of evaluation	questions with regard to usage and user satisfaction, general app effects, benefits and insights, reflection scale, reflection support of the app, learning outcomes and behavior
interviews	end of evaluation	feedback to the overall experience, subjective feeling of the application's acceptance within the team, capturing mood, benefits and insights, general comments
KPIs	start, end of and 1 month after evaluation	Average Rating, Net Promoter Indicator, Call Taker Satisfaction, Recap (see details in Table 4.12)
log data	end of evaluation	interactions with the application, e.g. clicks per visualization
app data	end of evaluation	captured moods, notes and context

The impact on work performance was measured by using the existing Key Performance Indicators (KPIs) of one call center. Customers receive automatic SMS messages from the call center to elicit feedback after they have spoken to the call takers and the KPIs are calculated based on the collected feedback. Table 4.12 lists the KPIs, their description and their rating in detail. The company imposed restrictions on the access to KPIs. Due to the different systems used to track and monitor KPIs, *Average Rating* was made available at an individual level, while *NPI*, *Call Taker Sat* and *Recap* were available on a team level.

A paired-samples t-test was conducted to compare the individual KPI metrics before the usage of the MoodMap App and after it. Concretely, the metrics were provided at three reporting periods:

(a) Before using the app: August 1, 2013–October 21, 2013 (81 days)

(b) Immediately after having used the app: October 21, 2013–December 19, 2013 (59 days)

(c) After having ceased using the app for a month: January 6, 2014–February 7, 2014 (32 days)

Table 4.12.: Investigated Key Performance Indicators

KPI	Description	Scale
Average Rating	Average of customer satisfaction rating	0–100
Net Promoter Indicator (NPI)	Based on customer advocacy and reflects the answers to the question: *How likely are you to recommend our services to others based on your recent experience with us?*	-100%–100%
Call Taker Satisfaction (Call Taker Sat)	Indicates the customer overall satisfaction with the call. Customers answer in a scale 1–10 and the percentage is calculated depending on how many customers score the call taker and what the score is.	1–10
Recap	Indicates whether the call takers proactively summarized the call to the customer (objective is lowering the amount of repeat calls they receive as a business). Question answered by customers is: *Did the last call taker recap what had been agreed on?*	0–100

4.9.2. Results

The results will be reported according to the four levels of Kirkpatrick and Kirkpatrick [2006], as described above.

Reaction and Usage

The participants used the MoodMap App on 31 consecutive days. Except for 5 days in which the app was not used at all (corresponding to days off), the app was used by all users for 8 hours and 42 minutes ($SD = 0.09$) on average per day. During that time, users were entering the MoodMap App repeatedly and using the different available features.

In total, 991 moods were captured during the whole evaluation period. On average, users captured 17.39 moods (*SD* = 24.50) during the whole evaluation period, with a range of 1 to 136 moods per user. Considering the moods captured in each team, an average of 23.72 (*SD* = 34.45) moods were captured per person in active_1 Team, 21.00 (*SD* = 24.52) in active_2 Team, 10.62 (*SD* = 11.91) in inactive_1 Team and 9.25 (*SD* = 10.95) in inactive 2 Team. These results show that users in teams active 1 and active 2 captured twice as many moods than teams inactive 1 and inactive 2, on average.

Regarding the notes attached to the moods, a total of 946 non-empty notes were captured by the users and served as annotation for their affective states. Table 4.13 offers an overview of the data gathered per team.

Table 4.13.: Overview of teams composition and data collected

Team	ct/mrg/ coach*	No. moods	Avg. moods	No. notes	Pre-quest.	Post-quest.	Both quest.
active_1**	19 / 1 / 1	427	23.72	423	5	13	4
active_2**	17 / 1 / 1	315	21.00	302	13	4	3
inactive_1	15 / 1 / 0	138	10.62	137	12	8	7
inactive_2	14 / 1 / 0	111	9.25	84	13	13	12
Total	65 / 4 / 2	991	17.39	946	43	38	26

*No. of call takers, managers and coaches pro team

**These teams additionally conducted interviews and provided KPI data

The analysis of the moods captured in each team revealed that the number of moods per user followed a similar distribution in all teams (see Figure 4.25). Each team had a percentage of its members (approximately 25%) who actively captured a higher number of moods (from 20 in the inactive teams to 136 in the most active team), as well as another percentage of people (also approximately 25%) who captured fewer moods (from 1 to 5 in all teams) but were instead checking the visualizations. This fact is also mirrored by the high standard deviations shown above.

Users also had to enter a context to each captured mood; i.e., in which situation the mood was captured. Figure 4.26 shows the distribution of all captured contexts ($N = 991$) among the four available categories; i.e., after a call, after a break, after a coaching session, and other. In order to get more insights about this 62% of *other* situations, the notes of those moods were analyzed. This analysis revealed the following contexts as the most common ones: start or end of shift, before break/lunch, back from lunch or a certain event, problem or issue (crash, waiting for other departments), feeling better after dealing with a problem, successful events, feeling tired, or having finished a certain task.

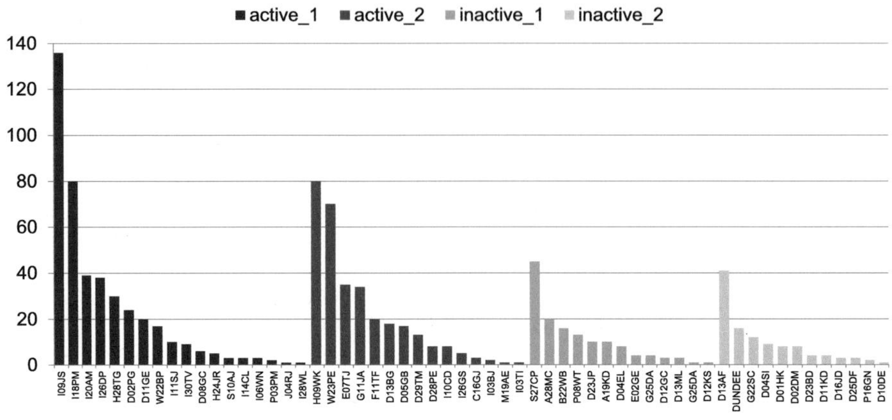

Figure 4.25.: Absolute number of moods captured by each participant of every team

An analysis of notes and contexts revealed information regarding in which situations call takers captured their moods and which reasons were behind them. Figure 4.26 to the left shows the distribution of all captured contexts ($N = 991$) among the four available categories. From the available categories, "others" was, unexpectedly, the most used. Therefore, in order to get more insights about these 617 moods with unknown context, the corresponding personal notes were analyzed and several categories were identified (see Figure 4.26 to the right).

From all the participants that were registered in the MoodMap App, 53 used the available visualizations during their working shift and a total of 1914 interactions were logged. Each of these users had on average 36.11 interactions with the application ($SD = 60.63$) during the whole evaluation period. Such a high standard deviation shows that the usage of the app was very polarized, having users who were very active, whereas others almost did not use the app at all.

Table 4.14 shows the usage of the views in the MoodMap App extracted from the log files. From the three available live visualizations which provide direct feedback in real time, *Timeline* ($M = 10.02$) and *Compare Me* ($M = 10.23$) were the most used. According to interviews and questionnaires, the *Compare Me* visualization was especially mentioned as the most important feature, as participants attached a high importance to the direct comparison of their mood to the teams' average mood. This confirms our hypothesis that comparing themselves to the team in a quick and intuitive way may be supportive and useful, both in terms of creating curiosity in the users as well as allowing users to detect discrepancies that can initiate a reflective process. In contrast, neither the *Collaborate* visualization ($M = 1.21$) nor either both available daily reports ($M = 0.08$) were used by the participants. From the Team Views which were only available for managers and coaches, the report with the smileys was the most used visualization.

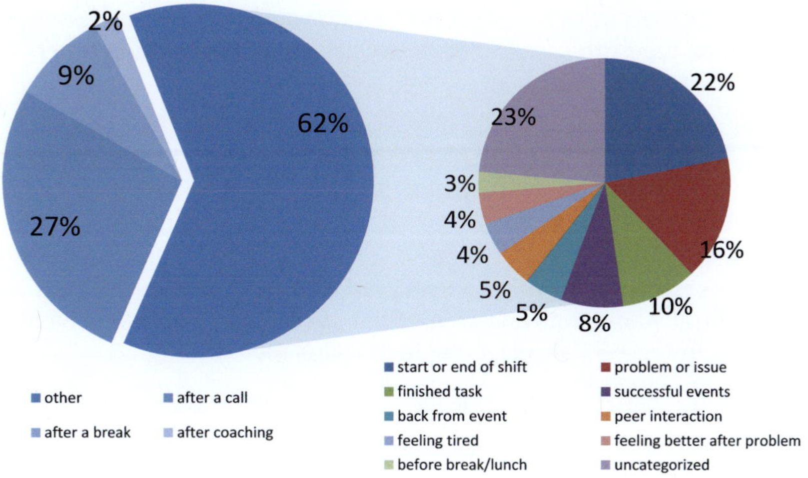

Figure 4.26.: Distribution of context categories among all users (left) and categorization of notes related to contexts of type "other" (right)

Table 4.14.: Descriptive statistics of the usage of the different views of the MoodMap App: three live views and two retrospective views

View	*Min*	*Max*	*Mean*	*SD*
Timeline	0	143	10.02	23.03
Compare Me	0	91	10.23	19.32
Collaborate	0	8	1.21	1.75
Meeting Report	0	3	0.08	0.43
Meetings & Me Report	0	1	0.04	0.19

The answers (N = 38) to the open questions of the post-questionnaire that referred to the acceptance of the MoodMap App and participants' reaction to it showed that the users' opinions were very amvibalent - from very positive over neutral to negative.

Regarding the situations in which it was useful to capture a mood, the responses range from *"It was interesting to capture moods at the start and end of shifts, depending on how much work was left to do etc."* to *"difficult to use an app when calculating mood because I FEEL. I do not need a technology to validate it."* If the users would or would not share their moods with managers was also very diverse. Some would especially share their mood about an awful call or a bad situation others would not share such a mood at all.

The final comments from the participants regarding the MoodMap App in general showed their different attitudes towards the application again. Four participants provided positive feedback like *"the mood map was fun to use and did lift team spirit for those that used it but I wouldn't say it has impacted on my day to day work or performance"* or *"I really enjoyed it. To make it more fun, we would use a # in the same way as twitter. It helped to improve mood further."* Five of the participants provided neutral statements and four of the participants' opinions were rather negative; e.g., *"I think BT should spend their money more wisely."*

The post-questionnaire covered questions regarding the self-reported capturing method used. Participants slightly agreed that the data gathering was accurate, effortless, relevant and timely, with a higher score in the active teams ($M = 3.78$) than in the less active teams ($M = 3.57$). The app was considered intuitive and easy to use without the need for further guidance ($M = 4.02$). Overall satisfaction with the app was also higher in the active teams than in the less active (see Table 4.15).

Figure 4.27 (satisfaction) shows that the participants ($N = 38$) stated that they have slightly agreed to be satisfied with the MoodMap App. If we consider this score for each individual team, it shows that the teams who have used the MoodMap App at most (Team active_1 and Team active_2) agreed to be more satisfied with the MoodMap App than those who had not used the application so intensively (Team inactive_1 and Team inactive_2). The overall score regarding the long-term usage of the MoodMap App during work (Figure 4.27, long-term usage) is rated rather neutral. Again, the two teams Team active_1 and Team active_2, who have intensively used the application, agreed that they would like to continue using the MoodMap App. In contrast, the scores of the two teams with the lower usage, namely Team inactive_1 and Team inactive_2, rated the long-term usage neutral or slightly disagreed to it. The future usage was rated neutral or slightly positive. In this case, the mean score represents also three of the individual teams except Team inactive_1.

A Pearson product-moment correlation coefficient was computed to assess the relationship between several variables from level 1. Concretely, the number of captured moods, interactions with the application, subjective usage, self-expressiveness of feelings and social media attitude were investigated. Due to the difference between the data available for each participant, it has to be taken into consideration that only a selection of the users could be considered in this analysis; i.e., the users who had data available for each of the variables involved and mentioned below.

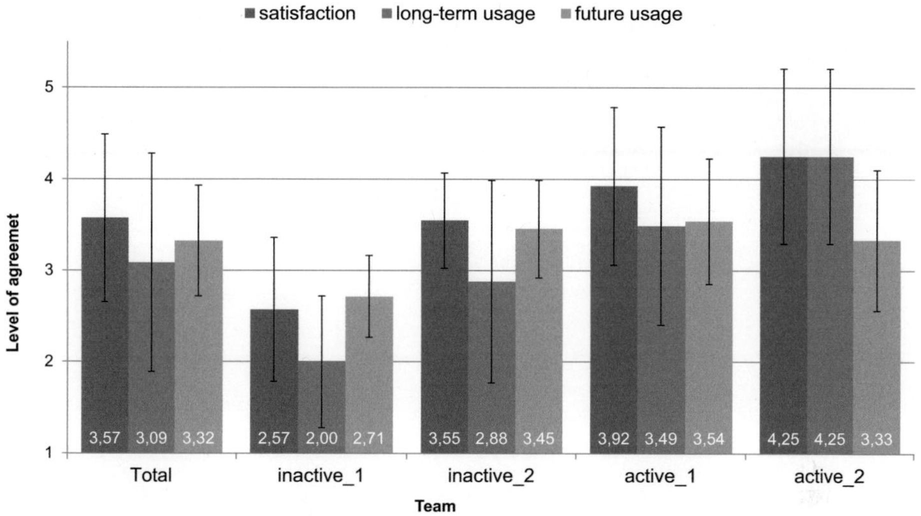

Figure 4.27.: Mean scores of satisfaction, long-term usage and future usage, in total (all participants) and per team

There was a very strong positive correlation between the number of captured moods and the number of interactions in the MoodMap App ($r = .870$, $p = .002$, $N = 64$). That means that users who captured more moods were also using the visualizations more often. A significant moderate positive correlation was also found between the number of interactions and subjective usage ($r = .496$, $p < .001$, $N = 35$). Finally, a strong positive correlation between captured moods and subjective usage was determined, too ($r = .626$, $p < .001$, $N = 35$). This result indicates that all three variables are correlated. This outcome is the expected result, as a higher usage of the app produces the capturing of more moods. It also shows that users could properly assess how often they used the app during their work and were aware of the introduction of the app in their daily practices. We also found that users' ease at expressing their feelings at work is correlated with captured moods and app interactions. There is a moderate positive correlation between interactions and expression of feelings ($r = .411$, $p < .014$, $N = 35$) and a weak positive correlation between captured moods and expression of feelings ($r = .384$, $p < .023$, $N = 35$). We found no correlation among the other level 1 variables mentioned above; e.g., social media attitude, which we expected to correlate with the usage of the app. This was also confirmed by an interview, where a highly active user in the MoodMap App stated not having any account in social media platforms.

Figure 4.28 shows the scores of the possible barriers of using the MMA including general barriers such as not having time, not having physical space, not having seen any advantage, or not having motivation to use the app. Users rated these barriers with neutral to slight disagreement, which also corresponds to each single team.

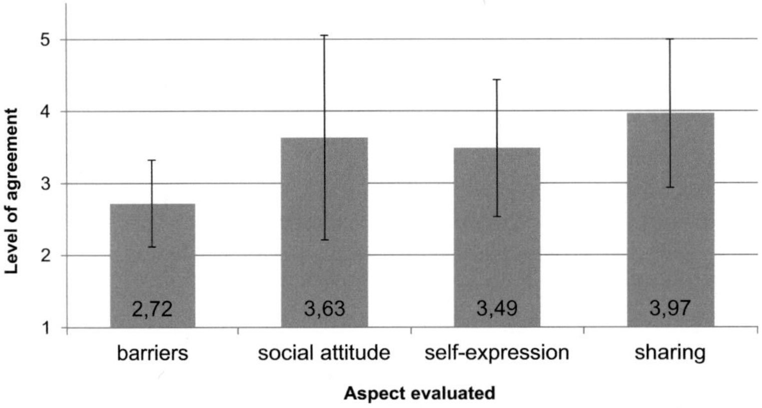

Figure 4.28.: Mean ratings for possible barriers including general barriers (time, space and motivation), social attitude, self-expression and sharing

The social media attitude (Figure 4.28, social attitude); i.e., how likely it is that they use social networking platforms (e.g., Facebook, Twitter, LinkedIn, Google+ or MySpace) was rated slightly positive, which means that the social media attitude is not a barrier for using the MoodMap App. Regarding their comfort with the self-expression of feelings (Figure 4.28, self-expression) in general and during work, the participants rated it neutral or slightly agreed. Having a look at this aspect at team level, only one team slightly disagreed with being comfortable in expressing their mood (Team inactive_1: $M = 2.50$; $SD = 0.80$), all other teams stated their self-expression rather positive. Sharing of emotions (Figure 4.28, sharing) with managers and coaches was not seen as a significant problem. The concerns of participants regarding the privacy they submit on social networking sites (rated with a 4-point Likert scale: not at all–a little–somehow–highly) shows that the participants are only little to somewhat concerned about their social privacy ($M = 2.47$; $SD = 0.95$).

From the open questions of the post-questionnaire we received many different responses regarding the barriers of the MoodMap App usage. Responses from the 13 participants who have answered this question show that they either do not see any direct barriers for using the MoodMap App, that they perceived the MoodMap App as easy-to-use, that the app could become part of their normal working day, or that the app only has a clear benefit for the coaches and managers but not for the call takers.

Call takers were also asked if they could imagine using the app in the future: 32.35% would use it if their manager or coach thinks it is important, 23.53% if their colleagues attach importance to it, 17.65% of them would use the app regularly, 2.94% from time to time, and 23.53% would not use it at all.

Learning

The post-questionnaire included seven app-specific questions of the evaluation toolbox. Figure 4.29 presents the mean ratings (in a 5-point Likert scale) of the app-specific reflection questions per team. The overall mean shows that the participants slightly agreed that the application has potential to initiate reflection by capturing data relevant for reflection and visualizing data to reconstruct working experiences as well as capturing learning outcomes. The rating of each team proved very interesting. While Team inactive_1 ($M = 2.09$; $SD = 0.99$) and Team inactive_2 ($M = 2.70$; $SD = 1.48$) rated the app-specific reflection questions rather neutral or slightly disagreed, the other two teams Team active_1 ($M = 3.44$; $SD = 0.69$) and Team active_2 ($M = 4.25$; $SD = 0.96$) rated it very positive. The results show that the teams with higher MoodMap App usage also gave higher ratings with respect to the app's potential to support reflection.

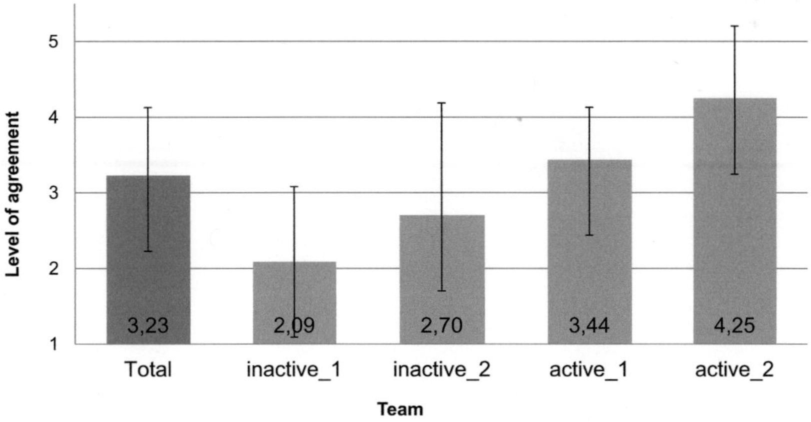

Figure 4.29.: Mean ratings per team for the seven application specific reflection questions

In order to investigate if self-reflection has taken place during the usage of the application, we analyzed the 946 inserted notes with a coding scheme for reflective content [Prilla and Renner, 2014]. Three different researchers conducted the first rating of the notes independently. The inter-coder reliability exceeded an average compliance in each of the following categories: Category 1 - Experience or issue/problem report: 87%, Category 2a - own emotions: 91%, Category 2b - emotions of customers: 93%, and Category 3 - interpretation and justification: 92%. A low number of notes were assigned to categories 4 and 7; therefore, no inter-coder reliability can be reported. After the first categorization round, the researchers discussed all the notes where their ratings differed. In this second categorization round, a 100% accordance was achieved.

Each note could be assigned to more than one category. From the total number of notes, 239 notes could be identified as individual reflective items. The remaining 707 notes were not work-related and could therefore not be assigned to any of the categories. Figure 4.30 shows a summary of the number of notes in each category. The categorization resulted in: 185 notes referring to the expression of own emotions, 141 notes classified as experiences or issue/problem report, 50 as emotions of customers, 17 as interpretation and justification of actions taken during work, 3 as linking an experience explicitly to other experiences, and finally 1 note as giving solution suggestions.

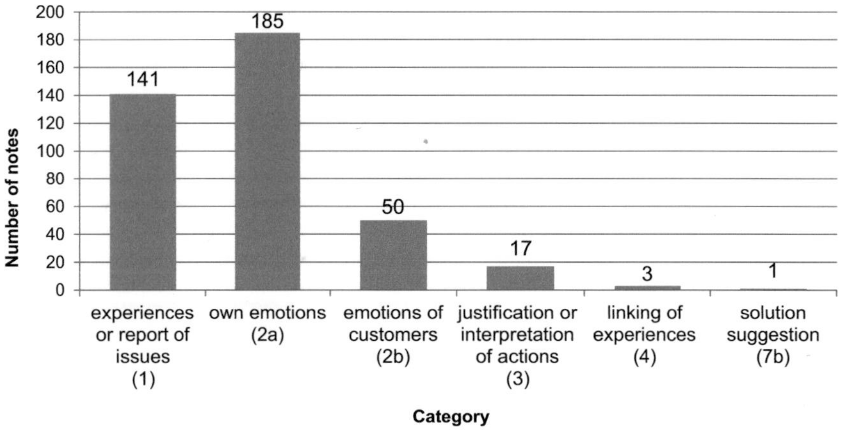

Figure 4.30.: Number of notes in each reflection category according to the Reflection Coding Scheme

The average ratings of questions that addressed reflection and its impact on participants' work are summarized in Table 4.15. The support of the MoodMap App regarding emotional awareness and identification of issues worth reflecting was rated with higher scores by the active teams than by the inactive ones.

Table 4.15.: Average values for items from the post-questionnaire: satisfaction, awareness and reflection (N = 38)

Questionnaire Item	Active Teams	Inactive Teams
I am satisfied with the MoodMap App.	4.00 (SD = 0.87)	3.17 (SD = 1.35)
The app helped me to become aware of my own mood.	4.06 (SD = 0.83)	3.11 (SD = 1.28)
The app helped me to become aware of my colleagues' mood.	3.88 (SD = 0.93)	3.06 (SD = 1.06)
The app helped me to identify significant situations worth reflecting.	3.71 (SD = 0.85)	2.83 (SD = 1.10)
The app helped me to identify significant mood changes worth reflecting.	3.65 (SD = 1.00)	2.72 (SD = 1.07)
Capturing my mood between calls with customers is useful to reflect and think about my dealing with call issues and customers.	3.65 (SD = 0.86)	3.17 (SD = 1.10)

As seen in Table 4.15, participants in the active teams agreed with the app helping them be aware of their colleagues' moods. This fact was also supported by the interview with a call taker: *"we sort of discussed it [the app] just to get a better time offline, you know, the wait-time in between calls and, speaking to my colleagues, they find it very positive [...]"*. A manager also confirmed: *"It improved communication within the team. [...] It opened the channels of communication around call drivers, energy dips and fluctuation in moods."* We also asked participants if the mood self-tracking app had increased their ability to reflect collaboratively. Results show that participants in the most active teams agreed with their ability being increased (M = 3.82), while the less active teams remained neutral (M = 3.28).

Participants were asked in pre- and post-questionnaires whether reflecting on their work and on their emotions helped them to improve their customers' satisfaction. After the evaluation, participants were more confident that reflection on *their work* has an impact on customer satisfaction, but less confident with respect to the impact of reflecting on *their mood*. This shows that reflection on mood alone is not enough to affect work. Rather, mood entries serve as trigger to start reflecting on work or working processes.

The questions of the Short Reflection Scale (SRS) were posed in the pre- as well as in the post- questionnaire with the goal of finding out if the usage of the application contributed to improve the reflective practices of the participants (N = 26). We found no significant differences between the pre-questionnaire (M = 3.98; SD = 0.49) and post-questionnaire (M = 3.89; SD = 0.53) mean ratings for the SRS. The values of the pre-questionnaire show that the willingness to reflect was rather high right before app usage and did not show any significant improvement after the evaluation. An explanation of this phenomenon is that most of the participants see themselves as reflective persons, and since the initial value was rather high it is more challenging to show an improvement. Another possible explanation for this would be the relative short evaluation period, as we have no evidence how likely it is that the answers to these questions significantly will change in 4 weeks.

We evaluated the results with respect to learning outcomes through two questions in the post-questionnaire. To the question if users had made a conscious decision about how to behave in the future (CL1[10]), the participants remained neutral with an average $M = 2.91$ ($SD = 1.09$). This was also the case for the question asking participants if they had gained a deeper understanding of their work life (CL2[11]), which was rated with $M = 2.85$ ($SD = 1.14$).

Considering the answers of each team separately, only Team_active 2 differs from the scores mentioned above. This team—with $M = 4.25$ ($SD = 0.96$) for CL1 and for CL2—agreed to have gained a deeper understanding with regard to their work-life and what to change about their work behavior. However, this polarized result may also be influenced by the fact that only four participants of this team have filled in the post-questionnaire.

We also asked participants about examples and further details about what they had changed or learned. Decisions taken by participants included being more positive; e.g., *"I realized I have been annoyed and consciously made the decision to let things affect me less"*, *"not to allow myself to jump to anger as often"*, or *"more positive attitude towards negative situations"*; and improving their behavior with respect to others; e.g., *"try and be more positive regarding distressed customers"*, *"to remain calm and not bring it to the next customer"*, or *"just how to change how I deal with people in general out of work as well as at work."*

Participants gained a deeper understanding about their feelings; e.g., *"nobody wants to see sad faces and low moods so it lifts your moods"* or *"when I notice the mood app is showing low energy...."* They learned also about how their mood affects their work; e.g., *"larger work load, causes more stress at different times of the day"*, *"I can see how my mood can change over the day depending how busy we are"*, or *"I could see that I was in a worse mood in the morning, but would work hard to push through the bad mood"*; and about what things they remember best; e.g., *"I would be more prone to remembering the things that went wrong rather than what went right."*

[10] CL1: "After using the MoodMap App, I made a conscious decision about how to behave in the future."

[11] CL2: "After using the MoodMap App, I gained a deeper understanding of my work life."

Behavior Change

Behavioral change (measured by question CB1[12]) was rated by the participants with $M = 2.77$ ($SD = 1.27$), which implies that the participants tend to state neutral or slightly disagreed that the MoodMap App helped them to improve their work at the call center (e.g., during the shift, after customer's calls, during and after coaching sessions, during team meetings, or in other situations). This result shows that—from a subjective perspective—participants tend to underestimate the positive influence of the app on their work performance, besides having recognized changes in their behavior in some cases and having improved their scores in the Key Performance Indicators (see Section 4.9.2). Nonetheless, 35% of the participants agreed with the MoodMap App helping them to improve their work performance and mentioned that their work is improved by becoming aware through the app. They stated that if their mood was low, they tried to lift it, that they would try to have a more positive attitude towards negative situations. A participant also mentioned that he or she would use the MoodMap App to state how much work they had completed.

We also asked the participants if they had recognized any improvements in the attitude of their managers and coaches. Most of the answers stated that the attitude of the four managers and their coaches was already great, being approachable, supportive and easy to interact with, so they had not noticed any further improvements. Nonetheless, in Team inactive_1 a participant recognized that their manager had shown a little more concern about their current moods and in Team inactive_2 another participant confirmed having recognized improvements but, unfortunately, did not give any further details.

Further questions on work improvement were divided according to the participant's role. Coaches and managers were asked if they had noticed any improvements in the work performance of their call takers since they started using the application. Answers to this question were available from teams inactive_2 and active_1, both from the manager and a coach respectively. Although the opinions differed (one coach and one manager agreed by rating 4, whereas the other coach and manager disagreed by rating 1), we could appreciate a direct relationship with the question on making a conscious decision about how to behave in the future mentioned above (Learning Outcomes). The manager and coach who agreed with having made a conscious decision and behaving differently also noticed improvements in the work of his or her call takers, and vice versa.

Table 4.16 shows the mean and standard deviation for several questions related to participants' behavior. For the comparison of the pre-test and post-test situation, only the answers of the 26 participants whose data for both questionnaires

[12] CB1: "The MoodMap App helped me to improve my work performance."

is available were taken into consideration. As the results show (see coaching sessions in Table 4.16) the perception of the participants was slightly improved. Average rating to the question regarding if being aware of own emotions during customer calls helps to reduce the call taker's customer repeats (number of times a customer has to call again to solve an issue, which should be always solved "Right First Time"; see customer repeats in Table 4.16) was also slightly reduced. Participants were also asked whether reflecting on their work and on their emotions helps them improve their customer satisfaction. The comparison between the answers before and after the evaluation (see work customer and emotions customer in Table 4.16) show that participants were more confident after the evaluation regarding reflection on their work, but they were less confident with reflection on their moods getting to affect customers' satisfaction.

Table 4.16.: Results to questions from the post-questionnaire regarding participants' behavior, with a 5-point Likert scale ($N = 26$)

	Pre-questionnaire	**Post-questionnaire**
coaching sessions	M=3.87; SD=1.45	M=4.00; SD=1.26
cover coaching	M=3.87; SD=1.45	M=3.87; SD=1.45
customer repeats	M=3.80; SD=1.16	M=3.43; SD=1.43
feedback processes	M=3.68; SD=1.03	M=3.68; SD=1.03
reflect feel	M=3.40; SD=1.34	M=3.40; SD=1.34
work customer	M=3.32; SD=1.33	M=3.80; SD=1.16
emotions customer	M=3.74; SD=1.54	M=3.32; SD=1.33

Additionally, the conducted Pearson correlation showed that there is a positive correlation between the customer's average rating of the participants after the usage period of the MoodMap App and how comfortable the users felt with expressing feelings in general ($r = .635$, $p < 0.026$ for $N = 12$). This shows that the usage of the app may have a positive impact on better communication with emotions and call taker's empathy, resulting in a better rating of the services by the customers.

Regarding the Short Reflection Scale score of the participants and the customer's average rating of the participants, it was also proved through a Pearson test, that they positively correlate with a score of 0.586 ($p < 0.035$) for $N = 13$. This implies that for these 13 participants the rating for this KPI is higher when the user has a higher reflection score. That means that the usage of the app has a positive impact on both parameters, although this interpretation can only be confirmed for those 13 participants whose data was available.

Additionally to the feedback gathered with the questionnaires, gained insights and behavioral changes were collected through several interviews. Interviews with two managers and one call taker were conducted. Feedback from both managers was very positive, especially regarding the insights they gained about their teams and how this positively affected the teams' work. The call taker from Team active_2 perceived the experience with the MoodMap App as very positive and he learned some insights when comparing himself to the team. Possible changes a manager was considering thanks to the MoodMap App were modifying the time or maybe even the organization of the huddles themselves if the call takers were in a low mood, or also defining some new tasks or activities for certain points in a day where the mood dropped. A manager also mentioned insights regarding their individual mood: *"As the moods were easily visible, this allows the managers to incorporate their coaching style to reflect the current mood"* and these insights made him also change his behavior at work: *"When my energy level is low, I leave the desk and do something else until my level is up again. Then I return to my desk."*

Insights for uptake in other teams were also discussed: *"I think it definitely improved my insight into my team. And I think it would also be useful for managers that have like a team that work away from the offices, that work at home so you can't always see them, but you can see what kind of moods they are in—and how they're feeling and stuff. You know, if I wasn't in the office, I can still see how my team is feeling. [...] It is definitely an improvement for me."*

The interviewed call taker commented on insights he had gained by reflecting on his mood and highlighted the fact that he could see the mood of his colleagues and compare himself to them: *"Yeah, I like the way you can see the team members as well; you can see where they are, or you sort of wonder yourself why are they there, or why are they are up there and I am down here or vice versa. So you sort of wonder and I ask these things to myself if they just had a really bad day or had a bad call or are just generally feeling unavailable [...] it is quite a good thing to look at, and I always compare myself to others."* He also mentioned that reflecting on a certain call helped him move on to the next customer feeling better and not being affected by past negative experiences.

The call taker also admitted not having used it in his coaching sessions, but being willing to use it: *"I think we should use them more in coaching, I think we should incorporate it in peer-coaching, but make it positive, don't reflect on a negative thing, [...] So everybody likes positive feedback; nobody likes negative feedback, so I think that by using it in coaching you should always make it positive...."*

Work Outcomes

For the first period, during which the MoodMap App was used (from October 21, 2013 until December 19, 2013), the results of the paired-samples t-test for the individual KPI *Average Rating* are shown in Table 4.17. To test the normality of the data, we previously conducted Kolmogorov-Smirnov tests. All variables related to the periods *before* and *during* usage of the MoodMap App were normal distributed.

There are statistically significant differences at the .01 significance level in pre-test to post-test scores in team active_1. The average rating delivered by the customers increased 8.20% during the period where the MoodMap App was used, which is a positive result. Regarding team active_2, the average rating slightly increased, but these results are not statistically significant. In the follow-up rating, KPIs were slightly reduced in both teams, but the reduction was not significant according to the t-test (Team active_1 -0.06%, team active_2 -8.62%).

Table 4.17.: Comparison of KPI *Average Rating* of active teams *before* and *during* the usage period: descriptive statistics and t-test results.

Team	Period	*M*	*SD*	*n*	*t*	*df*	*p*
active_1	before	82.79	7.98	19	-3.39*	18	.003
	during	89.58	5.81				
active_2	before	82.82	8.24	17	.06	16	.95
	during	83.00	11.86				

$^{*}p < .01$

For the second period, during which the MoodMap App was not used anymore (December 19, 2013 to February 7, 2014), we measured the metrics at individual level, summarized in Table 4.18. The intention of these measurements was to follow up if the identified improvement in the KPIs could be maintained for longer periods of time after the usage of the app. Again, Kolmogorov-Smirnov tests were conducted to test normality. Two out of the four variables were not normal distributed (concretely, the variables corresponding to the period *after* usage for both groups). Consequently, using a non-parametric test was more appropriate and robust. As we were dealing with paired groups, two-tailed Wilcoxon Signed-Rank tests for the individual KPI *Average Rating* were conducted. Since the p-value is greater than 0.05 in both tests (see Table 4.18), we conclude that the means have remained essentially unchanged (we accept the null hypothesis); there is no significant difference between the metrics during and after app usage.

As displayed in Table 4.18, the *average rating* scores suffered a slight reduction in both teams (Team active_1 -0.06% and Team active_2 -8.62%), whereas the median scores increased or remained. However, according to the Wilcoxon test, these changes are not significant.

Table 4.18.: Comparison of KPI *Average Rating* of active teams *during* and *after* the usage period: descriptive statistics and Wilcoxon test results.

Team	Period	*M*	*SD*	*Mdn*	*n*	*W*	*Z*	*r*	*p*
active_1	during	89.58	5.81	92	19	75	0.806	0.185	0.432
	after	89.33	13.46	95					
active_2	during	84.27	8.20	86	15	73.5	0.768	0.198	0.459
	after	77.00	21.69	86					

The Key Performance Indicators at team level are reported in Table 4.19.

Table 4.19.: Results for change in percentage of team KPIs during and after the app usage period, for active teams

	NPI		Call Taker Sat		Recap	
Team	**during**	**after**	**during**	**after**	**during**	**after**
active_1	40.00	17.14	7.14	-1.11	4.71	-3.37
active_2	16.67	-34.29	1.19	-3.53	3.80	-1.22

The metrics from team active_1 show that NPI increased 40.00% (from a score of 25 to 35 points) during the app usage period, whereas its improvement afterwards was only 17.14% (from 35 to 41). The metrics from team active_2 show a similar behavior. However, the difference between the usage period and the period after usage regarding the *NPI* is greater, having an improvement of 16.67% with the MoodMap App and a decrease of 34.29% during the period after the cessation. Regarding *Call Taker Sat* and *Recap*, the same behavior was detected in both teams: the metrics were slightly improved during the MoodMap App period, but they decreased minimally after the usage cessation.

The question related to the loyalty metric was only answered by a low number of participants ($N = 38$) and these were users who were not so active in the app, while we lack the answers from the most active users. Due to this fact, the loyalty metric could not be taken into consideration for the analysis and the Net Promoter Score (NPS) could not be accurately calculated.

Two managers (from teams active_1 and inactive_2) have filled in the post-questionnaire respectively. Their answers provided positive insights into the Team Views and how they helped to improve collaboration with their teams. The smileys visualization made them especially aware of the mood of each single team member and helped them gain insights about each team member ($M =$

4.5). The Weekly Timeline View made them aware of the mood development of the team and where actions need to be taken to increase the overall team's mood ($M = 4.25$). This positive attitude was also acknowledged during one of the interviews: *"I see the smileys, like I can always tell how people are feeling and if someone is having a really hard time or someone has done something really good."* and confirmed through the appraised log data. Discussions with the second level management revealed three possible reasons: this view shows what is happening at the present moment, it allows exploring the daily work development of each team member, and it is the most user-friendly and easiest to understand.

Managers confirmed in their interviews that they also got new insights with regard to their teams. They appreciated seeing how their individual call takers were feeling at a glance, especially when not having direct contact with each of their team members every day. This allowed managers to be more proactive; e.g., by directly contacting a call taker who was in a bad mood and offering support or further encouraging if necessary. Furthermore, the managers directly discussed the moods with their call takers on the floors during work and asked if there was anything to discuss in-depth or where the manager might provide further assistance. At team level, the managers also recognized that there were certain points in a day where the mood dropped: mid-afternoon and after lunch. So they were looking if there was anything they could put in place in order to change that and to increase the average team mood.

In order to confirm the design decision taken about sharing of the data after the first study, we asked call takers their opinion on sharing and the benefits it can bring. They slightly agreed ($M = 3.77$) with the fact that sharing their moods with their manager and coaches is fine for them. Regarding the goal pursued by sharing the data; i.e., that managers know the feelings of their team members to help them identify problems and directly help the appropriate person, participants restated their agreement ($M = 4.16$).

The interviews with the two managers of the most active teams shed insight on the opportunities provided by mood tracking. One of them explained an illustrative example about how he used the app and reacted on the mood of one of his call takers: *"I sit in a little corner of the office so I don't actually get a chance to interact with all of my team all the time. So I find the MoodMap App very useful to see how everyone was feeling because, obviously, not everyone comes to tell you how they are feeling and I had one guy, he sits quite far away from me and he was on a really hard time with a difficult customer. All said and done, by the way, he made a comment on the MoodMap App about having a really hard time and that he was not feeling like he was getting any help. So, straight away, I went over to him and asked what I could do to help him and an hour later his mood had gone from, like, really low to really high because I had gone over to help. [...] I would have never known about that and he would have probably struggled on, sitting there without me knowing anything."*

4.9.3. Discussion

Our study indicates that mood self-tracking increased cohesion in the team and supported reflection, what finally led to improvements on work performance. We discuss factors that have contributed to our research, challenges encountered, and resulting implications for the introduction and design of a mood self-tracking application at work in a wider sense.

Minimizing Capturing Efforts

Self-tracking is a voluntary activity driven by both intrinsic and extrinsic motivations [Gimpel et al., 2013] that requires, besides preparation, collection and integration, additional effort for reflection about and action on the data [Li et al., 2010]. By definition, subjective mood can only be collected via manual tracking and this results in additional efforts. Our work aimed to build a tool that lowers the user burden, which helps users easily track data and increase awareness. Besides the required efforts, the resulting adaptation of the MoodMap App led to a tracking interface which participants considered quick and easy to use.

Guidance for Capturing through Contextualization

Useful data must be easy to understand and linked to the work process. In our field study, we identified calls, coaching sessions, and breaks as the main tasks of call takers processes with potential to be related to mood data. This direct link to their daily tasks was intuitive and, at the same time, guided the capturing phase by showing examples of situations worth reflecting upon. However, the high percentage of moods captured outside the predefined tasks showed the importance of freedom for the appropriation of self-tracking tools by employees. Furthermore, the collaborative setting requires that moods have to be contextualized to be understood by others.

Comparison as Motivation Cue

Findings on activity tracker users showed that data tracking is often social and collaborative driven rather than personal [Rooksby et al., 2014], but this is exploited in the sense of competition (e.g., rankings) or showing success (e.g., announcing achievements in social media). However, in the call center sharing of data achieved cohesion in the team as well as empowerment of employees rather than competition or recognition, by increasing emotional awareness and providing meaningful triggers to collaboratively solving problems and improving work. As call takers confirmed in the questionnaires, being aware of their colleagues' mood is relevant for them. The log data also shows that the *Compare Me* visualization (which can only reflect updated values if the user captures his or her mood in that moment) was the most used feature. We see that this *curiosity of call takers in the mood of colleagues has not only contributed to motivating call takers to use the visualizations, but also to capturing more moods*. Therefore, our results extend the insights from Church et al. [2010] on sharing of mood within distributed groups of friends to employees in an open-plan office.

Trade-off between Sharing and Privacy

In many QS tools, sharing of data is exploited in the sense of competition (e.g., rankings) or showing success (e.g., posts about achievements in social media). In the call center, sharing of data achieved cohesion in the team as well as empowerment of employees. Privacy was expected to be a major barrier for self-tracking at the workplace and was targeted by questionnaires before and after the study. For participants, the benefits outweighed any privacy concerns because sharing and visualizing the annotated mood data led to clear benefits for both parties; i.e., team cohesion and empowerment of employees. Nonetheless, some employees may be uncomfortable with the fact of sharing their mood data and therefore *the decision on what and when to track should be left to each individual user*. Generalizing a positive attitude regarding privacy to other domains should be carefully considered; call takers are used to being monitored during their work (e.g., calls are recorded) but this is not the case for all professionals. These challenges also apply to the organizational culture, which in our case fitted with the approach of mood self-tracking very well, but we may find this initial predisposition lacking in other work settings.

Work Process Integration

It is necessary to discuss identified opportunities for reflection with all involved parties in order to integrate them in work processes and reduce barriers from the beginning. Although coaching sessions were seen as a promising venue to embed reflection, participants confirmed in the interviews that the app was not integrated. Some call takers expressed their willingness: *"I think we should use it more in coaching, [...] incorporate it in peer-coaching."* However, during the interviews, two possible causes for the lack of usage in coaching were suggested: (i) no integration of mood data with call center data in joint reports, and (ii) managers did not achieve to sufficiently motivate and engage coaches.

Lack of Time for Reflection

Work done in HCI has confirmed the importance of emotions, not only for personal self-tracking purposes, but also in work related settings to better support the re-evaluation of past working situations based on emotions [McDuff et al., 2012], as well as to improve communication in work environments [De Choudhury and Counts, 2013; Dullemond et al., 2013]. However, due to time and business constraints in call centers, time and space to review their gathered data was not given to call takers. In this respect, one manager stated: *"We think in numbers and money. If we give 2 minutes per day per person, that is 10 minutes per week and if I have 200 people online... that means... a lot of time and a lot of money. It is about the business."* This is an attitude that is unlikely to change because reflection is seen as of secondary importance to work tasks. Managers have always placed a higher value on action than on reflection [Daudelin, 1996].

Challenges of Reflection-on-action

The major challenge was not the capturing state of the tracking process, but the motivation and priorities of participants to take time to review the gathered data. As Choe et al. [2014] mention, the *"ultimate goal is to reflect upon one's data, extract meaningful insights, and make positive changes, which are the hardest part of QS"*. The low usage of the available mood reports as well as the fact that no dedicated time for reflection was made available showed that there is little evidence that reflection-on-action [Schön, 1984] has taken place.

Success of Reflection-in-action

Our results confirmed that people make sense of data especially when they collect it [Choe et al., 2014]. Furthermore, reflection should not be a stand-alone activity but a component of a holistic experience where an activity is ongoing [McCarthy and Wright, 2004]. Reflection-in-action [Schön, 1984] took place directly during the MoodMap App usage, as indicated by (i) the identification of reflective content in approximately a fourth of all notes gathered when capturing moods and (ii) the higher usage of those visualizations that offer a quick view of what is happening in the moment (e.g., *Compare Me* or *Smiley Team View*) or what has happened (e.g., *My Timeline*). These visualizations provided on-the-fly and real-time insights they could directly react upon.

Improvements in Work Performance

With respect to the work improvements investigated in RQ4, results show that some of the participants could recognize a clear benefit for themselves, but they could identify this benefit especially for the coaches and managers, if they can see how each individual call taker of the team is feeling and react to it. Some of the call takers, coaches, and managers mentioned that they have gained a deeper understanding with regard to their work-life and what to change about their work behavior. The call takers stated that they try to be more positive regarding distressed customers and to the decision to let things at work affect them less. Two of the managers and coaches also confirmed having taken conscious decisions to change their work behavior. Individual and team work performance improved in correlation with app usage as shown by KPI measurements. For strong usage in team active_1, this correlation was statistically significant and is further supported by the slight decline of the KPIs in the follow-up measurements. The impact of the application in their work environment cannot be isolated completely and other factors may affect the development of the KPIs. However, interviews with the management did not reveal any other concrete factor that may have influenced these positive results.

Improvements in Inter-Role Relationships

The introduction of the MoodMap App positively affected the communication between managers and call takers. Managers increased their awareness of their team's emotional state [García et al., 1999]. This allowed them to react quickly towards each individual member of the team. The fact that managers work in separate offices and are not always present in the common working space of call takers provided additional value to the insights gained from mood tracking. Feedback of call takers revealed that the app allowed them to vent and to quickly communicate problems to their manager when they had no immediate solution on their own and needed further support. As described above, a call taker's mood triggered a change in the manager's communication patterns and ultimately led to improvements in his employee's work performance. This shows how, with simple interventions implemented through self-tracking, the "reporting upstream" [Colombino et al., 2014] can be enriched so that employees' input can trigger changes in established work processes.

The differences of usage that we encountered in active versus inactive teams showed a direct connection with the different management styles as confirmed by discussions with the second level management. Whereas the active teams had managers who were engaged with the MoodMap App, encouraged their teams and proactively reacted to the data; managers in the inactive teams adopted a more passive attitude. For the active teams, this was seen as a direct benefit which enables later long term benefits of reflection.

Limitations

One of the main challenges was to achieve a complete dataset for the questionnaires, as well as a control group. Such methodologies are not usual in their work environment and there are many barriers to achieve these two conditions. Although the organizing manager at BT tried numerous times to get back the questionnaires (through the respective managers) and to find a control group, his efforts were unfortunately unsuccessful. This was also the case for the KPIs regarding teams inactive_1 and inactive_2, which could not be made available. As a result, the interpretation of the gathered data within the application itself, the usage of the MoodMap App derived from the log files, as well as the pre- and post-questionnaires was rather difficult. The prime reason is that the users who used the application most and the users who filled in the pre- and post-questionnaires were partially not the same. Therefore, we had to decide which available combination of data can be meaningfully used for which type of evaluation result and interpretation purposes. Due to this fact, only 26 participants delivered answers for both questionnaires and therefore analysis of pre- and post- situation was rather limited.

In the case of Team active_2, only 4 out of 18 participants have filled in the post-questionnaire, although this team was one of the two most active ones. Due to the low number of participants the obtained results might not completely mirror the whole team. On the other hand, we had conducted two very positive interviews with the manager and one call taker of the team. The positive attitudes of these two participants as well as the low numbers of filled in questionnaires may suggest that significant positive results regarding the benefits of the MoodMap App were not visible. The fact that teams active_1 and active_2 captured twice as many moods as the other two teams is also remarkable.

4.10. Summative Evaluation II: Italian Software Company

The use of the MoodMap App was initially identified by the human resources manager of the company with the goal to provide a possibility for self-reflection, self-development and stress detection during work. Therefore, they embedded the MoodMap App directly in their working processes with the aim of integrating it in their daily working routines. The MoodMap App should give the individual the possibility to reflect on his or her own mood as well as the mood of the whole department.

In this first trial, the MoodMap App was not integrated in their systems, but it was made accessible directly from the employees' desktop (through an icon). During the introduction of the MoodMap App, the Regola's manager responsible for the evaluation made the participants aware to use the application in different situations and significant work-related activities; e.g., if the service desk has to deal with a particular request. Very short meetings with the corresponding managers were planned in order to find out how the mood or particular things according to the results of the MoodMap App can be improved. Additionally, Regola had interest in investigating which daily activities are most suitable to introduce mood self-tracking.

This evaluation took place in collaboration with Know-Center Graz in the context of the EU project MIRROR.

4.10.1. Procedure

The summative evaluation of the MoodMap App at Regola started on February 12, 2014 and lasted until March 31, 2014. The MoodMap App was introduced to all five departments by the responsible project manager of Regola. During this introduction, the project manager described the usage of the MoodMap App and presented a success story which emerged during the MoodMap App evaluation at BT (see Section 4.9), in order to show them a meaningful insight and a clear benefit. Additionally, the department members were asked to fill in a pre-questionnaire including the MIRROR consent form. During the application usage period, all participants of the trial were asked to insert their moods during their working shifts and to reflect on their inserted moods and notes individually. The managers were additionally instructed to use the team visualizations in order to reflect on the mood development of their departments and take actions if necessary. At the end of the trial, all participants were requested to fill in a post-questionnaire. Additionally, seven participants of the evaluation took part in an interview with the researchers with the aim of gaining more insights about the evaluation and the usage of the MoodMap App at Regola.

Participants

Out of 38 employees of Regola, 35 have participated in the MoodMap App evaluation. The reasons for not participating were not related to the evaluation itself, but it was due to personal or professional reasons. The 35 participants were split over five departments, following the structure of the company (see Section 4.1.3). This resulted in the following departments and number of participants:

- Department Am (Administration): $N = 4$
- Department Co (Sales and Marketing): $N = 4$
- Department Qu (Support and Service Desk): $N = 6$
- Department Pm (Production): $N = 5$
- Department Sv (Development): $N = 16$

Among the participants, 27 were male and 8 were female. Participants in the evaluation were between 20 and 59 years old, with 9% of them aged between 20 and 29, 77% between 30 and 39, 11% between 40 and 49, and 3% between 50 and 59. They had worked on average $M = 6.77$ ($SD = 1.52$) years in their current position, ranging from participants with less than one year and to a maximum of 15 years in that position. The average years in a similar position were $M = 4.14$ ($SD = 2.96$). 80% of the participants are working full-time, 17% are working part-time, and one participant has not stated his job scope.

All participants have filled in the pre-questionnaire and the post-questionnaire. Two of the participants have filled in the pre-questionnaire after the trial, so only demographic data was used for analysis (questions regarding reflection practices and expectations were not considered). One participant has filled in the post-questionnaire with invalid data; therefore, these answers were also removed from the dataset. A total of 32 participants have filled in both questionnaires and their answers constitute the dataset used for comparisons of pre- and post-questionnaire variables.

Evaluation Tools

Analogous to the previous summative evaluation, we investigated relevant indicators for reflective learning and their impact for individuals and teams, as well as the organization as a whole. We used the summative evaluation toolbox developed in the framework of the MIRROR Project [Knipfer et al., 2012], which defines four analysis levels: reaction and usage, learning, behavior, and work outcomes.

Except for the Key Performance Indicators (KPI), we used the same evaluation tools as in the previous summative evaluation. A detailed description of these tools can be found in Section 4.9.1. KPIs could not be provided by the company. Therefore, concrete questions about their KPIs were asked to the different departments before and after the evaluation (e.g., number of bugs per week or number of hours dedicated to a certain task). The post-questionnaire included additional questions about employee satisfaction as well as improvement of work performance at individual and collaborative level.

4.10.2. Results

Following the levels of the toolbox, we report the results according to the four levels of Kirkpatrick and Kirkpatrick [2006].

Reaction and Usage

The participants used the MoodMap App on 48 consecutive days. Except for 12 days during which the app was not used at all (corresponding to days off), on average 10 hours and 32 minutes (SD = 0.129) lie between the first and the last logged event of every day. During that period, users were entering the MoodMap App repeatedly and using the different available features. A total of 2,250 moods were captured by the 35 participants during the usage of the MoodMap App. On average, users captured 64.29 moods (SD = 33.27) during the whole evaluation period, ranging between 12 and 143 moods per user. Considering the moods captured in each department, on average 41.50 (SD = 39.71) moods were captured in Department Am (N = 4), 38.75 (SD = 21.20) in Department Co (N = 4), 59.17 (SD = 29.17) in Department Qu (N = 6), 79.20 (SD = 38.62) in Department Pm (N = 5), and 73.63 (SD = 30.54) in Department Sv (N = 16). These results show that participants of the departments Pm and Sv captured an average of approximately twice as many moods per member than any of the other three departments. Regarding the notes attached to the moods, a total of 226 non-empty notes were captured by the users and served as annotation for their affective states. The contextualization of moods was not used regularly, as only a total of 31 contexts were captured by all participants.

Table 4.20 contains the distribution (absolute numbers) of captured moods, notes and context for each department that participated in the evaluation.

All 35 participants who were registered in the MoodMap App used the app during their working shift and used the main features of the app a total of 1767 times. Each of these users had an average of 50.49 interactions with the application (SD = 101.56) during the whole evaluation period. Such a high standard deviation also shows that the usage of the app was very polarized; having users who were very active, whereas others hardly used the app. Figure 4.31 shows the average usage of the main visualizations of the MoodMap App. The three features that were most used were the *Capture Mood*, *Timeline*, and *Compare Me* visualizations. This was also confirmed by the interviews and the questionnaires. The preferred visualization for the users was the *Compare Me* visualization, where employees could compare their own mood with the mood of their colleagues. This confirms the results obtained in the first summative evaluation (see Section 4.9); i.e., comparing themselves to the team in a quick and intuitive way is supportive and useful, both in terms of creating curiosity in the users as well as allowing users to detect discrepancies that can initiate a reflective process.

Table 4.20.: Absolute numbers of moods, notes, and context captured by each department

Team	*N*	No. Moods	Avg. Moods	No. Notes	Avg. Notes	No. Context	Avg. Context
Dept. Am	4	166	41.50	11	2.75	0	0.00
Dept. Co	4	155	38.75	43	10.75	4	1.00
Dept. Qu	6	355	59.17	32	5.33	2	0.33
Dept. Pm	5	396	79.20	67	13.40	6	1.20
Dept. Sv	16	1178	73.63	73	4.56	19	1.19
Total	35	2250	64.29	226	6.46	31	0.89

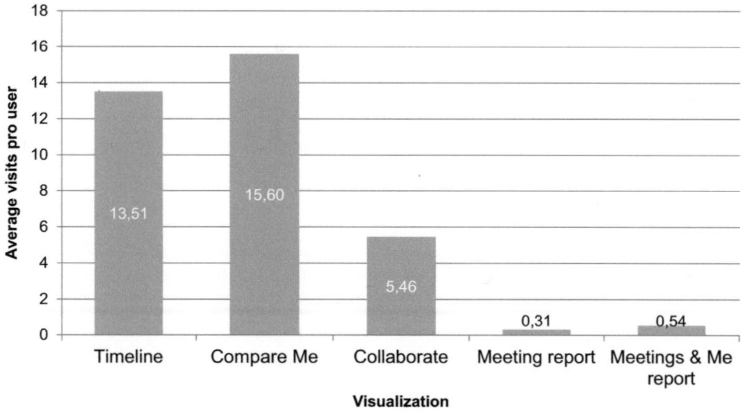

Figure 4.31.: Usage of the main visualizations of the MoodMap App. For each feature, average among all users is depicted.

The following mean scores were all rated on a 5-point Likert Scale (strongly disagree–strongly agree). Participants stated that they are neutral or slightly agree to be satisfied with the MoodMap App ($M = 3.24$; $SD = 0.85$). Four departments mirror the overall mean scores. Only Department Pm was not satisfied with the application ($M = 2.20$; $SD = 0.84$), although they have captured the highest number of moods per participant during this trial. This could be explained with the fact that they have neither used the available reports in the application nor conducted any meetings to reflect on their moods within their team to gain explicitly any insights or benefits. Furthermore, many of them did a lot of traveling during the evaluation period and seemed to be the ones under the most stress. Therefore, they mainly captured their moods and kept on working but could not perceive any benefit for themselves. The overall score regarding the long-term usage of the MoodMap App during work is rated rather neutral ($M = 2.94$; $SD = 1.00$). While Department Co agreed to continue using the MoodMap App ($M = 3.58$; $SD = 0.32$), the other four departments rated the long-term usage neutral or slightly disagreed with it.

The future usage of the MoodMap App was rated with an average value of $M = 2.76$ ($SD = 1.35$). Department Co especially agreed to continue using the MoodMap App in the future ($M = 4.00$; $SD = 1.41$). The other departments Department Am ($M = 2.75$; $SD = 0.96$), Department Pm ($M = 2.40$; $SD = 0.89$) and Department Sv ($M = 2.47$; $SD = 1.36$) slightly disagreed with this fact. For all values, the standard deviations are rather high; this shows that the participants diverge in their opinions regarding the future usage of the app.

A Pearson product-moment correlation coefficient was computed to assess the relationship between several variables from level 1. Concretely, the number of captured moods (notes and context), interactions with the application, subjective usage, self-expressiveness of feelings and social media attitude, as well as sharing, satisfaction, long term usage, the motivation to reflect alone or in the team, learning outcomes, change in behavior, and KPIs were investigated.

There was a positive correlation between the number of captured moods and the number of interactions with the visualizations in the MoodMap App ($r = .489$, $p = .003$, $N = 34$). This analysis reveals that most active users (e.g., the ones who visited the visualizations) were also the ones who captured more moods. Self-expression of feelings in general and during work clearly emerged ($r = .710$, $p < .001$, $N = 34$). This reflects that people who are usually comfortable to express themselves do not encounter additional barriers to do it at work, and vice versa.

Additionally, we see a strong positive correlation between the motivation to reflect on work in general and the opinion that the app helped them deal with their emotions ($r = .720$, $p < .001$, $N = 34$). This result indicates that the MoodMap App could help them deal with emotions, especially for people who are more motivated to reflect on work. A strong positive correlation exists between the number of captured moods and the subjective application usage ($r = .489$, $p < .001$, $N = 34$). This suggests that users were aware of their activities done in the MoodMap App regarding the capturing of moods. Participants who were more comfortable with sharing their moods with managers also inserted more notes in the MoodMap App, as it is shown by the positive correlation between these two variables (r = .488, p = .006, N = 30). Finally, we also found a positive correlation between moods and notes (r = .395, p = .019, N = 35) and notes and context (r = .377, p = .025, N = 35).

The scores of the possible barriers in relation to not having time, not having physical space, not having seen any advantage, or not having motivation to use the app, were rated with neutral to slight disagreement M = 2.66 (SD = 0.58) by all departments. The social media attitude; i.e., how likely it is that they use social networking platforms (e.g., Facebook, Twitter, LinkedIn, Google+, MySpace, etc.), was rated on average with M = 3.50 (SD = 1.08). This means that they slightly agreed to use such platforms and that the social media attitude is mostly not a barrier to use the MoodMap App. While four of the departments mirror the average score, Department Co rated this item with M = 4.50 (SD = 0.58). This shows that the participants of Department Co strongly agree to use social networking platforms.

In contrast, the social privacy concerns (evaluated with a 4-point Likert scale: not at all–high) are rated with M = 2.68 (SD = 1.17). This shows that the participants are only from a little to somewhat concerned about their privacy on social networking sites in general, which is therefore not seen as a major barrier to use the MoodMap App. Department Qu and Department Sv are more concerned about their privacy than the other three departments. Department Cu is least concerned regarding privacy, which again matches with their overall social media attitude. Regarding the self-expression of feelings in general and during work, the participants rated it neutral or slightly agreed that they feel comfortable with this fact (M = 3.41; SD = 0.84). While Department Co rated the self-expression very high, Department Pm rated it rather low. The other three departments stated their self-expression rather neutral. Sharing of emotions with managers or department members was rated with M = 3.53 (SD = 0.86), which means that sharing of individual moods was not seen as a significant problem. In this case, the average value represents the scores for all five departments.

Additionally, the participants mentioned several situations when they would share their moods with their managers; for example, *"upon the occurrence of important working events that make my mood change considerably"* or *"in the situations where a manager is able to listen constructively the issues/problems identified in the work processes."* One manager refused to share his moods at all: *"Never. The moods are extremely personal and depend on thousands of factors. I would not want to share it to work."* Situations where the participants would not share their moods with their managers encompass mostly non-work related private issues and situations where users are discontent or dissatisfied with their work. However, the manager mentioned before did not consider any potential situation for sharing: *"Never. It is not ethical to ask to share the mood in the workplace."*

From the open questions of the post-questionnaire we received many different responses regarding the barriers of the MoodMap App usage. This question was left blank by 26 participants, who did not identify further barriers for usage. Three of the participants did not see any barriers to use the MoodMap App at all. Four of the participants mentioned that they have no time to use the MoodMap App because of urgent and tight timelines. One participant stated that he would like to have a faster approach to insert his moods; e.g., in form of a widget. And one participant stated that *"the graphical interface is not usable."*

Summarizing the answers of the open question of the post-questionnaire about the usage of the MoodMap App, we identified ambiguous opinions among the participants. On the one hand, we obtained several positive statements which refer mainly to the managers' perspective and that they could use the MoodMap App to better support their team; e.g., *"To be useful it should be used by managers to check the mood of its staff and possibly implement appropriate corrective actions"* or *"it's a great project but maybe the effectiveness was a bit limited by the lack of time to make meetings on the subject."* A participant gave insights on the general attitude he had experienced: *"MMA and the concepts in which it is based are intelligent. But the Italian culture and mentality, especially in working environments, do not give any importance to feelings/energy/health/stress of people so the use of MMA has showed little profit and 'was seen as a waste of time'."* This statement reflects that, despite the existence of laws dictating that companies have to verify the level of stress of their employees, this has not been included in their organizational culture yet. Additionally, we also received some ideas for improvement; e.g., *"The app should be made much more streamlined and straightforward [...] use a faster instantiation, maybe a widget on your desktop."* In contrast, there were also some critical statements regarding the usefulness of the MoodMap App, especially from one manager: *"The objectives of the MoodMap are unrealistic. The idea of thinking about the one's own mood is good, but I just consider it inapplicable [...]."* He also mentioned several reasons why users would never state their real mood into such a tool (e.g., ethical reasons, non-work-related personal bad feeling or depressions) and questioned what one should do if mood is not optimal: *"What happens if an employee is going through a bad time?"*. This fact suggests that the purpose of supporting reflection with the MoodMap App in order to detect and improve such situations was not properly transmitted to him.

Learning

The post-questionnaire included nine app-specific questions of the evaluation toolbox, eight regular questions and one control question. Figure 4.32 presents the mean ratings (from 5-point Likert scales) of the app-specific reflection questions. The overall average $M = 2.86$ ($SD = 0.80$) shows that the participants were neutral, that the application has potential to initiate reflection by capturing data relevant for reflection and visualizing data to reconstruct working experiences as well as capturing learning outcomes. While Department Pm disagreed that the application has potential to initiate reflection, the other four departments answered this question neutrally. These ratings are also very interesting with regard to the application usage and how many moods per participant and department were captured during the whole evaluation period. The results show that departments having captured fewer moods slightly agreed that the application has potential to trigger reflective learning; departments with higher app usage stated the opposite. These results are also aligned with the insights gained from the interviews: especially the managers did not use the application for other purposes than for capturing moods. Therefore, they could not exploit the capacity of the different visualizations regarding reflective learning about their own moods nor on the moods of their department. Furthermore, they did not include the application in their meetings, so in those situations the potential to trigger reflection was also missed.

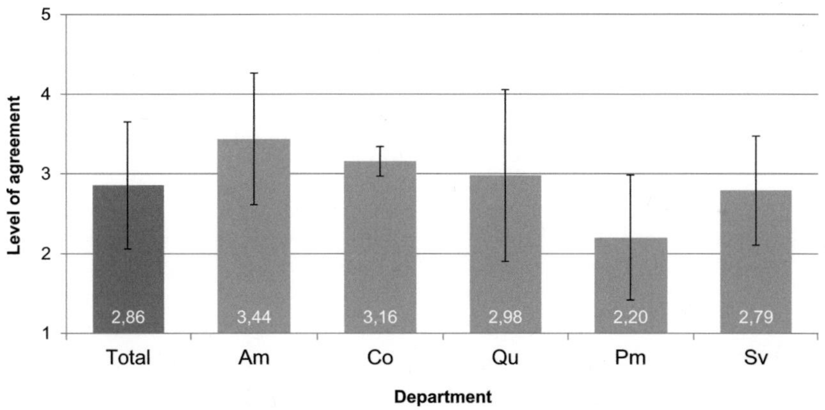

Figure 4.32.: Mean rating of the application specific reflection questions per department

All eight items were on average rated neutrally covering mean values between 2.71 and 3.29. Department Co with an average of $M = 4.50$ ($SD = 1.67$) strongly agreed to become aware of their own mood and also stated to become more aware of their colleagues mood with a $M = 4.00$ ($SD = 1.17$).

Regarding the identification of significant situations, significant mood changes or topics worth reflecting upon, it was positively rated by Department Am with $M = 3.42$ ($SD = 0.42$) and Department Co with $M = 3.58$ ($SD = 0.89$) and negatively rated by Department Pm with $M = 2.27$ ($SD = 0.89$). In addition, only Department Am agreed that the MoodMap App guided them to reserve space for reflection (M = 3.50; SD = 0.58). Department Am agreed with the MoodMap App helping them to gain a better understanding of the department and its members (M = 3.75; SD = 0.50), but Department Pm disagreed with this fact (M = 2.00; SD = 0.71). Only Department Am with an average of M = 3.58 (SD = 0.79) agreed that the app helped them to better understand their emotions, how their emotions affect their work, or to deal better with their emotions. The other departments remained neutral with respect to this fact. That the capturing of moods during their daily work is useful to reflect on and think about their work performance was confirmed by Department Am (M = 3.75; SD = 0.50) and Department Co (M = 3.75; SD = 1.41).

Participants were asked to capture their mood during the day. The usefulness of capturing the mood at the beginning of the day was rated with M = 3.50 (SD = 1.05), in the middle of the day with M = 3.62 (SD = 1.10), and at the end of the day with M = 3.59 (SD = 1.10). Regarding further situations in which it was useful to capture a mood, the responses range from during or after meetings until stressful situations, including "moments of tension" or "during/after the execution of tasks that require concentration and accuracy", and in phases where the user was feeling particular fatigue or tiredness.

The defined coding scheme for reflective content [Prilla and Renner, 2014] was used to analyze the content of the 225 notes. Each note could be assigned to more than one category. 208 notes could be identified as individual reflective items while the remaining 17 notes had non-reflective content. Beside the categories defined in the reflection coding scheme, a new category "Category 2ap" was included. This is a subcategory of "Category 2a" (own emotions) and represents the expression of physical condition (e.g., pain, illness) related to own emotions. Figure 4.33 shows the total number of notes which were assigned to each category. The categorization resulted in: 168 notes classified as experiences or issue/problem report, 54 notes referring to the expression of own emotions, 18 as expression of physical condition, 0 as containing emotions of customers, and finally 14 as interpretation and justification of actions taken during work.

The Short Reflection Scale (SRS) was evaluated for those participants who have filled in both questionnaires (N = 32). We found no significant differences between the pre-questionnaire (M = 3.78; SD = 0.40) and post-questionnaire (M = 3.72; SD = 0.46) mean ratings for the SRS. A two-way ANOVA with the factors time (pre- vs. post-questionnaire) and type of reflection (individual vs. team) revealed no effect of time but a significant effect of reflection type (df = 1 [31], F = 60.52, $p < .001$). Post-hoc related t-tests show that individual reflection scores are significantly higher than team reflection scores at both times (pre-/post-questionnaires: t[31]=6.2/5.7, both $p < .001$).

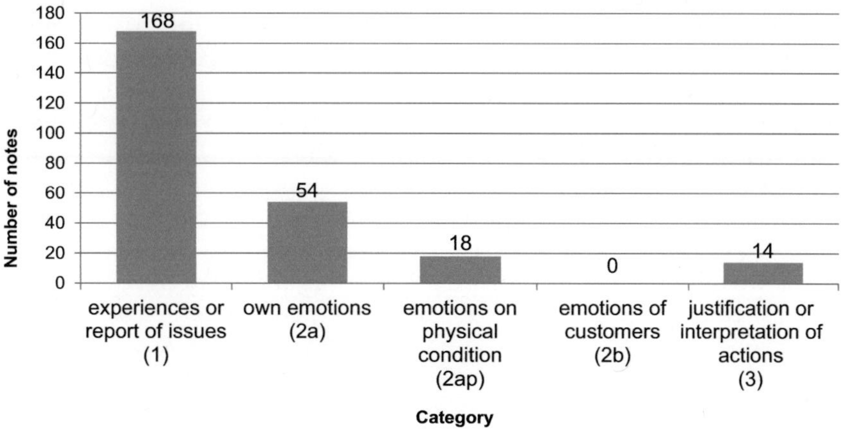

Figure 4.33.: Number of notes per each reflection category according to the Reflection Coding Scheme

Several variables from level 1 (reaction and usage) and level 2 (learning) correlate regarding the long-term usage in general. The long-term usage covers questions with regard to the long-term advantage of using the application (long-term 1), the wish to continue the usage of the app as part of the work-life (long-term 2) and to the practicality of continued use of the application during work-life (long-term 3). Sharing of moods with managers positively correlates with all long-term variables which indicate that following moods over a longer period of time might positively influence the collaboration between managers and employees. The motivation to reflect on work in general as well as to deal better with emotions are also increased by a longer usage of the MoodMap App. Additionally, recommending the app to others would increase if it is used longer and more clear insights and benefits are gained on an individual level. These correlations confirm our second hypothesis, that these four factors influence the long-term usage of the MoodMap App. Table 4.21 presents the detailed correlations.

A moderate positive correlation between the users' satisfaction with the application and seeing the long-term advantage of using the application was also found ($r = .494$, $p = .003$, $N = 34$). With regard to the user's satisfaction with the application we also saw a strong positive correlation to the motivation to reflect on work in general ($r = .729$, $p < .001$, $N = 34$), to deal with emotions ($r = .592$, $p < .001$, $N = 34$) and the recommendation of the application to others ($r = .704$, $p < .001$, $N = 34$).

The learning outcomes stated within the post-questionnaire ($N = 34$) were seen as nearly neutral to slightly disagree ($M = 2.66$; $SD = 0.95$); i.e., participants were not in agreement whether they gained a deeper understanding of their work life and what to change about their work behavior, with or without regard to their work within their department. While four of the departments mirror the average values, Department Pm with an average of $M = 2.10$ ($SD = 0.89$) clearly stated that they did not perceive any deeper understanding of their work life or did not consciously make a decision about how to behave in the future. The analysis of the open questions from the post-questionnaire provided few more details about their understanding of their work life and their conscious decisions of what to change in the future. Only two to four participants answered the open questions regarding their learning outcomes. Regarding the conscious decision of what to change in future, one participant stated to *"focus/concentrate on a certain working outcome"*, while a manager mentioned that he will *"give a greater attention to the mood of the staff in my team."* With respect to getting a deeper understanding of the own work life, one participant stated to care about *"appropriate moments in which to take a break."* Other participants gained a deeper understanding about the *"importance and influence of encouragement from the team of colleagues and especially their superiors (managers)"* and *"in the management of the business in relation to the moods, especially in times of stress."*

Table 4.21.: Correlation between long-term usage and sharing, motivating to reflect, dealing with emotions and loyalty metric ($N = 34$)

	long-term advantage (LT1)	**continued usage (LT2)**	**practicality during work-life (LT3)**
sharing	$r = .605, p < .001$	$r = .702, p < .001$	$r = .590, p = .001$
motivation to reflect	$r = .464, p = .006$	$r = .507, p = .002$	$r = .467, p = .005$
dealing with emotions	$r = .647, p < .001$	$r = .566, p < .001$	$r = .516, p = .002$
loyalty metric	$r = .711, p < .001$	$r = .645, p < .001$	$r = .488, p = .003$

Behavior Change

Behavioral change (through question CB1[13]) was rated by the participants with an average of $M = 2.53$ ($SD = 1.02$), which implies that the participants tend to slightly disagree that the MoodMap App helped them to improve their work. Department Pm strongly disagreed ($M = 1.60$; $SD = 0.89$) that the MoodMap App has helped them to improve their work, while the other four departments (Am, Co, Qu, and Sv) represent the average score mentioned above. The post-questionnaire only confirmed that they have not noticed any improvements

[13] CB1: "The MoodMap App helped me to improve my work performance."

regarding their work. A Pearson product-moment correlation coefficient was computed to assess the relationship between the variables from level 2 (learning) and 3 (behavior change). As shown in Table 4.22, strong positive correlations were found between making a conscious decisions of how to behave in the future (CL1[14]), gaining a deeper understanding of the work life (CL2[15]), the improvement of work performance (CB1[13]) and level 1 variables like the user's satisfaction with the application, the long-term advantages, the motivation to reflect on work, better dealing with emotions and the recommendation of the application to a colleague (loyalty metric).

Table 4.22.: Correlation between variables from levels 2 (learning) and 3 (behavior change) ($N = 34$)

	CL1	**CL2**	**CB1**
satisfaction	$r = .613^*$	$r = .524^*$	$r = .685^*$
long-term advantage (LT1)	$r = .619^*$	$r = .718^*$	$r = .526^*$
continued usage (LT2)	$r = .569^*$	$r = .737^*$	$r = .572^*$
practicality during work (LT3)	$r = .487$ $p = .003$	$r = .736^*$	$r = .457^*$ $p = .007$
motivation to reflect	$r = .665^*$	$r = .669^*$	$r = .754^*$
deal with emotions	$r = .809^*$	$r = .773^*$	$r = .775^*$
loyalty metric	$r = .659^*$	$r = .608^*$	$r = .679^*$

*Significant at $p < .001$

Additionally to the feedback gathered with the questionnaires, gained insights and behavioral changes were also collected through several interviews. Seven interviews were conducted with the following participants: the manager of the Department Am, the manager and one of the two staff members (who coordinated this evaluation from Regola's side) from the Department Pm, two staff members from the Department Co, one staff member from the Department Am, and another staff member from the Department Sv. Below some representative statements of the conducted interviews are presented.

Generally, the feedback from managers and staff was very positive, as it is shown for example in the following statement from a manager: *"It was an interesting experience as a user because in a way it is my company that becomes interested in my work. They try to be aware of my goals during my work activities and I think that it is a really positive thing...."* Further statements from the staff showed the positive

[14] CL1: "After using the MoodMap App, I made a conscious decision about how to behave in the future."

[15] CL2: "After using the MoodMap App, I gained a deeper understanding of my work life."

experience: *"Yes, it is a positive experience... I think it was a useful tool to access this state of mind at any given time of the day and particularly during work and activity"* or *"I thought that the usage of the MoodMap App could help and support the entire company and team work."*

An interview with one of the three persons who were responsible for introducing the MoodMap App at Regola provided very important insights regarding the preparation and conduction of such an evaluation. For him it was very difficult to convince the employees to use the MoodMap App on a regular basis, but he still sees a clear benefit the MoodMap App could have for a company like Regola: *"Managers push you and they want you to finish on time. Usually they don't ask you if you are stressed, you are happy or in a good mood and low energy. I must say it is very positive that maybe someone now, I hope that our managers thinks about that also and not about only finishing the work and so. Because I think that if the staff is happy and working well the work is finished in time...."* Some of the participants also perceived a clear benefit or insight for themselves; e.g., *"to express my feelings and in general and at work—it is possible that the MoodMap App helped me in this regard for activities with my colleagues or my team activities in general"* or *"I am a person who is very angry after a meeting. I used to go happy to the meeting and feel angry afterwards. The MoodMap App allowed me to have a look—how can I switch my mood directly after the meeting."* On the other hand, limitations were also mentioned about how to get something relevant out of the captured data: *"I collected a lot of data information and my trend. I had learned something more on my approach to the work. But then... maybe I did not realize it or I am still missing something that triggers and makes me shine on new perspectives."*

Work Outcomes

In order to detect differences between the situation before and after the usage period, we asked participants in both questionnaires (pre-test and post-test) about their job satisfaction and the impact of reflection on their job. Regola could not provide KPIs from their organization. Therefore, data regarding team specific KPIs were planned to be collected through the questionnaires, but the data from the post-questionnaire could not be obtained due to a technical problem. Consequently, a comparison with the KPIs collected before the evaluation period was not possible. Further alternatives to collect this data were not possible; therefore, we focus our results on the job satisfaction, and the work improvement on an individual as well as team level, which were collected in the pre- and post-questionnaires.

Participants' rating about job satisfaction improved during the app usage, from an average of $M = 3.31$ ($SD = 1.34$) to $M = 3.79$ ($SD = 1.08$). Participants were also asked whether reflecting on how they feel could both individually and collaboratively help them to improve their work performance. Expectation before the evaluation ("Reflecting on how I feel could help me to improve my work performance.") was compared with the actual experience during the evaluation ("Reflecting on how I feel improved my work performance."). The comparison of the average values (pre: $M = 3.52$; $SD = 0.74$ and post: $M = 3.28$; $SD = 0.92$) shows that participants were slightly less confident after the evaluation regarding reflection on own individual work. This was also the case with reflection and discussion on their moods getting to improve their team performance (pre: $M = 3.76$; $SD = 0.64$ and post: $M = 3.14$; $SD = 0.83$).

As mentioned above, the average job satisfaction improved after the evaluation. Therefore, job satisfaction at department level was analyzed. Figure 4.34 below shows the average work satisfaction of each department, before and after the app usage. All departments except for Department Qu reported an improvement of their work satisfaction. Results show an increase in the average satisfaction value as well as a decrease of the standard deviation for each department (see Figure 4.34). Department Qu has shown a very low satisfaction both before ($M = 2.25$; $SD = 1.71$) and after the evaluation ($M = 2.00$; $SD = 1.41$).

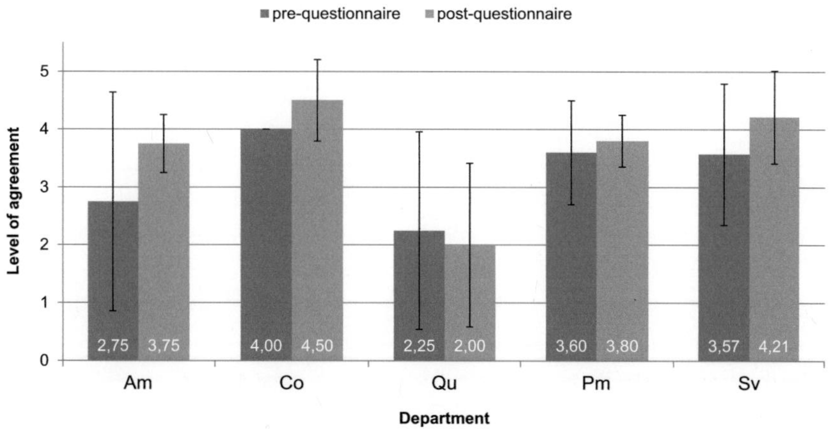

Figure 4.34.: Job satisfaction of each department obtained in the questionnaires before and after the usage of the MoodMap App

Average rating the question regarding individual reflection on how an individual feels helps to improve his or her work performance slightly varied among departments (see Figure 4.35). Whereas the agreement on this question decreased in four teams (Am, Co, Pm and Sv), it was increased in the case of the Department Qu. Interviews with members of the different departments indicated that especially this Department understood how reflecting on emotions can improve work and in which way the MoodMap App could support it. We can also derive from the interviews that the remarkable decrease in Department Pm (formed by the project managers in Production) may be related to the lack of time for usage as well as the attitude that most of the managers adopted with respect to considering emotions at work. This fact is later discussed in further detail.

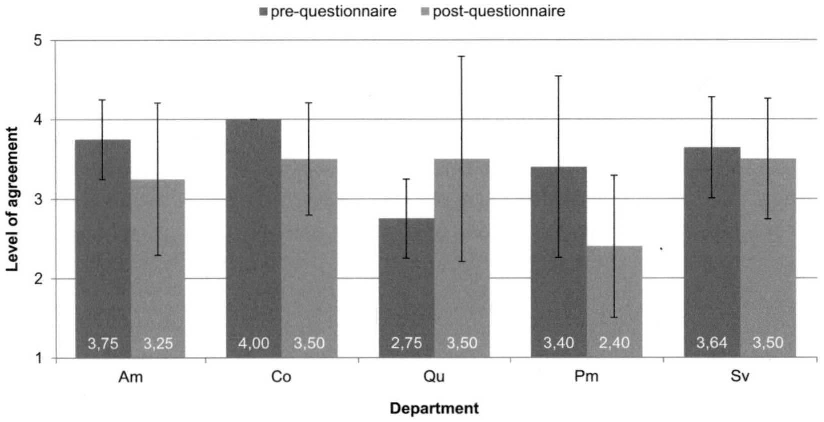

Figure 4.35.: Subjective impact of individual reflection on work improvement per department before and after the usage period

The results of the loyalty metrics ($N = 34$) look as follows: 3% are promoters, 26% are passives and 69% are detractors. That implies a computed Net Promoter Score (NPS) of -68%. This low score reflects the difficulties experienced at Regola to introduce the MoodMap App as a support for reflective learning.

A Pearson product-moment correlation coefficient was computed to assess the relationship between the variables from level 4 and variables from other levels, which may have had an impact on the subjective KPIs. KPI 1 representing the satisfaction with one's own work was not correlated with any of the variables investigated below, however, this was the case for the KPIs related to the impact of reflection on work (post-questionnaire answers).

There are positive correlations between KPI 2 (reflecting on own feelings helps to improve work) and both, expression of feelings in general ($r = .464$, $p = .007$, $N = 33$) and expression of feelings at work ($r = .684$, $p < .000$, $N = 33$). This fact shows that there is a strong influence of self-expressiveness of the participants and their trust on reflection to improve their work performance. A significant moderate positive correlation between two of the subjective post-questionnaire values of the KPIs and the average value of the app-specific questions was found.

The belief that reflecting on how one feels helps to improve work (KPI 2) has a moderate correlation with the app-specific mean ($r = .505$, $p = .003$, $N = 33$). This is also the case for reflection and discussion on their moods getting to improve their team performance in relation to the app-specific mean ($r = .499$, $p = .003$, $N = 33$). By calculating the correlations between the KPIs and the variables from levels 2 and 3, we can investigate the Hypothesis 3, that people who learned due to the usage of the MoodMap App and also changed their behavior thanks to it also rated the KPIs with a higher value. This hypothesis was confirmed, as shown in the following Table 4.23. Both KPIs' improvement, individual work performance and team work performance, correlate positively with questions on making a conscious decision about how to behave in future (CL1), gaining a deeper understanding of one's own work life (CL2) and improving one's own work performance (CB1).

Table 4.23.: Correlation between post-values of the KPIs and variables from levels 2 (learning) and 3 (behavior change) ($N = 33$)

	CL1	**CL2**	**CB1**
KPI2	$r = .488, p = .004$	$r = .360, p = .040$	$r = .588, p < .001$
KPI3	$r = .456, p = .008$	$r = .407, p = .019$	$r = .583, p < .001$

Strong and moderate correlations were also found with variables that had an influence on the app usage and the reflection on the data. These variables include the satisfaction with the MoodMap App (App satisfaction), the motivation to reflect on work in general (Motivation to reflect), and the belief, that the app helped them collaboratively to deal with their emotions (Dealing with emotions). Table 4.24 shows an overview of these correlations.

Table 4.24.: Correlation between post-values of the KPIs and app satisfaction, motivation to reflect, help to deal with emotions and loyalty metric ($N = 33$)

	App Satisfaction	**Motivation to Reflect**	**Dealing with Emotions**	**Loyalty Metric**
KPI2	$r = .698, p < .001$	$r = .480, p = .005$	$r = .452, p = .008$	$r = .721, p < .001$
KPI3	$r = .589, p < .001$	$r = .602, p < .001$	$r = .507, p = .003$	$r = .573, p < .001$

Finally, the loyalty metric has a strong and moderate correlation respectively with the KPIs referring to the impact of reflection on work.

4.10.3. Discussion

The employees of all departments declared that their job was very stressful and that they had to meet many project deadlines during that period. Nevertheless, a high number of moods were captured during their working days, but they had nearly no time and/or space to reflect on the captured data. Therefore, on the one hand, they did not see a real benefit for themselves but, on the other hand, it was not mentioned after the evaluation that the capturing of moods was seen as a "waste of time" (as one participant had in the expectations asked in the pre-questionnaire).

As part of the evaluation, very short meetings with the corresponding managers were planned in order to find out how mood or particular things according to the results of the MoodMap App could be improved. However, these meetings to conduct reflection sessions about the captured moods with their managers or within the team could not be scheduled. Such planned sessions with the project responsible would have shown the managers how to deal with the captured data and might have given them some insights regarding their whole team or single team managers. From the managers' side, the staff members did not receive any feedback nor did the managers take any direct actions with regard to their team members. This could also be explained with the fact that the managers had no time to deal with the moods of their team members and to try out the whole functionality of the MoodMap App, because this would have increased their work load again in the end.

One of the main barriers for adoption was the fear of stating their mood honestly, as it may affect their working position in the company. This suggests that it is important to convince the participants that the goal of the application is not to use the data inserted against them, but in their favor. Such a conviction is only possible if the managers, as well as the organization, are committed to such principles. Another factor that may have influenced the usage of the application is the low number of members that some departments had. From the experience gained in other evaluations, bigger teams see an additional advantage when the manager can attend to each member individually and the MoodMap App can help raise awareness. However, in the case of Regola, having small teams may have led to perceived intent of control instead of support. The company decided themselves that the structure of the company should be respected and therefore participants were divided in teams according to their departments. To avoid that the size of the teams affected the anonymity and appearance of control, an alternative team structure to aggregate moods and annotations should be discussed.

Regarding the MoodMap App features, the participants were very satisfied with it and they had no technical problems at all. They stated that the capturing of moods was very easy and they thought the application was complete. The favorite visualization was the *Compare Me* View, because there they could directly compare their mood to the mood of the whole department at one glance. The user prompts were sometimes ignored, but most of the times they were mentioned as very positive and useful.

Besides having captured 2,250 moods, participants only introduced 225 notes, 207 of which were categorized as reflective items. The analysis revealed that only 14 of these notes achieved category 3, where the learner interprets or justifies an action. Therefore, the evidence for reflection while capturing their moods, by immediately identifying the cause of it or relationship to work tasks, was considerably low.

The whole summative evaluation was conducted in a time when Regola was in a very busy period (e.g., a lot of hard project deadlines fell into the trial period) which adds additional challenges to the introduction of a new application. The introduction of the evaluation was organized within a one hour lasting workshop for all employees together. After the evaluation, the project managers on site mentioned that it would have been much better to organize different meetings with each single department in order to give a more detailed and better suited introduction for the corresponding participants and their job roles, by both analyzing their work processes and embedding the MoodMap App on them. Additionally, they might have also given support on how to reflect on the data and how they could derive some benefits or insights for themselves. We see this as one of the major lessons learned for the introduction of reflection tools in an organizational setting. It is of crucial relevance to prepare the introduction of the application very well, to show all participants a clear benefit and accompany all departments during the whole evaluation process. This is necessary to guide them to include reflection on their working processes but also to support them to gain all benefits of the MoodMap App usage.

Summarizing the progress of the evaluation, participants were very active in capturing their moods but it seems that the purpose of this capturing was not understood. Due to diverse constraints, time and space for reflection was not facilitated although this was part of the evaluation plan and suggested by the researchers. Consequently, reflection on the data was not fully achieved as expected. As the usage data reveals, some users who were very active in capturing moods only visited the visualizations a few times, so they may have considered the capturing more as a reporting to the company instead of a way of reflecting on their work.

4.11. Related Work

Mood has shown its potential to trigger reflection and learning from it, not only in theory [Boud et al., 1985], but also in practice [Carmichael, 2012; Cousins, 2010]. Mood is in the top five of the most popular items tracked by Q-Selfers [Choe et al., 2014] and numerous applications for mood tracking exist in the QS[16].

Self-tracking of mood is an example in which the benefits of tracking are not limited to individual behavior but can have an impact at organizational level too, as affective states can influence a variety of performance-relevant outcomes including judgments, creativity, helping behavior, and risk-taking [Brief and Weiss, 2002].

While research has concentrated on identifying the impact of self-tracking at individual level [McDuff et al., 2012; Morris et al., 2010; Ståhl et al., 2009] and studying how affect is conveyed with technology [Church et al., 2010; De Choudhury and Counts, 2013; Huisman et al., 2013], the impact of mood tracking in a real collaborative work environment has been less considered until now.

Before continuing with the review of related work, we briefly summarize our statement on terminology regarding affect. There is a vast amount of research on defining, modeling and measuring emotions in the area of psychology, leading to numerous different theoretical models of assessing and representing emotional states [Baumeister et al., 2007; Scherer, 2005; Russell, 1980; Schlosberg, 1954]. The word 'emotion' is often applied to a wide variety of phenomena, such as moods, sentiments, temperament, and passions. Although these words are regularly used interchangeably, they do in fact refer to specific but different affective states. In line with existing research, we understand emotions and moods as defined in the work of Scherer [2005] and Frijda [1994]. Emotions are affective reactions to an event, typically short-lived and directed at a specific object or event. The differences between emotions and moods are that emotions are less diffuse and have a clear cause or object, are shorter in duration (seconds to minutes) and more focused and intense [Frijda, 1994]. Scherer [2005] defines moods as *"diffuse affect states, characterized by a relative enduring predominance of certain types of subjective feelings that affect the experience and behavior of a person."* Emotions can contribute or influence the mood of an individual, whereas moods tend to affect which emotions are experienced [Brave and Nass, 2003].

More recent work has been done on the relationship between emotional components and mood, as well as the relation between behavior and emotions. Baumeister et al. [2007] present an emotional theory consisting of feedback and retrospective appraisal of past situations, which leads to a model on how emotions shape behaviors including reflection and learning through reflection.

[16] E.g., `http://www.moodjam.com`, `http://www.moodscope.com`

Other approaches of how affect can be conceptualized and objectively used for measurement can be found in Russell [1980], which is also the basis for the mood representation in our own MoodMap App (see also Section 4.2).

4.11.1. Tracking and Representing Mood

Latest work includes using technology for tracking emotions through user-initiated approaches. For example, Church et al. [2010] have studied how mood changes the working behavior when using a PC and what its effect is on group communication.

In Gay et al. [2011], a user study is conducted on Aurora, a mobile phone-based emotion sharing and recording system, which was applied in various health settings to use emotions for getting a better outcome (e.g., weight reduction, alcohol cessation). A mobile emotional messaging system named eMoto was developed to send messages combined with emotions [Sundström et al., 2007]. In this approach, a special type of sensor captures emotion-related gestures and renders the background of the SMS in the fitting color.

In order to investigate the potential of a mobile phone application to extend access to cognitive behavioral therapy techniques, Morris et al. [2010] developed an application for emotional self-awareness based on illuminating data trends and self-regulation through certain interventions offered by the application. Another mobile sensing platform for social psychology studies is Emotion-Sense [Rachuri et al., 2010], which deals with individual emotions, activities and verbal/proximity interactions.

In summary, the main difference with our work is that these approaches have focused their investigation on a human-computer interaction perspective and have mainly studied how moods can be represented and communicated. In our work, we based the representation of moods in established theories provided by psychological research and concentrated on studying the impact of mood tracking on self-reflection.

4.11.2. Automatically Detecting Mood

Conscious of the vast amount of HCI research on emotion recognition/estimation (which is not our goal), we concentrate here on discussing work on the relationship between emotions and work behavior. On the other hand, there are approaches for automatically detecting emotions. An approach to collect data about the emotional states of users in everyday life was done in Healey et al. [2010]. They used different sensors to capture the emotional state, namely a heart rate sensor and a galvanic skin response sensor. Additionally, they asked participants to log their affective states (with a mood map based on Russell [1980]) and add corresponding annotations. Putting the captured mood in connection to the sensor data, they were able to recognize high and low as well as positive and negative emotions in real life settings. Based on the two-dimensional map of Russell [1980], Kaiser and Oertel [2006] enhanced an e-learning system with a sensor system to capture emotions. The major goal was to support users in handling situations, when they were in a bad mood during learning.

Not directly moods, but cues about how people are feeling or behaving in certain work situations have been captured and analyzed. In [Byun et al., 2011], a system to sense and analyze "honest signals" was developed and experimentally evaluated in 1–1 conferences where participants played several roles in conversations of several types (e.g., negotiation or brainstorming). Their results show that non-verbal signals could be accurately assessed and that users found the feedback valuable for modulating their video conference conversation. The work of DiMicco [2005] has demonstrated that visualization of the amount of time attendees are talking during a meeting influences people's behavior too. While these are automatic methods to recognize moods and emotions, our approach is deliberately based on manual self-tracking. On the one hand, automatic methods lower the tracking effort, can raise awareness, and influence behavior. But on the other hand, reflection requires the cognitive focus to analyze and understand the data. Therefore, we see the manual mood capturing itself as a reflection opportunity.

4.11.3. Research on Mood at Work

All these approaches address mood awareness and self-regulation for mood improvement mainly in Human Computer Interaction (HCI) context and in the health sector. Nonetheless, some work has been conducted in work-related settings, but none of the encountered approaches considers mood awareness to promote reflective learning and improve future experiences.

The relationship between work routines and how they influence mood has gained some attention; e.g., Matic et al. [2010] monitored parameters like localization, sound, or speech to uncover correlations with mood states assessed through two rating scales (POMS[17] and PANAS[18]). In their study, online versions of the questionnaires were used and no further interfaces for mood assessment

[17] The Short Form of the Profile of Mood States (POMS-SF) is a multi-dimensional mood scale to assess psychological distress through a 37-item questionnaire [Curran et al., 1995]

[18] The International Positive and Negative Affectivity Schedule (PANAS) Short Form is a cross-culturally validated measure of emotional states proposed by Thompson [2007], which consists of two independent 5-item adjectival rating scales.

were designed. In [Müller et al., 2011b], the authors describe a study with nurses and physicians of a stroke unit who were equipped with a wearable electrocardiography (ECG) and acceleration sensor during their everyday work in order to make them aware of stress and support the recalling of experiences to identify stressors. Finally, in Saari et al. [2008], a mobile application for facilitating emotional awareness in knowledge work teams is described. This application is a prototype that gathers emotional, social and informal information on a group of knowledge workers to improve their group performance, but it has not been tested in a real work setting.

Dullemond et al. [2013] investigated a microblogging and mood sharing system to facilitate knowledge sharing in distributed organizations and showed that members of software development teams feel more connected to each other when they are able to share activities and moods. The relationship between affect and different types of communication have also come under examination. In [De Choudhury and Counts, 2013], social media has been used to understand the mood of employees in organizations; e.g., to assess employees' reaction to important organizational changes. In [Mark et al., 2014], an in situ study of the comparison of online and face-to-face interactions regarding how they have an effect on people's mood in a work environment is described.

In conclusion, though mood self-tracking has been investigated in many lab settings or with knowledge workers, to our knowledge no study has examined the impact of introducing mood self-tracking in a real work environment. In our work, we combine aspects of individual mood tracking and awareness of own mood with the collaborative aspects of mood sharing and awareness of others' mood to investigate reflection in work settings. Through this combination, new possibilities such as using the team mood as baseline for "assessing" own mood become possible.

4.12. Conclusions

Our studies with the MoodMap App have shown the benefits of mood self-tracking and have provided valuable insights on its introduction and adaptation to diverse work settings. The first trial allowed us to explore different tracking and visualizing interfaces, and served as driver towards the development of the first MoodMap App prototype. With the first formative evaluation in virtual meetings we were able to assess the feasibility of the whole approach and explore its benefits for work settings lacking non-verbal communication. The first results obtained from this evaluation as well as the insights gained in the subsequent design study drove the development of the second prototype of the app. We could evaluate the benefits and socio-technical challenges in a real work environment as well as assess the requirements that the app should fulfill to be used, not only in virtual meetings, but also in a call taker setting and a software development company. The final summative evaluations delivered valued insights on the benefits of mood tracking and the practices of users to embed it at the workplace. Additionally, taking into consideration the results from both summative studies we could identify what are major barriers for adoption and use in each of the targeted work settings.

In order to answer our research questions RQ2 and RQ3 (see Section 1.2), we investigated which visualization techniques foster reflection as well as which motivation techniques obtain better results. Results show that by using a self-reported approach as in the MoodMap App, users make sense of the data when collecting it. This is an important step towards embedding reflection in work processes, as time to review the gathered data is neither available nor provided. This retrospective review of the data would be the lone possibility for users if the considered approach would have been based on automatic methods (e.g., a hardware sensor). Additional efforts required from a self-reporting approach did not affect the adoption and integration of the MoodMap App. The results from all conducted studies have additionally highlighted the easy-to-use data gathering approach.

Implementing active prompting at capturing stage to explicitly ask users what activity they have been doing proved to (i) immediately trigger reflection on the relationship between their feelings and the work task, and (ii) facilitate the link to work processes that helps to reconstruct past experiences in retrospect. These results obtained in the first summative evaluation at the call center were contrasted with the experience gained in the second evaluation at the software company. In the later use case, this explicit link to work processes was left to optional personal free notes. Therefore, a lower number of notes with work context were achieved and this fact resulted in a lower evidence of reflection taking place.

Moreover, the interviews with participants of the summative evaluations revealed that mood self-tracking can achieve improvements in the communication channels within the teams and awareness of the mood of their colleagues. These collaborative aspects are crucial for the long-term usage of the app. More than 50% of the participants in the call center made reference to collaboration, be it if managers and coaches attach importance to the usage of the MoodMap App, or if their colleagues do it. Therefore, future applications should exploit this cohesion in teams and ensure that further benefits are provided at team level, not only for the individuals.

With respect to RQ4; i.e., which improvements can be achieved by learning on mood and work data, we could observe that participants at the call center made small changes in their behavior; e.g., talking to customers in another manner or introducing a break in their working routine. Improvements were achieved also at interpersonal level, as mood tracking positively affected the communication between managers and call takers in the call center. Feedback of call takers revealed that the app allowed them to vent and to quickly communicate problems to their manager when they had no immediate solution on their own and needed further support. As described above, a call taker's mood triggered a change in the manager's communication patterns and ultimately led to improvements in the employee's work performance. However, as shown in our last summative evaluation, the lack of tangible changes at management and team level can lead to a sense of controlling.

5. Use Case II: Reflecting on Emotions in Trading

In the previous use case, the measurement of the outcomes of reflection transferred to changes in behavior and work performance has proven to be challenging, especially in real work environments. Therefore, in order to measure the impact of reflection in a controlled environment, we designed an experiment to evaluate mood tracking in an experimental asset market. Extensive research on markets and trading has shown that mood and emotions as well as their regulation play a central role in traders' decision processes [Fenton-O'Creevy et al., 2011]. In a laboratory experiment consisting of an asset market, an adaptation of the MoodMap App which allows capturing and reflecting on mood was designed and evaluated. This study was motivated by the fact that an experimental asset market offers a controlled environment, where the quality of the work performed by the participants can be linked to the creation of price bubbles and therefore it becomes measurable. Parts of this chapter have been included in Rivera-Pelayo et al. [2015].

5.1. Work Context, Requirements and Challenges

Financial decisions of traders and investors can be affected by their emotional states [Cohen et al., 2008]. Therefore, learning approaches to increase emotional awareness and regulation play an important role to improve financial decision performance.

The first approaches to experimental market bubbles go back to the late twentieth century, when Vernon L. Smith and his team of researchers analyzed investors' dividend expectations in stock markets [Smith et al., 1988]. Among a variety of experiments to explore the functionality of markets, they analyzed experimental spot asset markets, which are used to investigate the behavior of participants in the context of market decisions. One of their major research objectives was to detect which factors are influencing the decision-making process and choice behavior of individuals. In the former experiments of Smith, it was observed that asset prices rise and fall like in real markets. Moreover, market bubbles appeared and burst during the experiments.

This development of market bubbles is similar to rare events in the real market. Many varied experiments have shown that the formation and development of market bubbles depends on different factors, such as the experience or liquidity of traders, or the novelty of the environment. Further factors which can influence the development of market bubbles are emotions. There is sample evidence that the decision-making process is not only affected by subjects' experiences, but also by emotions or the mood state of a subject [Cohen et al., 2008]. Markets are well known for eliciting high levels of emotions in a setup where participants have to put their decision-making skills in practice [Cetina and Preda, 2005]. As Fenton-O'Creevy et al. [2011] conclude in their qualitative investigation of the influence of emotions on the decision-making of traders in four City of London investment banks, emotions and their regulation play a central role in traders' decisions.

In experimental asset markets, there have already been some investigations on the effect of mood and the development of price bubbles [Andrade et al., 2012; Gross and Levenson, 1995]. However, research shows that until now, traders' response was mainly assessed through questionnaires or by measuring physiological response [Astor et al., 2011, 2013; Hariharan et al., 2013]. Most of the scientific market experiments from the literature investigated the effects of different market conditions, such as dividend structure, buying on margin, or the possibility of short selling. They have been also investigated to figure out if a modification of subjects' characteristics is a triggering market bubble factor. Some studies investigated the influence of induced mood or the changed risk-perception by presenting missed profits on a market bubble.

However, the mood development of subjects and its potential to support reflective learning processes has not been investigated yet. None of the many research studies investigated how the mood develops during a market experiment where a market bubble often arises or how the reflective learning process in interaction with a mood overview can decrease the magnitude effect of the bubble.

5.2. MoodMarket

The MoodMarket constitutes the adaptation of the MoodMap App (see Section 4.2) to the context of asset markets. The interface for capturing mood remains the same, but the type of visualization that is shown to users differs. Therefore, the two-dimensional mood map with a colored background is used to capture the mood from users.

Analogous to the interface used in the MoodMap App, the mood map is based on the Circumplex Model of Affect by Russell [1980] and its arrangement of colors refers to Itten's color system [Itten, 1971]. On the two-dimensional map, the user can indicate the state of valence from negative to positive and the current level of arousal from low energy to high energy. In this way, one has the opportunity to assess the mood numerically, instead of providing discrete choice options. When the user clicks on a certain area of the mood map, a combination of the two metrics, arousal and valence, is recorded.

After a certain amount of time, the user can take a look at the recorded data and review the mood development. A mock-up of the chronological arrangement of the mood development in each period is shown in Figure 5.1.

Figure 5.1.: MoodMarket development: Mock-up of the personal view

The smileys are used to visualize the mood development. The smiley's appearance, color and size vary according to the user's captured mood in each period. The classification of different smileys with respect to the two dimensions of the mood map is shown in Figure 5.2.

Figure 5.2.: Classification of the smileys in the mood map

Depending on the valence, the sad look on the left side changes to a happy one on the right side. The smiley's size increases, according to the level of arousal, from small at the bottom of the mood map to a big smiley at the top side. The color of the smiley is equal to the certain point on the mood map where the user clicked. The mood map itself is sectioned into different smiley classifications which are invisible for the mood map user. This serves the purpose of generating a better overview of the mood development for the subjects and over time. The metrics are subdivided into five different sections, resulting in 25 sections.

5.2.1. MoodMarket: IMRLQS Support Dimensions

Being a simplification of the MoodMap App, the MoodMarket offers support for a subset of the IMRLQS dimensions, which are summarized in Table 5.1.

Table 5.1.: Dimensions of the IMRLQS that are supported by the MoodMarket

Support Dimension	Characterization	MoodMarket
Tracking	Tracking means	Software sensor (web-based application)
	Tracked aspects	Emotional (mood)
	Purposes	Increase emotional awareness, improve trading, reduce bubbles
Triggering	Active	-
	Passive	Mood timeline (mood in each period)
Recalling & Revisiting	Contextualization	Historical context (mood in each period)
	Data fusion	Self
	Data analysis	-
	Visualization	Timeline showing the mood of the user at the end of each period

5.2.2. Treatment Design

The experiment is conducted as a double auction asset market following the implementation of Smith et al. [1988]. Subjects are trading assets in a way that it is very likely to observe the occurrence and burst of speculative bubbles during the experiment. The first treatment is strictly following the approach of Smith et al. [1988] and the second one is complemented with a simplified version of the MoodMap App. Subjects in the second experiment have to use the mood map application between the market periods during the experiment.

Once the experiment is executed, it is possible to determine how the mood states have influenced the subjects, and if the mood map application has led to a difference in the subjects' behavior. The auction market is organized around trading periods, 15 in this case. Users enter their moods before each period and therefore a mood can be assigned to each of them. When the user clicks on a certain area of the mood map, the selected mood is mapped to a smiley and appears in the timeline. The timeline with the mood development during the past periods can be reviewed after having entered the current mood.

In the following, the different parts of the experiment are described. These parts will be the treatment design of the double auction market itself and a questionnaire that will be asked at the end of the experiment. The implementations of the experimental design are explained consecutively. The experiment consists of two different treatments which are slightly different from each other. Treatment number one (T1) is a double auction asset market similar to the experiment conducted by Smith et al. [1988]. Treatment number two (T2) is exactly the same as T1 but distinguishes itself through the added mood evaluation method.

The experiment is based on a double auction asset market. During this experiment subjects are able to trade assets for 15 market periods. One period lasts 240 seconds. When the market experiment begins, the subjects can place bids or asks, as well as buy or sell assets for an experimental currency (henceforth EC) during each market period. Furthermore, an important aspect is that each asset in the portfolio of the subject pays a dividend to the asset owner after each trading period. However, the subjects do not know the dividend level in advance. The dividend level is the same for everyone and depends on the dividend structure of the experiment. In this particular case, it is 0.00 EC; 0.08 EC; 0.28 EC; 0.60 EC. In this instance, the dividends are drawn from a uniform distribution. Therefore, the expected average dividend is 0.24 EC. An important aspect of this experiment is the fundamental value which is directly dependent on the average dividend. The fundamental value is the amount of money which reflects the actual value of one asset. In this experiment, the fundamental value of one asset is equal to the remaining expected dividends. At the beginning of the experiment the fundamental value of one asset is equal to 3.60 EC. During the ongoing experiment the fundamental value of each asset declines by 0.24 EC each trading period until it reaches the value of zero at the end of the experiment (see Figure 5.3).

The dividend structure and the declining process of the fundamental value are exactly explained to the subjects in the instruction of the experiments. At the beginning of the experiment a certain amount of money and assets is given to each subject as an opening stock. There are three different endowment classes for nine traders in total (see Table 5.2). Three traders are in each endowment class and each endowment class has the same total amount of ECs.

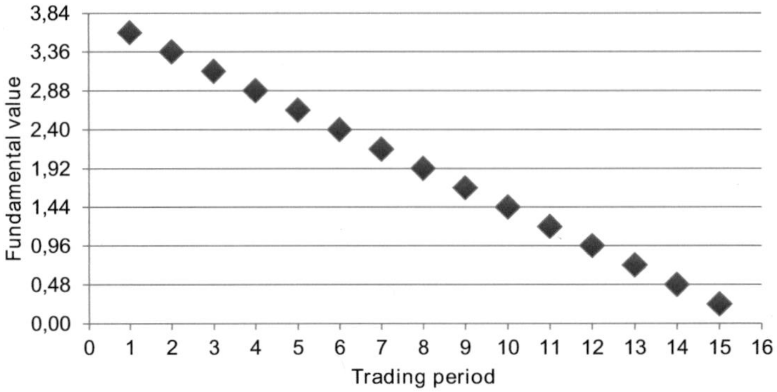

Figure 5.3.: Development of the asset's fundamental value

Table 5.2.: Endowment classes

Class	Money	Value of shares*	Total
I	2.25 EC	10.80 EC	13.05 EC
II	5.85 EC	7.20 EC	13.05 EC
III	9.45 EC	3.60 EC	13.05 EC

*Worth of shares = number of share multiplied by the fundamental value of 3.60 EC

Although there is not a consensus for the bubble-crash pattern characteristic of the SSW experimental design, we can identify three main factors that affect it. Traditionally, reasons have been attributed to individuals' characteristics. Work by Dufwenberg et al. [2005] has proved that if some or all traders are experienced, bubbles are reduced. Smith et al. [1988] argue that the lack of common rational expectations in early to mid periods despite common information causes the burst of bubbles. For example, a risk neutral trader should be willing to pay exactly the expected dividend of the asset times the number of periods remaining in the experiment session. For instance, 3.60 EC should be payed in the first trading period, 3.36 EC in the second, and so forth. However, other work has investigated the market design itself. According to Johnson and Joyce [2012], the reason for markets being prone to bubbles and crashes is based on a design characterized by a rapidly decreasing fundamental value.

Figure 5.4 shows the market screen, as it is visible for the subjects. At the top of the screen, the number of periods and the remaining time of one period are displayed. As explained above, the market periods are from 1 to 15 and the time is displayed as a countdown, beginning from 240 seconds. Below, the market screen is divided into three different parts: (i) Personal data, (ii) trading information, and (iii) own history.

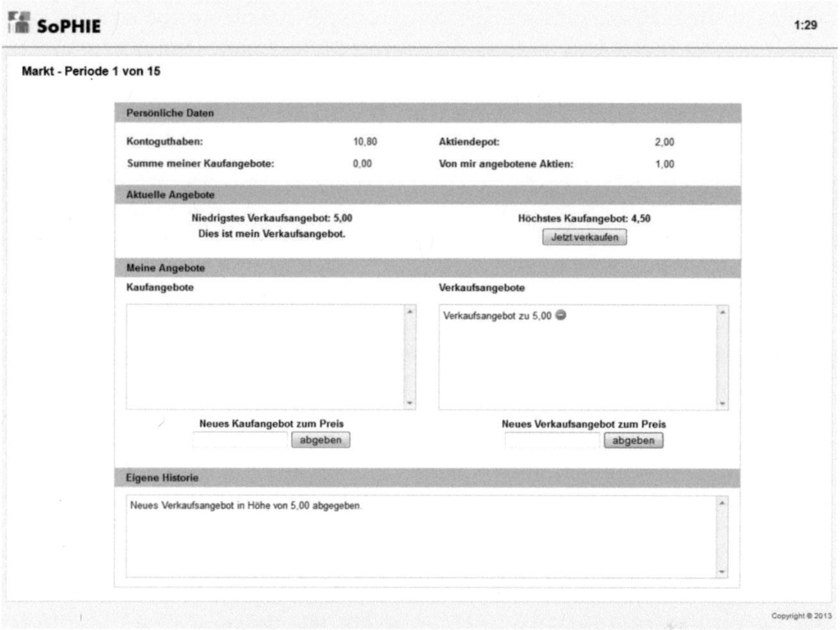

Figure 5.4.: Subject's market trading screen

In the personal data section, the user can see the account balance (10.80 EC in the example in Figure 5.4) and the number of assets in the portfolio (2.00 assets in the example) which are transferred from one period to the next period. Additionally, the sum of bids and the assets offered by the subject (in the example, 0.00 EC and 1.00 asset respectively) are displayed. If the subject submits a bid to the market, the sum of bids increases and the account balance decreases in the same amount. If the bid is not accepted (either because the subject withdraws the bid or the bid is still open at the end of the period), it is automatically canceled and the account balance of the subject updated to the previous stand.

The trading part is divided in two sections. The upper part (*"Aktuelle Angebote"*) shows the current lowest offer for sale (5.00 EC in the example) and the highest bid (4.50 EC in the example). The system ranks the offers and bids automatically and shows the respective highest or lowest prices, according to the trading activity of the subjects. Below each of them, a button allows the subject to accept the offer or bid by clicking on it. These buttons only appear if the offers are not submitted by the subject him or herself. If the subject presses one of the buttons, the system shows a confirmation request before the transaction is concluded. Subjects can only buy assets if they have enough credit in their account balance. Likewise, assets can only be sold if their portfolio has the necessary amount. In the lower part (*"Meine Angebote"*), the subject's offers for sale and bids are displayed. To the left, the subject can make a bid by entering the desired amount and pressing the offering (*"Abgeben"*) button. The same procedure applies to creating an offer for sale, by pressing the button in the right-hand part. As soon as the offer is successful, it is shown in the corresponding list. The offers of the subject disappear from the lists automatically, as soon as another market participant accepts it or the subject who offered them decides to retire them. The red symbol next to the offers in the lists allows subjects to delete them (see the offer for sale at 5.00 EC in the example in Figure 5.4). The system asks for confirmation and, finally, deletes the offer.

The lowest part of the screen (*"Eigene Historie"*) shows the subject's history; i.e., what they have already done during one market period. All submitted asks and bids as well as all successful sales and purchases are shown. This part is cleared at the end of every period and all asks and bids which could not find any attraction are reset.

After 240 seconds, a trading period is finished and the trading screen changes directly to an intermediate trading screen until the next trading period starts. Figure 5.5 illustrates the intermediate trading screen. Firstly, the intermediate trading screen shows the current account balance and number of assets of the subject. Secondly, the market information for the price of one asset in the recently ended trading period is shown (maximum, minimum and average prices). Finally, subjects get some information about their current bank account, the dividends received by the subject and the dividend draws of the last period.

The market trading and the intermediate trading screen are the same for both treatments. The difference between T1 and T2 is that in T1 (control group) a new trading period starts after the intermediate trading screen, whereas in T2 (MoodMarket) the mood map application appears after the intermediate trading screen (for details refer to Section 5.2.3 below).

As mentioned before, the subjects in the experiment trade with experimental currency (EC). The exchange rate between EC and Euro is 2 to 1. Consequently, a participant would receive 1 euro for every 2 EC won in the experiment. At the end of the experiment, participants receive the profit that they have generated in cash.

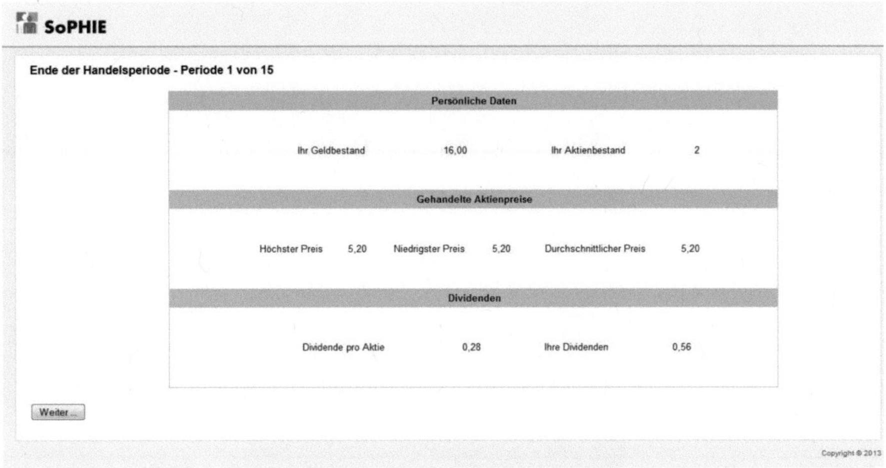

Figure 5.5.: Intermediate trading screen

5.2.3. Mood Map

The Mood Map is shown to the subjects of T2 between periods, in order to enter their mood and reflect on the past periods. They are asked to submit their mood state by clicking on a point of the mood map. Therefore, the subjects in T2 can see the mood map as well as an overview of their mood development. The new trading period starts twenty seconds after the last mood has been captured (i.e., all subjects have entered their moods). Figure 5.6 illustrates the mood development of two trading periods. The red point on the mood map indicates the current mood entered by a subject. As soon as the cursor moves across the mood map, the given values of arousal and valence shown below the mood map indicate the current point in the map.

5.2.4. Implementation

The MoodMarket was implemented in an existing platform called SoPHIE—Software Platform for Human Interaction Experiments—developed at the University of Osnabrück. SoPHIE is a web-based system which allows the implementation of different configurations of auction asset markets for experimental purposes. For further details about the architecture of the SoPHIE platform, the reader can refer to Hendriks [2012].

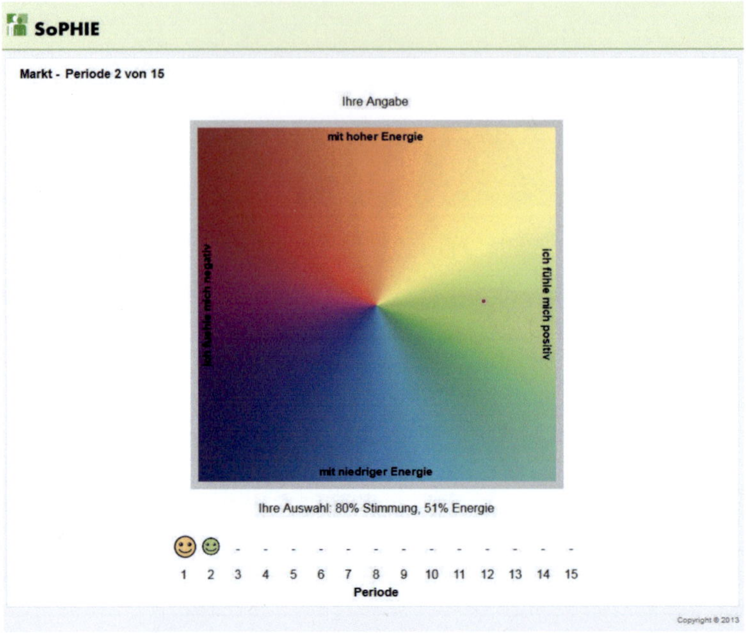

Figure 5.6.: Visualization of the mood map and the mood development in T2

5.3. Experimental Study: Asset Market

As shown in previous studies with the MoodMap App (see Sections 4.9 and 4.10), one of the main challenges is the difficulty to measure the outcomes of self-reflection with confidence; i.e., how the processes and work of individuals was improved. In the context of an experimental asset market, we are able to measure individuals' performance by the behavior of participating subjects and the development of market bubbles. In this study, we investigate if subjects' decision behavior can be improved as far as the efficiency of trading is concerned, by giving them the chance to reflect on and re-evaluate the previous decisions. The experiment was conducted in August 2013 and it was a joint collaboration with the Institute of Information & Market Engineering (IISM–KIT) and the University of Osnabrück.

The main hypothesis we explore is that the potential resulting market bubble should be reduced by the influence of self-reflection on mood and its relation to subjects trading behavior. The possibility for the individual self-reflection process of subjects is implemented between trading periods, by giving subjects the opportunity to evaluate their mood and review their mood in past periods. This should support the re-evaluation process, as subjects could conclude from their emotional state that their former decisions were right or wrong. From these new insights, behavioral changes may be observed, in comparison to a market not providing a self-reflection process. Additionally, the mood evaluation of the self-reflection process should indicate whether the asset prices and the overall market development are dependent on or independent of the subjects' mood. Indeed, a measurable indicator should be present, as several studies revealed that market bubbles are more likely to occur and are significantly larger and longer when subjects are in a positive mood [Isen et al., 1988]. Therefore, the overall goal of this experiment is to study the relationship of market players' moods, self-reflection, and subjects' decision behavior. On the one hand, the influence of mood on the subsequent decision-making behavior of subjects will be investigated. On the other hand, the impact of a mood self-reflection tool on subjects' decision behavior will be analyzed.

Consequently, we formulated the following research questions:

- Is it possible to alter subjects' decision behavior with a self-reflection tool such as the Mood Map?
- How is the development of price bubbles when introducing mood self-reflection in the market's trading process?

5.3.1. Procedure

Participants in the experiment were divided in two groups: subjects participating in a market session with treatment T1 (without the Mood Map) and subjects participating in a session with treatment T2 (MoodMarket; i.e., with the Mood Map). In both experimental asset markets, subjects had 15 trading periods where assets were sold and bought. Mood capturing and reviewing was introduced after each period of the MoodMarket treatment, where the user could also see a summary of the trading performance.

Participants

A total of 108 participants took part in the experiment. The experiment was composed of 12 sessions with 9 participants each. The sessions were divided in experimental group (6 sessions in treatment T2, where mood capturing was used) and control group (6 sessions where they played the treatment T1, without mood capturing).

Subjects in the experiment were 87 men and 21 women. Their ages were between 17 and 37, with an average of 23.81 years old ($SD = 3.36$).

Evaluation Tools

Subjects in the experiment had to answer a questionnaire at the end of the session. The questionnaire included items on personal characteristics (demographics) as well as standard questionnaires to assess personality variables. Questions were answered in a 5-point or 7-point Likert scale. Both scales were varying from strongly disagree to strongly agree. As the questions used in previous studies were mainly oriented to evaluations conducted in a real work context and not in lab settings, they were slightly adapted. We included additional questions based on standards to assess need for cognition and tendency to reflect. A personal ID given to each subject allowed for the association of data from the experimental asset market and the questionnaire. The questionnaire for T2 included additional questions related to the Mood Map.

The general questions are investigating the experimental asset market and the use of the mood map application itself and the attitude of the subjects towards it. Furthermore, the questionnaire should reveal how convenient the use of the mood map application is and whether subjects think that the use of the mood map application has changed their behavior. Questions with respect to the experience of traders were also included, since previous studies showed that the experience of traders is an important aspect for the results of the experiment. The following questions focused on the usability and experiences subjects gained using the Mood Map application during the experiment. These questions appear only in the questionnaire from the second treatment and they are a subset of the MIRROR Evaluation Toolbox [Knipfer et al., 2012].

The part of the questionnaire with general questions is followed by the assessment of subject's reflection attitude and need for cognition. The Short Reflection Scale [Knipfer et al., 2012] assesses participants' general tendency to reflect and the importance they place on reflection. The need for cognition is related to the subject's affinity to solve complicated cognitive problems. A questionnaire about the need for cognition can give some indication of how subjects manage tasks and social information. In the context of the experimental asset market, reflective learning is a highly cognitive process because subjects have to re-think and re-evaluate their behavior. For this reason, the information about need for cognition is material for the analysis of the experiment. The questions to assess need for cognition are based on the work by Cacioppo et al. [1984].

In order to evaluate the magnitude and development of the market bubble in each treatment session, several metrics were calculated. The first evaluated metric is the maximum deviation from fundamental value, defined by Caginalp et al. [2001] as "the most important quantity." A very low value would indicate that the bubble is essentially eliminated in the market. The relative deviation is calculated as the deviation related to the fundamental value. The maximum deviation from the fundamental value is computed as in the following Equation 5.1:

$$Deviation = max_t(P_t - f_t) \tag{5.1}$$

where:

P_t is the market price in trading period t
f_t is the fundamental value in trading period t

A second measurement is the boom duration of a market bubble, which is defined by the number of periods that the market bubble lasts. It is calculated as the highest count of consecutive market periods where the median market price (P_t) is above the fundamental value (f_t).

The market activity can be determined by the turnover. This Key Performance Indicator (henceforth KPI) of turnover quantifies the trading volume of assets which are traded on the market. This can either be calculated for one trading period or for the whole market experiment. The formula for only one trading period is defined as the number of exchanged assets divided by the total stock of units which can be traded by experimental market participants (Total Stock

Units, TSU). To evaluate the turnover at market level, the summation of all traded assets of the whole market experiment has to be considered. This is denoted as follows in Equation 5.2:

$$Turnover_{Total} = (\sum_{t=1}^{i} q_t)/TSU \tag{5.2}$$

where:

i is the total number of periods
q_t quantity of units of the asset exchanged in period t
TSU is the Total Stock Units

Finally, we measured the amplitude of the produced market bubbles. The amplitude is a measure of overall price changes during the market experiment. The price changes are evaluated relative to the fundamental value (f_t). High amplitude can be interpreted as a market bubble or as a tendency not to track the f_t. It is calculated as indicated in the following Equation 5.3:

$$Amplitude = max_t \{(P_t - f_t)/f_t\} - min_t \{(P_t - f_t)/f_t\} \tag{5.3}$$

where:

P_t is the market price in trading period t
f_t is the fundamental value in trading period t

5.3.2. Results

Differences between Treatments

The personality variables for each treatment were analyzed to gain insights on the profiles of the subjects and the differences between the two groups. The results of an independent two tailed t-test revealed that there was a statistically significant difference with respect to Need for Cognition. This indicates that, on average, people in the MoodMarket group readily engage in thinking about topics as they are presented, enjoy the thinking process, and are motivated to apply their thinking skills with little prompting. There were no significant differences regarding the reflection capacities of the subjects (Short Reflection Scale). Therefore, we can conclude that the groups were homogeneous groups with respect to reflection and are a valid sample to investigate our hypothesis. Table 5.3 summarizes the results of the t-tests analysis.

Table 5.3.: Results for Need for Cognition and Short Reflection Scale in both treatments

	Control Group (T1)		MoodMarket (T2)		
Treatment	*M*	*SD*	*M*	*SD*	*p*
Need for Cognition	4.67	8.58	8.33	9.32	.032
Short Reflection Scale	3.06	7.39	3.37	5.57	.790

Regarding the questions about the impact of the Mood Map, subjects do not state that tracking their mood between periods influences them significantly (see summary of main values in Table 5.4). In summary, subjects agreed that they had reviewed the development of their moods in the timeline with the smileys. However, they remained neutral when they were asked if they had reflected about their mood after each period.

Table 5.4.: Average values for items from the post-questionnaire regarding the Mood Map App ($N = 54$)

Questionnaire Item	*Mean*	*SD*
With the given instructions, I could find out how the MoodMap App worked by myself.	4.37	0.76
Gathering of my mood data with the MoodMap App was easy.	3.87	0.85
I was not motivated to use the MoodMap App.	3.11	1.19
The frequency of mood capturing with the MoodMap App between periods was suitable.	3.50	0.88
I examined my mood trend visualized in the smileys' timeline.	3.48	1.18
I have reflected at the end of each period about the development of my moods.	2.76	1.20

Reduction of Price Bubbles

In order to define the effects of the market experiment on the decision behavior of market players, we determined the magnitude of the market bubble through several metrics. The mean deviation per period was on average higher in the control group ($M = 1.28$; $SD = 1.47$) than in the MoodMarket ($M = 0.95$; $SD = 1.19$). Both the deviation and relative deviation at market level (i.e., per session) are depicted in Figure 5.7, for each type of treatment.

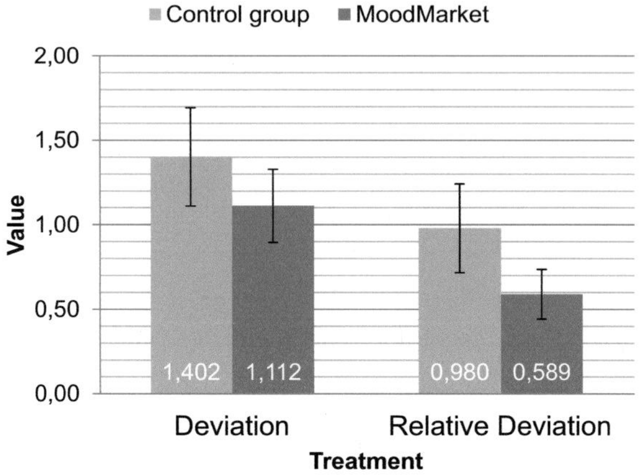

Figure 5.7.: MoodMarket: Deviation and relative deviation of the market bubble in each type of treatment: MoodMarket and Control group

Table 5.5 shows the results of the conducted independent-samples t-test to compare the bubbles' deviation and relative deviation of both types of treatment (control group and MoodMarket). The conducted Levene's tests indicated that the groups do not have equal variance (Deviation: $F = 6.565$; P-value = 0.011; Relative Deviation: $F = 14.818$; P-value = 0.000). Therefore, we conducted the corresponding t-test assuming unequal variances. There is a significant difference (at a 5% level) in the scores for relative deviation, whereas the scores for deviation do not present a significant difference. These results suggest that reflecting on mood has an effect on players' trading. Specifically, our results suggest that it reduces price bubbles in the market and therefore improves the decision behavior of the participants.

The amplitude of the market bubble in each treatment was also measured. Figure 5.8 shows the average values of both types of treatment (i.e., control group and MoodMarket), revealing that the bubbles' amplitude was on average higher in the control group than in the MoodMarket.

We conducted an independent-samples t-test (see Table 5.6) to compare the amplitude of the MoodMarket treatments with the control group treatments in detail. The conducted Levene's tests indicated that the two groups do not have equal variance ($F = 8.415$; P-value = 0.004). Therefore, we conducted the corresponding t-test assuming unequal variances. There is a significant difference at a 5% level between both types of treatment. These results suggest that the usage of the Mood Map had a positive influence on the amplitude of the price bubbles; i.e., the amplitude of the price bubbles was reduced.

Table 5.5.: Deviation and relative deviation: Descriptive statistics and t-test results.

Metric	Treatment	*n*	*M*	*SD*	*Var*	*t*	*df*	*p*
Deviation	Control Group	87	1.402	1.369	1.874	1.586	158	0.115
	MoodMarket	85	1.112	1.005	1.010			
Relative Deviation	Control Group	87	0.980	1.234	1.523	2.578	134	0.011
	MoodMarket	85	0.589	0.680	0.462			

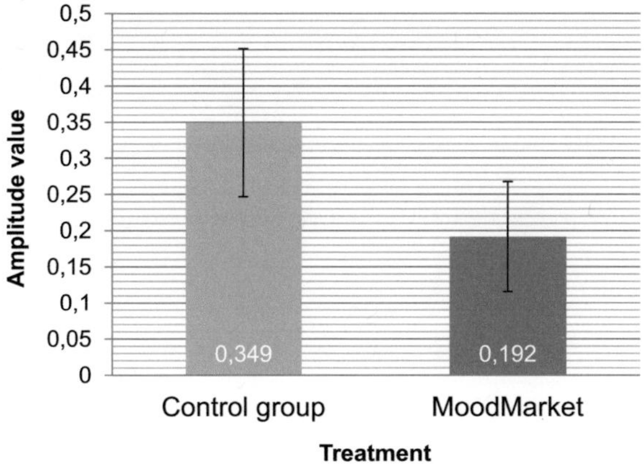

Figure 5.8.: MoodMarket: Amplitude of the market bubble in each type of treatment: MoodMarket and Control group

Summarizing the results obtained from the analysis of the economic data, the relative deviation and amplitude of the price bubbles present significant differences between the control group and the experimental group. However, no significant differences were observed in the absolute deviation measurements. In order to gain further insights about the development of the price bubbles, we analyzed the behavior of the mean asset value during the experimental sessions. Figure 5.9 shows the mean asset value in each period of the 12 sessions belonging to the corresponding treatment of each experiment session. This development illustrates the development of the price bubble in the market.

The periods with no values (break in the line) indicate that participants did not handle in that period. In order to facilitate the comparison with the expected behavior of the asset values (as explained in Section 5.2.2), the fundamental value of the assets is also depicted through a discontinuous line The comparison of the amplitudes of the price bubbles show a tendency toward lower values in the MoodMarket treatment.

Table 5.6.: Amplitude of the price bubbles: Descriptive statistics and t-test results.

Metric	Treatment	*n*	*M*	*SD*	*Var*	*t*	*df*	*p*
Amplitude	Control Group	87	0.349	0.480	0.230	2.462	158	0.015
	MoodMarket	85	0.192	0.351	0.123			

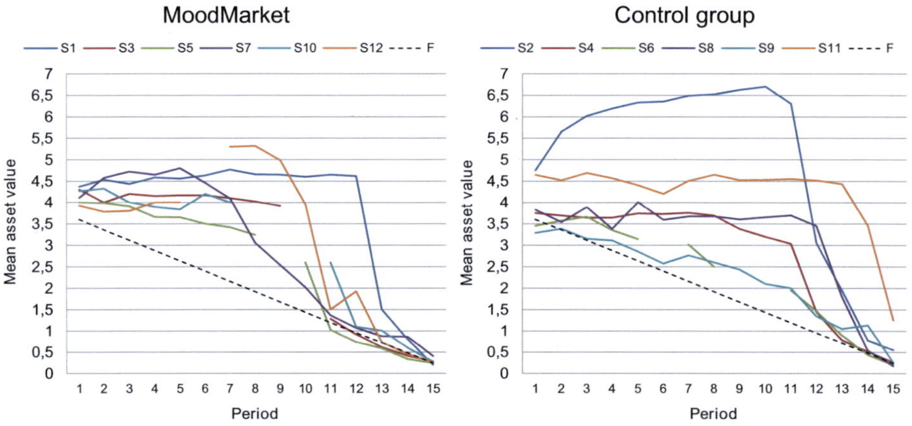

Figure 5.9.: Mean asset value in each period of MoodMarket and control group

The measurement of the total turnover in each market reveals that it was higher in the control group ($M = 3.824$; $SD = 2.206$) than in the MoodMarket ($M = 2.935$; $SD = 0.672$). This indicates there was a lower trading volume in the MoodMarket, and therefore we can conclude that participants were potentially more rational in their decision-making behavior.

We also analyzed the development of the auction course by comparing its global behavior in both treatments. Figure 5.10 shows the average development of the asset value in all experiment sessions of each treatment type; i.e., MoodMarket and control group.

The analysis shows that the participants in the experimental group, on average, realized that the negotiating price of the auction was too high a whole period earlier (see periods 9–10 in Figure 5.10), and ,consequently, that they were riding in a bubble. In conclusion, market price bubbles were not different in absolute size (maximum), but reflection via mood capturing helped subjects to recognize the price bubble earlier and hence, to adapt their behavior accordingly.

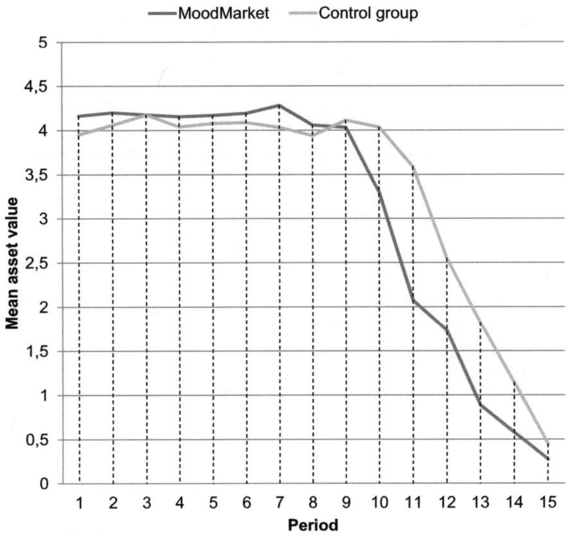

Figure 5.10.: Development of the mean asset value in each period of every market session (MoodMarket and control group)

In order to investigate if there is any relationship between the observed behavior of the price bubbles and the mood of the subjects in the MoodMarket, we analyzed the gathered mood data. Figure 5.11 shows the average mood value of the participants in each period. This was calculated taking into account the individual mood of each participant in all the MoodMarket sessions.

As it can be seen in Figure 5.11, a clear change in the trend of both valence and arousal was observed exactly in the same periods where subjects realized that they were riding in a bubble (see periods 9–10). This relationship enforces our hypothesis that reflecting on moods contributed to this improvement in their trading behavior.

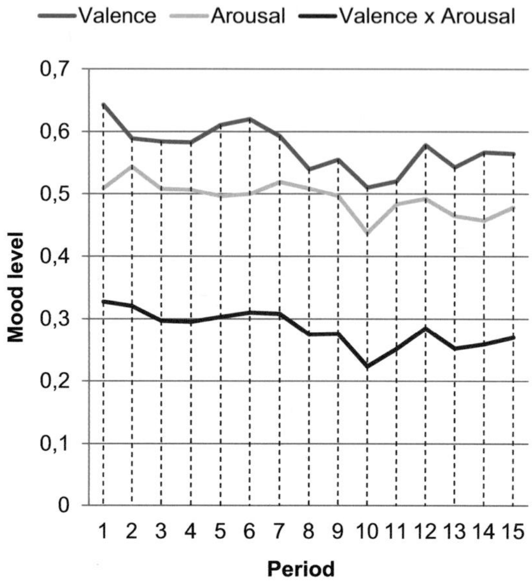

Figure 5.11.: Average mood trend in each period among all sessions of the MoodMarket

5.4. Related Work

The effect of mood and the development of price bubbles in experimental asset markets has been a key research topic in the last years [Andrade et al., 2012; Schoenberg and Haruvy, 2012]. In the experiments carried by Andrade et al. [2012], subjects had to watch a mood inducing film prior to the experimental market game. Former research by Gross and Levenson [1995] showed that it is possible to induce a certain type of mood across an ethnically diverse sample of subjects. For this research about the influence of a mood state on a market bubble, four different films were selected to elicit four different emotional states. The analysis of these experiments revealed that larger asset bubbles arise on markets where subjects watched exciting videos. In general terms, possible reasons for this behavior could be found in subjects who were too expectant about the market development or who neglected necessary market information as an important component of future market expectations.

According to Andrade et al. [2012], this behavior change is justified as follows. As partially mentioned above, there is evidence that emotions are changing the cognitive process of information-processing. Another reason could be the misattribution of arousal [Pham, 1998]. The misattribution of arousal is defined as a process where people evaluate the false cause—making them aroused. In this study, it means that people feel aroused because of the market game instead of the basic reason, the mood-eliciting film. The last possible reason would be an altered risk perception of subjects [Hogarth et al., 2008]. The combination of these three reasons, belonging to different types of psychological processes, can lead to the effect that positive feelings decrease risk aversion [Kuhnen and Knutson, 2005]. This in turn results in higher bids and larger market bubbles.

A similar study is the one by Schoenberg and Haruvy [2012], which is related to the SSW study where market bubbles arise. In this study, the emotion is not induced by films prior to the market game, but by relative performance information' during the experiment. Subjects are able to compare themselves either to the best or the worst trader. Therefore, the subject's account status screen with information about the best and worst trader is shown to the experiment participants. One can assume that the comparison with other subjects causes a mood which is positive if the result is close to the best or even is the best, or a negative mood if the performance is bad. As a result, Schoenberg and Haruvy [2012] could show that perceived performance relative to others has significant effects on subjects' behavior, just like prices are higher and boom durations are longer during a market bubble. This observation is caused by changed risk perception, since traders within an upward-reference market conceive the difference to the leader as a loss and therefore they are more risk seeking.

Research on emotions suggests that auction outcomes may elicit an aversive "frustration of losing" and a rewarding "joy of winning" response. Taking into consideration these patterns of winning joy and losing regret, Astor et al. [2011] investigated emotional processes in auctions with varying feedback information and provide an approach that combines an auction experiment with psycho-physiological sensors to indicate emotional involvement. In subsequent work of these authors [Astor et al., 2013], they investigated the intensity of these emotional reactions.

The xDelia[1] project has also built tools and conducted studies to measure psychophysiological parameters and mirror the results back to traders in financial markets. Astor et al. [2014] investigated how a serious game can improve decision-making by boosting decision-makers' awareness to their emotional state and improving their skills for emotion regulation. The game, which was evaluated in two laboratory experiments, displays the players individual emotional state (biofeedback) and adapts the difficulty of the decision environment to this emotional state. Also under the premise that emotions are a key factor in decision-making, Hariharan et al. [2013] studied how a system that incorporates affective information in the form of physiological signals can lead to better decision behavior.

[1] http://www.xdelia.org

In conclusion, there is a vast field of research that investigates trading behavior and which factors affect the development of price bubbles, including emotions as one of the factors examined. However, the potential of a self-reported approach to track mood data and reflect on it has not been examined yet.

5.5. Discussion and Conclusions

Participants were neutral regarding mood capturing having a significant influence on their decision-making behavior. However, as it has been shown above, subjects did change their trading behavior and performed better in the MoodMarket than in the control group. This suggests that the effect of mood capturing on decision performance was potentially subconscious and that the perception of the impact of the app differs from the real impact. These were positive first results regarding the effect of mood capturing on decision-making.

The analysis of the mood data shows a clear change in the mood trend in the same periods where the trading behavior of the subjects leads to a decrease of the market bubbles. The fact that these data show this coincidence gives evidence that there is a relationship between reflection on moods and their trading behavior. This contributes with valuable insights to our RQ4 (see Section 1.2). We can draw the conclusion that by reflecting on their moods, subjects in the MoodMarket improved their trading behavior.

The obtained economic results, both at market and period level, show positive results in the direction of our hypothesis. However, some of the results were not significant. This fact is also affected by the small sample and, therefore, further experiments should be conducted in order to confirm the obtained promising results at a higher significance level.

6. Use Case III: Reflecting on Feedback in Lectures and Presentations

For lectures and conferences—one of the main daily activities of researchers, professors, lecturers and students—there is currently little or no support for learning by reflection, even though in these scenarios there seems to be a great potential to improve professional skills and presenters' performance by learning from personal experience.

6.1. Work Context, Requirements and Challenges

It is not easy for presenters to know how their performance is perceived by the audience (e.g., is the lecture difficult or easy to follow? Is the presentation too fast or too slow?). Especially in mass lectures, virtual courses or conferences, reliable feedback from the audience is missing and the speaker lacks support to quickly evaluate the overall course of the presentation and react accordingly.

In this context, we identified the potential of tracking feedback and helping professionals who participate in presentations to improve their skills and performance when addressing an audience. Such data would help the speaker to reflect on the differences between his or her own perspective on an event and how his or her performance is perceived by the participants. This need for learning from others' perspectives motivated the design and development of a tool to support reflection on audience feedback. To realize technical support for the reflection in this concrete scenario, we have to consider issues like how to present individual feedback of a large group of participants so that it can be interpreted while avoiding excessive cognitive load.

Traditionally, conventional surveys after the lectures or conferences are finished have been used as feedback channel. These surveys are usually oriented towards the content of the course/talk and the understanding of the students. In many cases the surveys also include feedback about the presenter's performance. However, they are performed once the event is finished or even some weeks later.

Therefore, the presenter cannot incorporate the lessons learned in the current lecture. Reflecting on captured feedback data may help users to continuously learn from their performance and improve their skills.

There are several approaches related to capturing data in education [Duncan and Mazur, 2005; Hadersberger et al., 2012; Kundisch et al., 2012; Rubner, 2012], as well as in business [Teevan et al., 2012], with the purpose of increasing the interaction with the audience, but none of them focus on using the captured data to review the presenter's performance and improve by reflecting on it.

6.2. Live Interest Meter

We designed the Live Interest Meter (LIM App) for scenarios that involve a person addressing a large audience; e.g., in a lecture or a conference (see Figure 6.1). Its goal is to quantify and track abstract feedback from an audience (e.g., emotions and thoughts especially referred to their perception of the event in which they participate) and to provide this information as live feedback to the presenter so that he or she can evaluate and learn from their experiences while performing the talk (reflection-in-action) as well as after it (reflection-on-action). At the same time, the LIM App aims at improving attendants' attitude, attention and concentration during a lecture or conference through reflection.

The LIM App has a central part consisting of a meter, which allows users to track and aggregate any quantifiable aspect as seen by the audience, like comprehension (Is it difficult or easy to understand?) or performance (Is it too fast or too slow for me?). The development of the feedback is displayed graphically in the "Evolution Graph" (see Figure 6.3). This way, the speaker can quickly evaluate the overall trend and react accordingly ("Adaption/Reaction" in Figure 6.1). Moreover, members of the audience can compare their own ratings with the group aggregation, and reflect on the trends or deviations and differences or similarities of the data ("Peer comparison" in Figure 6.1). That is how the LIM App provides an integrated feedback and reflection loop for both the presenter and the audience. In order to increase the interactivity between audience and presenter, the tool additionally offers a group chat, instant polls and rated questions. Apart from being used on their own, these features also help contextualizing the evolution-data from the meter.

In the described work situation, three use cases can be defined. First, a presenter can use the application to gather feedback (a) which can be evaluated and learned from while holding the presentation (reflection-in-action). Having the role of an audience member, users can give feedback (b) during the presentation and, while doing that, improve their own attitude, attention and concentration.

Lastly, after a presentation has taken place, the presenter can evaluate (c) and reflect on the gathered data (reflection-on-action).

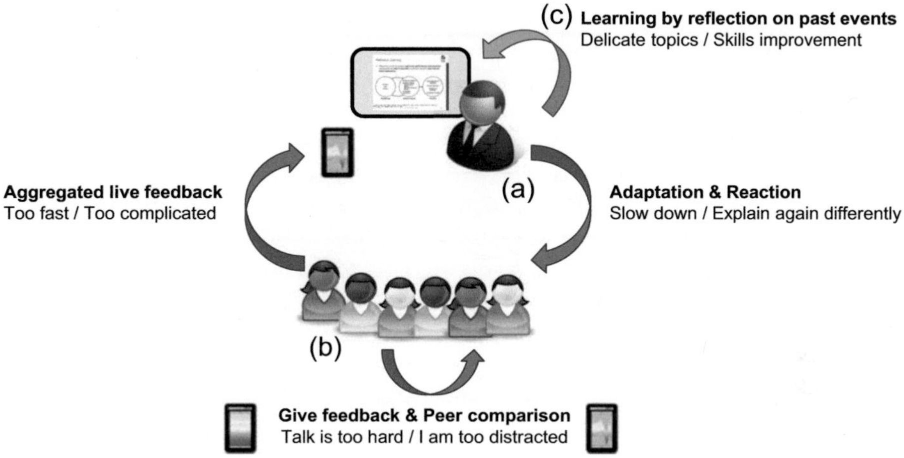

Figure 6.1.: Scenario and use cases of the LIM App

6.2.1. Live Interest Meter: IMRLQS Support Dimensions

In the following, we describe how the LIM App supports reflective learning according to our Integrated Model of Reflective Learning and Quantified Self (IMRLQS, see Chapter 3).

- **Tracking.** Tracking is based on *self-reporting* through the LIM App. The tracked aspect are mainly *abstract thoughts and opinion*, which are quantified through the meter. This feedback can be any aspect related to the presentation or lecture; e.g., interest of the topic, comprehension of the talk, velocity of the presenter, etc., and it may be included in the category of emotional data because of its abstract nature. The *purpose* to track feedback through the LIM App is to measure own learning, as well as to express an opinion and share it with the presenter and thereby to offer other perspectives which may be useful for both lecturer or presenter and audience.
- **Triggering.** Triggering refers to the starting of the reflective learning process, by raising awareness or detecting discrepancy. The LIM App supports *passive triggering*, as it relies on the user to visualize the graph showing the evolution of the feedback and evaluate it in its context (topic, questions, polls). Besides, in the case of the audience, the comparison to the average

feedback value has also a big potential to trigger reflection, as it shows the contrast of different perspectives. *Active triggering* is implemented by notifications shown to the speaker if the feedback values achieve particular low or high thresholds.

- **Recalling and Revisiting.** In the LIM App, users can review all the data and reflect on it after the event. *Contextualization* of the data is provided by topic markers, questions, polls, and chat. According to the model, data can also be augmented with information about the social context of the user. This is offered by the LIM App by comparing the users' values to the group's average values, what may provide new perspectives on experiences and offer new abstraction levels. Presenters can also use this contextualized feedback for subsequent reflection on the difference between the participants' perception of events and their own experience. Additionally, *sharing* data related to feedback in a social context and experiencing how others give their opinion can motivate people to do it also by themselves and thereby to capture their own data. With the *visualization* of the evolution graph, users can detect upward or downward trends or identify deviations from a certain norm that may indicate progress or a problem. By exploring the graph, it is possible to detect topics where a user's capability or speed of understanding deviates from the other classmates. The presenter can assess if a theory needs further explanation and examples in order to be comprehensible for the majority of the audience.

The implementation of the support dimensions in the LIM App described above is summarize in Table 6.1. Following, Table 6.2 shows an overview of the developed prototypes and the main added or modified features in each prototype.

Table 6.1.: Dimensions of the IMRLQS that are supported by the Live Interest Meter

Support Dimension	**Characterization**	**Live Interest Meter**
Tracking	Tracking means	Software sensor (mobile and web-based application)
	Tracked aspects	Emotional aspects and activity
	Purposes	Aggregate different perspectives, improve communication skills
Triggering	Active	Notifications
	Passive	Feedback, live visualizations, event reports
Recalling & Revisiting	Contextualization	Social context (sharing and comparing), historical context, and task (topic markers, questions, polls)
	Data fusion	Subjective data (self) and group data
	Data analysis	Mathematical and graphic aggregation
	Visualization	Timelines with feedback trends and comparison with other users, topic markers, bar charts with polls results, questions posed with respective rating

Table 6.2.: Overview of the LIM App prototypes

Prototype Version	**Release Date**	**Added/Modified Features**
LIM 0.6	June 2011	Quantifying feedback Feedback evolution graph Topics Polls Questions Chat Group configuration
LIM 1.0	November 2012	UX Design & dashboards User management Written feedback (comments) Notifications Event data reports Chat removed

6.2.2. Live Interest Meter 0.6

The LIM App is available as a JavaScript-based application as well as an Android App. Whereas the first one provides a broader access from any device (e.g., tablets and laptops), the second version offers a more unobtrusive user interface (accessible from smartphones). In the following, we provide an overview of the first prototype of the LIM App and its features.

The Meter

The meter component, illustrated in Figure 6.2, is the core of the application and consists of a colored surface with an input slider that allows introducing the desired value. It has a title explaining what is being assessed and two captions representing the positive (top) and negative poles (down); all three captions are set up by the presenter (master) at the beginning of the session. For the visualization of the meter, we chose the blended colors of traffic lights; i.e., a negative rating is colored red, yellow means neutral and green is a positive rating. Users can update their feedback at any time. A given value stays valid for a specific amount of time, in order to maintain a certain timeliness of the feedback. The timeout value can be set up by the presenter to match the event's pace. The meter input component is closely related to the evolution graph, which visualizes time series of the meter-values. Additional features include polls with instant evaluation, a question system with user rating, and a group chat.

Evolution Graph

The evolution graph (see Figure 6.3) shows three different aspects of the meter-values in a timeline (x-axis): (a) the feedback value of the user is depicted through a red line, (b) the black line displays the group average feedback, and (c) the colored area spans between the 10th and 90th percentile of the group values. In the top-right corner the number of currently valid user-votes is displayed—important to estimate the relevance of the given feedback. The time range of the display can be adapted locally by each user. The red circles at the bottom represent topic markers. In this first prototype, the presenter (master) as well as the audience (clients) can see all the data in a graphic live. This fact can help presenters to react to their audience and adapt themselves while giving the talk. In the case of the audience, they can compare themselves with the average and percentiles (10th and 90th) of all participants. Average and percentiles are established measures which are typically used to compare and analyze data and are suitable to explain to the public. Therefore, these measures were chosen for the comparison of feedback levels with other participants.

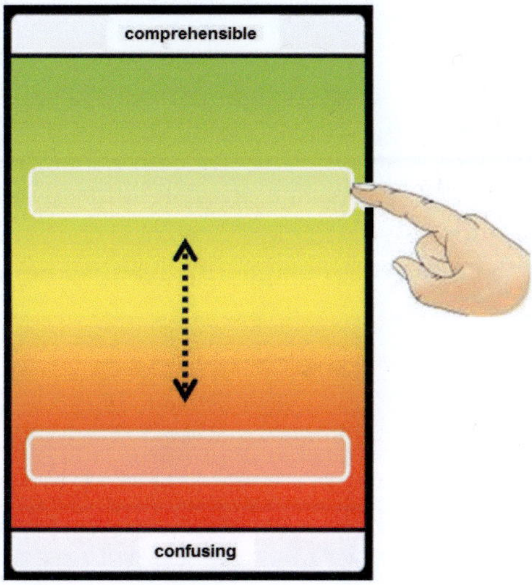

Figure 6.2.: Meter with one dimension, provided with a slider for input values

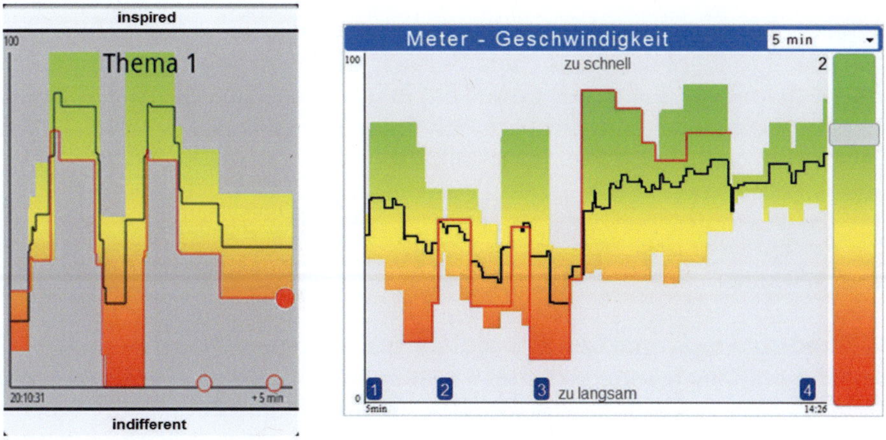

Figure 6.3.: Evolution graph showing the feedback over time in the Android interface (left) and the JavaScript interface (right)

Polls

Presenters have the possibility to set up polls before or during their presentations. Audience members can also suggest polls, so that an assistant can prepare special polls during the actual presentation. The presenter then only has to accept and open the suggested poll. Opened polls automatically show up as pop up on the participants' side. As soon as participants provide their answers, they can see the overall results. If the poll votes change, the results are immediately updated in the user interface.

Questions and Chat

The LIM App implements a question system that allows participants to ask questions visible to everyone, as well as a means to rating questions. It is accessible through the settings menu and lists all current questions, each decorated with a star rating bar, through which the participants can rate the question and in this way indicate and reaffirm a question's importance and urgency. The number of votes for the respective question is shown in parentheses so that both presenters and audience can get an idea of how many people rated a certain question. Especially in a large audience, everybody can ask questions without hindering global progress. Based on the star rating, the presenter can decide if and when to react. The question system itself is only intended for questions directed at the presenter, who is supposed to answer them verbally at some point of the event. But probably a lot of questions could be answered by members of the audience without disturbing the global flow. That is where the chat component comes into play. It enables communication with the whole audience, without the need to disturb the global attention to the talk. The chat is currently only available in the web-based front end.

Topic Markers

We introduced topic markers as a tool for the presenter to label periods of the presentation. This feature provides a better contextualization of the gathered feedback. Topic markers can be the slide titles, slide numbers or any other set of titles corresponding to the development of time. Once the group is set up and the topic markers are defined, the presenter only needs to release a given marker, when the matching point in time is reached. Topic markers show up in the evolution graph of all users as numbered dots, with the full title showing when it is clicked on (see red circles in the mobile version and numbered blue rounded squares in the mobile version shown in Figure 6.3).

Master Control

Through the web-based front end, users can join a group as participant or create a new group as master, indicating the group name and a password to protect it from unauthorized changes. When creating a new group, presenters can configure the meter to the kind of feedback they would like to collect. The title of the meter and its captions for the two opposite poles can be specified. Furthermore, they can prepare a list of topic markers and polls for their immediate availability during the presentation.

Android Version

This version of the LIM App is implemented for Android devices. When users enter the app and, after logging in to the group, they can touch the screen and capture their feedback with the meter. By tapping on the evolution graph (Figure 6.3) the participants move to the slider input (Figure 6.2) where they can provide and update their feedback value by just moving a finger somewhere on the screen relative to the y-axis. This value reflects their current opinion or perception without even looking at the device.

Figure 6.4 shows some additional screens of the Android application. The first screen (Figure 6.4a) is the start screen that welcomes the user after starting the application. The second screen (Figure 6.4b) shows an example of a possible poll that the master may open for the audience. Finally, after users have answered a poll, they can see the aggregated votes of other users (Figure 6.4c).

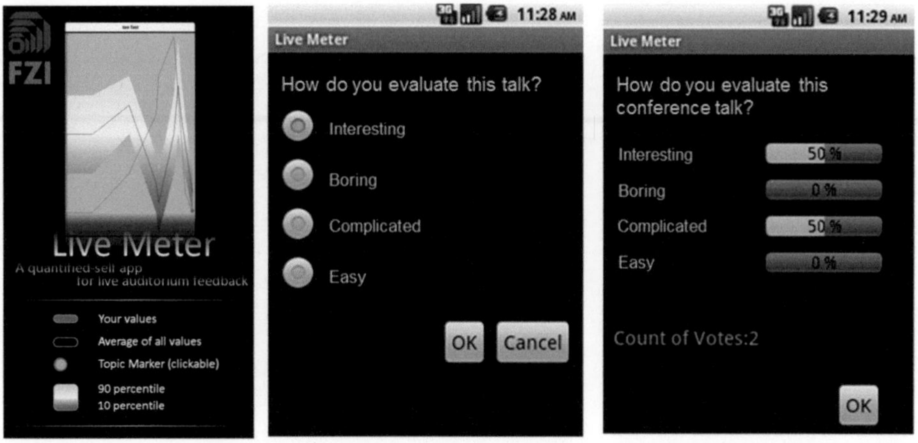

Figure 6.4.: LIM Android App: Welcome screen (left); poll example (center); poll votes (right)

JavaScript Version

This client version of the LIM App (see Figure 6.5) is a web-based front end that allows users to access the LIM from any browser. The screen is divided into four areas showing the meter component (top left), the questions (top right), the chat (bottom left) and the polls (bottom right).

The master's function to set up a group is available through the web-based front end. First, it allows the master (presenter) to activate/deactivate the chat, polls and questions; as well as configure the lifetime of the values and the update interval for the meter (see Figure 6.6 to the left). If any of the features (chat, polls, or questions) are deactivated, the app is automatically updated and they do not appear in the view of the JavaScript clients (participants in the audience). Second, the master can enter the topics that he or she will address and go through them with the Previous, Repeat and Next buttons (see Figure 6.6 to the right). This will set and show the topics as markers in the history graphic and the chat (topics attached to their timestamps are shown in blue, see Figure 6.5).

The values lifetime specifies the time in seconds that a given vote is valid, in order to ensure a certain feedback remains current (a value entered; e.g., 20 minutes ago is not considered as a current value). The vote update interval is an essential parameter for the update behavior of the whole system. In order to prevent vote flooding and system overload, both client and master check for changes to their values only with that interval and send updates only when a value actually changes. That means that the clients meter value is not sent immediately when the user moves the slider, but when the value timer triggers and detects a changed local value (for further details about the implementation see Section 6.2.4).

The meter can be configured by the master. In the setup window, he or she can specify the title and values of the meter (Figure 6.6 center). Two values are specified (top and bottom parts of the meter) which are shown as captions in the meter and/or history graphic. Besides, the time span showed in the history graphic can be configured through a drop-down menu showing the available time in minutes.

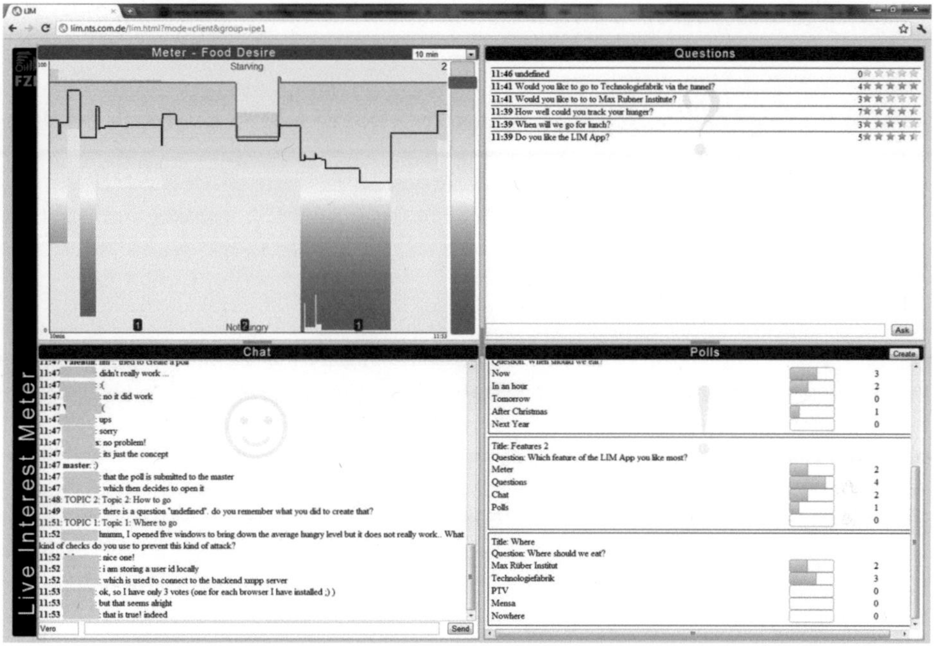

Figure 6.5.: JavaScript version of the client: meter and evolution graph (upper left), questions with ratings (upper right), chat (bottom left) and polls (bottom right). Screenshot obtained during an internal test.

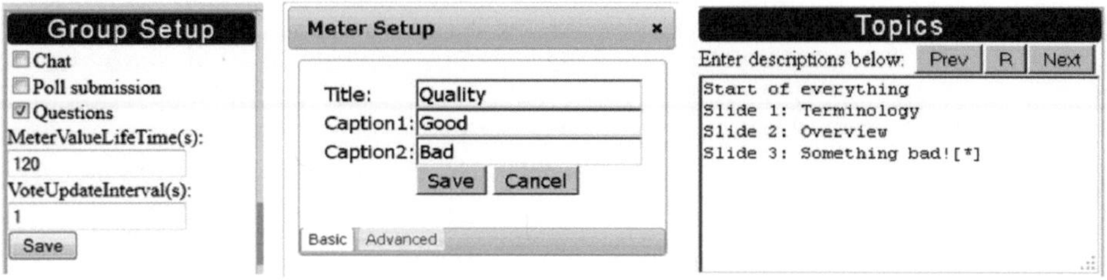

Figure 6.6.: Master view with configuration of the group (left), configuration of the meter (center) and topics stamps (right)

6.2.3. Live Interest Meter 1.0

The second prototype of the LIM App focused on supporting the revisiting and recalling of past events. In order to facilitate the review of the captured data, the development of the application considered the accessibility from as many types of devices as possible. As a result, the second prototype of the LIM App is developed as a web application, accessible from desktop, tablets, and mobile browsers. In addition to the web application, the Android app was also further developed in this second prototype, but it only includes functions that can be used by the audience during the presentation.

Based on the conclusion of our first formative study (Section 6.4) and the subsequent evaluation (Section 6.5), the new version of the LIM App improved existing features and added new ones, especially for the review of data gathered in past presentations. Anonymous questions to the presenter and polls with several options are still available, whereas the chat was removed. Additionally, the audience can send anonymous comments related to the feedback that they are giving in the meter, which can be very constructive for the presenter. Regarding the polls, prior to the presentation the presenter can prepare and save poll templates they would like to ask later on.

The risk of displaying too much information to the presenter while he or she performs the talk was an identified challenge and was also confirmed by our previous studies. Therefore, we decided to define a dashboard for the presenter that visualizes the most important items. It displays the current values of the meter as well as the number of currently active participants that use the meter for giving feedback. As suggested by participants in previous studies, a countdown timer is also available. Below the timer, a notification area is situated which shows different notifications based on the current group average meter value.

To facilitate the revisiting of past events, the enrichment and presentation of the gathered data was implemented. Our results showed that not all presenters were able to react and reflect during the presentation and therefore the major potential for reflection lies in recalling and revisiting past events in retrospective. Users can go to the *My Events* page and explore the reports of their presentations, including the meter feedback, polls, questions, and written feedback comments.

In the following, we detail the LIM web application and its whole functionality. At the end of this section, we describe the mobile version of the LIM App (available for Android platforms) is described.

The Meter

The meter was maintained as the main component of the LIM App. However, we identified that there are cases where the default color scheme (see Figure 6.7a) is not suitable; e.g., when feedback about the speed of the talk is given. In such an example, "too fast" would appear in green and "too slow" in red indicating the wrong color meaning. In such cases, this second prototype offers a different color scheme with a blue gradient (see example in Figure 6.7b) which can be chosen by the presenter.

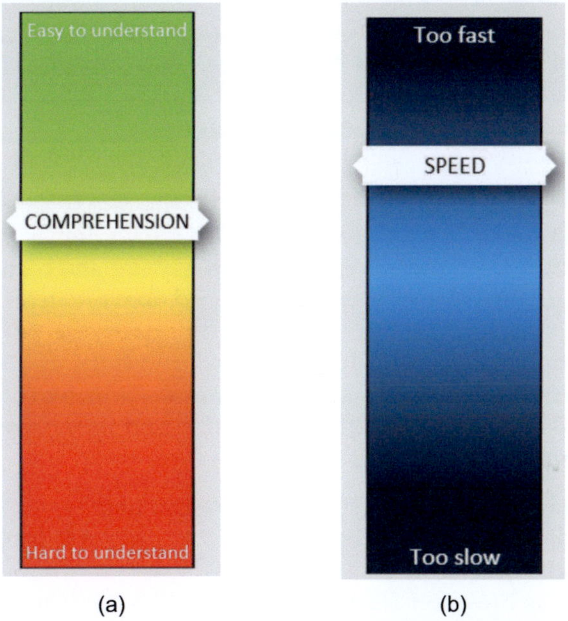

Figure 6.7.: Configurable color schemes for the LIM Meter: (a) default and (b) alternative

User Management and Groups

In this second prototype, user management was added to the LIM App and users had to register in order to have a personal profile with all the presentations where they have participated. When using the web app, the user can either join a group as participant (client) or create a new group as presenter (master), indicating the group name and a password to protect it from unauthorized changes. The menu bar in the upper part allows joining a group to give feedback, hosting a group as a presenter, visiting the reports of the events in *My Events*, or opening the personal menu to log out or see information about the app itself.

In order to join a group and give feedback as member of the audience, the user has to enter the name of the group. The user will be redirected to the audience dashboard (see Section 6.2.3). Users can only join groups that are active; i.e., the presenter has created the group and it is still open (see Section 6.2.3 about how to create a group).

Creation of Groups

If the user wants to create a group to receive feedback while giving a talk, he or she has to select the menu Host group (see Figure 6.8, left). The configuration screen will appear automatically, where the presenter or lecturer can configure the meter to the kind of feedback he or she would like to receive.

In the setup window, the presenter can specify the title (Figure 6.8, *Meter title*) and values of the meter. Two values are specified (*Upper caption* and *Lower caption*, respectively) which are shown as captions in the meter and history graphic. The type of meter; i.e., the color scheme as explained above, can also be configured (see meters *type A* and *B* in Figure 6.8). Additionally, the permissions of the group can be configured, including polls and questions. It allows the master (presenter) to activate/deactivate them. If any of the features (polls or questions) is deactivated, the app is automatically updated and they do not appear in the audience dashboards.

Finally, the user has to give a name and a password to the group. This password is only set for configuration of the group and to protect it from unauthorized changes from other users. By clicking on the *Create Group* button, the user will be redirected to the Presenter Dashboard (see Section 6.2.3) and the presentation can start. After this, any user can join the group and give feedback from the audience, as explained in the previous section.

Polls, Questions and written Feedback

Additional features include polls with instant evaluation, a question system with user rating, and anonymous written feedback (see Figure 6.9). Polls and questions have the purpose of contextualizing the data from the meter, as well as offering a better integration with features that may be necessary in such kind of scenarios (a lecture or a conference talk) and raise the interactivity between audience and presenter.

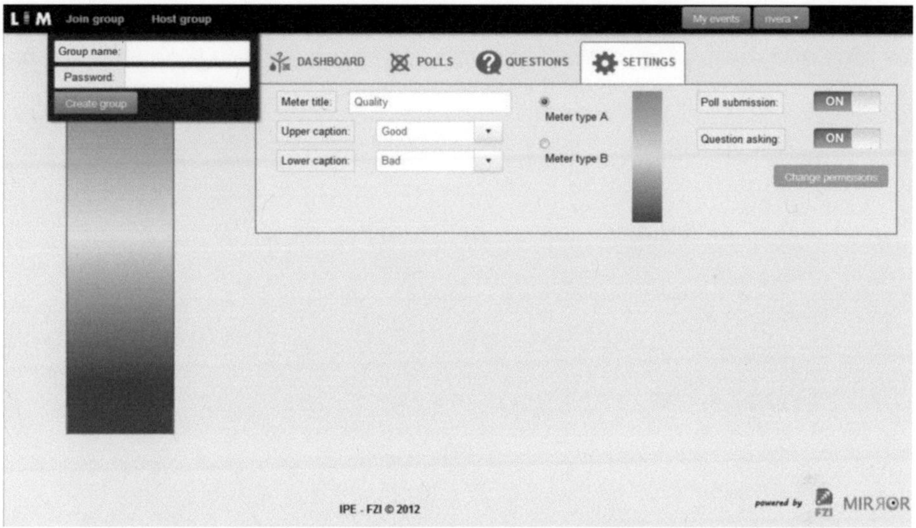

Figure 6.8.: Configuration of the group as master (presenter or lecturer)

Presenters have the possibility to set up polls before or during their presentations. Incoming polls automatically show up as a notification in the polls tab and users can select one of the available options (see Figure 6.9a). As soon as participants provide their answers, they can see the overall results. If the poll votes changes, the results are immediately updated in the user interface. The members in the audience can also suggest polls to the presenter, who will decide if a certain suggested poll is suitable and should be open to the rest of the audience in order to be answered.

The LIM App implements a question system that not only allows any participant to ask a question visible to everyone, but also provides the means of rating every question (see Figure 6.9b). Users have a list of the available questions, each decorated with a star rating bar, through which the participants can rate the question. Next to the rating, the number of votes for the respective question is shown. Especially in a large audience, everybody can ask questions without hindering global progress and people who lack confidence to raise their hand and ask can do it anonymously with this feature. Based on the star rating, the presenter can decide when to react. The question system itself is only intended for questions directed at the presenter who is supposed to answer them verbally at some point of the event.

Finally, written feedback in the form of text can be sent to the presenter (see Figure 6.9c). This allows users to contextualize the meter feedback and send any comments to the presenter. In order to avoid an information overload as well as an excessive distraction of the presenter, these comments are not visible to the presenter during the presentation, but will appear later in the corresponding generated report in the personal area of the user.

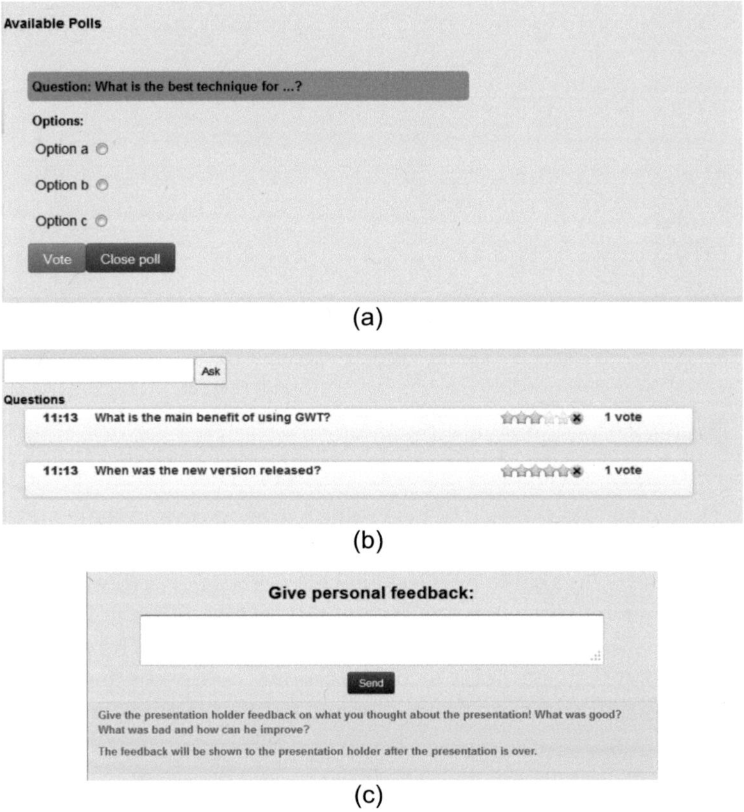

Figure 6.9.: (a) Polls, (b) questions and (c) written feedback in the LIM web version

Audience Dashboard

The audience dashboard (see Figure 6.10) is available for all the members in the audience and gives access to the feedback meter as well as the functions presented above. On the left, the user can give feedback through the meter, by simply using the slider. Below the meter, the "Give Feedback" button allows users to give anonymous written feedback by sending a comment to the presenter (with the text written in the text input field).

On the right, there is the tab panel where the user can access the rest of functions: evolution graph, polls, questions, and written feedback. By going to the corresponding tabs, the user has access to polls and questions as explained in Section 6.2.3. If a new poll is sent to the users or a new question is asked, there will be a number in red indicating the notifications. Regarding the evolution graph, users can see the evolution of their feedback as well as that of the other members in the audience. While the audience is giving feedback through the meter during the presentation, the aggregated live group feedback can be seen in the evolution graph (see Figure 6.10). The graph displays the personal meter value (red line), group's minimal, maximal (colored area) and average values (black line) in any particular point in time during the presentation. As the audience members analyze and evaluate their own data with the aggregated group data, the observed differences or similarities can trigger reflection.

Feedback data can be contextualized by adding interesting topics; e.g., "What is the presenter talking about right now?", "Which slide is being shown?" This feature can be accessed on the right-hand side of the dashboard, as depicted in Figure 6.10. Users can also share these interesting topics with others, if they activate the option "Share with others". These topics are also displayed in the evolution graph as green points. Contrary to the previous LIM prototype, instead of letting the presenter define important topic marks, the task was delegated to the audience. With that change, it was intended that much more contextualization would be brought into the presentation and at the same time some workload is lifted from the presenter.

Finally, the time span showed in the history graphic can be configured through a drop-down menu showing the available time in minutes.

The polls and questions features, which were already part of the first prototype, can be accessed through the tabs in the panel on the right side of the screen. Their purpose is to improve the interaction between presenter and audience and contextualize the feedback captured with the meter. Asking questions anonymously was one of the most appreciated features during the first evaluations, whereas the chat function was considered as too distracting and therefore removed from this new prototype. Finally, the audience can also send anonymous comments related to the feedback that they are giving in the meter.

Presenter Dashboard

The dashboard of the presenter, shown in Figure 6.11, visualizes the most important items in order to minimize the distraction during the presentation. The decision to define this dashboard was driven by the fact that presenters may not be able to actively interact with the LIM App during a presentation, as was confirmed by our previous studies.

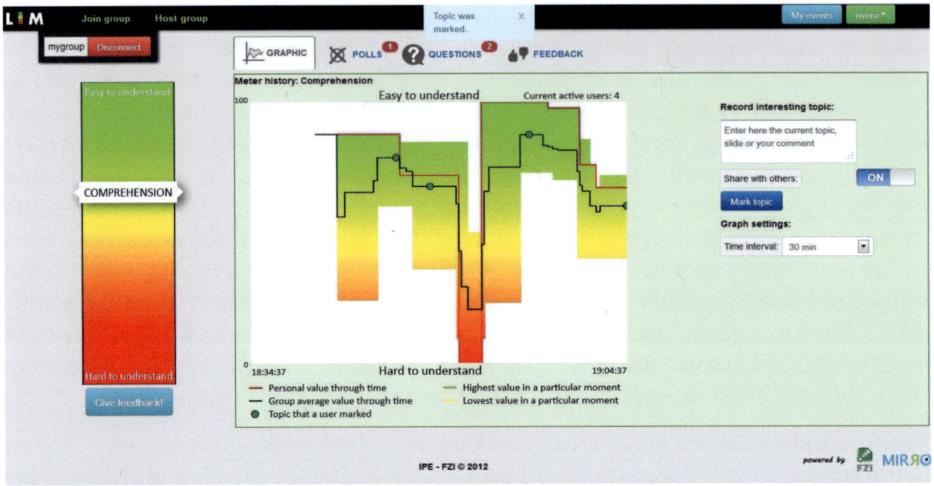

Figure 6.10.: Overview of the LIM audience dashboard during the presentation

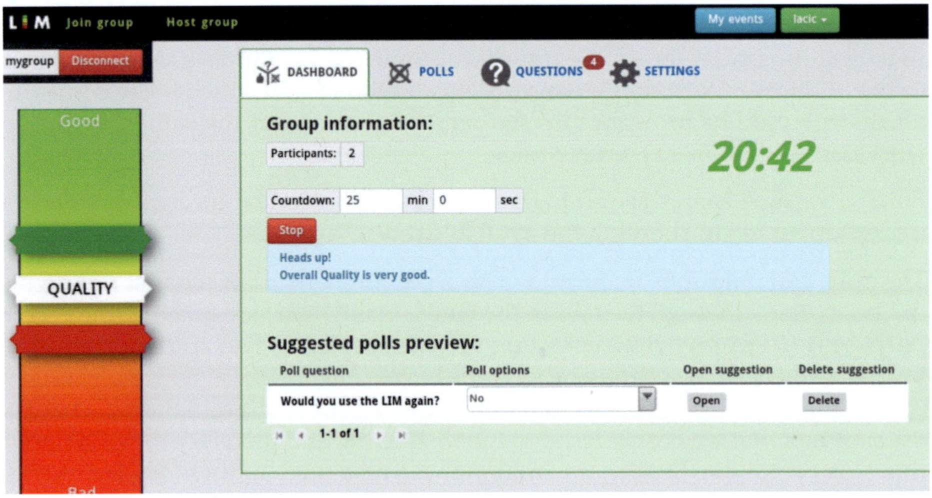

Figure 6.11.: Overview of the LIM presenter dashboard during the presentation

In the left part of the dashboard, the dashboard displays the current value of the meter, including the average value (white slider), the minimum (red slider) and the maximum (green slider). In the right part, the number of active participants that use the meter to give feedback is shown. This is important to estimate the relevance of the given feedback. A countdown timer is also available, so that the presenter can keep track of the time. Below the timer, a notification area is situated, which shows different notifications based on the current group average meter value. Also contained on the dashboard is a quick preview table of suggested polls. The preview table can be especially useful for creating a previously saved poll template. The displayed summarized data, along with the meter component (as seen in Figure 6.11) encapsulates the most relevant data to passively trigger reflection and allow the presenter to adapt while holding the presentation.

On the right, analogous to the audience dashboard, is the tab panel where the presenter can access the rest of the functions: polls, questions, and settings. By going to the corresponding tabs, the user can access polls and questions, as explained in Section 6.2.3. If a new poll is sent to the users or a new question is asked, there will be a number in red indicating the notification.

The presenter has a built-in functionality to mark a question as answered and the audience can vote which questions are the most relevant ones. With that, as seen in Figure 6.12, the presenter can keep track of which questions are already answered and which are still relevant. The pollution of too many questions being asked (be it real questions regarding the context of the presentation or just spam) can be easily countered; once a question is marked as answered it is removed from the list of displayed questions.

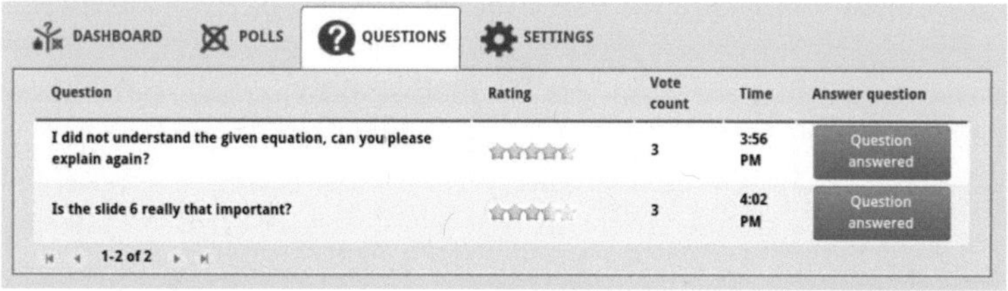

Figure 6.12.: Questions asked during the presentation, as seen by the presenter

Regarding the polls, prior to the presentation the presenter can prepare and save poll templates he or she would like to ask later on. During the presentation, members of the audience can also propose polls which be sent to the presenter, who will decide if they are suitable to be opened to the rest of the audience.

My Events

To facilitate the revisiting of past events, the enrichment and presentation of the gathered data is needed. Results presented in Section 6.6 also showed that not all presenters were able to react and reflect during the presentation and, therefore, the greater potential for reflection lies in recalling and revisiting past events in retrospective (the third dimension defined by the IMRLQS, see Chapter 3).

After a presentation is finished, the user can go to the *My Events* section and select a group session in which he or she participated as either the presenter or audience member. A summary of the selected presentation will be shown, containing the feedback given or received, the questions asked, and the polls answered by the audience. On the left, as seen in Figure 6.13, the user can see a list of the presentations divided in *Hosted Groups* (i.e., the groups where the user was the presenter) and *Joined Groups* (i.e., the groups where the user gave feedback as a member of the audience). After selecting a group, the user can choose which session he or she wants to explore by selecting the date and time in a drop-down menu.

The report of an event is divided into three sections. The displayed data (see Figure 6.13) firstly consists of a timeline depicting what was tracked during the presentation and what the trends were through four different lines. In the figure, the feedback regarding the speed of the talk is depicted. The three main lines display the gathered group's minimal, maximal and average values at a particular point in time. If the user was a member of the audience in that presentation, the fourth line will show his or her own meter-values during the presentation. In the case where the user was the presenter, the fourth line will show how many audience members were actively participating at any point of time when feedback was given. With this information, better conclusions can be made about the meaning of a particular aggregated meter value at a point in time. Additionally, the timeline displays the topics that were marked as shareable and their corresponding information. To further narrow down the time interval that should be displayed, a time filter is available. Below the timeline, polls that have been asked and answered are shown. Furthermore, anonymously asked questions are also available and can be sorted based on their corresponding ratings, votes, and time of asking. Lastly, the anonymous feedback is displayed at the bottom of the report. With these feedback comments from the audience, additional information about the presentation that could not be covered with the default LIM App functions can be found out.

Android Version

This version of the LIM App is implemented for any device with Android[1] operating system (version 2.2 and up). The Android app is focused on ease of use to provide an unobtrusive and seamless way of participating and giving feedback. Because of the small screen that mobile devices tend to have, the Android version does not allow reviewing the data in *My Events*. In the following, the interface and functionality of the Android app will be briefly presented. It can be noticed that this is a subset of the features from the web application.

[1] `http://android.com`

When users enter the app, they can log in and register. After logging in, they are redirected to the screen that allows joining a group (see Figure 6.14a). Once they are logged in to the group, users can touch the screen and capture their feedback with the meter. By tapping on the screen which constantly shows the evolution of the feedback (Figure 6.14c), the meter appears and the participants can move the slider for feedback input (Figure 6.14b). This way, they can update their feedback value by just moving a finger somewhere on the screen relative to the y-axis. This value reflects their current opinion or perception without having to look at the device. The history graph shows three different aspects in a timeline, as described before. The blue bubble (bottom right corner of the graphic) allows users to track interesting topics or leave comments about things that happen during the presentation (certain topic, certain slide, etc.).

All the functions of the LIM App are accessible via the menu of the mobile device (see Figure 6.15a). It allows selecting the time scale of the evolution graph, logging out, disconnecting from the current group, and accesssing polls, questions, and feedback. When a presentation or event is over and the presenter (master) closes the group, all users of the application are notified accordingly (see Figure 6.15b).

Figure 6.16 shows some additional screens of the Android application. The first screen (Figure 6.16a) allows users to create a new poll and suggest it to the presenter. The second screen (Figure 6.16b) shows the list of questions asked by the audience and their ratings. At the bottom, the user can suggest new questions. Finally, the last screen shows the written feedback feature which allows sending anonymous comments to the presenter which will be available in the event report (Figure 6.16c).

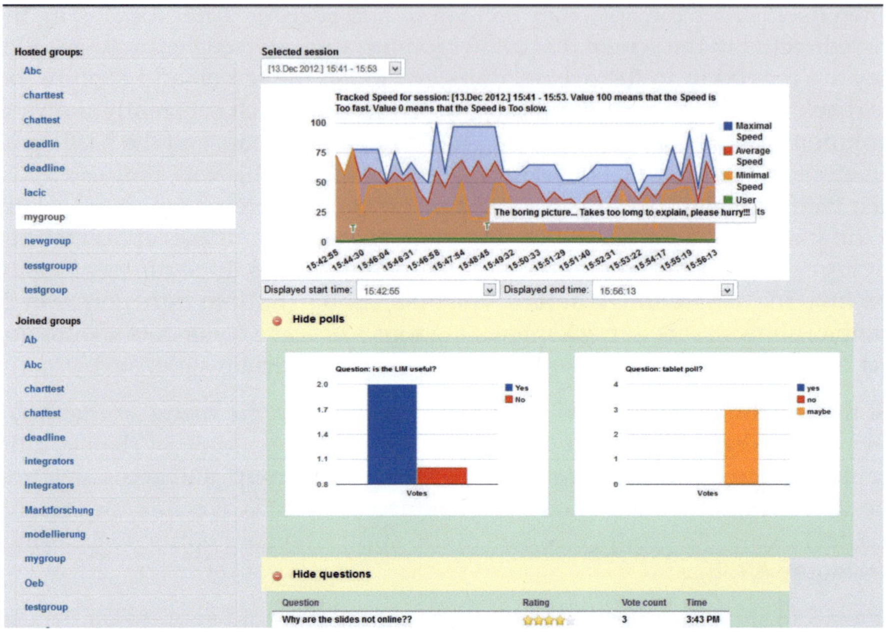

Figure 6.13.: Feedback Report of a presentation, showing the feedback timeline, asked polls and posted questions

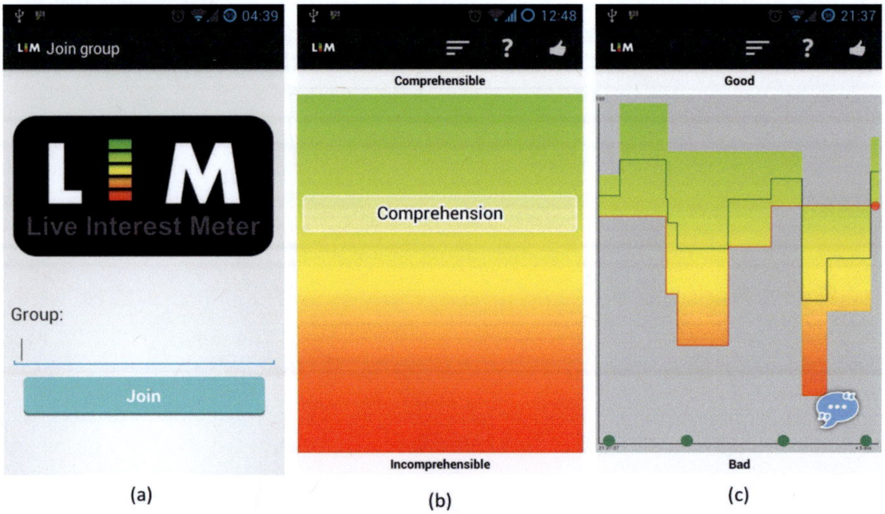

Figure 6.14.: LIM Android App: (a) Joining a group, (b) meter with slider for value input, and (c) evolution graph with topic marker

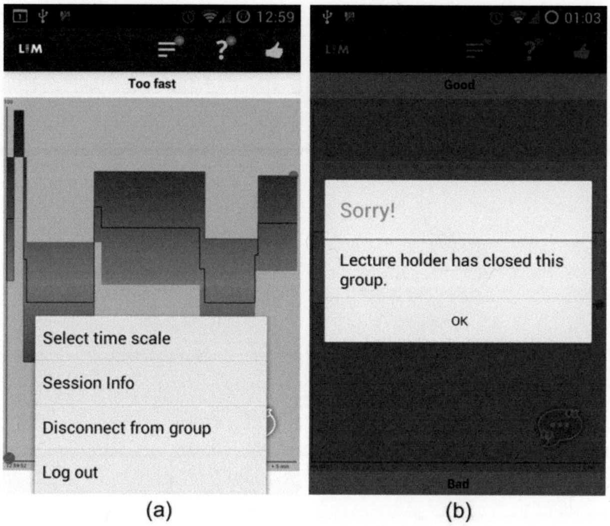

Figure 6.15.: LIM Android App: (a) Menu to access the several functions and (b) notification received by members in the audience when the presenter closes the group

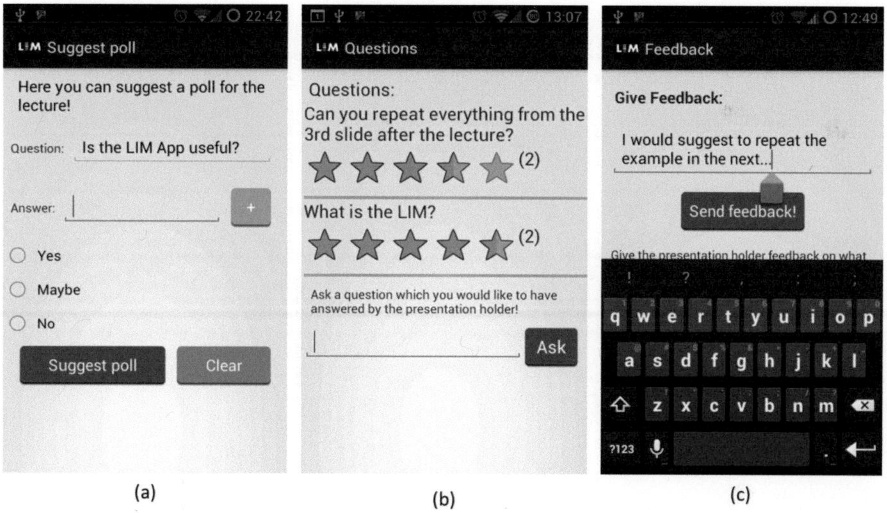

Figure 6.16.: LIM Android App: (a) Suggesting a poll to be opened by the presenter, (b) list of questions asked and ranked by audience members, and (c) written feedback that can be sent to the presenter

6.2.4. Implementation

The LIM App is implemented as an application that follows a three-tier architecture, as shown in Figure 6.17.

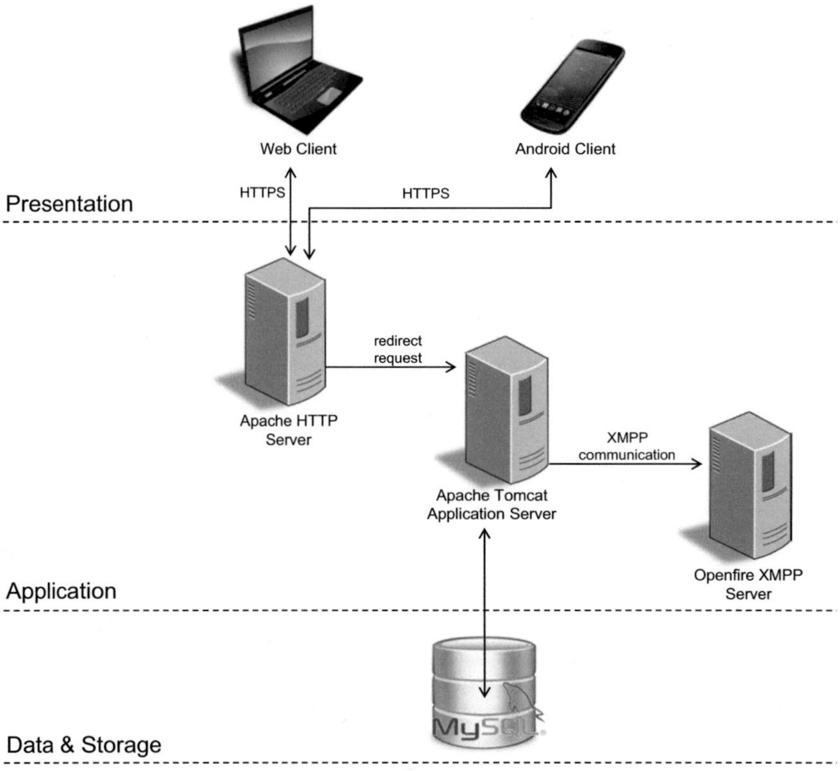

Figure 6.17.: Architecture of the LIM platform

Presentation

There are two interfaces available for the LIM App: a web application and a mobile application. The LIM App was initially developed as an Android application, which has been implemented in Java. Additionally, a JavaScript (JS) client was developed in order to make the LIM available for other devices and platforms (tablets, laptops, etc.). It is implemented in Java and is compiled into a deployable web application based on JavaScript and CSS using the Google

Web Toolkit. This JS client allows users to connect to the Java application server (Apache Tomcat[2]). Client and server communicate via HTTPS requests.

Application

The LIM App communication is based on the Extensible Messaging and Presence Protocol (XMPP[3]), a communications protocol for message-oriented middleware based on XML (Extensible Markup Language). The JS client uses Bidirectional-streams Over Synchronous HTTP (BOSH[4]) as an extension to push messages to clients as soon as they are sent. All communication in the system occurs from client to master or the other way around, and there is no direct communication between clients. The Smack[5] (web) and asmack[6] (mobile) libraries were used as client libraries for XMPP. XMPP was chosen as the communication protocol for the LIM App because it provides a simple mechanism to create and manage groups with a bi-directional communication. The data messages exchanged through the XMPP protocol between master and clients are coded in JSON[7] format. In the case of the JS client, google-gson and jQuery are used in order to parse the JSON messages. Decoding and encoding of messages in the Android application is done using the Gson library.

Data and Storage

The LIM App stores the data from the group sessions in a MySQL[8] database. The data layer is implemented using the object-relational mapping library Hibernate[9], which provides a framework for mapping the object-oriented domain model to the relational database. The implemented data model can be seen in Figure 6.18. The data about the creator of the group (presenter), the questions asked, and the polls conducted are associated with the group session. The meter configuration, meter feedback, and topic data are associated with a group client. The relationships between the tables ensure that users can access the data gathered of all presentations where they have participated in, either as presenter or as audience member.

[2] http://tomcat.apache.org/download-70.cgi
[3] http://xmpp.org
[4] http://xmpp.org/extensions/xep-0124.html
[5] http://www.igniterealtime.org/projects/smack
[6] https://code.google.com/p/asmack/
[7] http://www.json.org
[8] http://www.mysql.com
[9] http://hibernate.org/

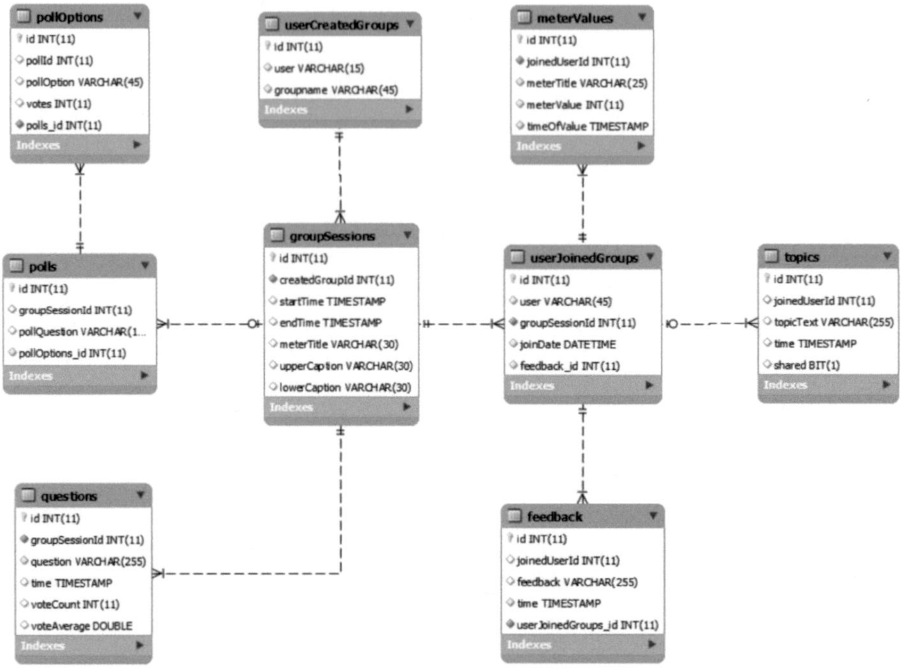

Figure 6.18.: Data model implemented in the LIM App

6.3. Evaluation Approach

First tests with an initial prototype proved that the LIM App is especially valuable for settings where there is a numerous audience or the event is done virtually, as the presenter lacks a direct personal communication with the members of the audience. We also identified that events where there is not a defined presenter but which are based on informal discussions among many participants do not offer the appropriate conditions to use the LIM App.

We evaluated the main concept of feedback tracking with the first prototype of the LIM App (see Section 6.2.2) in an initial formative evaluation, conducted in a project meeting (Section 6.4). Afterwards, with the aim of refining and further developing the application, we conducted a design study consisting of interviews with end users and an online survey (Section 6.5).

The development of the second prototype (see Section 6.2.3) focused on the review of the data after the presentations, by implementing user profiles and data reports. This second prototype was evaluated in two formative user studies in several work contexts, including lectures, research and business (see Sections 6.6 and 6.7). The LIM App did not undergo major changes after these last formative studies, but they served to prepare the application for the summative evaluation (see Section 6.8), both from a technical and usage perspective.

In this particular use case, members in the audience are the ones who are providing feedback to the speaker. Therefore, these should also perceive a benefit in order to be motivated to gather the data. In order to assess this, the conducted evaluations included not only feedback from the speaker (e.g., the lecturer) but also from the audience (e.g., students).

A chronological overview of the studies and evaluations conducted with the Live Interest Meter (LIM App) is given in Table 6.3. In the following sections, the procedure and the results of each evaluation are described in detail. In total, five studies with 294 participants involved were conducted with the LIM App.

Table 6.3.: Overview of the LIM App evaluations

Type of Evaluation	Organization/ Setting	App Version	Participants	Start–End
Formative	Project Meeting	0.6	10 researchers	28-06-2011
Design Study	HSKA*	0.6	39 lecturers 48 students	21-05-2012 27-06-2012
Formative	HSKA and KIT**	1.0	3 lecturers 44 students	01-07-2012 20-12-2012
Formative	Business, academic and scientific***	1.0	6 presenters 14 customers	16-04-2013 16-01-2014
Summative	German university	1.0	1 lecturer 129 students	24-03-2014 11-06-2014

*HSKA: Hochschule Karlsruhe

**KIT: Karlsruhe Institute of Technology

***Involving British Telecom, Tracoin Quality, Cyprus University of Technology, KIT, and FZI

6.4. Formative Evaluation I: European Project Meeting

This first formative study was conducted to evaluate the main concept behind the LIM approach and refine the investigated use case. We collected feedback on usability, intention of use, and usefulness. Additionally, as the LIM App is used while performing a presentation and this can result in a high cognitive load, we evaluated the subjective mental workload that the application requires. It consisted of an informal test of the LIM App in a project meeting. This study has been partly presented in Rivera-Pelayo et al. [2013a].

6.4.1. Procedure

The first study with the LIM App was conducted during a project meeting of a European Project. The meeting had a duration of two days (from June 28 to June 29, 2012) and the application was used during the first day. The meeting was organized to analyze the progress and discuss further activities. The project was constituted by 12 international research institutions from Great Britain, Spain, Austria, Switzerland, and Germany. In total, 20 project members were part of the meeting. Out of these, 10 participants used the LIM App and participated in the evaluation.

At the end of the app usage, we distributed a questionnaire to evaluate participants' feedback. The main topics assessed with the questionnaire were the influence on the presentation, effects on distraction, benefits of feedback capturing, and peer comparison. All questions were evaluated with a 5-point Likert scale. Finally, we used an unweighted or Raw NASA-Task Load Index (RTLX) [Hart, 2006] to assess the subjective mental workload of the application. The RTLX is a multi-dimensional scale designed to estimate mental workload while performing a task. The workload is estimated as the combination of six independent subscales: Mental Demand, Physical Demand, Temporal Demand, Frustration, Effort, and Performance. The subscales, ranging from 1 as optimum and 20 as worst value, were averaged to calculate the overall workload score.

6.4.2. Results

The first questions of the questionnaire referred to the overall influence and usage of the LIM App in the meeting. The overall influence[10] of the LIM App in the meeting sessions was rated with an average value of $M = 2.6$ ($SD = 0.97$),

[10] "How would you rate the overall influence of the LIM App on the sessions?"

indicating a neutral influence on the meeting. The distraction[11] caused by the LIM App (assessed with a scale from 1 = not at all to 5 = very distracting) was evaluated rather low ($M = 2.4$; $SD = 1.07$).

We investigated the purposes for which the LIM App was used as well as for which purposes it was more suitable according to the participants. Figure 6.19 shows a summary of the obtained results. Participants had the option to add additional purposes, but other purposes besides the ones in the provided list were not suggested.

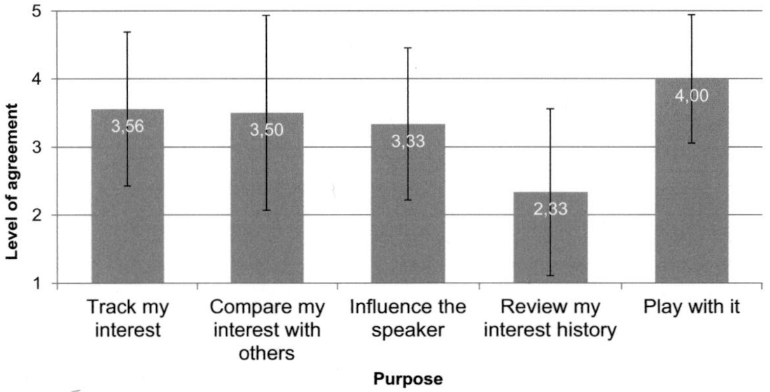

Figure 6.19.: Mean and standard deviation for each purpose for which the participants used the LIM App (1 = very bad to 5 = very well)

The results show that this first prototype of the LIM App succeeded in its main purpose; i.e., to track the interest of the audience. The meter interface, conceived to track interest, appeared to be easy to use and intuitive. The lowest rating was given to the review of the interest history. This may be affected by the fact that the user has to explicitly go to the history mode after the event and many of the users concentrated on using the app mainly during the presentation. A remarkable result is the high rating that participants gave to the purpose of playing with the app. Being the first time they use such a tool and using the novel analogy of being a meter may have contributed to this fact. It was intended to be a dynamic, appealing and fun application, but we have to consider this carefully in order to avoid too much distraction during its usage.

The questionnaire also contained questions about the usefulness of the group feedback for both speaker and audience[12], rated with a 5-point Likert scale (1 = negative to 5 = positive). The usefulness of the group feedback for themselves

[11] "Did the LIM App disturb you or distract your attention during the meeting?"
[12] "Please rate the usefulness of the group feedback for yourself/the speaker."

($M = 4.00$; $SD = 0.82$; $N = 7$) was clearer for the participants than the usefulness for the presenter ($M = 3.50$; $SD = 0.53$; $N = 10$). The usefulness for the presenter was influenced by the type of meeting as well as by the fact that it was only used during a short period of time during the meeting and not in several presentations/meetings or to review how the meeting was thereafter.

Regarding the user interface (UI), the users considered that the history graph reflects well the interest evolution of the meeting ($M = 3.80$; $SD = 0.92$; $N = 10$). Suggestions made to improve the UI included having a bigger dot for indicating the interest, displaying a larger average line, and providing a scrollable navigation history.

We asked participants if they would like to use the LIM App regularly and why. We received a negative answer from 20% of the participants (*"Added value not easy to see"*), whereas 50% would maybe use the app regularly (*"Might be interesting if the speaker reacts on feedback," "to influence the speaker"*) and 30% confirmed that they would definitely use it in the future (*"I like the idea of instant and interactive feedback"*).

We obtained valid answers to the NASA-RTLX scale from nine participants, which are summarized in Table 6.4. We obtained an overall workload score of 4.61. Examining the subscales, *frustration* and *physical demand* achieved the best results. On the contrary, the poorest results were obtained for *effort* and *mental demand* needed, though with a high standard deviation that indicates disagreement among participants.

Table 6.4.: Descriptive statistics for each subscale of the Raw NASA-TLX scale and the user score calculated by participant among all subscales

	Min	*Max*	*Median*	*Mean*	*SD*
Mental demand	2	14	4	5.78	4.15
Physical demand	1	4	3	2.78	0.97
Temporal demand	1	12	3	4.44	3.24
Performance	1	11	3	4.78	3.83
Effort	1	20	4	6.11	5.95
Frustration	1	10	4	3.78	2.82
RTLX User Score			3.5	4.61	1.95

At the end of the questionnaire, participants could give some final comments. They highlighted the simplicity of the app as well as the ease of use and understanding of the app concept. One participant suggested that it would be very useful for the presenter to see the time of the presentation. With respect to the usage scenario, they emphasized that it would be better for conferences or lectures, and mentioned that, for such a meeting, a web interface would be very useful; e.g., to prepare polls for the presentation. The duration of the battery in some of the participants' mobile phones was the main technical problem.

During the evaluation we could also gather some informal feedback and suggestions from the participants. One user said that he or she would like the app to remind him or her about introducing his interest; for example, the application could vibrate to attract his attention. They also suggested that conferences or lectures may be more suitable scenarios to use the LIM App, compared to discussion-oriented sessions as the one they had. Some comments on the UI referred to the possibility of ranking the polls and showing them again in the end or showing a summary to the presenter (master) when all polls are closed. From several informal discussions during the meeting, we perceived that all participants liked the concept of the LIM App and found it was a good and innovative idea.

6.4.3. Discussion

In these informal tests, we gained the first insights about the Live Interest Meter. Summarizing these insights and the comments of participants, we can conclude that the LIM App is suitable for big audiences where personal contact is not established but it is not suitable for events which are discussion-driven, as then the role of the presenter is not well defined. Participants needed an adaptation phase to achieve the integration of the app in their ongoing work tasks. Some technical problems with the Wi-Fi and high battery consumption could have influenced the answers of the participants and introduced biases, especially in questions referring to distraction or influence on the meeting.

The evaluation results show that the introduction of a Quantified Self approach to quantify feedback in the form of a meter value can be successful and is initially well accepted. The users recognized the advantages of tracking their interest and saw the potential of reflecting on the tracked data. In this first study, we used only a mobile version of the LIM App for Android. It was proven that a mobile version is beneficial for tracking as it allows interacting with the meter while doing other tasks. However, for features that require the input of text (e.g., creating a poll) a web interface may be more practical.

These insights were taken into account in the subsequent studies and evaluations as well as in the further development of the LIM App.

6.5. Design Study I: Hochschule Karlsruhe

The aim of this user study was to investigate the acceptance and perceived usefulness of the LIM App, as well as the refinement of the features of the first prototype. Therefore, this study was not an evaluation of the tool but a study to inform the further development of the tool based on the users' needs. It was conducted in mid 2012 and its results contributed to the development of the second prototype of the LIM App as well as to the understanding of the support of reflective learning in presentations and lectures. The study reported herein was published in Rivera-Pelayo et al. [2013a].

6.5.1. Procedure

The study was divided in two phases. Firstly, we performed several interviews with target users and subsequently we conducted an online survey. It was designed around the following research questions:

- RQ1: *In which scenarios and how can the quantification of feedback performed by the LIM App support reflective learning?*
- RQ2: *Which features are more appreciated by users, both presenters and audience?*

Interviews

Initially, 20 qualitative interviews with groups of the LIM App end users were conducted in order to investigate the use case scenarios and the application of the LIM App itself. The interviewees were end users including professors, teachers, and students (from both faculties of pedagogy and informatics). In this way, we covered both groups of presenters and audience. These interviews not only enabled us to get qualitative feedback, but served as input for the design of the subsequent online acceptance study.

The goal of the interviews with presenters and lecturers was to find out which methods they used to get feedback in their presentations, which aspects of the LIM App they like best for the collection of feedback, and which results are the most interesting for them. Furthermore, which features are obstructive and which other new features the presenters and lecturers would like to have. Likewise, the interviews with the potential audience intended to collect suggestions and opinions regarding positive and negative aspects of the LIM App as well as to get to know which expectations they have for the use of the application.

Survey

In a second phase, we conducted an online survey based on our experience and the feedback from the interviews. The survey contained questions related to the use case of the LIM App as well as to the application itself. Our aim was to get to know the disposition, opinion, and ideas of potential users. For that purpose, we explained them the concept of reflective learning and its support with the LIM App (including screenshots), before asking them several questions for assessment and evaluation.

Participants

The survey was online for a month (from May to June 2012) and 120 people participated. In total, we obtained 87 valid and complete datasets. Due to the first selective questions about the role of the participants regarding their participation in presentations (as presenter or audience), we intentionally skipped people who did not fit one of the two roles. With this intentional constraint, we aimed at reaching potential users that know and understand the context of our work and the use of the LIM App.

From the total number of participants ($N = 87$), 39 (44.82%) give presentations professionally; e.g., as a teacher, professor, or in conferences; whilst the other 48 (55.17%) participants do not give presentations but attend them. In order to diversify the participants' background, we distributed our survey through various channels: personal relations to professors, colleagues and institutions, social media, and our website.

Participants in the survey do presentations in different contexts: teacher at school (7.69%), lecturer at a university (41.02%), speaker in conferences (56.41%), or presentations as part of their professional work (56.41%). Regarding their audience, only 12.81% speak before more than 60 people, whereas the majority of the participants have audiences of 11-30 (46.15%) or 31-60 (25.64%) people.

The 48 participants who do attend presentations do it as students (89.58%), in their free time (8.33%), in conferences (6.25%), and/or at work (22.91%). The age distribution of the participants was the following: 17-24 (36.78%), 25-35 (41.37%), 36-50 (12.64%), and more than 50 years old (9.19%). Regarding their educational background, 48.27% of the participants had a technical and 37.93% an economical background, whereas 6.89% had studied pedagogy or other disciplines (6.89%).

6.5.2. Interview Results

Many speakers or lecturers already collect feedback from their presentations and lectures, but they do it in conventional ways, through written questionnaires or direct contact with their attendants. Technology-supported feedback systems were not used among the participants and the idea of having a system like the LIM App, which allows them to give and get feedback, was very well received.

This was also true for the audience, who was willing to give feedback not only after but also during lectures. Additionally, according to participants, feedback anonymity would result in higher audience participation and students would voice their own opinion more openly, without the fear of contradicting opinions or ideas. Some students mentioned that giving negative feedback anonymously would make sure that their grades would not be affected, while they could still give the teacher honest feedback.

The poll function was considered especially useful for lectures, because it allows lecturers to quickly evaluate the knowledge of their students. This would help lecturers and professors adapt their lecture to the participants' knowledge; i.e., whether a certain topic is unclear and therefore needs further explanations or the presenter can move on to the next topic. On the other hand, the chat was considered unnecessary, as it allows a higher level of interactivity in the audience which may end up to be a higher distraction.

All interviewees who usually give presentations had concerns regarding the use of a system to give feedback during the event. Many of them were afraid of the distraction to both presenter and audience, if they focus more on the application itself than on the content of the lecture. From our experience, not everybody trusts themselves to be able to react to the response of the audience and adapt the course of a presentation on the fly. This might prove to be a source of frustration, as people in the audience may expect a fast adaptation, whereas the presenter may only be able to show a long term improvement.

Regarding the anonymity of the users, on the one hand, this allows a higher level of participation but, on the other hand, it can be misused. One interviewee suggested that people in the audience could agree on giving a certain feedback to the presenter (e.g., intentionally giving negative feedback) and this would lead to a corruption of the results. The sincerity and credibility of the feedback cannot be proven in such a situation. Another point was the possibility of making the feedback more constructive in order to contribute to the presenter's development or improvement.

Many interviewees agreed that reflection needs time and, therefore, they would prefer reflecting after the event had taken place than during the presentation while feeling under pressure.

Finally, some interviewees remarked that the use of such a system would be possible in universities and colleges, but not in schools, due to the fact that the use of laptops and smartphones is not so widespread and even prohibited in some cases.

6.5.3. Survey Results

The first part of the survey contained questions about the use case in which the LIM App is used and how it can influence and provide benefits for the end users. Questions referring to the role of the presenter (e.g., in which context their talks are given) were only asked to participants who had confirmed that they give talks and presentations, whereas other questions concerning the role of the audience (e.g., which criteria they would like to evaluate) were only answered by the rest.

From the presenter's side, nearly 90% of the participants would like to get feedback after each presentation, whereas around 72% would also agree to get feedback during the event, for example after each section (see Figure 6.20). Receiving feedback live during the whole presentation was chosen as ideal by 12.82% of the participants and as OK by 25.64%, but 33.33% were indecisive, 10.26% considered it to be tight (just enough), and 17.95% thought that collecting feedback during the whole presentation is insufficient.

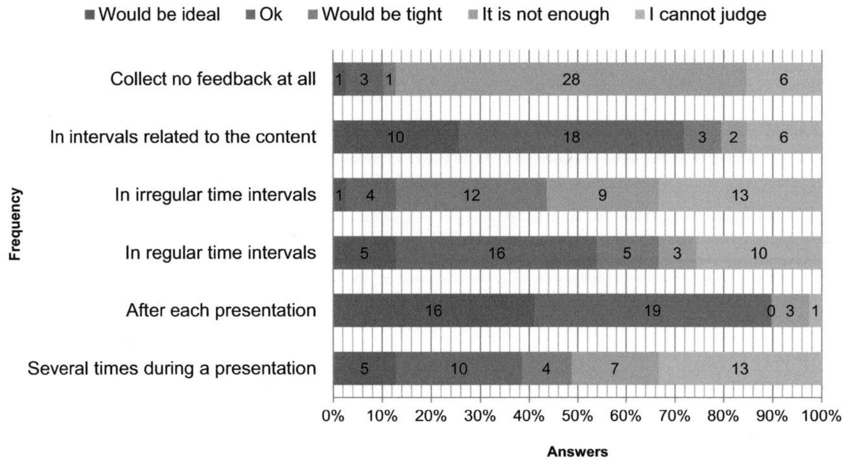

Figure 6.20.: How do you evaluate the following periods of time to receive feedback (as presenter)?

Figure 6.21 shows how likely presenters consider that they will react to the feedback they are receiving. Although the pressure for immediate feedback adaptation was a concern among many participating presenters, 53.84% think that they could achieve it during the presentation. Reacting to the feedback periodically (e.g., some days later) and in relation to the content blocks (e.g., between content blocks) seems to be the most popular option (76.91%), what may be directly related to reflective learning practices from the data they gathered in past events.

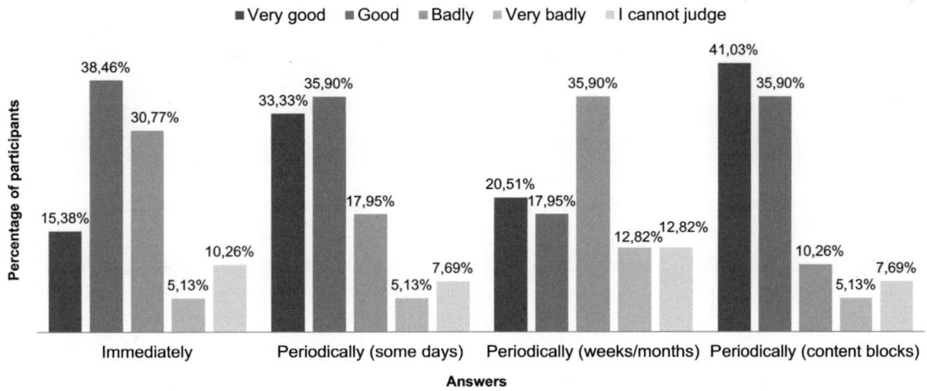

Figure 6.21.: What do you consider realistic regarding how you can react to the feedback (as presenter)?

All respondents expressed their opinion regarding several aspects of the LIM App, like if the adoption of a tool like this would completely distract the audience (18.39%: strongly agree, 56.32%: agree, 20.68%: disagree, 1.14%: strongly disagree) or if feedback must be anonymous in order to be reliable and honest (41.37%: strongly agree, 27.58%: agree, 26.43%: disagree, 3.44%: strongly disagree).

In the survey, we also asked about the capturing of the feedback data. In this regard, 64.36% of the participants agreed with data collected live and continuously being better and more significant than only periodically collected data (see Figure 6.22).

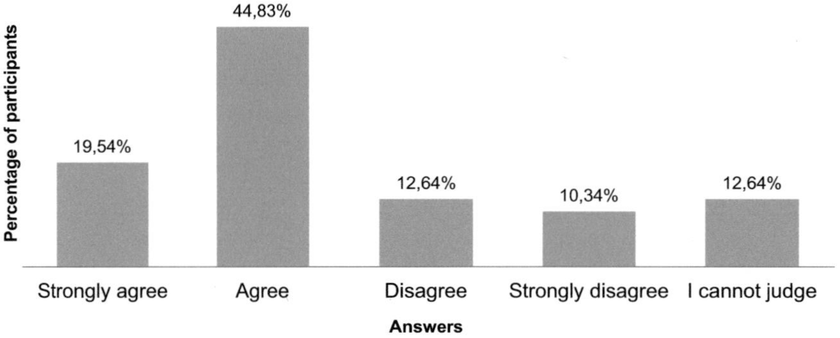

Figure 6.22.: Data collected live and continuously is better and more significant than only periodically collected data.

The second part of the survey contained questions about the concrete characteristics that the LIM App offers and which new features would improve the application. The chat function in the LIM App was considered unnecessary (4.59%: very meaningful, 16.09%: rather meaningful, 43.67%: unnecessary, 33.33%: absolutely unnecessary, 2.29%: I cannot judge). On the contrary, the participants appreciated polling questions (34.48%: very meaningful, 54.02%: rather meaningful, 8.04%: unnecessary, 3.44%: absolutely unnecessary) and also the possibility to review old polled questions (28.73 %: very meaningful, 50.57%: rather meaningful, 13.79%: unnecessary, 2.29%: absolutely unnecessary, 4.59%: I cannot judge).

We also investigated the differences between the information the speakers would like to know about and the information that people in the audience are willing to evaluate and give feedback about. Figure 6.23 shows that speakers and audience members agree on pace and clarity of examples being important, but disagree regarding the slides and documents of the lecture.

Finally, as Figure 6.24 depicts, participants considered the comparison among presenters and their performances more meaningful for them than comparing the feedback given by the students. Regarding this issue, comparing different presenters and their lectures is not our main objective, because they do not share the same context and therefore feedback would be difficult to be meaningful as would be learning something from it. Nevertheless, our approach is twofold: from the presenter's perspective comparing all events where one person has participated in and, from the audience's perspective, comparing all events where one person has given feedback in.

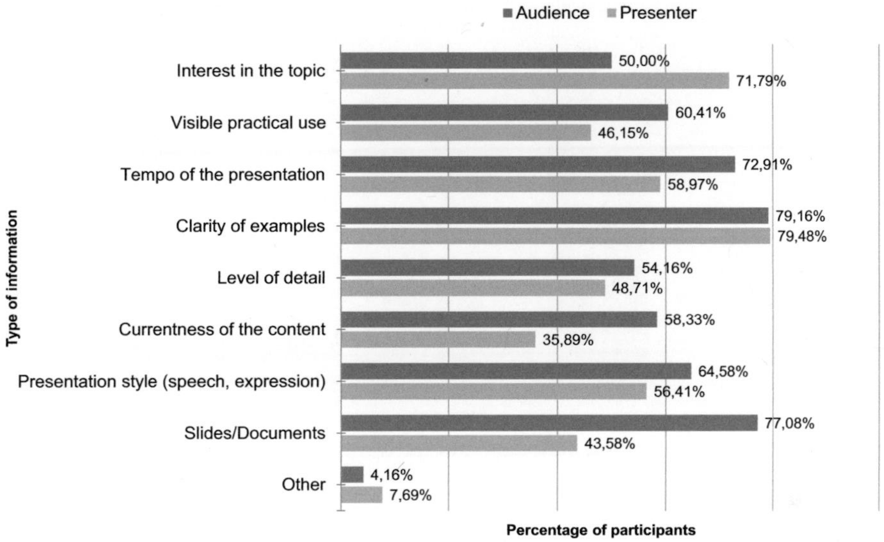

Figure 6.23.: Which information would presenters like to know about and which information does the audience want to evaluate?

Participants in the acceptance study also gave their general opinion about any functionality they would like to have or any comment they had on the LIM App. Some of them agreed that the application should be kept as simple as possible and should be easy to use. One respondent expressed concern regarding the misuse of the application and therefore did not consider full anonymity a possibility, but rather the use of nicknames or pseudonyms. Regarding the scenario where the LIM App is used, two participants would also like to have support for practical lectures or labs, which are more interactive and the role of the presenter is less relevant. However, the LIM App was designed and is more suitable for the scenario described above (see Section 6.2). There were also very interesting and useful suggestions regarding the interface of the LIM App; e.g., showing a clock with the time or countdown or having templates for polls with yes/no answers, etc. Finally, one participant found the LIM App an exciting project, despite having concerns about the confidence of the presenter to react and adapt to students' requirements.

Summarizing the positive results, more than 3/4 of the participants (78.16%) in the survey found the idea behind the LIM App very positive and found advantages in using it. More than half of them (57.47%) would like to test the Live Interest Meter application.

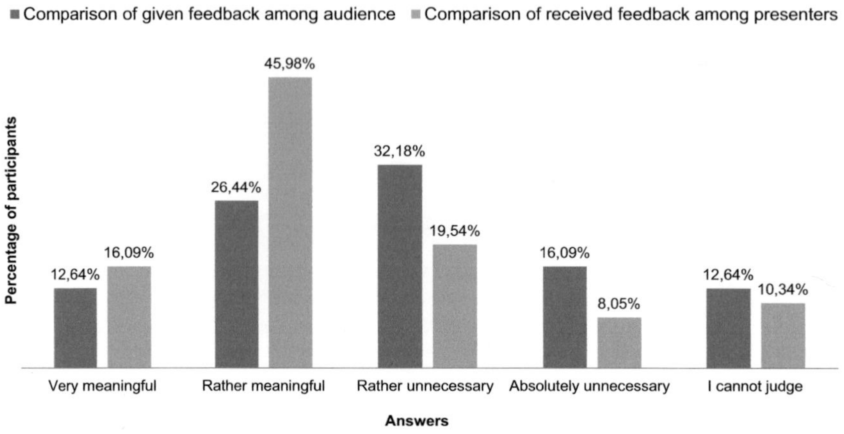

Figure 6.24.: Evaluation of the significance of comparing between members of the audience and between presenters

6.5.4. Design Choices

Taking into consideration the results of this study, the LIM App was redesigned and subsequently the second prototype was implemented. The resulting design choices were instantiated through mock-ups, which served as (i) basis for discussions and (ii) guide for the development of the prototype.

Figure 6.25 shows a representative sample of the generated mock-ups. The notes on the side of the mock-ups contain details about the interaction and dynamic components of the UI. New dashboards were designed to satisfy the needs of both roles involved; i.e., members of the audience (see Figure 6.25a) and presenter (see Figure 6.25b). In both dashboards, questions and polls were accessible through a menu or tab system situated in the upper part. When selecting the corresponding icon, the panel with polls or questions appears (see Figure 6.25c and d). The interesting topics were added to the audience dashboard, as they would be responsible for contextualizing the feedback in this prototype (see Figure 6.25e). Finally, with the creation of the *My Events* section, the display of the gathered data in a report was designed (see Figure 6.25f).

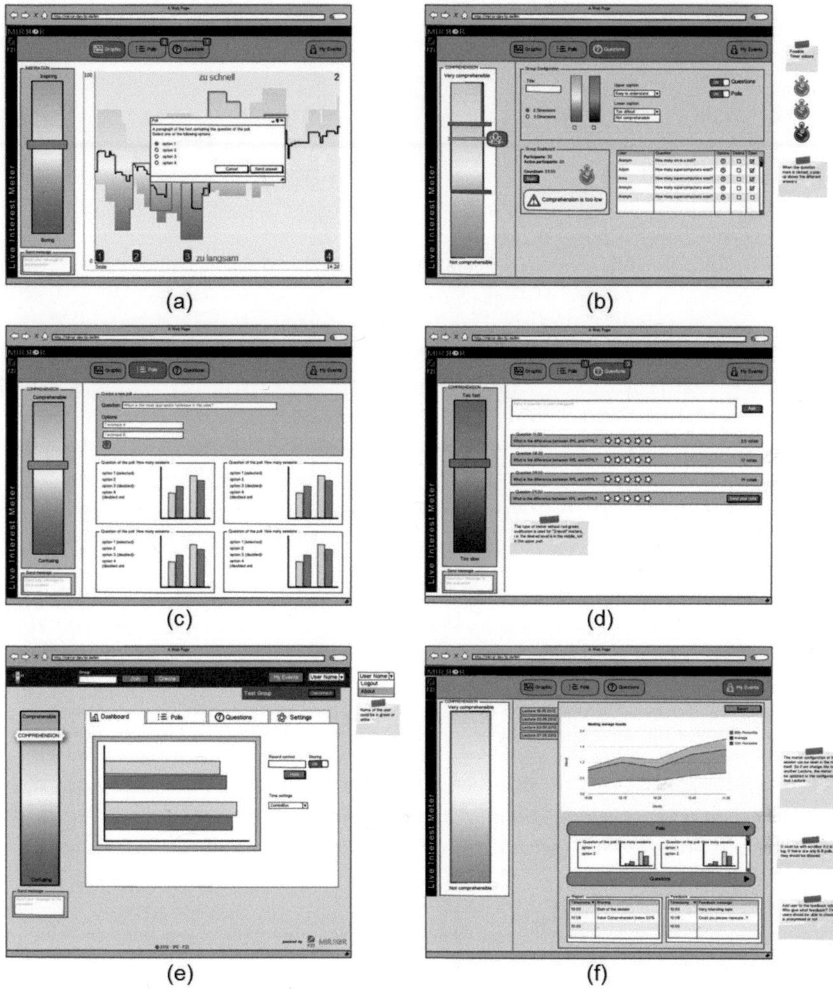

Figure 6.25.: LIM mock-ups used to discuss evaluation results and guide further development: (a) Audience dashboard with poll, (b) presenter dashboard, (c) polls panel, (d) questions panel with notifications, (e) audience dashboard with topic markers, and (f) report of a presentation.

6.5.5. Discussion

We conducted a user study to investigate the acceptance, perceived usefulness, and potential improvements of the LIM App. This user study delivered a highly positive resonance and the idea of using a technology-driven feedback system was well received. Test subjects recognized the advantages of the feedback system, both during and after the lecture, and saw a possible benefit in its use.

We also confirmed one of the main fears of end users: the potential distraction of the audience, by concentrating on the application instead of the presentation itself. In order to improve this, we addressed this issue in different directions; e.g., by keeping the application as simple as possible to demand the minimum cognitive effort from users. To this end, the next prototype only showed the necessary information to the users or we offered an introductory training to teachers in order to show them how to integrate the LIM App in their lectures and make the best of it. Nonetheless, the success of related approaches [Teevan et al., 2012; Munday, 2012] that achieved engagement of users instead of their distraction opens the door to minimizing this issue.

The captured data are not only useful for reflection-in-action (live), but for the subsequent reflection-on-action as well [Schön, 1984]. In order to support the last one, the reviewing of past events becomes crucial. Our efforts in developing the next prototype of the LIM App focused on improving the support of recalling and revisiting past events, by creating a platform that allows users to explore their gathered data retrospectively. Additionally, further improvements based on the feedback from the user study were adapted; e.g., alternatives to the chat functionality were explored and features to support the presenter, such as notifications in relevant situations or a time reference were adopted. With the new prototype (see Section 6.2.3), we were able to evaluate the real use of the application in the field and, in this way, validate our current results, which show the expectations and opinions of the end users of the LIM App.

6.6. Formative Evaluation II: Hochschule Karlsruhe and Karlsruhe Institute of Technology

We conducted a first formative evaluation of the second prototype of the Live Interest Meter. This evaluation took place between July and December 2012 and was conducted at the Karlsruhe Institute of Technology (KIT) and the Hochschule Karlsruhe (HSKA). The main goal of this evaluation was to evaluate the added benefits of the features implemented to support the recalling and revisiting of past events; i.e., *My Events*, which allowed users to explore their gathered data retrospectively.

For further details about this formative evaluation, the reader can refer to its publication [Rivera-Pelayo et al., 2013b].

6.6.1. Procedure

The LIM App was tested and evaluated in three different lectures (see a summary in Table 6.5). The main lecture (Group M) was using the LIM App during its sessions in three consecutive weeks and, besides the lecturer, consisted of 19 students aged 19 to 25 years. It was a Computer Science lecture with undergraduate students. In the first and last lecture session, the tracked meter value was "Speed", whereas in the second lecture the meter title was "Comprehension."

The other two lectures used the LIM App only in one session. The first one (Group S) had a highly active and small audience (13 students). From the 13 Masters students that participated, 11 filled out the questionnaires. The age distribution of the students goes from 20 to 26 years. The lecturer also configured the meter to track the "Speed" of the talk. This was a mathematics lecture and, besides having a small group, the lecturer and her students already knew each other for several semesters.

The last lecture (Group L) had a large audience with much less student activity. From the 50 students that used the LIM App, only 15 of them filled out the questionnaire at the end of the lecture, whereas the rest had given feedback in a verbal manner. This lecture was part of a Bachelor of Science in Management and Economics. The tracked value was "Quality."

Table 6.5.: Description of the three lectures participating in the evaluation

Group	Sess.	Partic.	Degree – Field	Tracked aspects
S	1	11/13	MS – Mathematics	Speed,
M	3	18/19	B – Computer Science	Speed, Comprehension
L	1	15/50	B – Mgmt. and Economics	Quality

*No. of valid responses / Total number of students in the lecture

At the end of the trials, a questionnaire was distributed to lecturers and students. The questionnaire addressed four main topics: features of the LIM App, level of participation, thoughts about learning by reflection, and outcomes and work assessment using the LIM App. One researcher of the LIM team was present at the lectures to assess the presenter and students as well as to follow the course of the evaluation.

6.6.2. Results

The LIM App was used for 83 minutes on average. The polling function was only used by the presenters in Group M and L. Every presenter used the question functionality at least once in their lecture, and there were 17 questions in the lecture with the greatest attendance (Group L). After every lecture's end, all presenters checked the *My events* page to explore the data and reflect on past presentations.

One presenter agreed strongly with the LIM App helping her reflect on experiences from work. On the statement that the LIM App has helped by providing information relevant for the decision to reflect, as seen in Figure 6.26, one presenter did not agree (Group S), but the other two did. The same two presenters agreed that the LIM App helped them remember and reconstruct an experience. It can be also seen in Figure 6.26 that the two presenters agreed on the statement that the LIM App helped them collect information relevant to reconstructing work experiences. They also agreed that relevant content is provided for the reflection to take place, where the presenter from Group S remained neutral. Allowing the audience members to send general feedback has proved to be a great support for reflection.

Related to the main goal of using the LIM App, all three presenters agreed that it is important to improve their presentation skills. When asked if they would use the LIM App regularly, every lecturer gave a different answer. In the case of Group M, the lecturer stated that he would use it regularly, as it allows the comparison of different teaching strategies. In the case of Group L, the answer was maybe, because it was not clear if the LIM App has distracted the students following the lecture. As for Group S, the answer on regularly using the LIM App was negative, being affected by the high interaction already existing in the group.

The evaluation results from the perspective of the audience were overall positive. In the informal interviews we had with them, Group M stated that it was a nice way to give some instant feedback and ask questions anonymously during the presentation. It was also discussed that, to truly benefit from the LIM App, a longer and more frequent use would be needed. Group S thought that it improves lecture participation and that they would rather be able to control the speed of the presentation to some degree.

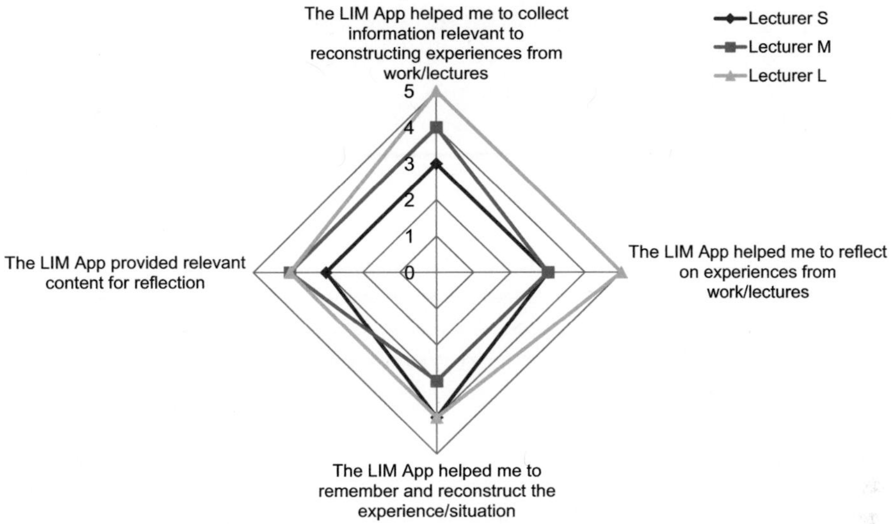

Figure 6.26.: Evaluation of reflection questions answered by the presenters—from 1 (strongly disagree) to 5 (strongly agree)

In Group M, when asked if the LIM App provided help in collaborating with other members of the audience, only 4 (22.22%) disagreed whereas 7 agreed and 2 agreed strongly (making it together 50%). Such results prove that by removing the chat, as suggested in our previous evaluation (Section 6.5), the level of useful collaboration did not drop. Additionally, 7 (38.88%) students stated that the LIM App guided them in re-evaluating an experience. When taking into consideration the average value of how many times the LIM App and its *My events* page were used, a correlation can be determined between agreeing on questionnaire statements and the frequency of using the LIM App.

In the feedback section at the end of the questionnaire, some students suggested embedding presentation slides in the application as it would result in using the LIM App more frequently. When asked if they would like to use the LIM App regularly, 4 (22.22%) students said yes and 11 (61.11%) students said maybe, also stating that (i) the LIM App is fun, (ii) better than the usual way of giving feedback, (iii) provides a possibility to participate personally in the lecture, (iv) allows asking questions and giving feedback anonymously, and (v) it is good to use it frequently so the lecturer is able to adapt to the needs of the students.

As for the Group S, to the statement that the LIM App was helping them pay more attention to the held mathematics lecture, 3 (27.27%) students strongly disagreed, 1 (9.09%) disagreed, 4 (36.36%) remained neutral, 1 (9.09%) agreed and 2 (18.18%) students did not answer at all. The majority, with 6 (54.54%)

students, agreed and 1 (9.09%) student strongly agreed on the statement that it is important to get involved in the lecture and contribute with feedback. However, it was experienced that the LIM App was not needed in such highly interactive small lectures.

Regarding Group L, the meter component was used during the entirety of the presentation. The general feedback functionality had a high usage and polls were used by the presenter as introduction in the topic. On providing help in collaborating with audience members, similar to Group M, 3 (27.27%) disagreed, 3 (27.27%) remained neutral, 5 (45.45%) agreed on the statement. When asked if the LIM App is guiding them in re-evaluating an experience, 5 (45.45%) students agreed and 4 remained neutral (36.36%). As for using the LIM App regularly, out of 10 students answering the question, 30.00% answered with maybe and 40.00% said yes, arguing in one case that it provides good reflection on the situation. Finally, students from all groups mostly agreed that it is important for presenters to constantly improve their presentation skills.

From the additional suggestions, four students stated that the topics shown on the evolution graph should display the additional information with which the topic was annotated on mouse click, as implemented in the *My events* page. One of the most suggested improvements was to incorporate the presentation slides in the LIM App and to correspondingly adapt the topic marking functionality because it would allow the audience members to take notes for a specific slide.

Being present during the lectures also provided some general insights on which factors are promoting or affecting the use of the LIM App. One interesting thing could be noticed in all groups regarding the motivation of data sharing. Taking Group S as an example, roughly five minutes after the lecture had started, the first topic was marked by a user. In a short while, three additional topic marks came, which were followed by two more in a few seconds. A topic mark by one user has clearly triggered the attention to the presentation context by the other users which they also recognized to being something important to remember later. Also, in one session of Group M, the LIM App was not once mentioned during the lecture and the presenter did not look at the LIM App at all which resulted in a very low usage of the application during the lecture. This fact showed that in order to get major benefits from the LIM App it is necessary to integrate the application in the lecture's normal workflow.

6.6.3. Discussion

In this evaluation, it was shown with the developed Live Interest Meter application how learning by reflection can be supported with a Quantified Self tool. This was the first evaluation of the LIM App in the field and allowed us to confirm the feasibility of the approach in a classroom setting. In accordance to the results of the analysis, reflection took place by the users who used the LIM App often. A key factor in collecting data for reflection is the presenter itself and how he or she engages the audience to participate and integrate the LIM App in the lecture. This relation was deducted from analyzing the questionnaires and seeing that the users who agreed with statements referring to the reflection support are the ones who actually used the LIM App most, during and after the presentation. This fact also suggests that a brief training would be needed in order to introduce the LIM App and optimally integrate it in the lecture. Taking the results into consideration, it is clear that the target areas for the LIM App are indeed presentations with a large audience number and little or no student-lecturer interaction.

6.7. Formative Evaluation III: Business, Research and Lectures

Before conducting the final summative evaluation, a formative evaluation with several professionals from the business, academic, and scientific branches was conducted. The goal of these small tests with end users in different work settings was twofold: (i) to widen the scope of usage of the Live Interest Meter and (ii) to refine the application and conduct the necessary preparations for the long-term summative evaluation. Additionally, some trials had to be performed and technical issues had to be solved in order to achieve a stable version that can be used in several university lectures during a long period of time.

These trials consisted of the usage of the Live Interest Meter for one to five sessions and were carried out in several settings: two business events organized by British Telecom and Tracoin Quality, two lectures at Karlsruhe Institute of Technology, a lecture at Cyprus University of Technology, and two presentations at FZI Research Center for Information Technology. The evaluation tools used to gather feedback from the participants include questionnaires and informal feedback from the speakers, depending on each concrete test.

A total of six professionals used the LIM App during their presentations. Table 6.6 shows an overview of tests that were conducted and, in the following, we explain the procedure and obtained results in detail.

Table 6.6.: Overview of formative trials: participants, time period, number of presentations, and evaluation tools used

ID	Profession	Country	Period	No.	Evaluation Tools
A	Managing Consultant	Netherlands	16-04-2013	1	Interview
B	Project Manager and Consultant	Netherlands	16-04-2013	1	Interview Audience feedback
C	Lecturer at University	Germany	02-07-2013 to 09-07-2014	2	Interview
D	Professor at University	Germany	21-10-2013 to 11-11-2013	3	Questionnaire Interview
E	Researcher and Lecturer	Cyprus	01-11-2013 to 07-11-2013	2	Questionnaire Interview
F	Researcher	Germany	16-01-2014	1	Questionnaire Interview

6.7.1. Tests in Business Context

The LIM has been tested twice in business scenarios. The first test took place on January 30, 2013 at the Learning Technologies Conference 2013, where one member of British Telecom (BT) gave a talk about MIRROR and "The role of reflection in learning." The second test was at the MIRROR Roadshow that British Telecom and Tracoin Quality organized on April 16, 2013 in the Netherlands. Presenters from the MIRROR team used the LIM App to get feedback from the members in the audience during their presentation. Informal feedback and comments were gathered in both events in order to inform the use of the app in business scenarios. Figure 6.27 shows a screenshot of the data report resulting from the MIRROR Roadshow event.

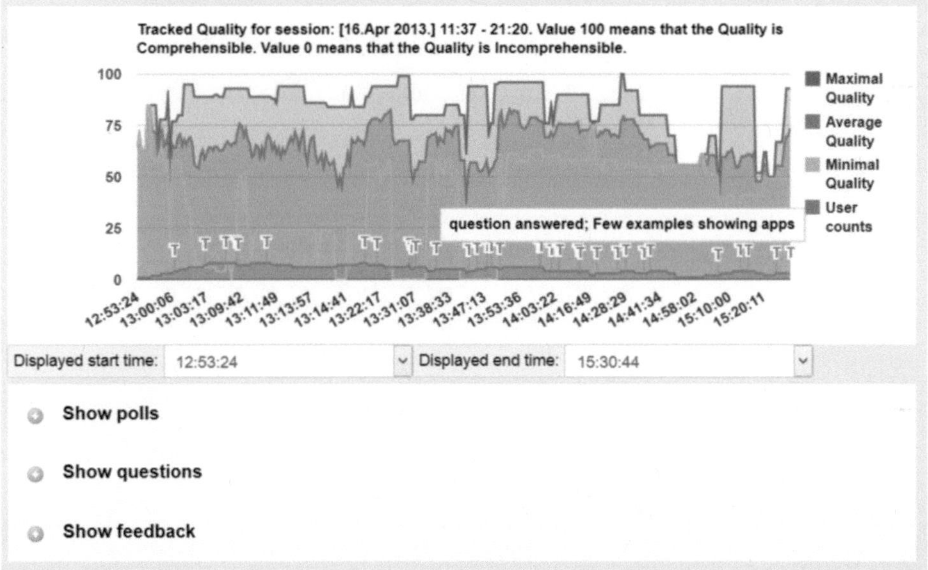

Figure 6.27.: Screenshot of the data report resulting from the MIRROR Roadshow presentation. Feedback trend and one of the gathered topics are displayed.

Seven members of the audience answered a survey with questions about their experience with the LIM App. These participants were 4 consultants (2 of them training consultants), 1 trainer/coach, 1 product manager, and 1 managing director. Out of these 7 participants, 5 considered it important to contribute with feedback to the presenter during his or her presentation. Some of their arguments were that *"a presenter could look at what the interest was in the things he or she was telling about. Therefore, the next time he or she could change these things in to more interesting ones or put a movie/picture between long texts,"* *"easy to follow and interpret,"* or *"great to submit questions."* The remaining two participants who did not agree stated their reasons: *"I think the presenter has to be coached, because you can also get very nervous if the feedback is negative. And the presenter must have the skills to change his way of presenting during the presentation. So maybe as part of a training session?"* and *"I find it difficult to listen and react at the same time."*

Two participants mentioned that the features they liked most where rating and feedback, and the history graphic, because *"you can see what other people think about the presentation and in which parts you thought differently."* Figure 6.28 shows the obtained results to the remaining questions, which were answered by 5 out of the 7 participants.

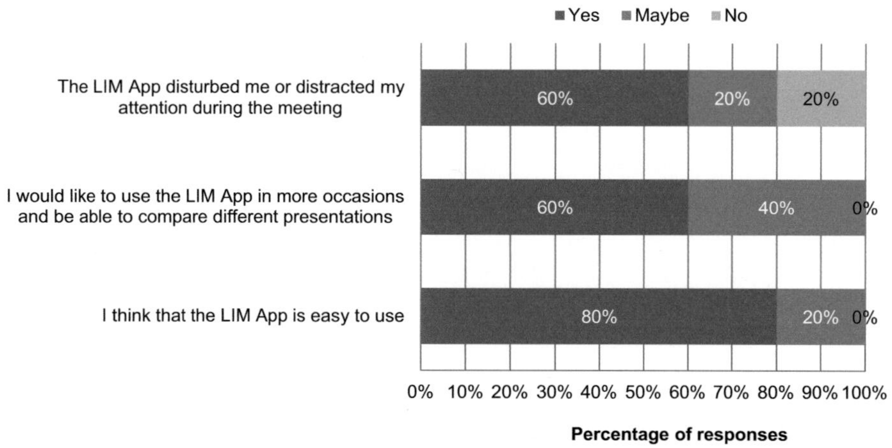

Figure 6.28.: Responses regarding usage of the LIM App ($N = 5$)

At the end of the meeting, we asked participants what they thought about improving performance by reflective learning apps on a team and organizational level. Some participants had a positive attitude:

"Working with apps is yet future for our organization. Gaming should be also introduced in teaching. A good start."

"People learn all the time just by doing their work. But people are not aware of this all the time. Reflective learning apps give tools to—on a structural basis—be aware of your learning activities, be proud on what you did very well and learn from challenging situations. And it gives the management or departments like ours the opportunity to decide which inventions are necessary to offer (to individuals, groups, teams, etc.)"

"I think these apps could really be of good use, because you can learn from your co-workers and also communicate about experiences. I think it will connect people and also make

them see that they are not alone in struggling trough difficult situations. I think the apps will make people talk more to each other about these difficult situations. Because the tools are simple to use, they can be very helpful for learning on demand."

However, other participants still had doubts about it:

"I think this can only be answered after I have tested 1 or 2 apps."

"It gives more tools, but I feel it could also shift the attention to the tool or the apparatus supporting it."

6.7.2. Tests in Scientific and Academic Contexts

Participants D, E and F answered a questionnaire to evaluate their experience with the LIM App. In the following, we summarize the main results of the questions included in the questionnaire (evaluated on a 5-point Likert scale, from 1 = strongly disagree to 5 = strongly agree).

Participant E agreed with the LIM App helping him or her to reflect on experiences from presentations, whereas Participants D and F remained neutral. To the question regarding whether they gained a better understanding of their audience, we obtained mixed results (Participant D = 2, Participant E = 3, and Participant F = 4). For all of them, capturing feedback during their presentations is useful to reflect and think about their presentation skills ($M = 3.67$; $SD = 0.58$). While Participants E and D agreed with the feedback chart in the data reports helping them to remember and restructure what happened during the presentation, Participant F disagreed. The lack of topics gathered by the audience and therefore visible in the report (there was only one topic mark) was the main reason for this.

Figure 6.29 shows the answers of the three participants to the app-specific questions which refer to the support of reflective learning. Results show that the advantages of the app were recognized mainly by participants E and F. The long-term usage and higher motivation to use the LIM app was rated higher by Participant F, than Participants D and E. One of the main issues behind these results is that participants D and E used the same network to connect to the Internet (which is offered by the university itself) and they had technical issues. However, Participant F did not experience any technical problem with the LIM App.

The three participants would recommend the LIM App to a friend or colleague. Two of them added a final comment to the questionnaire. Participant E mentioned that *"this is a great application that certainly has great potential to both students and instructors. The issues that I had were due to technological constraints (Wi-Fi issues etc). In general, I liked the application and I would certainly use it in other courses."*

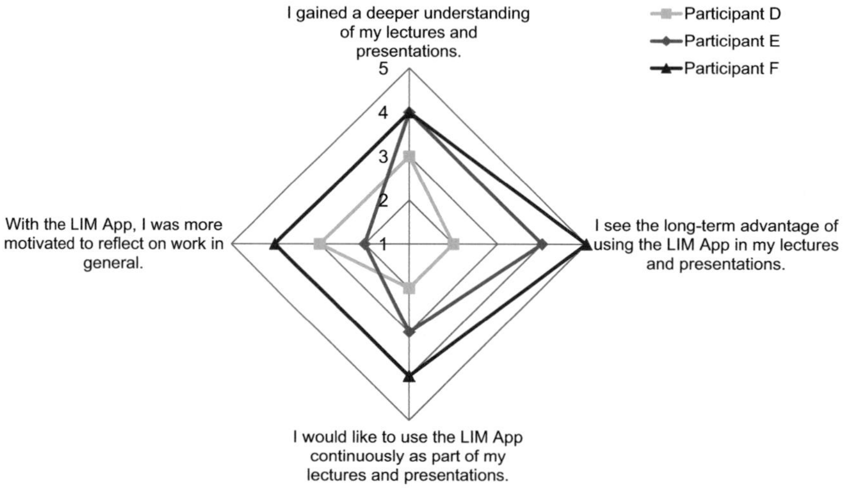

Figure 6.29.: Post-questionnaire results regarding the app-specific questions referring to reflective learning support

Participant F, who used the LIM App during a presentation in a research institution, commented on the usage of the app during the presentation itself: *"I did not use the app during the presentation because I was afraid I would be distracted. Further instructions would have been good before my presentation, because then I would have used it also during the presentation."* In this case, the speaker received a quick introduction before her talk, which was not enough to understand how much effort would be needed. Especially in sporadic uses of the LIM App (in contrast to presenters using it during; e.g., a whole semester), it is important to give clear instructions to avoid excessive fear of distraction from the speaker.

Questionnaires from Students

In the trial with Participant E, we distributed a questionnaire among the students ($N = 7$). All questions measured their agreement with the questions on a 5-point Likert scale (from 1 = strongly disagree to 5 = strongly agree). An exception to this was the technology acceptance, which was evaluated by a subset of the items contained in the Technology Acceptance Model (TAM) [Davis, 1989; Venkatesh and Davis, 2000; Fishbein and Ajzen, 1975] and using a 7-point Likert scale. The average score of the 15 items related to the lecturer's presentation skills was very high ($M = 4.70$; $SD = 0.69$). Students were satisfied with the lecture ($M = 4.43$; $SD = 0.53$) as well as with the interaction between them and the lecturer ($M = 4.86$; $SD = 0.38$). They felt motivated and admitted usually reflecting on what they had learned in past lectures (both $M = 4.00$; $SD = 0.58$).

They remained neutral to the statement that the comparison of their own feedback with the overall group feedback gave them useful information ($M = 3.20$) and that seeing other classmates giving feedback made them also want to do it ($M = 2.80$). They scored the LIM App helping them to pay more attention at the lecture slightly above the neutral value ($M = 3.20$). They were neutral with the fact that their classmates had asked questions which they would normally not ask ($M = 3.40$) and that they had asked questions by themselves ($M = 3.20$). Data gathering with the LIM App was considered as slightly relevant ($M = 3.60$).

Table 6.7 shows the descriptive values of the Technology Acceptance questionnaire, which was answered in the post-questionnaire only by the users who had used the LIM App in the two sessions ($N = 5$). The remaining two users stated why they had not used the app: *"Lecture purposes, I feel very good about the lectures and the lecturer!"* and *"I knew about it too late."*

Table 6.7.: Descriptive values (mean and standard deviation) for each construct of the technology acceptance questionnaire

Construct	***Mean***	***SD***
Perceived Enjoyment (PE)	4.20	1.52
Perceived Usefulness (PU)	4.24	1.33
Perceived Ease of Use (PEU)	4.35	1.31
Behavioral Intention (BI)	4.25	1.33

Interviews

Several interviews were conducted at the end of the trials, which are summarized in the following.

An interview with Participant E shed light on their experience and the feedback from the students. The things they liked most during the use of the LIM App were the feedback meter and the anonymous questions. They would like to use the former feature especially in cases where they are in a big auditorium and they are embarrassed to address questions to the speaker. The least clear aspects for them was the username that they had to use, as there was a pattern to follow in order to uniquely identify the users in the evaluation (as defined by the MIRROR Participant Code[13] used in our other evaluations). They would recommend the LIM App to friends and classmates, especially in cases of being in a big auditorium. Regarding future suggestions, they would suggest having a

[13] According to Knipfer et al. [2012], the MIRROR Participant Code consists of the following five characters: the first letter of the user's place of birth, the user's day of birth (two digits), the first letter of the user's father's first name, the first letter of the user's mother's first name.

type of notification or status symbol that indicates if they are connected to the right course (e.g., in case there are technical problems with the Wi-Fi).

Participant C is a lecturer at a German university and teaches very technical lectures which are part of a degree on Computer Science. Approximately 100 students were attending his lecture and 50% of them used the LIM App during two lecture sessions. In an interview with Participant C, he provided details about his experience with the app and the benefits it brings for him: *"In my specific case, I don't think that I can take profit of the Live Interest Meter, because the lecture is about predicate logic. For me it is clear that the comprehension of the topic can go down really fast and I am already aware of the parts that are difficult. In other words, if I put the limitations that a certain content has to be explained in 1.5 hours, the app does not help me change it."* Regarding his reaction to the feedback and potential changes that he could make, Participant C did not know what he could actually do: *"I cannot react/respond to the students during the lecture and afterwards I did not know, how I could explain things differently or better. I could not find any hint in the topics that the students captured."* Besides the belief that nothing could be changed, he came to some alternatives during the interview: *"I can only think of two possibilities: to lift the restrictions and for example have more time available to explain the content. This would need the adaptation of all the content as well as other lectures that build on this one. A second option would be using other didactic methods, different to the ones I am using. For example, the 'inverted classroom model' may be a suitable one."* In his opinion, he could imagine using the LIM App in other type of topics, which are more about hypothesis and arguments.

6.7.3. Discussion

In this formative study, we aimed at widening the scope of the LIM App and also investigating concrete benefits and challenges in other settings beyond the classroom. Results revealed that lecturers and presenters see an advantage in using the application and it helps them to know their audience better.

Major insights gained from these trials are related to the introduction of the application and other factors affecting its usage, rather than contributing to make design changes in the application. Nonetheless, the results obtained were of major significance to provide a basis for the execution of the subsequent summative evaluation.

6.8. Summative Evaluation I: Lecture at a German University

The goal of this summative evaluation was to study the impact of tracking and reflecting on feedback in lectures during a longer period of time. Through the usage of the Live Interest Meter (LIM App), we analyzed the acceptance of the tool, the support for reflection, and the impact on the lecturer's presentation skills. This summative study was conducted at a German university[14].

6.8.1. Procedure

The evaluation started on March 17, 2014 and lasted the whole semester, until June 25, 2014. One university professor who is teaching in two lectures participated in the evaluation. Both lectures were about Computer Science (Databases) and had a very similar content. The first lecture (Lecture A) took place on Wednesdays from 8:00 to 9:30 and was part of a Bachelor's degree on International Management. The second lecture (Lecture B) was scheduled on Mondays, also from 8:00 to 9:30, and was part of a Bachelor's degree on Business and Industrial Engineering.

The first day of each one of the lectures were introductory days, where students get to know the lecturer and the subject. Therefore, the LIM App was introduced by the professor himself on the second session. He was provided with a set of slides that described the LIM App and its usage, including registering, joining a group, giving feedback, using polls and questions, and visiting the data reports. The LIM App was used in every session of the lectures, except for those sessions which were canceled for external reasons (exercises session, vacation, or lecturer absence).

Participants

The lecturer is a male aged between 40 and 49. He has a full professor position and has been for 4 years in that position. He used the application during his teaching in two lectures: Lecture A with 52 and Lecture B with 77 students.

From all participants, 113 have answered the corresponding pre-questionnaire, containing demographic data. Out of these participants, 44 were students from Lecture A and consisted of 33 men and 11 women. All of them were between

[14] The name of the university is kept anonymous for privacy issues, in order to avoid the identification of the lecturer that participated in the evaluation.

20 and 29 years old. These students had studied on average for 6.27 (*SD* = 0.66) semesters, ranging from participants with 5 and to a maximum of 8 semesters studying. In Lecture B, 69 participants answered the pre-questionnaire, consist-ing of 20 men and 49 women. They were between 20 and 39 years old, with 99% of them aged between 20 and 29. Students in Lecture B had studied on average for 7.31 (*SD* = 1.01) semesters, ranging from participants with 4 and to a maximum of 9 semesters studying.

Evaluation Tools

As in previous summative evaluations (see Sections 4.9 and 4.10), we used the evaluation toolbox developed in the framework of the MIRROR Project [Knipfer et al., 2012], based on a modification of the Kirkpatrick model [Kirkpatrick and Kirkpatrick, 2006]. As mentioned before, members of the audience should also perceive a benefit in order to be motivated to give their feedback. Therefore, our evaluations not only considered the opinion of the professor, but also delivered insights about how the audience, concretely students, could also (i) improve their learning experiences by assessing their own learning and comparing themselves with their peers and (ii) assess the improvements on the presentation skills of the professor.

In the second lecture of the semester, professor and students were asked to fill in a pre-questionnaire including their consent form. During the semester, they were asked to use the LIM App to give feedback to the lecturer, and ask questions or answer polls whenever there was the need to do it. At the end of the semester, all participants were requested to fill in a post-questionnaire.

Table 6.8 provides an overview of used evaluation tools. Pre- and post-questionnaires measured agreement with questions on a 5-point Likert scale (from 1 = strongly disagree to 5 = strongly agree). The used questionnaires (pre- and post-) can be found in Appendix B. We used log data for descriptive statistics about app usage, and interviews to gain rich information about the evaluation.

The technology acceptance was evaluated through a subset of the items contained in the Technology Acceptance Model (TAM) [Davis, 1989; Venkatesh and Davis, 2000; Fishbein and Ajzen, 1975].

Table 6.8.: Live Interest Meter Summative Evaluation: evaluation tools used

Tool	Professor	Students
pre-questionnaire	consent form, demographic data, expectations regarding the app, lecture satisfaction, presentation skills, reflection scale	consent form, demographic data, expectations regarding the app, lecture satisfaction, presentation skills
post-questionnaire	usage and user satisfaction, lecture satisfaction, presentation skills, benefits and insights, reflection support, learning outcomes and behavior, reflection scale	usage and user satisfaction, lecture satisfaction, presentation skills, benefits and insights, technology acceptance, reflection support
final interview	feedback to the overall experience, subjective feeling of the application's acceptance within the students, capturing feedback, benefits and insights, general comments	-
log data	interactions with the application; e.g., times given feedback, questions asked, polls answered	

6.8.2. Results

Analogous to the summative evaluations presented in previous chapters, firstly, we report the results of the lecturer's questionnaire according to the four levels of Kirkpatrick [Kirkpatrick and Kirkpatrick, 2006]. Afterwards, we give details of the analysis conducted with the students' questionnaires. Finally, the feedback received in the interview with the lecturer is summarized.

Results: Lecturer's Assessment

An overview of the data gathered in each lecture (Lecture A and Lecture B) is offered in Table 6.9.

Table 6.9.: Overview of the number of students and the data collected in each lecture

	Lecture A	Lecture B	Total
Total no. of students	52	77	129
Pre-questionnaires	44	69	113
Post-questionnaires	34	51	85
Both questionnaires	20	32	52
Regularly used LIM*	22	16	38
Registered in LIM	50	56	106

*Answered 'yes' in the post-questionnaire

Reaction and Usage

The LIM App was used in a total of seven sessions in Lecture A and nine sessions in Lecture B. In two sessions (one of each lecture), the LIM App could not be used because of technical problems. The log data are summarized in Table 6.10, which indicates how many times the different features were used in each of the lectures.

Table 6.10.: Data gathered through log and application data

Feature	Lecture A	Lecture B	Total
Join group	81	178	259
Send feedback	1176	1629	2805
Ask question	3	1	4
Rate question	11	13	24
Answer poll	20	18	38
Add topic	1	1	2
Send written comments	1	3	4
Review data reports	8	64	72

Feedback on reaction and usage was not only analyzed with the logs, but also investigated through the post-questionnaire of the professor. Some of the important factors are the barriers that users encounter when using an application. We obtained satisfactory results regarding the possible barriers concerning the tool usage and reflection support. The participant disagreed (all ratings = 2) with all the mentioned barriers; i.e, not having time to use the app, not finding physical space to use it, not seeing an advantage in using or not being motivated to use the LIM App, and needing further training to get to know how it works.

The pre-questionnaire of the professor also included which expectations he had on the usage of the LIM App. He would like to receive from his students *"hints for concrete improvements (in contrast to general remarks)."* Among his expectations from such an application were having a simple tool for him and his students, being able to collect several types of comments, requiring a low interpretation effort, synchronizing with presentation material, and integrating it with tools he generally uses; e.g., PowerPoint.

At the end of the evaluation, the professor evaluated his satisfaction with respect to the LIM App. He disagreed with being overall satisfied. His comments at the end of the questionnaire revealed the main reasons for this: *"There are several important points missing in the app to make it really useful in my setting. To name what I believe are the most important three: (i) Automated tracking of presented material along the feedback stream: which was the slide that made students' attention decline? (ii) Automatic setup of courses without the need to stay online during the whole lecture. (iii) Built-in incentive scheme for participating students: I like to motivate my students for my lecture content and not for a feedback tool."*

Learning and Behavior Change

The measurement of the Short Reflection Scale (SRS) revealed a minor improvement when comparing the answers of the pre- and post-questionnaire (from a value of 3.1 to 3.2). There were mainly two aspects in which the participant improved his attitude: (i) the importance to him of good presentation skills and improving his lectures, and (ii) talking to colleagues about how to improve presentation skills.

We evaluated the learning outcomes through two questions in the post-questionnaire. To the question if he had made a conscious decision about how to behave in the future (CL1[15]), the participant disagreed. This was also the case for the question asking participants if he had gained a deeper understanding of his work life (CL2[16]). To the question if with the LIM App, he was more motivated to reflect on work in general, the participant remained neutral.

The overall attitude of the participant regarding the support of the LIM App was rather neutral. On the one hand, he agreed with capturing feedback during his presentations being useful to reflect and think about his presentation skills. He was also positive with respect to the overall goal of the LIM App and agreed

[15] CL1: "I made a conscious decision about how to behave in the future during my lectures and presentations."

[16] CL2: "I gained a deeper understanding of my lectures and presentations."

that it helped him reflect on experiences from his held lectures. On the other hand, he disagreed with the LIM App helping him identify significant concrete topics worth reflecting on. He remained neutral regarding the support of the data reports for gaining a better understanding of his students. Therefore, this was one of the main topics addressed in the subsequent interview.

In order to evaluate changes in behavior, the lecturer was asked in the post-questionnaire if the LIM App had helped him improve his work performance. He disagreed with this fact. This is in line with the previous questions on making a conscious decision and gaining a deeper understanding and, therefore, it follows the logic that no improvements can be achieved if these improvements are not previously identified.

Work Outcomes

We analyzed the data from the official evaluation survey conducted by the university at the end of each semester. Comparing the data from the previous semester with the semester during which the LIM App was used, there were no significant changes in the scores received by the lecturer.

Results: Students' Assessment

In the following, we present the analysis of the students' questionnaires. As in this particular scenario the students act as customers, their feedback also reveals insights on potential improvements on work outcomes, especially regarding his presentation skills.

From the 44 participating students in Lecture A, 22 (50%) answered in the post-questionnaire that they had regularly used the LIM App. In the case of Lecture B, which had 69 students participating in the evaluation, this number was 16 (23%). Therefore, only this subgroup of students answered the questions related to the LIM App usage. They remained neutral to the statement that the comparison of their own feedback with the overall group feedback gave them useful information ($M = 2.95$) and that seeing other classmates giving feedback made them also want to do it ($M = 2.74$). They did not agree that the LIM App had helped them pay more attention to the presentation/lecture ($M = 1.82$). They disagreed ($M = 1.97$) with having asked questions by themselves which they would normally not ask, but rated with a higher score ($M = 2.45$) the fact that their classmates had done it.

The post-questionnaire of students also covered questions regarding the self-reported capturing method used and the gathering of the data with the LIM App. Their answers are summarized in Figure 6.30.

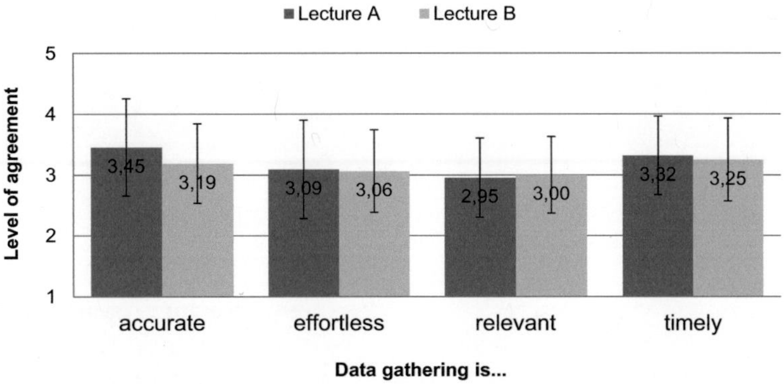

Figure 6.30.: Data gathering by the LIM App evaluated by students: accurate, effortless, relevant, and timely

Table 6.11 shows the descriptive values of the Technology Acceptance questionnaire, which was answered in the post-questionnaire only by users admitting to having used the LIM App regularly ($N = 38$).

Table 6.11.: Descriptive values (mean and standard deviation) for each construct of the technology acceptance questionnaire

	Lecture A ($N = 22$)		**Lecture B ($N = 16$)**	
Construct	***Mean***	***SD***	***Mean***	***SD***
Perceived Enjoyment (PE)	3.83	1.17	3.29	1.22
Perceived Usefulness (PU)	2.65	1.18	2.59	1.10
Perceived Ease of Use (PEU)	4.42	1.56	4.41	1.34
Behavioral Intention (BI)	3.07	1.34	2.83	1.38

In order to establish a comparison of the lecture before the usage of the LIM App and after it, we asked in the pre- and in the post-questionnaire questions regarding several aspects of the lecture, the presentation skills of the lecturer, and the attitude of the students. In the following, we show the results of these answers, taking into consideration only participants who answered both questionnaires ($N = 52$). Table 6.12 shows the answers to the questions related to the lecture itself. Table 6.13 shows the answers to the questions related to the lecturer and his presentation skills.

Table 6.12.: Average values for items from the post-questionnaire regarding their attitude towards the lecture (*N* = 38)

	Lecture A (*N* = 20)		Lecture B (*N* = 32)	
Questionnaire Item	**Pre**	**Post**	**Pre**	**Post**
I am in general satisfied with this lecture.	4.15 (*SD* = .49)	4.15 (*SD* = .59)	3.94 (*SD* = .62)	4.16 (*SD* = .51)
I am satisfied with my participation during the lecture.	3.55 (*SD* = .60)	3.40 (*SD* = .82)	3.44 (*SD* = .62)	3.66 (*SD* = .79)
I am satisfied with the interaction between me and the lecturer.	3.85 (*SD* = .75)	3.70 (*SD* = .66)	3.50 (*SD* = .72)	3.69 (*SD* = .78)
I always pay attention during the lecture.	3.50 (*SD* = .69)	4.00 (*SD* = .46)	3.47 (*SD* = .88)	3.66 (*SD* = .75)
I easily get distracted during the lecture.	2.50 (*SD* = .89)	2.40 (*SD* = .68)	2.94 (*SD* = .84)	2.81 (*SD* = .78)
I am usually very active during the lecture.	2.30 (*SD* = .73)	2.50 (*SD* = .89)	2.47 (*SD* = .76)	2.53 (*SD* = .84)
I feel confident about asking questions during the lecture whenever I need to.	3.40 (*SD* = .68)	3.90 (*SD* = .55)	3,41 (*SD*=1.01)	3.59 (*SD* = .95)
I feel socially integrated in the lecture.	3.65 (*SD* = .59)	3.95 (*SD* = .51)	3.59 (*SD* = .71)	3.78 (*SD* = .55)
I feel motivated in the lecture.	3.70 (*SD* = .73)	4.05 (*SD* = .76)	3.56 (*SD* = .95)	3.59 (*SD* = .71)
I usually reflect about what I learned in past lectures.	2.95 (*SD* = .83)	3.45 (*SD* = .89)	3.09 (*SD* = .89)	3.34 (*SD* = .87)
Total average	3.36 (*SD* = .89)	3.55 (*SD* = .91)	3.34 (*SD* = .89)	3.48 (*SD* = .88)

Table 6.13.: Average values for items from the post-questionnaire regarding the presentation skills of the lecturer ($N = 38$)

	Answers ($N = 52$)	
Questionnaire Item	**Pre**	**Post**
The speed/pace of his/her speech is always appropriate.	3.73 (*SD* = .89)	3.87 (*SD* = .84)
His/Her vocal expressiveness (volume, pronunciation, tone) in his/her talks is adequate.	4.19 (*SD* = .66)	4.35 (*SD* = .48)
He/She always seems to feel confident during his/her presentations and lectures.	4.44 (*SD* = .61)	4.38 (*SD* = .66)
He/She always finishes the presentations on time and achieves to present all the contents.	4.04 (*SD* = .68)	3.92 (*SD* = .62)
He/She always uses clear examples in the presentations.	3.92 (*SD* = .81)	4.13 (*SD* = .66)
In his/her talks, the lecturer uses a comprehensible/understandable speech.	4.06 (*SD* = .73)	4.15 (*SD* = .64)
The slides are always appropriate to the audience (format and style).	3.83 (*SD* = .81)	3.79 (*SD* = .75)
I am always motivated and interested in his/her talk.	3.69 (*SD* = .83)	3.65 (*SD* = .79)
I am always engaged and participate in his/her presentations.	3.25 (*SD* = .71)	3.40 (*SD* = .75)
He/She always establishes eye-contact with the audience.	4.13 (*SD* = .60)	4.27 (*SD* = .63)
His/Her presentations have always a very high quality and look professional.	4.13 (*SD* = .56)	4.25 (*SD* = .56)
The lecturer collects feedback about the lecture and his/her performance.	4.31 (*SD* = .67)	4.02 (*SD* = .73)

In order to gain insights about the main barriers for usage, we asked participants who did not regularly use the LIM app (12 from Lecture A, 35 from Lecture B) what the reasons behind their decision were. We obtained information from 37 out of these 47 users. After analyzing the comments, we now present a summary of the main reasons in Table 6.14.

Table 6.14.: Reasons of students for not using the LIM App during lectures, classified in users and non-users

Reason	Non-users	Users	Total
Device issues: too old, not smartphone or iPhone	14	2	16
Distraction	8	3	11
Internet connection	7	3	10
Battery or data volume insufficient	6	3	9
Problems with the app (login or other type)	5	4	9
Too complicated/stressful	5	0	5
No interest, no motivation or no need	3	2	5

Finally, students could add any comments about the evaluation and the usage of the LIM App. Some of them highlighted the problems that they encountered and their answers are summarized in Table 6.14. Other users commented on the issues that had worked well or they liked in the LIM App; e.g., *"I found it very useful for questions after the lecture"* or *"one of the best lectures this semester; the lecturer always made sure that everybody is on track."*

Interview with the Lecturer

At the end of the evaluation, we conducted an interview with the lecturer, summarized below. The goal of the interview was to gain further insights about the general experience of using the LIM App, which improvements he would suggest, how well the features of the LIM App worked, and what the impact on reflection was.

General experience with the LIM App
He liked the idea of having a back-channel to get feedback from the students. However, he was missing mainly three things:

- The method was too invasive in terms of group configuration: *"At the beginning of the lecture, I had to set up the group and configure the parameters. In some lectures, I had no need to connect to the Internet because I only had the slides. I had to go online in order to log in to the LIM App, configure the group and set up the timer. That meant too many steps and it was the same procedure every time."*
- *"The network was unfortunately too unreliable. Therefore, the application was often stopped."* The professor would like to have a new session mechanism that is independent of the lecturer. The perfect solution for him would be *"a calendar view where I can register when I have a lecture. Then I should only configure everything at the beginning of the semester and then it would work automatically. This way, I could just go to the lecture and say 'the LIM App is active so please everybody log in to the group'."*
- The incentive mechanism seems to be too weak. He mentioned that the lecture is already very good and the students do not have many issues or complaints to communicate during the lecture. They know they can evaluate the lecture in the official final evaluation: *"students do not want an extra effort as they know there is an official channel. In the official evaluation, I just received little criticism to the didactic, but rather about the content of the lecture (for example, not being interested in it)."*

The interviewee continued explaining how the evaluation method works at his university: *"The incentive mechanism for the official evaluation is also very weak. We do a lottery among students. We give cards with IDs to the students so that they can answer anonymously. Only 50% of the 116 cards that they distributed were used to answer the evaluation survey."* Additionally, he mentioned that students from Lecture B have more interest in Informatics because they are studying a more technical degree and therefore give better assessments.

He explained that, at the beginning, many people started using the LIM App, around 30-35 users. Afterwards, it started to decrease until approximately 15 students remained active in the third week. And he also added: *"I motivated my students to follow my topics, but I could not motivate them to use the app."*

Figure 6.31 shows an example of a report that the professor described during the interview: *"I could identify a pattern. In the beginning it goes up, then it goes down. After 45 minutes I always do a break and you can recognize this in the data. In the breaks, I used to show the data to my students and comment on it. It would make sense to show it in the main screen live because I did not have a second monitor where I could look at it."*

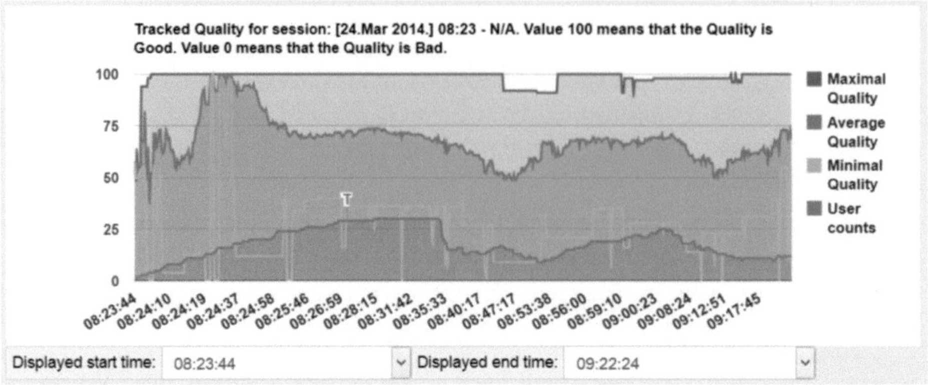

Figure 6.31.: Screenshot of a LIM data report of one of the lectures during the evaluation

Potential improvements

We started talking about the reports and what could be improved: *"When exploring the reports, I could actually identify when something happened; e.g., where the attention of my students went down. The problem was more to reconstruct where exactly it was. I have shown the reports to my students and we had a look at them together. They could reconstruct the situation well, but I could not. I can identify where there are holes but the mapping to the concrete content is missing."*

One of the proposals he did was having a tool where you could upload the PDF of the presentation to the browser. This way, everything would be in the system and we could do a mapping between each slide and the feedback being given. Regarding technical issues, he also mentioned that one of his students told him that the Android app consumed a high data volume and therefore this could be improved.

"I liked the mechanism to get feedback and especially doing it in big groups (80-90 people). Maybe I would not do it in each lecture, but choose some of them (e.g., 3–4 times in a semester). This would also contribute to the motivation of students." He liked the fact that there are a web application and an Android application available. However, he missed a version for iOS.

Methodology for the LIM App usage

We discussed with the professor the methodology that we had followed in this evaluation. In this case, we had given him the tool without influencing how he uses it; e.g., not not making him to set goals at the beginning of the semester or fixing which aspects he wants to get feedback on. He mentioned that having a kind of consulting around the app that guides the lecturer would only bring something for new colleagues and added that *"it also depends on the type of person, but I don't think it may be necessary. For example, there are lecturers that have been working for many years, and either they do a lot of lectures and they master them or they have experience but they don't care about having a good lecture... and therefore such a consulting would not be suitable for them."*

Exchange with students
"I talked to them after the breaks and told them when I had noticed something relevant in the report." He also mentioned that sometimes he noticed that they had not understood a certain slide and he repeated the explanation. When discussing the types of issues mentioned by students, he added: *"Whenever I received feedback about the app it was because of technical problems."*

Usage of features
With respect to his preferred feature, he mentioned: *"The timeline in the report. However, I would really like to have the link to the slides."* He explained afterwards that he had a meticulous control of the slides that he has planed for each lecture and how many he actually achieves to explain. He could usually achieve around 80% of the slides he had prepared for a certain lesson.

He also commented on the usage of the reports: *"At the beginning I used to check the reports very often, but later I did not do it so often because students were not participating so actively. I used to check them on Sundays before preparing the next lecture."*

Changes at work
"I cannot think of any big change. However, I took the time to reflect on it and think about possible improvements. The stimulus or push was already there, because you get it explicitly displayed and you can confirm it." He mentioned that he could more or less identify which slides were really bad and he then changed them, but did not do a big didactic reorganization or change in methodology. However, he confirmed that *"using the LIM App prompted the initiative of making small changes."* The interviewee made further comments on the general necessity of receiving concrete suggestions for professional development (e.g., in courses or training), if a lecturer wants to make big changes in his or her didactic method; e.g., getting to know what works better nowadays with students. He could envision such a methodology supported by the LIM App: *"I could imagine analyzing several sessions automatically in the app and suggesting the suitable didactic method for it. For example, if it is detected that the feedback goes down after 20 minutes in several lessons, then the system would suggest doing an exercise after 20 minutes."*

6.8.3. Discussion

Summarizing the results of this evaluation, the lecturer reflected on the gathered data and which potential changes he should do thanks to the use of the LIM App. Although he did not make major changes in the lecture, he did perform small changes in his daily presentations.

Some technical problems limited the experience, which caused the students' satisfaction with the application to be rather low. The professor did not actively react to changes in the students' feedback during the lectures and this may have also influenced their motivation.

It was suggested that the most suitable methodology would be using the LIM App three to four times per semester, as a kind of measuring tool. This may also function as an additional incentive to increase the participation of the students.

One of the solicited features is automatic integration of the presented material along the feedback stream; i.e., keeping track of which slide was presented at each point in time. Another suggestion was providing automatic setup of courses. However, this would turn the LIM App into a more complex system that cannot be used as an add-on in every presentation.

In previous studies, we had identified some concerns regarding the students voluntarily participating and giving feedback. Although this was not the case in all the scenarios where the LIM App was used, this was definitely one of the main challenges in this summative evaluation. To this extent, we investigated the impact of gamification—'the use of game design elements in non-game contexts' [Deterding et al., 2011]—to increase the motivation of students to use the Live Interest Meter App. Based on an extended literature review on gamification, we conducted an online experiment to analyze the users' intention to use an adapted version of the Live Interest Meter with and without gamification. The results show that perceived fun has a positive effect on the motivation to use the LIM and the motivation to use the application with gamification is significantly higher than for the application without it. Therefore, gamification seems to be an appropriate enabler to engage people in using QS approaches as personal learning tool for improving learning experiences. For further details about this online experiment, the reader can refer to its publications [Morschheuser et al., 2014a,b]. Regarding the limitations of this study, the sample size was insufficient to validate the hypothesis with a between-subject test. However, meaningful tendency for gamification was indicated between-subject and the performed within-subject analysis showed high significant results. Furthermore, the measurement was hypothetical and self-reported. In order to implement the gamification concept in the LIM App, the implementation of what we dubbed

"LIM-Community," a platform to review previous presentations, analyze the personal learning behavior and interact with other users, was needed. This would have limited the work settings that were targeted by the LIM App; i.e., support in business and research settings would not be possible anymore. Therefore, larger experiments of the gamified LIM App in real classroom settings could not be conducted. Nonetheless, this study provided a first important contribution to the successful use of gamification approaches for improving interaction and supporting individual reflective learning with Quantified Self tools to gather audience feedback.

6.9. Related Work

The Live Interest Meter has some functions in common with what are known as Audience Response Systems (ARS). Despite these partially overlapping features, there is a substantial difference with respect to the goal we pursue. ARS aim at improving interaction between speakers and audience in formal settings, but do not address the support of reflective learning to improve one's presentation skills and, therefore, work performance. Other application-oriented approaches aim at supporting reflection in formal settings (e.g., school, university) but the collected data are mainly related to the students' activity. In the following, we review these approaches and outline existent similarities and differences between them and our work.

6.9.1. Audience Response Systems and Real-Time Feedback

Audience Response Systems (ARS), also known as clickers, enable instructors in a large lecture class to instantaneously collect student responses to a posted question, generally multiple choice. The answers are immediately tallied and graphically displayed on a classroom projection screen where both students and instructor can see and discuss them [Caldwell, 2007]. These systems generally aim at improving student outcomes such as improved exam scores or passing rates, student comprehension, and learning, as well as student attendance and interest on the course. Clickers have evolved from the original hardware versions with remote control [Barber and Njus, 2007; Bunce et al., 2010; Debourgh, 2008] to more recent mobile and web-based versions [Andergassen et al., 2012; Duncan and Mazur, 2005; Kundisch et al., 2012; Rubner, 2012].

The review of available tools has revealed that there has been and still is quite a lot of research and development done on Audience Response System and their challenges, both from a technical and pedagogical perspective. Especially since 2013, a growing interest in ARS has taken place in the research community and universities worldwide, but also from a business perspective[17]. The aim of these tools and their evaluations was usually to encourage students (i) to have richer interactions with their lecturers/presenters [Ada, 2013; Holzer et al., 2013], (ii) to support teaching methods like peer instruction from a pedagogical perspective [Kundisch et al., 2012; Quibeldey-Cirkel et al., 2013] or (iii) to study the technical introduction of mobile devices and smartphones in university environments [Scheele et al., 2003; Wessels et al., 2007; Feiten et al., 2013]. However, our work is the first approach to investigate the usefulness of the data for reflective learning purposes and therefore addresses the existing gap on research which has concentrated on supporting students' interaction. With our work, we investigate the main challenges of reconstructing experiences for reflective learning as well as quantifying data which is mainly abstract and has not been available for learning processes until now.

Classic Polling Systems

There are also some approaches that explore questions and answers (Q&A) in a bidirectional way; i.e., not only the lecturer can create questions to evaluate students, but students can also pose questions. The digital back-channel Backstage [Hadersberger et al., 2012] provides microblog-based communication for fast information exchange among students as well as from audience to lecturer. In learning settings with a large and typically passive audience, the goal of Backstage is to foster active participation and facilitate collaboration akin to small learning groups. They also present an approach to aging of microblog messages, based on the back-channel activity, to ensure that attention during a lecture is directed to recent and active messages.

A system called mbclick has been developed by the University of Manchester. It offers the basic functionality of any ARS; i.e., ask questions to the audience but this system is designed around the idea that giving feedback closes the learning gap between what students already know and what their instructor wants them to know. Therefore, the system allows further explaining why a particular response is correct or not, which are delivered directly to individual students after they have answered.

In Akbari et al. [2010], the authors describe and evaluate MiRA, which is also a microblogging-based system designed to enable all way communication between participants of a mass lecture. Their main goal is to support a more active learning experience, in spite of the size and layout of large lecture halls. It can be

[17] http://letsfeedback.com
http://www.gosoapbox.com
http://www.questionpress.com

accessed and used both during and after a lecture to track and solve problems and questions. To give feedback to the lecturer, it is suggested that an assistant collects the questions and problems during the lecture and proposes them in a short break.

From a formal learning perspective, audience response systems have been typically used as technical support for an interactive teaching method called Peer Instruction, coined by Harvard Professor Eric Mazur [Mazur, 1997]. This is the case of PINGO—"Peer Instruction for very large groups"—, a web-based classroom response system that has been developed at the University of Paderborn [Kundisch et al., 2012; Beutner et al., 2014]. PINGO is intended to be a polling system and, therefore, only allows creating and sending questions that should be answered by the audience (e.g., single or multiple choice questions).

Another example where the use of ARS was studied from a didactic point of view is the browser-based mobile clicker implemented and integrated in the learning and communication platform of the WU—Vienna University of Economics and Business. A pilot study of this clicker with the aim of activating students during lectures is presented in Andergassen et al. [2013].

In this category of tools and in the academical context, there are also some available products. For example, ShakeSpeak[18] is a plug-in for MS PowerPoint that allows users to insert questions in the slides. During the lecture, students can vote and answer the presenter's questions by sending an SMS, accessing the Internet, or writing a message on Twitter. During the presentation, it is possible to show a graphic with the responses of the audience to a question. A similar approach is also Poll Everywhere[19]. Another example is Socrative[20], an online mobile student response system that empowers teachers to engage their classrooms through a series of educational exercises and games via smartphones, laptops, and tablets. It allows teachers to send different types of questions to their students; i.e., multiple choice, true/false and short Q&A, as well as pre-prepared quizzes. Reports on the students' answers are available for the teacher in different forms.

Real-Time Feedback at University

Besides the clickers discussed above, there are other projects that have developed systems to support real-time feedback during lectures at university. Notebook University Karlsruhe (NUKATH) [Bonn et al., 2003] was a project funded by the German BMBF from 2002 to 2003, aiming to develop and assess a multitude of

[18] http://www.shakespeak.com
[19] http://www.polleverywhere.com
[20] http://www.socrative.com

possible usages of notebooks in academia. NUKATH had 10 subprojects, one of which was AMSULA (Applications of mobile systems), which conducted a large survey among over 1,000 students on the concepts and goals of a notebook university. The results showed that most students would welcome electronic aids. AMSULA also developed several tools for cooperation, which enabled electronic feedback, electronic hand-raising, and multiple choice polls with live results. Those tools were developed mainly for notebooks, but a web client for PDAs was tested, although PDAs were not as common as today's smartphones. Currently, the NUKATH tool has been updated and it is called nuKIT. The NUKATH platform received little interest on the student side until about 2011, when apparently due to an increased availability of mobile devices such as smart phones, laptops, or tablets in the classroom, the platform achieved a major revival [Pfeiffer-Bohnen et al., 2013]. The main goal of nuKIT is to serve as a polling service during the lecture, allowing also giving feedback about the speed of the lecturer.

WIL/MA Toolkit—Wireless Interactive Learning Mannheim— is another project related to real-time feedback; it is developed at the University of Mannheim. Its aim is to facilitate a bidirectional and synchronous communication between lecturer and students, as well as to offer an interactive lecture [Scheele et al., 2003; Wessels et al., 2007]. It allows the presenter to define several rating scales for any parameter they would like to asses; e.g., the speed of the lecture or noise in the environment.

Most of these systems were either obsolete or developed later, in parallel to the LIM App, as it is shown by the publications of these colleagues from other universities. This shows the contemporary relevance of building systems that gather feedback from students in university lectures. However, the main difference between these projects and our work is the use of the data to support reflective learning and improve professional work performance, rather than to enhance interaction during lectures.

Integrated Feedback Commercial Solutions

Many of these commercial solutions are the update of the old clickers (based on hardware remote controls) to current society trends and the growing availability of mobile devices.

A commercial classroom response system called GoSoapBox[21] is offered by Go Education, LLC with the aim of enhancing students' engagement in class. This tool has a confusion barometer where students can state if they do not understand something, social Q&A to post a question at any point during the

[21] `http://www.gosoapbox.com`

lecture, discussions that the instructor suggests and students can discuss a certain topic, anonymous polls posed by the instructor, and quizzes which can be sent by e-mail later. In Munday [2012], the author presents a case study to explore the use of GoSoapBox. A survey of students using this classroom response system in class found that they enjoyed using the tools provided, from discussions to question and answer sessions, and recommended continued use of the program. At a first sight, GoSoapBox and the LIM App offer similar functions. However, GoSoapBox was created to manage the whole dynamic of a lecture as well as students' knowledge. Therefore, data from functions like the confusion barometer, which would be helpful for the speaker to reflect upon, is only available during the lecture and stored data only includes questions, polls, and quizzes.

Piazza[22] is a wiki style format platform for questions and answers (Q&A) that allows both lecturers and students to add any post to the system wall. A post can be a note (a comment which does not need an answer), a question, or a poll with several options for answers. Posts can be addressed directly to the instructor or to the whole audience. Piazza aims to offer support both during and after lectures, by allowing instructors to manage their lecture content and student communication.

Out of the educational context and with the goal of helping audience members engage fully in enterprise presentations, Teevan et al. [2012] have developed a mobile application to provide real-time feedback. Aggregated feedback is displayed in a visualization during the presentation, with notifications on interesting feedback events. The interface allows providing positive feedback using a green *thumbs up* button and negative feedback using a red *thumbs down* button. Participants in their study conducted in a large enterprise meeting report that providing feedback helped them pay close attention to the presentation and enabled them to feel connected with other audience members.

Most of the related work about clickers explores and focuses on giving a benefit for students and are tightly related to the content of the lectures and the knowledge they acquire, being limited to polling of questions and answers in many cases. This is associated with the fact that their main goal is to improve the learning process of the students (formal learning), while our work is focused on workplace learning. Therefore, we consider the lecturers and presenters as the center of the scenario and focus on the improvement of their presentation skills and performance with the use of the LIM App. In this case, students play a very important role, as they are the ones who provide feedback that serves for the reflection process and, therefore, they also have to perceive a benefit on the tool. The feedback meter function was enriched with other features that support the

[22] `http://piazza.com`

lecture like polls and questions and are intended to improve the lecture itself, but also to add context to the feedback given to the lecturer.

In order to identify the similarities and differences between the LIM App and other available tools, we analyzed and compared eight different tools: nuKIT[23], ARSnova[24], Tweedback[25], Pingo[26], ShakeSpeak[27], Piazza[28], Socrative[29], and GoSoapBox[30]. The first analysis of tools was done in 2011. Afterwards, the analysis was updated in 2012 and published in Rivera-Pelayo et al. [2013a,b]. We have updated the analysis in August 2014 to ensure an up-to-date review of existing research. The analyzed tools were selected among the related work according to their level of maturity (e.g., studies that have been conducted with the tools) and their higher degree of similarity with the LIM App (e.g., we discarded the tools that only allow sending polls to the audience or solely receiving anonymous questions from them). Tables 6.15, 6.16, and 6.17 give a comparative overview of these tools and the last prototype of the LIM App with respect to their characteristics, purpose, and use case.

[23] http://elearning.studium.kit.edu/179.php
[24] https://www.arsnova.eu
[25] http://www.tweedback.com
[26] http://pingo.upb.de
[27] http://www.shakespeak.com
[28] http://piazza.com
[29] http://www.socrative.com
[30] http://www.gosoapbox.com

Table 6.15.: Comparison of ARS: LIM App 1.0, nuKIT, ARSnova

Category	Criterion	LIM App 1.0	nuKIT	ARSnova
General	Provider	FZI Research Center for Information Technology	Karlsruhe Institute of Technology (DE)	Technische Hochschule Mittelhessen (DE)
	Application type	Web and mobile (Android)	Web and mobile (Android)	Web
	Goal	Quantification of abstract feedback, reflection support	Lightweight communication tool for within-lecture use	Support PI, live feedback and just-in-time teaching
	Communication	Presenter - Audience Audience - Audience	Presenter - Audience	Presenter - Audience
	Application time	Live & retrospectively	Live	Live
	Target group	Universities, conferences, speakers	Universities	Universities
Feedback	Type(s)	Configurable parameter	Speed	Speed
	Representation	Line chart with max, min, avg and own value	Bar chart	Bar chart
Functions	Polling	✓	✓	✓
	Quiz	✗	✓	✓
	Ask questions	✓	✓	✓
	Question rating	✓	✗	✗
	Chat	✗	✗	✗
	History	✓	✗	✗
	Written feedback	✓	✗	✗
Data	Storage	✓	-	-
	Data reports	Feedback, polls, questions, comments, topics	-	-

Table 6.16.: Comparison of ARS: Tweedback, Pingo, ShakeSpeak

Category	Criterion	Tweedback	Pingo	ShakeSpeak
General	Provider	University of Rostock (DE)	University of Paderborn (DE)	Shakespeak
	Application type	Web	Web and Android app	Web
	Goal	Allow feedback from students in very large lectures	Involve students in the lecture by answering questions	Let students ask / answer questions with mobile devices
	Communication	Presenter - Audience	Presenter - Audience	Presenter - Audience
	Application time	Live and retrospectively	Live	Live
	Target group	Universities	Universities	Universities
Feedback	Type(s)	Panic-button	-	-
	Representation	Line chart	-	-
Functions	Polling	✓	✓	✓
	Quiz	✓	✗	✗
	Ask questions	✓	✗	✗
	Question rating	✓	✗	✗
	Chat	✗	✗	✗
	History	✗	✗	✗
	Written feedback	✗	✗	✓
Data	Storage	✓	✓	✓
	Data reports	Quiz results, chatwall	-	Excel/PDF with aggregated results

Table 6.17.: Comparison of ARS: Piazza, Socrative, GoSoapBox

Category	Criterion	Piazza	Socrative	GoSoapBox
General	Provider	Piazza Technologies	Socrative, Inc.	Go Education, LLC
	Application type	Web, iOS / Android app	Web, iOS / Android app	Web
	Goal	Community-edited Q&A platform during / after lecture	Engage and assess students with educational activities	Increase students' engagement during lectures
	Communication	Presenter - Audience Audience - Audience	Presenter - Audience	Presenter - Audience Audience - Audience
	Application time	Live and retrospectively	Live	Live
	Target group	Schools, Universities	Schools	School, Universities
Feedback	Type(s)	-	-	Confusion barometer
	Representation	-	-	Absolute number, history
Functions	Polling	✓	-	✓
	Quiz	✗	✓	✓
	Ask questions	✓	✗	✓
	Question rating	✗	✗	✓
	Chat	✓	✗	✓
	History	✓	✗	✗
	Written feedback	✓	✗	✓
Data	Storage	✓	✓	✓
	Data reports	Wall with all posts	Excel with students' answers	Excel with students' answers to polls, quizzes, and questions

The feedback mechanism is the central element of the LIM App and was intended to be its greatest benefit. After having analyzed several tools, we can see that the quantification of feedback is one of the major differences and no other tools capture and represent users' feedback by using an analogy such as the meter. The LIM meter gives audience the flexibility of a scale and at the same time an easy-to-use and intuitive interface. For speakers, it provides the freedom of choosing which time of feedback is desired and detailed analysis of the current status during the presentation as well as the feedback trends in retrospective. In contrast to other tools, the LIM App does not offer further features to support interaction between the members of the audience like allowing members of the audience to answer others' questions (like GoSoapBox) or having an online forum (like Piazza). Our studies revealed that these features, despite adding interaction could also be a high source of distraction. This, along with the fact that such forums or chat do not add valuable information to reflect upon, guided the decision of not including it in the final prototype of the LIM App. Compared to other tools, one of the weaknesses of the LIM App is not allowing users to create quizzes or polls before opening the presentation session (i.e., some hours before). However, this feature had no influence on our research work and, therefore, it received a lower priority. Finally, to our knowledge, none of the available applications target the support of reflective learning for lecturers and speakers and, therefore, make an emphasis on creating reports with the data that has been gathered during the presentation. Tools that provide similar reports concentrate on pedagogical evaluating measures like individual students' activity, right or wrong answers to polls, and posted questions.

6.9.2. Enhancing Reflection

In the field of Technology-Enhanced Learning, there are few approaches to support self-reflection and increase awareness for learners and teachers, mainly centered on the activities of the students. One such system is the Student Activity Meter (SAM) [Govaerts et al., 2012], which provides a set of visualizations to be used in digital learning platforms (or LMS) where teachers and students can not physically interact. The system aggregates the data to calculate different metrics like total time spent and number of resources used by a student. It aims to provide teachers a way to assess their students' performance and to give students a way to compare their own progress with the group's, as well as the teachers' expectations. Another example is the EnquiryBlogger presented by Ferguson et al. [2011], which is an extension of a blog developed to support awareness and reflection for enquiry-based learners. It offers three different plug-ins which give visual feedback on when the learners have reflected on their blog posts.

The approach presented by Santos et al. [2012] focuses on capturing the activity of students outside learning management systems using existing tracking tools. Santos et al. [2012] describe their research on the development of a dashboard with visualizations of activity data about the students' use of several tools (like Eclipse IDE or websites). The visualizations are goal-oriented and intended to increase motivation of students and help them reflect on their learning process.

The work we have conducted with the LIM App differs from the above related work in that it explores and focuses specifically on the improvement of the lecturer and it also considers presentations in a business context. With the combination of realtime capturing and analysis of the data during the event as well as after it, we offer both possibilities to support reflective learning on-action and in-action [Schön, 1984]; i.e., adaptation during the event as well as subsequent reflection on the data. The use case we are considering takes the lecturer and speaker as the center of the scenario and focuses on professional performance improvement. In this case, students play a very important role, as they are the ones who provide feedback, but they are not strictly the only participants to benefit from the tool. In contrast to this, most of the related work explores and focuses on providing a benefit for students and is closely related to the content of the lectures and the knowledge they acquire.

6.10. Conclusions

The Live Interest Meter was evaluated in formative and summative studies. The majority of the participants would recommend it and would use it in the future. The Net Promoter Score calculated among all participants who answered a questionnaire in the last two evaluations (see Sections 6.8 and 6.7) reveals a score of 25%.

Regarding reflection on the gathered data and which visualizations fostered reflection (RQ2, see Section 1.2), participants preferred exploring the data of the reports in retrospective instead of reacting to the data while performing the presentation. This indicates that further efforts should be invested in enriching the feedback data with context that contributes to reconstruct past experiences. For future versions of the LIM App, participants saw potential in linking the feedback to the concrete slide being presented.

Tracking feedback data has proven to be relevant and beneficial. However, one of the major requirements to achieve these benefits is the gathering of enough context data in order to support the sense-making process. This is highly dependent on the engagement of the audience and therefore the socio-technical perspective of the LIM App has to be considered. This is also linked to the additional challenges that arise with respect to motivating users (RQ3, see Section 1.2). In the considered scenario, not only the speaker has to be motivated to reflect, but the members in the audience have to be motivated to create the basis for this reflection. However, insights gained from the different evaluations show that there is a direct proportional link between the motivation from lecturers and speakers to reflect and the motivation of the audience. In other words, if members in the audience do not engage sufficiently and provide the content for reflection, speakers and lecturers lose their motivation because they do not have a solid basis to derive new insights and achieve reflection outcomes.

With respect to changes in and improvement of one's own work (issues addressed by RQ4, Section 1.2), results show that feedback tracking can lead to small changes in speakers' performance. However, from a sociological perspective, further coaching and training may be needed in order to offer solutions to speakers. Some participants in our studies expected having solutions to their problems directly from the students or would like to get them from the system. Nonetheless, the goal that we pursue with the LIM App is that these solutions are found thanks to the self-reflection of participants. We could show the data gathered by the LIM App is indeed a first step towards supporting reflection on lectures and presentations. From a methodological perspective, our results suggest that the usage of the LIM App in selected sessions and presentations, instead of a continuous usage, is the most suitable strategy.

To achieve a satisfactory regular use in the future, technical work on compatibility with Wi-Fi infrastructures in public institutions is needed. The results obtained with the LIM App, especially during the long-term summative evaluation, were considerably affected by the technical problems caused by certain Wi-Fi infrastructures. Despite numerous tests and technical evaluations, this could not be completely solved. In some networks, the connection of a high number of users at the same time was not feasible. In other networks, the communication between a random subset of clients and the server of the LIM App was interrupted because of the weakness of the network.

7. Insights from the Empirical Validation of the Holistic Approach

Following a methodology guided by the IMRLQS, we developed three different QS prototypes, which were evaluated in distinct work contexts. Table 7.1 offers a summary of the three use cases that were investigated and the learning spectrum that was covered. We analyze the introduction and use of QS apps from a socio-technical perspective. Studies conducted for the elaboration of this work revealed how several factors have an impact on the usage of the apps and on reflective learning in work environments.

Table 7.1.: Investigated use cases and learning spectrum

	MoodMap App (Chapter 4)	**MoodMarket** (Chapter 5)	**LIM App** (Chapter 6)
Tracked Aspect	Emotions	Emotions	Feedback
Tracking	Self	Self	Observer
Work Context	Virtual meetings Call centers Software dev.	Experimental asset market	Lectures Public speaking
Goal	Emotional awareness, communication, work performance	Trading behavior, reduction of price bubbles	Presentation skills
Reflection	in-action: between work tasks on-action: end of meeting/day	in-action: between trading periods on-action: end of market	in-action: during presentation on-action: end of lecture/presentation

In the following, we perform a joint analysis of the results obtained in the user studies. The user studies detailed in Chapters 4, 5, and 6 and the comparison between their results are taken into consideration for this analysis. The goal of this chapter is to provide a body of empirical application-oriented insights which serve as validation of the holistic approach and can be applied beyond the concrete investigated work settings.

The insights identified and presented below provide a basis of successes and pitfalls and thereby inform the future design of Quantified Self applications to support reflective learning at work. First, we analyze and discuss insights related to our research question RQ2, addressing self-reporting and observer-reporting as tracking mechanisms (Section 7.1). Second, we continue our joint analysis with the results related to RQ3, including sense-making of data (Section 7.2), data visualization (Section 7.3), and motivation (Section 7.4). Finally, we provide insights regarding learners' improvements and other work-related aspects targeted by our RQ4. This includes measuring outcomes (Section 7.5), adapting apps to workplaces' requirements (Section 7.6), setting learning goals (Section 7.7), and considering privacy concerns (Section 7.8).

7.1. Self, Peer and Group Tracking

As mentioned in our theoretical model, one important aid to the reflection process is the fusion and comparison of objective (measured by sensors), self-reported (data from the user), and peer or group assessment (reported data from others about a user). Therefore, developers have to be aware of which perspective on the data is useful in every scenario. In this respect, we investigated self-reporting and observer-reporting (peer and group) as tracking mechanisms.

- *Self-reporting* of data relies on the active effort of users to report on events and capture their subjective impressions. Users' involvement introduces bias in the data, but this can be minimized by adopting user interfaces that simplify the tracking. For example, in the MoodMap App (Chapter 4) and the MoodMarket (Chapter 5) we restricted the input to a single click in a two-dimensional map. Self-reporting can be used in a wide variety of scenarios, but requires the cooperation and acceptance of users. The amount and quality of captured data are determined by the engagement of users, and therefore motivation plays an important role (see Section 7.4).
- *Observer-reporting* involves other individuals capturing the data about the learner's experiences by using self-reporting means. With these observers' data, insights on peer and group assessment is possible. Although each observer provides the data related to the experience from a subjective

perspective, it can become more objective by aggregating data from multiple observers. For instance, the Live Interest Meter (Chapter 6) supports speakers by tracking feedback from each member of the audience and the aggregation of this feedback contributes to offering an objective perspective of the presentation. However, as observers have to capture data by themselves, their motivation is crucial for success. In the case of the LIM App, although we leverage the audience interest to listen to an engaging talk, we observed that this may not be enough to ensure long term usage and that there are other factors influencing observers' motivation. In such cases, where the intrinsic motivation of the observers is not enough, alternative extrinsic motivations may be a solution. For instance, we investigated the use of gamification to improve students' participation in the LIM App.

Further differences between self- and observer-reporting could be identified in our studies. Gathering of data in terms of being accurate, effortless, relevant, and timely was evaluated with higher scores in the MoodMap App and MoodMarket than in the LIM App. This suggests that the motivation to give feedback had a high influence on gathering data. Finally, results have revealed that, when using observer-reporting approaches, the impact and changes on the learner's behavior have to be visible for the observers. Otherwise, the benefits will be nonexistent for them. For instance, members in the audience using the LIM App expected the speaker to react to their feedback or to show that, by reviewing the data, insights had been gained and changes had been applied. If this was not the case, students would lose both their motivation to use the app and the hope for better lectures.

7.2. Sense-Making of Data

Reflective learning requires that learners understand the meaning of the data in order to be able to reflect on it. The process of recalling and revisiting experiences engages the learner in making sense of the gathered data. In most of the investigated use cases, we used self-reporting approaches where the data are produced by the users themselves. The results of our studies reveal that this facilitates the understanding of the data and contributes to an easier interpretation of it. The previous process of selecting when and what to track, as well as interpreting the tracking user interface (e.g., the two-dimensional mood map in the MoodMap App and the MoodMarket, or the configurable LIM meter), contributes to an easier sense-making process. Moreover, it facilitates the relationship between the data and one's own experiences, which is already established at capturing stage.

On the contrary, applications that use automatic methods for data capturing (e.g., a hardware sensor) do not require users to actively contribute to the tracking phase. As a consequence, collecting data alone does not produce reflective learning, as it requires time to understand the data, especially when the data become richer and more complex [Müller, 2014].

7.3. Data Visualization

As we suggested in our theoretical framework (see Chapter 3), appealing and intuitive presentation forms and visualizations for the users should be chosen, which at the same time foster the analysis of the data. Otherwise, this can become one of the major barriers for triggering reflection and facilitating the recalling of experiences.

Data can be visualized from several perspectives, depending on the criteria taken into consideration. Visualizations of surprising data or unexpected perspectives can lead to cognitive dissonance [Festinger, 1957] and trigger reflection [Consolvo et al., 2009b]. Hence, designers should aim to outline deviations and help understand the underlying reasons.

We analyzed and proposed the most common visualization perspectives found in the QS community:

- social: comparing one's own performance/measurements with others' or aggregating data over multiple users
- spatial: the location of the user, allowing the understanding of the relation between place and behavior
- historical: comparison of current values to historic values
- meta-level: using item metadata that supports the understanding and interpretation of the data
- external perspective driven by other datasets: visualization according to data provided by other standard sources of information like, e.g., the weather.

In some cases, there are already established visualizations for these perspectives, which have proven to be intuitive and accepted; e.g., timelines for the historical or social networks for the social perspective. However, other types of context can result in more complex visualizations, which have to be adapted to the type of captured data as well as to the learner's background.

The visualization of data can benefit from the vast research on visualization techniques, but further research is needed to assess the added value of these visual approaches in terms of effectiveness, efficiency, and other criteria that pertain to learning [Klerkx et al., 2014], especially in informal learning. Consequently, visualizations to support learning need to be developed by using a user-centered design approach, resulting in several prototypes and iterations which are affected by the feedback of end users. The concrete background of learners, their work context, as well as their knowledge of the data have to be taken into consideration.

In our studies, we have identified some of the most important factors to consider during the design approach. For choosing the correct visualization, it is important to know from the end users which kind of questions they would like to get answered with the analysis of the data. This will guide the selection of the appropriate visualization. In our studies with the MoodMap App, we have experienced that employees would like to know how their colleagues are feeling and compare themselves to the team's affective state. Consequently, visualizations to easily establish this comparison were needed. Another important factor was the identification of mood and feedback trends. For such cases, the time component should be easy to interpret in the visualizations; e.g., by using an intuitive timeline. Timelines were especially appreciated in work environments where employees are accustomed to visualize data in this form; e.g., in the telecommunications and IT sector. Smileys were also well received by the call centers' employees because they were used to seeing them in other work tools and in social networks. Although some visualizations may seem more original or sophisticated (see the timelines of the MoodMap App 1.0 in Figure 4.6 as an example), they may be perceived by the end users as too difficult to interpret and not intuitive enough. Therefore, this indicates that the work context is an important factor which should be taken into consideration.

In summary, participants in our studies requested mainly three types of visualizations: status charts, comparison charts, and timelines.

Status charts offer a quick overview of the data and are usually related to the current status of the learner; e.g., by showing average values or progress made. Examples of status charts would be the average mood of a day, the number of tasks that have been completed, or the average current feedback from the audience.

Comparison charts show data from different instances and facilitate its examination in order to note the similarities or differences. For instance, data from different users or data between groups can be compared. Comparison charts can be used by learners to benchmark themselves against others in the sense-making process; e.g., the *Compare Me* visualization in the MoodMap App shows the contrast between the own individual mood and the team mood.

Timelines offer a historical perspective on the data. They are useful to analyze in depth what was happening (timelines with lower time spans) and identify trends during a certain period of time (timelines with a higher time span).

In these types of visualization, deviations from the standard trend, or identified unusual values can become a trigger for reflection and therefore lead to an analysis of the underlying reasons. In order to achieve the optimal visualization, an iterative user-centered design process is required to collect requirements from the end users. In this process, the background of the learner, as well as its knowledge of the data, has to be taken into consideration.

We also identified a categorization of the visualizations, dividing them in "live" and "retrospective." The observed preferences for "live visualizations", in contrast to "retrospective visualizations", were diverse. For instance, with the MoodMap App, the daily live views were used more often whereas the reports which are available afterwards were rarely visited. In the MoodMarket, we deliberately implemented simple visualizations embedded in the trading process. Within the LIM App, the opposite case was observed, and users usually preferred to review the reports in retrospective, and analyze not only the last lectures, but also previous lectures from past days. By analyzing these users' behaviors, we can conclude that live visualizations facilitated reflection-in-action, whereas visualizations that offer a report on past data aim at supporting reflection-on-action. The decision on which visualizations are optimal in each case will highly depend on the target work setting (see Section 7.6).

7.4. Motivational Cues

Our user studies have proven the feasibility and usability of self-tracking in work environments. However, one of the major challenges to overcome is the additional efforts that reflective learning requires. Users have to be motivated not only to reflect on the tracked data, but also to track the data itself. Therefore, several challenges were identified:

- Despite the widespread acknowledgment of the importance of reflective learning, our studies revealed that, due to time and business constraints, time and space for reflection is not given to employees. Additionally, employees themselves also consider that conducting their tasks has a higher priority than reflecting on their work. This attitude is unlikely to change because reflection is seen to be of secondary importance to work tasks. Therefore, we had to find external motivation or additional benefits provided by our applications in order to achieve a successful use.

- Reflective learning relies on re-evaluating past experiences and does not consider the definition of a concrete measurable goal that must be pursued. For instance, this would be the case in known examples from the QS, like losing weight or smoking less, where weight and cups of coffee become the measurable goal. Outcomes of reflection are unknown a priori and may result in unexpected insights. This open-ended nature without a goal to achieve adds difficulties to motivate users to reflect and therefore to use applications that support it (see also Section 7.7).
- In many cases, learning processes take place subconsciously and individuals are not aware of how they affect them and the changes in behavior that are produced. For example, participants in the MoodMarket (Chapter 5) were not aware of the influence that mood tracking had on their behavior. This lack of awareness constitutes an additional barrier for users' motivation.

Our results show that in order to overcome these challenges, certain motivation techniques have to be adopted. In the Quantified Self community, competition and peer recognition are the main mechanisms that bring people to track further data and feel motivated to improve themselves [Maitland et al., 2006]. At the workplace, collaboration and teams' sense of belonging has proven to be a powerful motivator. In our studies with the MoodMap App, communication within the teams was improved and managers changed their behavior to offer better support. This fact was also appreciated by the employees, who mentioned that the opinion of their colleagues and managers about the app is important for them and affects their decision on future usage. Additionally, as mentioned before, comparing one's data with the others' allows individuals to gain objectivity and awareness on others. Therefore, designers should consider and exploit the influence of teams and groups.

An alternative approach is to resort to external motivation techniques. One of the current most extended ones is gamification; i.e., the use of game design elements in non-game contexts. Involving gamification in the design of an application from the beginning and adapting it to the concrete work context where it is used can contribute to keep participants involved and engaged over time.

7.5. Measuring Outcomes

As described in the reflection model by Boud et al. [1985], the re-evaluation of experiences that takes part during the reflection process produces a final outcome. These outcomes can be new perspectives on experience, changes in behavior, readiness for application, or commitment to actions. The nature of these outcomes results in changes that may be intangible; e.g., a commitment to action that does not result in a final behavioral change or a new perspective that is not articulated and stays only in the individual's mind. Outcomes of cognitive or affective nature may be measurable only by asking individuals, whereas behavioral outcomes additionally might be measured by sensors or external indicators. Nonetheless, we have to account for the time required to evaluate changes in these indicators. Short-term benefits derived from reflection will be hardly unveiled by them.

As we have seen from the QS, for Q-Selfers a defined outcome is not always required. Not finding insights from data exploration or not achieving changes in own behavior do not produce a feeling of discouragement or failure. However, this is one of the remarkable differences we encounter when transferring QS approaches to work settings. In order to justify our approach to support reflective learning as well as to show employees that they achieve an improvement, measurable outcomes are required. As mentioned before, the nature of the outcomes itself makes this measurement challenging, but we found parameters that act as indicators for achieved outcomes; e.g., Key Performance Indicators. Alternatively, having an experimental environment as investigated with the MoodMarket (Chapter 5) let us measure changes in behavior in a controlled fashion.

Despite these efforts, even measuring visible changes in behavior remains a challenge because the achieved outcomes are not known a priori and, therefore, the measurement cannot be predefined. Consequently, in many occasions, improvements obtained from reflective learning will remain unmeasured or unrevealed but they will nonetheless contribute to the learning development of the individual.

7.6. Workplace-Specific

Building apps for a specific work context enables users to reflect with less effort and thereby improve their daily work. Our user studies on reflective learning aimed at creating a working socio-technical system that integrates the new technology and processes into the existing workflow. The introduction of the apps in real workplaces proved crucial. Developers need to have direct contact with end users in the development phase, as well as in the introduction of the app; e.g., data reports were implemented after the first usage of the LIM App in the field and new visualizations were implemented for the MoodMap App after the first trial at call centers.

Support for reflective learning has to be embedded in the daily work. If there are defined processes in place, analyzing these processes and adapting the designed applications is required. In the case of the MoodMap App, a successful integration was achieved by establishing a link between moods and concrete tasks performed by employees (e.g., calls or meetings).

However, these processes are not always clearly or explicitly defined or there are work settings where employees follow a more personalized and open structure. For instance, this is the case with the LIM App used in lectures and public speaking. Speakers have their own method and lecturers have their own teaching techniques. There is not an established process or steps defined that guide how they should do their work. In such cases, it may be useful to define a process that involves the usage of the app by integrating it from a pedagogical perspective. For example, learners could adopt learning processes that already include reflection as one of the basic steps. The professional learning processes suggested by Loucks-Horsley et al. [1998] (see Figure 7.1) is an example of an established process where the usage of reflection tools could be embedded.

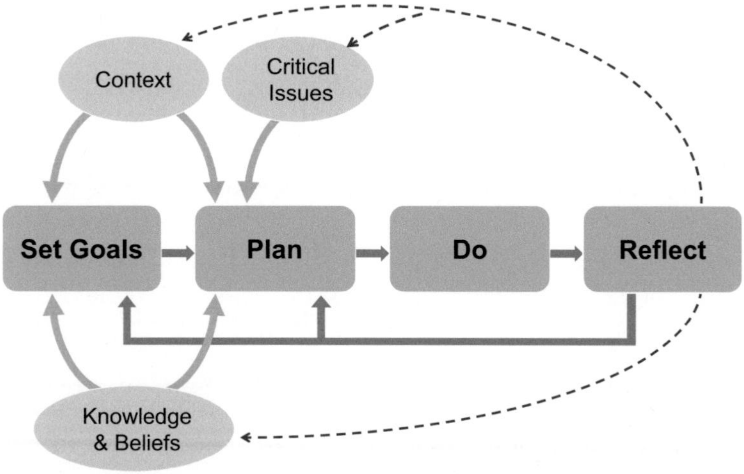

Figure 7.1.: Professional Learning Process adapted from Loucks-Horsley et al. [1998]

An integration of the apps also at technical level is crucial to achieve appropriation and the feeling of being part of their work. For instance, it was essential for the use of the MoodMap App to be integrated into the call taker system. Although a full integration was not feasible due to company constraints, call takers could reach the MoodMap App by pressing a button directly in the system that they use during their normal work. This small but important detail achieved that call takers reach the app easily and have the feeling that it as a part of their daily working environment. The integration of the LIM App in existing learning management systems (LMS) or other university tools would contribute to increasing its acceptance and regular use.

7.7. Goal Setting

Reflective learning does not necessarily follow a predefined goal but draws insights from past experiences which in our approach are represented by the tracked data. As mentioned in Section 7.5, the outcomes of reflection cannot be 100% measurable, despite adopting alternatives like KPIs or external evaluations, which should reflect the performed changes.

In the Quantified Self, their inherent curiosity about themselves drives them to explore and reflect on their data. In some cases, a goal-driven motivation is pursued (e.g., losing weight or controlling a particular disease). In many other cases, it is just the enthusiasm on technology and data that drives this quantifying behavior, without having identified in advance any concrete benefit from it (e.g., tracking any kind of social contact with other people or which streets of a particular city have you already passed by).

Our experience with supporting reflective learning at work confirms that learning goals and expected outcomes are difficult to define a priori. Though applications might be associated with the overall learning goal of getting a better understanding of work practices and changing behavior to improve work performance, the resulting outcomes depend on the particular work situations of individuals and teams. However, we can define the purpose of using the applications to the type of improvement we want to achieve. For example, in the case of the LIM App the goal is to improve presentation skills, the MoodMarket aims at improving trading behavior and therefore reduce price bubbles, and the MoodMap App targets improvements in communication and work performance in general. It is therefore critical, when designing tools for reflection, to find a balance between defining an overall learning goal (e.g., reflecting on a particular aspect of work) that allows us to choose relevant data and visualizations, at the same time leaving space for exploration during reflection. In some cases, reflective learning helps to identify these unknown goals in order to later pursue a defined one. For example, by reflecting on mood data one may discover that a certain task has negative effects. Hence, the learner may define the goal of reducing the number of times this task has to be performed.

7.8. Privacy Concerns

Privacy was expected to be a major barrier for self-tracking at the workplace, especially when part of the data was not anonymized. This was the case for the MoodMap App 3.0, which contained team views with non-anonymized data for managers and coaches. Therefore, privacy concerns were targeted by questionnaires before and after the studies. In the case of the call center (Section 4.9), the benefits outweighed any privacy concerns because sharing and visualizing the annotated mood data led to clear benefits for both parties; i.e., team cohesion and empowerment of employees. However, it must be taken into account that call takers are used to be monitored during their work (e.g., calls are recorded) but this is not the case for all professionals. Therefore, we cannot generalize this positive attitude regarding privacy to other domains.

One of the most important influencing factors is the organizational culture. Contrary to the call center setting, the initial predisposition to capture and share mood was not the same in the software company (Section 4.10). One of the main barriers for adoption was the fear of stating their moods honestly, as it may affect their working position in the company. The conviction that reflective learning could improve their work is only possible if the managers as well as the organization are committed to such principles. Another factor that may have influenced the usage of the application is the low number of members that some departments had. From the experience gained in the call center, bigger teams see an additional advantage when the manager can attend to each member individually and the MoodMap App could help to increase this awareness. However, in the case of Regola, having small teams may have led to a sense of controlling instead of support.

In general, privacy was considered important but not a requirement to be satisfied by the applications. In some cases, functionality aiming at enhancing the privacy was seen as a barrier to usage of the system. For instance, visualizations with anonymized data were seen as complex, hard to understand, and obstructing when trying to find underlying reasons.

Using self-reporting approaches allowed leaving the decision on what data to track to the users. Although this overcomes the privacy issues arisen with automatic capturing means, it is not enough to aim for a beneficial impact and designers should be prepared for a wide variety of attitudes [Müller et al., 2015]. Designers must be aware of the threats of using the apps in an undesired manner and this has to be communicated and discussed with employees and management. From a design perspective, it is required that employees are able to delete and manipulate the data as well as to decide which data they want to share (e.g., by offering functionality to configure sharing settings).

Results revealed how important it is to communicate insights and actions gained, as capturing and sharing data without perceiving usefulness on it can lead to a feeling of controlling. Hence, privacy functionality has to be a central part of the systems but adaptable to the needs of the specific work context, as privacy concerns vary across domains, countries, and cultures.

Part III.

Conclusions

8. Summary

Reflective learning is one of the core processes for improving work performance. Existing theories of reflective learning provide an understanding of the cognitive and social processes, but do not consider the use of technologies to enhance reflective learning processes. Inspired by the tools and methods of the Quantified Self (QS) community, we investigated the role of tracking technologies in the reflective process and presented a holistic approach to the design of self-tracking applications. As a result, we show how Quantified Self approaches can support reflective learning processes at the workplace, both from a theoretical and technical perspective. Our goal was to investigate the benefits of self-tracking at work, thereby extending research on self-tracking from private areas of life and "extreme users" to employees in work settings. To this end, we developed three self-tracking applications and evaluated them in distinct workplace settings. The validation of our holistic approach was conducted through a total of thirteen studies with more than 600 participants involved.

8.1. Contributions and Impact

In this thesis, we have developed a novel holistic approach that defines the use of tracking applications inspired by the Quantified Self to support workplace reflective learning. An Integrated Model of Reflective Learning and Quantified Self (IMRLQS) has been conceptualized to provide the required theoretical basis. In addition to ordering this strand of research, the IMRLQS model provides a systematization and understanding of the design space for future QS applications aiming at supporting reflective learning. This model has been explored in real workplace settings by designing and developing three self-tracking prototypes which were evaluated in different work settings. The studies conducted as part of the evaluation targeted not only design and technical aspects but also learning impact and social aspects. Our results show that participants using the implemented QS applications learned from their personal and work experiences, gained valuable insights about their work, and improved their work performance.

To achieve this thesis' goal of investigating if and how Quantified Self approaches can aid learning, we defined four research questions which led to the following core contributions.

An integrated model that constitutes a framework for technical support of reflective learning, derived from unifying reflective learning theory with a conceptual analysis of Quantified Self tools. The Integrated Model of Reflective Learning and Quantified Self answers our first research question (RQ1), which targeted how Quantified Self principles and tools can support reflective learning at work. The model defines three main support dimensions: tracking cues, triggering, and recalling and revisiting experiences. Each of these dimensions is characterized with explicit mechanisms and design choices that show how QS applications can implement reflection support. The IMRLQS has set a pioneering foundation for the systematization and understanding of the design space for QS applications aiming to support learning from employees' experiences. Therefore, the model not only is the conceptual foundation for the development of this thesis and the guide for the design of the subsequent developed prototypes, but also a solid basis for the design of future QS prototypes.

Design, implementation, and evaluation of three self-reporting QS applications. Based on the IMRLQS model, we built on an iterative user-centered design-based methodology to instantiate QS approaches to support reflective learning in specific work settings. The resulting prototypes are novel applications that have adopted QS techniques and adapted them in order to be successfully integrated in real workplace settings. We selected three work contexts where reflective practice is seen as promising but has not been integrated in their work processes yet. In each of the three investigated use cases, we addressed our second, third, and fourth research questions. These include whether self-reporting QS applications can capture and quantify data about our daily work activities as basis for reflective learning (RQ2), which different data visualizations and motivation techniques foster learning processes (RQ3), and which improvements can be achieved by reflecting on data from personal and work life (RQ4).

The first use case explored reflection on emotions in several work scenarios of the telecommunications and IT sector. We designed and evaluated the MoodMap App, a mood self-tracking application that aims at improving employees' performance by increasing emotional awareness and re-evaluating daily work experiences in relation to the impact of their emotions on work. We conducted a total of seven user studies, encompassing virtual meetings and teleconferences where non-verbal communication is missing, call centers where there is a constant relationship with customers, and software-technology development services in the emergency domain. These studies helped refine each of the three MoodMap

App prototypes and understand which features of the application achieved the desired support and lead to improvements in the learners' work. Results show that participants made small changes in their behavior, communication between employees was positively affected, and inter-role relationships were improved. In our study at the call center, Key Performance Indicators revealed a significant improvement of the call takers' work performance during the MoodMap App usage period. Results reveal that collaborative aspects like awareness of colleagues' moods are crucial for acceptance and long-term usage of the app. We also identified which factors contribute to a successful introduction of mood self-tracking in work environments. For instance, tangible changes at management and team levels are required to avoid a sense of controlling derived from the misuse of the data.

In the second use case, we conducted a study to evaluate the impact of mood tracking on decision-making. Experimental asset markets offer a controlled environment, where the quality of the work performed by the individuals can be linked to the creation of price bubbles and, thereby, it becomes measurable. A prototype called MoodMarket integrates mood tracking in the trading process, allowing individuals to capture and reflect on their moods between trading periods. The results show that participants who tracked their mood during the experiment improved their trading behavior. Participants were not aware of these improvements and did not expect mood capturing having an influence on their decision-making behavior. However, the analysis of the data at economical level shows that (i) price bubbles were smaller in amplitude, (ii) participants realized they were riding in a bubble earlier than the participants who did not track their mood, and (iii) there is a relationship between their trading behavior and their captured moods. Considering the overall results, they indicate that traders achieved improvements in their work performance as part of subconscious reflective learning processes.

The third use case investigated the tracking of feedback in lectures and professional presentations in order to improve presentation skills. The Live Interest Meter (LIM App) was designed and implemented to easily track feedback from the audience and compare the own perspective of the speaker with the perspective of the audience members. The LIM App was evaluated in five studies, being used by lecturers, students, researchers, and consultants. The evaluations considered not only the benefits and improvements for the speaker but also the acceptance and feasibility of the approach from the audience in their role of data providers. Our evaluation results show that feedback tracking can lead to small changes in speakers' performance. In the considered scenario, not only the speaker has to be motivated to reflect, but the members in the audience have to be motivated to create the basis for this reflection. Therefore, the improvements achieved by the speakers must be visible to the audience members and motivation techniques to maintain the engagement of the audience have to be considered. We were able to show that the data gathered by the LIM App is indeed a first step towards supporting reflection on lectures and presentations.

A framework of empirical application-oriented insights derived from the results obtained in the thirteen user studies. The resulting insights not only validate the holistic approach of applying Quantified Self approaches to support reflective learning at work, but also provide best practices and pitfalls from a socio-technical perspective and thereby inform the future design of this type of applications.

In conclusion, this thesis contributes with a promising approach for supporting reflective learning at work. We provide evidence that Quantified Self approaches can support the cognitive learning process at a theoretical, workplace-independent level. Our studies with three developed prototypes in selected work settings provide evidence that QS approaches can support reflective learning and achieve improvements at work. As predicted by reflective learning theory, the outcomes achieved by participants have been diverse, ranging from small changes in the slides of a presentation to improvements measurable by Key Performance Indicators. The nature of reflective learning and the requirements characteristic of workplace settings make the implementation of supporting applications challenging. However, the IMRLQS model and the insights gained through our studies with QS approaches provide a solid basis for the successful implementation of future applications.

8.2. Outlook

Applying Quantified Self practices and tools to support reflective learning is a novel approach that considers learning support from a technical, social, and theoretical perspective. The growing number of sensors and mobile technologies for personal data tracking as well as the ever-growing Quantified Self community point to promising future opportunities for integrating new sources of data and making them available for reflection. We have shown that Quantified Self approaches, despite having to be appropriately adapted to the workplace requirements, can be successfully used in work settings. Therefore, it appears to be reasonable to connect these adapted tools with their counterparts in the private life.

The envisioned potential for integration also includes combining data gathered by our QS applications with existing work data. Although we invested part of our efforts into integrating the applications in the systems of our target users and produce data reports which include company data, this could not be entirely fulfilled due to company restrictions. This definitely constitutes an interesting point for further research. For instance, the data from the MoodMap App could be linked to further details about the calls (besides the current call reference) and a relationship between moods and notes could also be established with the coaching needs of call takers. These options are currently under discussion with the managers of British Telecom. In the case of the LIM App, the integration with the slides used during the presentations or with other learning material would provide further context to the aggregated feedback.

The Quantified Self is considered a key contemporary trend emerging in big data science [Swan, 2013]. The growing number of smart devices and applications used are generating huge amounts of data about individuals' behavior. This vision towards a human side of big data based on information about personal behavior and private aspects of life is becoming a reality. With our work, we have extended the benefits of tracking data to improve private aspects of life (e.g., health and well-being) with the achievement of work-related improvements. We have set the foundation for a new type of Quantified Self applications that join the benefits of personal tracking with the requirements and aspirations of work settings, including collaborative aspects of teamwork, privacy concerns, and the focus on work performance in organizations. In the near future, the spread of Quantified Self approaches in organizations could also integrate personal data in the current upstream reporting used as mechanisms of performance management and accountability. In doing so, there is further potential for the combination of data following a bottom-up stream with the top-down information flows coming from organizational analysis.

In this thesis, we have investigated the overall approach of designing QS approaches in several work contexts in order to show the potential and provide evidence of the benefits. Our focus has been on the development of lightweight applications that are flexible enough to be adapted to several work contexts within a certain domain. Further research focusing on individual work contexts could integrate tracking approaches with context-specific metadata to achieve an adapted representation of personal experiences. This representation of experiences would be richer by adding semantics to the data. This would facilitate the integration of different systems as well as the smarter analysis of the tracked data together with domain data provided by other sources. The use of the applications and the tracked data could also be connected with on-site coaching processes. This would encourage employees to take actions and change their behavior in accordance to the achieved reflection outcomes.

In the particular use case of mood self-tracking, investigated in our first two use cases, there is a vast amount of research on automatic methods to recognize moods and emotions. On the one hand, automatic methods lower the tracking effort, can raise awareness, and influence behavior. On the other hand, our results show that reflection requires the cognitive focus to analyze and understand the data and therefore the manual mood capturing itself is a reflection opportunity. Taking into account this human-computer interaction perspective, there is a great potential for further research on interfaces for mood tracking adapted to the new workplace application areas.

Finally, a promising field of research is the investigation of motivation and incentives within QS approaches at the workplace. Our studies revealed the main motivations in the different work domains and these could be further built upon in future prototypes. Especially in work settings where other people contribute to tracking data (as it was the case in our Live Interest Meter use case), additional motivation techniques are needed to maintain the engagement of the users. We investigated gamification as one of the potential motivators to achieve this. However, further evaluations in several settings including lectures and business presentations are needed to investigate which techniques are more effective.

This thesis is the first research work that systematizes and transfers experimental approaches from the Quantified Self community to provide support for reflective learning at work and make use of its benefits for work performance improvement. The design, implementation, and evaluation of three QS applications have proven the feasibility, usefulness, and benefits of our approach. By unifying these two strands, Quantified Self and reflective learning, we have established a promising basis for a new kind of learning support in work environments.

Appendix

A. MoodMap App – Summative Evaluation I: British Telecommunications Call Centers

This appendix contains a printed version of the online questionnaires answered by the participants in the summative evaluation of the MoodMap App at the BT call centers in Dundee and Alness (see Section 4.9).

A.1. Pre-questionnaire

Print version

Questionnaire

1 Welcome page

Dear participant,

This data collection is part of research activities within the larger context of an EU-funded project named MIRROR - Reflective Learning at Work. The MIRROR project tries to develop tools to help employees to learn from their past work-related experiences. Today's study is the first step of the evaluation of the ***MoodMap App*** and this survey contains questions about reflection and your expectations regarding the apps.

The online survey will take approximately ten minutes to complete. There are no right or wrong answers. In fact, we are very much interested to know your personal experience and opinion.

Thank you very much for your cooperation and have fun taking the survey!

2 Core Questions

Your Participant Code*:

Kindly write down your participant code.
Your code consists of:

1. The first letter of your place of birth
2. Your own day of birth (two digits)
3. The first letter of your father's first name
4. The first letter of your mother's first name

Example: A person born in **L**ondon on the **7**th of July, with parents named **J**ake and **S**ue would enter: "L" (for London) in the 1st blank, and "07" (for the birthday on the 7th) in the 2nd blank, "J" (for Jake) in the 3rd, and "S" (for Sue) in the 4th blank. So this person's code would be: L07JS

If you don't know any of these, use "X" for the first letter of your place of birth, "00" for the date of birth, "Y" for the first letter of your father's name, and "Z" for the first letter of your mother's name.

☐ ☐ ☐ ☐

Gender*:

○ Male ○ Female

Age Group (in years):

○ <= 19
○ 20 - 29
○ 30 - 39
○ 40 - 49
○ 50 - 59
○ >= 60

Please indicate your role*:

○ Advisor ○ Coach ○ Manager

*compulsory questions

3 Core Questions Job

Job Scope*:

○ Full-time ○ Part-time

Department*:

____

Years in current position:

[ ] years

Years in current team (if applicable):

[ ] years

Years in current and similar positions (altogether):

[ ] years

4 Short Reflection Scale

Questions about reflection practices*

Kindly answer the following questions as they apply to you and indicate your agreement with the following statements. There are no right or wrong answers.

	strongly disagree	disagree	neutral	agree	strongly agree
I often reflect on my work in order to improve it.	O	O	O	O	O
We as a team often reflect on our work in order to improve it.	O	O	O	O	O
I think it is important to try to improve my work performance.	O	O	O	O	O
I frequently reflect on my work processes.	O	O	O	O	O
I frequently reflect on my emotions and how I feel during my work.	O	O	O	O	O
Reflecting on my work processes helps me to improve my task performance.	O	O	O	O	O
Reflecting on my emotions and that of my colleagues during meetings helps me to improve my work performance.	O	O	O	O	O
In team meetings we frequently talk about how we can improve our work performance.	O	O	O	O	O
Outside of meetings, I often talk with my colleagues about our work performance.	O	O	O	O	O
It is important to me to discuss frequently with others about our work performance.	O	O	O	O	O
Conversations with colleagues help me to improve my work performance.	O	O	O	O	O
Even a few days later, I can remember a certain situation (e.g. customer call or coaching session) well when I reflect on it by myself or with others.	O	O	O	O	O

5.1 App Expectations Advisor

Your expectations about the app usage and impact*

Which expectations do you have with a tool that allows to track and visualize your mood and the mood of your colleagues?

Which expectations do you have with a tool that allows to articulate your experiences made and challenges faced during your daily work?

Are you comfortable with sharing experiences and challenges with your coaches and manager?

6.1 App Expectations Coaches/Manager

Questions about expectations about the app usage and impact*

Which expectations do you have with a tool that allows to track and visualize your mood and the mood of your team members?

Which expectations do you have with a tool that tracks and shows you the performance of your teams (and coaches)?

7 App Expectations General

The following questions are related to the use of the *MoodMap App* in your daily work.

In which aspects could the MoodMap App help you or improve any aspect in the following situations?

During your daily work (shift):

Between customer calls:

During and after your coaching sessions:

In face to face meetings:

In which aspects could the MoodMap App improve your team?

During your daily work (shift):

Between customer calls:

During and after your coaching sessions:

In face to face meetings:

8 Satisfaction

How satisfied are you with your coaching sessions?*

Please answer the following question on a scale from 1 = very dissatisfied to 5 = very satisfied.

1	2	3	4	5
O	O	O	O	O

Please indicate your agreement to the following questions.*

	strongly disagree	disagree	neutral	agree	strongly agree
I feel my ideas to improve a process are addressed by my manager/coach.	O	O	O	O	O
Sometimes I notice a problem or room for improvement, but I don't communicate it to others.	O	O	O	O	O
My coaching sessions cover all my coaching needs.	O	O	O	O	O

Please indicate your agreement to the following sentences.*

	strongly disagree	disagree	neutral	agree	strongly agree
I'm generally aware of the coaching needs my teams have.	O	O	O	O	O
I can observe that the work processes are changing on the basis of the feedback from employees.	O	O	O	O	O
The organization encourages the articulation of ideas and improvements by employees.	O	O	O	O	O
Reflecting on how I feel could help me to improve my work performance.	O	O	O	O	O
Reflecting and discussing on how we feel could improve our team performance.	O	O	O	O	O
Being aware of my emotions during customer calls could help me to reduce my customer repeats.	O	O	O	O	O
Reflecting on my work could help us to improve our customer satisfaction.	O	O	O	O	O
Reflecting on my emotions could help us to improve our customer satisfaction.	O	O	O	O	O

9 Final page

You have reached the end of the survey.

Many thanks for taking part in the study.
You may now close this window.

A.2. Post-questionnaire

Druckversion

Questionnaire

1 Welcome page

Dear participant,

This data collection is part of research activities within the larger context of an EU-funded project named MIRROR – Reflective Learning at Work. The MIRROR project tries to develop tools to help employees to learn from their past work-related experiences.
Today's study is the second step of the evaluation of the ***MoodMap App*** and this survey contains questions about reflection and your evaluation regarding the app.

The online survey will take approximately 10 to 15 minutes to complete. There are no right or wrong answers.
In fact, we are very much interested to know your personal experience and opinion.

Thank you very much for your cooperation and have fun taking the survey!

2 Core Questions

Your Participant Code:

Kindly write down your participant code.
Your code consists of:

1. The first letter of your place of birth
2. Your own day of birth (two digits)
3. The first letter of your father's first name
4. The first letter of your mother's first name

Example: A person born in **L**ondon on the **7**th of July, with parents named **J**ake and **S**ue would enter: "L" (for London) in the 1st blank, and "07" (for the birthday on the 7th) in the 2nd blank, "J" (for Jake) in the 3rd, and "S" (for Sue) in the 4th blank. So this person's code would be: L07JS

If you don't know any of these, use "X" for the first letter of your place of birth, "00" for the date of birth, "Y" for the first letter of your father's name, and "Z" for the first letter of your mother's name.

Team-ID (your OUC):

Please indicate your role:

○ Advisor ○ Coach ○ Manager

3 Short Reflection Scale

Questions about reflection practices

Kindly answer the following questions as they apply to you and indicate your agreement with the following statements. There are no right or wrong answers.

	strongly disagree	disagree	neutral	agree	strongly agree
I often reflect on my work in order to improve it.	○	○	○	○	○
We as a team often reflect on our work in order to improve it.	○	○	○	○	○
I think it is important to try to improve my work performance.	○	○	○	○	○
I frequently reflect on my work processes.	○	○	○	○	○
I frequently reflect on my emotions and how I feel during my work.	○	○	○	○	○
Reflecting on my work processes helps me to improve my task performance.	○	○	○	○	○
Reflecting on my emotions and that of my colleagues helps me to improve my work performance.	○	○	○	○	○

In team meetings we frequently talk about how we can improve our work performance.	○	○	○	○	○
Outside of meetings, I often talk with my colleagues about our work performance.	○	○	○	○	○
It is important to me to discuss frequently with others about our work performance.	○	○	○	○	○
Conversations with colleagues help me to improve my work performance.	○	○	○	○	○
Even a few days later, I can remember a certain situation (e.g. customer call or coaching session) well when I reflect on it by myself or with others.	○	○	○	○	○

4 Usage

How often have you used the MoodMap App?

- ○ several times every day
- ○ once a day
- ○ several times in a week, but not every day
- ○ sometimes (less than once every week)
- ○ never

In a typical week, how likely are you to use social networking websites (e.g. Facebook, Twitter, LinkedIn, Google+, MySpace, ... etc.)?

not at all likely	slightly likely	moderately likely	very likely	extremely likely
○	○	○	○	○

In general, how concerned are you about the privacy of the information you submit on social networking sites?

not at all	a little	somewhat	highly
○	○	○	○

Please indicate your agreement with the following statements.

	strongly disagree	disagree	neutral	agree	strongly agree
I feel comfortable to express my feelings **in general**.	○	○	○	○	○
I feel comfortable to express my feelings **at work**.	○	○	○	○	○

5.1 Barriers

You indicated that you never used the MoodMap App.
Could you please tell us the main reason for your answer?

Please answer the following questions about barriers for using the MoodMap App.

	strongly disagree	disagree	neutral	agree	strongly agree
I did not have the time to use the MoodMap App.	○	○	○	○	○
I did not have the physical space (e.g.,necessary privacy) to use the MoodMap App.	○	○	○	○	○

I did not see an advantage in using the MoodMap App.	○	○	○	○	○
I was not motivated to use the MoodMap App.	○	○	○	○	○
The MoodMap App was intuitive and easy to use without the need for guidance..	○	○	○	○	○
I need more formal training with the MoodMap App.	○	○	○	○	○

What were other barriers to using the MoodMap App?

6.1 App specific

The following questions refer to the usage of the MoodMap App and its support for reflection.

	strongly disagree	disagree	neutral	agree	strongly agree
The MoodMap App helped me to collect information relevant for reconstructing my experiences from work.	○	○	○	○	○
The MoodMap App helped me to reflect on experiences from work.	○	○	○	○	○
The MoodMap App helped me to collect information that could help me decide when to reflect about my work.	○	○	○	○	○
The MoodMap App helped me to remember and reconstruct a work experience/situation with the help of different visualizations of moods and notes.	○	○	○	○	○
The MoodMap App helped me by capturing my reflection outcomes, e.g., new insights, decisions.	○	○	○	○	○
The MoodMap App helped me by making reflection outcomes, e.g., new insights, available for later use.	○	○	○	○	○
The MoodMap App guided me in capturing information about my work experiences.	○	○	○	○	○
The MoodMap App helped me by showing how many calls I had in a day.	○	○	○	○	○
The MoodMap App helped me to become aware of my own mood.	○	○	○	○	○
The MoodMap App helped me to become aware of my colleagues' mood.	○	○	○	○	○
The MoodMap App helped me to identify significant situations worth reflecting	○	○	○	○	○
The MoodMap App helped me to identify significant mood changes worth reflecting.	○	○	○	○	○
The MoodMap App helped me to identify significant topics worth reflecting.	○	○	○	○	○
The MoodMap App helped me to gain a better understanding of the team and its members.	○	○	○	○	○
The MoodMap App helped me to understand my emotions better.	○	○	○	○	○
The MoodMap App helped me to understand better how my emotions affect my work.	○	○	○	○	○
The MoodMap App helped me to deal better with my emotions.	○	○	○	○	○

6.2 App specific 2

The following questions refer to the usage of the MoodMap App and its support for reflection.

	strongly disagree	disagree	neutral	agree	strongly agree
Capturing my mood *during my work shift* is useful to reflect and think about *my daily work*.	○	○	○	○	○
Capturing my mood *between calls with customers* is useful to reflect and think about *my dealing with call issues and customers*.	○	○	○	○	○
Capturing my mood *during and after coaching sessions* is useful to reflect and think about *my daily work performance*.	○	○	○	○	○
Capturing my mood *during and after coaching sessions* is useful to reflect and think about *my coaching needs*.	○	○	○	○	○
Capturing my mood *after my breaks* is useful to reflect and think about *my daily work*.	○	○	○	○	○

In which other situations was it useful for you to capture your mood?

6.3 App specific 3

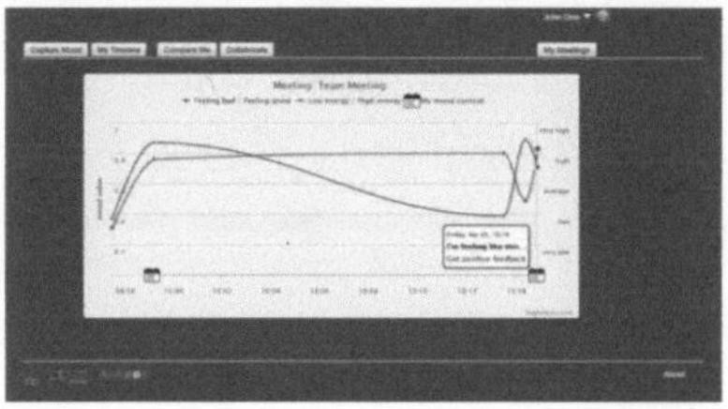

	strongly disagree	disagree	neutral	agree	strongly agree
Seeing the development of my mood in the Timeline visualization helps me to remember and restructure what happened during my work.	○	○	○	○	○
Seeing the development of my mood in the Timeline visualization made me reflect about my work.	○	○	○	○	○

6.4 App specific 4

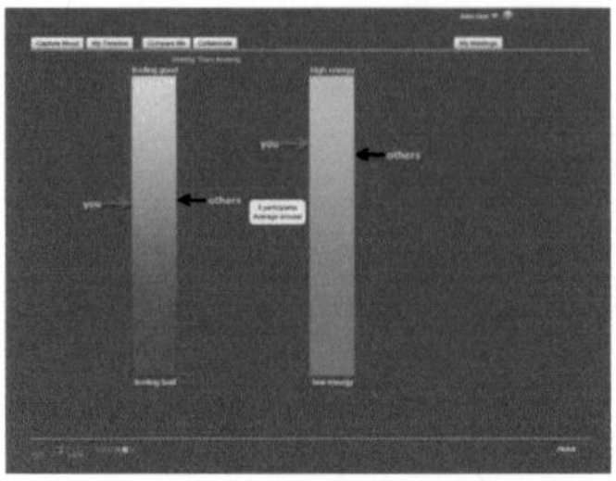

	strongly disagree	disagree	neutral	agree	strongly agree
The comparison of my mood with others, in the CompareMe Visualization, helps me to reflect about my work.	○	○	○	○	○

6.5 App specific 5

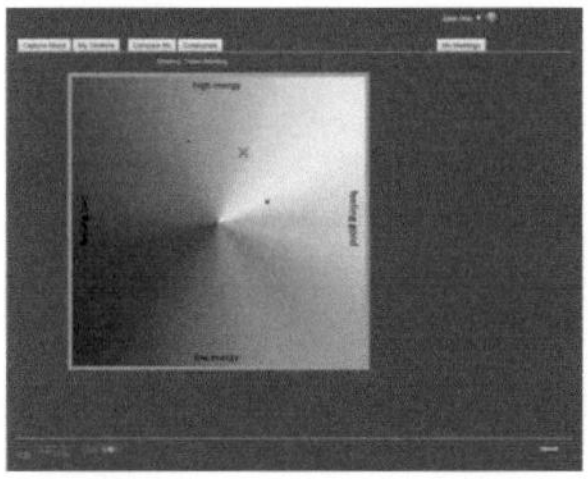

	strongly disagree	disagree	neutral	agree	strongly agree
The overview of my colleagues' mood in the Collaborate Visualization, helps me to reflect about my work.	○	○	○	○	○

6.6 New features (all) report

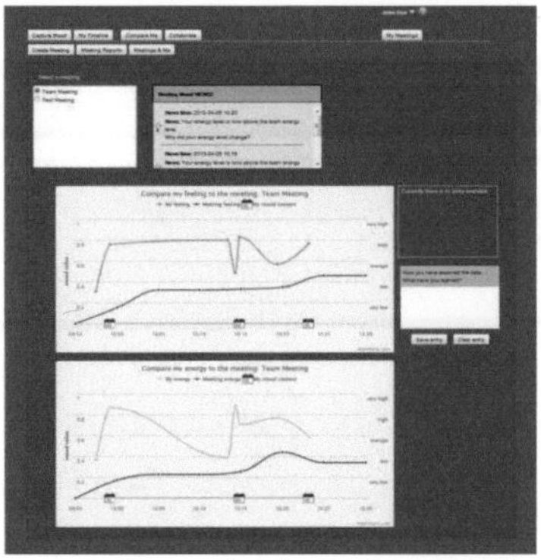

The following questions refer to the concrete features that the MoodMap App offers.

	strongly disagree	disagree	neutral	agree	strongly agree
The mood reports were very useful to recall my working shifts.	○	○	○	○	○
The comparison between my moods and the collaborative moods in the timelines of the mood reports were very useful to reflect on my work.	○	○	○	○	○
The contextualization (e.g. after a call, after a coaching session) of the moods helped me to associate my moods to a certain situation.	○	○	○	○	○
The contextualization (e.g. after a call, after a coaching session) of the moods helped me to recall my past experiences.	○	○	○	○	○
The activity (e.g. call, coaching session) associated to a mood helped me to better reflect about a past situation during a day.	○	○	○	○	○

6.7.1 Sharing (Advisors)

Sharing moods

Please answer the following questions about sharing moods

	strongly disagree	disagree	neutral	agree	strongly agree
Knowing the feelings of his/her team members can help managers and coaches to identify problems and directly help the appropriate person.	○	○	○	○	○
Sharing my moods with my manager and coaches is fine for me.	○	○	○	○	○

In which situations would you share your feeling and energy level with your manager and coaches?

In which situations would you not share your feeling and energy level with your manager and coaches?

6.8.1 New features: 2 smileys (Coach/Manager)

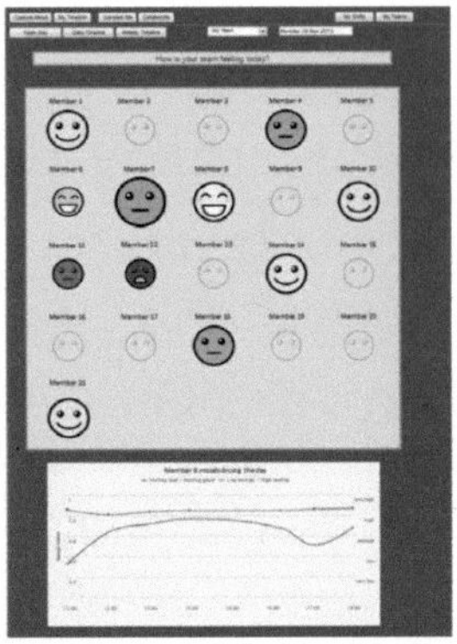

The following questions refer to the concrete features that the MoodMap App offers.

	strongly disagree	disagree	neutral	agree	strongly agree
The "My Teams" views makes me aware of the feeling and energy levels of each of my team members.	○	○	○	○	○
The "My Teams" views helps me gain insights about my team members and their work.	○	○	○	○	○
The "My Teams" views give me insights where my team members have some coaching needs.	○	○	○	○	○
The "My Teams" views are used to support directly the coaching sessions for my team members.	○	○	○	○	○

6.8.2 New features 3: my teams (Coach/Manager)

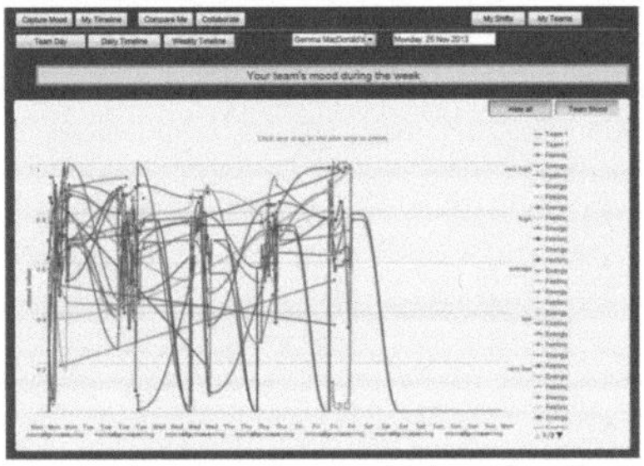

The following questions refer to the concrete features that the MoodMap App offers.

	strongly disagree	disagree	neutral	agree	strongly agree
The "My Teams" views give me insights about the development of the feeling and energy level during a week.	○	○	○	○	○
The "My Teams" views show me when there is need to take actions to increase the team's energy and feeling level.	○	○	○	○	○

6.8.3 New features 4: pie chart (Coach/Manager)

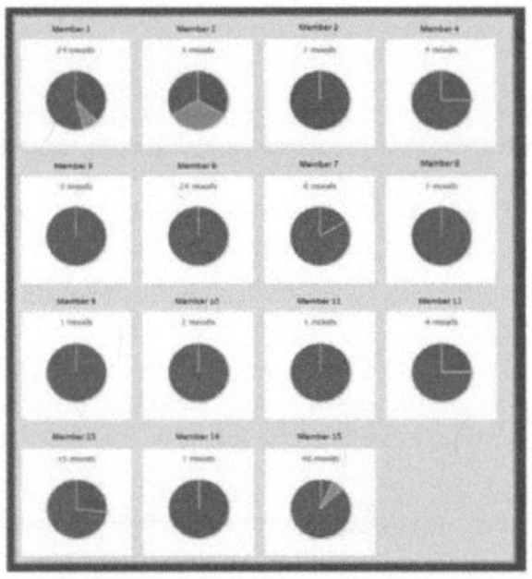

The following questions refer to the concrete features that the MoodMap App offers.

	strongly disagree	disagree	neutral	agree	strongly agree
The "My Teams" views help me to identify in which situations my team members captured their moods.	○	○	○	○	○
The "My Teams" views help me to identify how the moods of my advisors were in certain situations (e.g. after a call, a coaching session, etc.).	○	○	○	○	○

6.9 Reflection levels

	strongly disagree	disagree	neutral	agree	strongly agree
After using the MoodMap App, I made a conscious decision about how to behave in the future.	○	○	○	○	○

Which decisions did you take? Can you give any example?

	strongly disagree	disagree	neutral	agree	strongly agree
After using the MoodMap App, I gained a deeper understanding of my work life.	○	○	○	○	○

In which aspects did you gained a deeper understanding or learned something about your work?

	strongly disagree	disagree	neutral	agree	strongly agree
The app helped me to improve my work performance (e.g. during the shift, after customer's calls, during and after coaching sessions, during team meetings or in other situations).	○	○	○	○	○

In which aspects and situations could you improve your work performance?

	strongly disagree	disagree	neutral	agree	strongly agree
After using the MoodMap App within a coaching session, I made a conscious decision about how to behave in the future.	○	○	○	○	○

Which decisions did you take? Can you give any example?

6.9.1.1 Reflection levels (Coach)

	strongly disagree	disagree	neutral	agree	strongly agree
After using the MoodMap App within a coaching session as a coach, I made a conscious decision about how to behave in the future.	○	○	○	○	○

Which decisions did you take? Can you give any example?

	strongly disagree	disagree	neutral	agree	strongly agree
Did you notice any improvements in the work performance of your advisors since you started using the MoodMap App?	○	○	○	○	○

6.9.2.1 Reflection levels (Manager)

	strongly disagree	disagree	neutral	agree	strongly agree
After using the MoodMap App within a team meeting, I made a conscious decision about how to behave in the future.	○	○	○	○	○

Which decisions did you take? Can you give any example?

	strongly disagree	disagree	neutral	agree	strongly agree
Did you notice any improvements in the work performance of your advisors since you started using the MoodMap App?	○	○	○	○	○

6.10 Reflection levels 2

	strongly disagree	disagree	neutral	agree	strongly agree
I am satisfied with the the MoodMap App.	○	○	○	○	○
I see the long-term advantage of using the app in my work-life.	○	○	○	○	○
I would like to use the app continuously as part of my work-life.	○	○	○	○	○
It is practical for me to continue using the app in my work-life.	○	○	○	○	○
With the MoodMap App, I was more motivated to reflect on work in general.	○	○	○	○	○

Collaboratively, the MoodMap App ...

	strongly disagree	disagree	neutral	agree	strongly agree

... increased our ability to reflect.	○	○	○	○	○
... helped us to deal with our emotions.	○	○	○	○	○
... improved our coaching sessions.	○	○	○	○	○

6.11 Usage

	strongly disagree	disagree	neutral	agree	strongly agree
I did not have the time to use the MoodMap App.	○	○	○	○	○
I did not have the physical space (e.g.,necessary privacy) to use the MoodMap App.	○	○	○	○	○
I did not see an advantage in using the MoodMap App.	○	○	○	○	○
I was not motivated to use the MoodMap App.	○	○	○	○	○
The MoodMap App was intuitive and easy to use without the need for guidance..	○	○	○	○	○
I need more formal training with the MoodMap App.	○	○	○	○	○

What were other barriers to using the MoodMap App?

Data gathering with the MoodMap App was ...

	strongly disagree	disagree	neutral	agree	strongly agree
... accurate.	○	○	○	○	○
... effortless.	○	○	○	○	○
... relevant.	○	○	○	○	○
... timely.	○	○	○	○	○

6.12 Recommendation/Future Use

Recommendation

How likely is it that you would recommend the MMA to a friend or colleague?

not at all likely — neutral — extremely likely

I could imagine using the MoodMap App in the future for myself...

- ○ ...regularly.
- ○ ...from time to time.
- ○ ...if my manager or coach think it is important.
- ○ ...if my colleagues attach importance to it.
- ○ ...not at all.

7 Satisfaction

How satisfied are you with your coaching sessions?

Please answer the following question on a scale from 1 = very dissatisfied to 5 = very satisfied.

1	2	3	4	5
○	○	○	○	○

Please indicate your agreement to the following questions.

	strongly disagree	disagree	neutral	agree	strongly agree
My coaching sessions cover all my coaching needs.	○	○	○	○	○
Being aware of my emotions during customer calls helps me to reduce my customer repeats.	○	○	○	○	○

Please indicate your agreement to the following sentences.

	strongly disagree	disagree	neutral	agree	strongly agree
I'm generally aware of the coaching needs my teams have.	○	○	○	○	○
I can observe that the work processes are changing on the basis of the feedback from employees.	○	○	○	○	○
Reflecting on how I feel helps me to improve my work performance.	○	○	○	○	○
Reflecting and discussing on how we feel improves our team performance.	○	○	○	○	○
Reflecting on my work helps us to improve our customer satisfaction.	○	○	○	○	○
Reflecting on my emotions helps us to improve our customer satisfaction.	○	○	○	○	○

Did you recognise any improvements in the attitude of your manager with you?

Did you recognise any improvements in the attitude of your manager with the whole team?

Did you recognise any improvements in the attitude of your coach with you?

8 Final comments

Do you have any further comments on the MoodMap App or about this evaluation?

9 Final page

You have reached the end of the survey.

Many thanks for taking part in the study.
You may now close this window.

B. Live Interest Meter – Summative Evaluation I: Lecture at a German University

This appendix contains the questionnaires answered by the lecturer during the summative evaluation of the Live Interest Meter (see Section 6.8).

B.1. Pre-questionnaire

FZI

MIRROR

Questionnaire Live Interest Meter – LIM App

1. Your Participant Code

Please write down your Participant Code. Your code consists of the following 5 alphanumeric characters:

	The first letter of your place of birth	Your own day of birth (two digits)	The 1st letter of your father's first name	The 1st letter of your mother's first name
Your Code				

Example: A person born in **L**ondon on the **7**th of July, with parents named **J**ake and **S**ue would enter: "L" (for London) in the 1st blank, and "07" (for the birthday on the 7th) in the 2nd blank, "J" (for Jake) in the 3rd, and "S" (for Sue) in the 4th blank. So this person's code would be: L07JS.

2. Please write the current date (dd-mm-yyyy): ____________________

3. Your gender: ☐ male ☐ female

4. Your age group: ☐≤19 ☐20-29 ☐30-39 ☐40-49 ☐50-59 ☐≥60

5. Name of your lecture: ______________________

6. About your job

Department: ____________________

Position: ____________________

Scope: ☐Full-time ☐Part-time

Years in current and similar positions (altogether): _______ years

7. Please indicate your agreement with the following statements.

	strongly disagree	**disagree**	**neutral**	**agree**	**strongly agree**
I often reflect on my work in order to improve it.	O	O	O	O	O
We as a team often reflect on our work in order to improve it.	O	O	O	O	O
I think it is important to try to improve my presentation skills.	O	O	O	O	O
I frequently reflect on my lecture presentations.	O	O	O	O	O
Reflecting on held presentations helps me to improve my presentation skills in my lectures.	O	O	O	O	O
In team meetings we frequently talk about how we can improve our presentation skills.	O	O	O	O	O
Outside of meetings, I often talk with my colleagues about how to improve our presentation skills and hold a good presentation.	O	O	O	O	O
It is important to me to discuss frequently with others about how to improve our presentation skills and hold a good presentation.	O	O	O	O	O
Conversations with colleagues help me to improve my presentation skills.	O	O	O	O	O
Even a few days later, I can remember a certain lecture presentation well when I reflect on it by myself or with others.	O	O	O	O	O

Version 1.0 Page 1

8. Please evaluate the following sentences in relation to your lecture in this semester.

	strongly disagree	disagree	neutral	agree	strongly agree
I am in general satisfied with this lecture.	O	O	O	O	O
I am in general satisfied with my performance in my presentations.	O	O	O	O	O
I am satisfied with the participation of the students in my lecture.	O	O	O	O	O
I am satisfied with the interaction between me and my students.	O	O	O	O	O
I am satisfied with the motivation of my students for the lecture.	O	O	O	O	O
I am satisfied with the general attitude of the students during my lectures.	O	O	O	O	O

9. How many questions do you usually get from your students during your lecture?
- a. more than 3 in a session
- b. 2-3 questions per session
- c. 1 question every session
- d. less than 1 question every session
- e. 1 question during the whole semester
- f. never

10. Do your students give you general feedback or comments on your lecture?
- a. more than 3 in a session
- b. 2-3 comments per session
- c. once every session
- d. sometimes (less than once every session)
- e. once during the whole semester
- f. never

11. Please evaluate the following sentences in relation to this lecture and presentations.

	strongly disagree	disagree	neutral	agree	strongly agree
The speed/pace of my speech is always appropriate.	O	O	O	O	O
During my presentations and lectures I always speak clearly to my audience.	O	O	O	O	O
My vocal expressiveness (volume, pronunciation, tone) in my talks is adequate.	O	O	O	O	O
My speech is always fluent.	O	O	O	O	O
I always feel confident *before* my presentations and lectures.	O	O	O	O	O
I always feel confident *during* my presentations and lectures.	O	O	O	O	O
I always finish my presentations on time and achieve to present all the contents.	O	O	O	O	O
I always use clear examples in my presentations.	O	O	O	O	O

FZI

MIRROR

Questionnaire Live Interest Meter – LIM App

In my talks, I use a comprehensible/understandable speech.	O	O	O	O	O
My slides are always appropriate to my audience (format and style).	O	O	O	O	O
I always establish contact with my audience during the talk.	O	O	O	O	O
My audience is always motivated and interested in my talk.	O	O	O	O	O
My audience is always engaged and participates in my presentations.	O	O	O	O	O
I always establish eye-contact with my audience.	O	O	O	O	O
My presentations always have a very high quality and look professional.	O	O	O	O	O
I regularly collect feedback about my lectures and my performance.	O	O	O	O	O

12. Which specific feedback would you like to get from your students?

13. Which expectations do you have for a tool that gives you feedback about your lecture presentations?

14. In which aspects could the LIM App help you DURING and AFTER your lectures?

15. Which experiences do you have with getting feedback from your audience?

Many thanks for taking part in this study.

Version 1.0

Page 3

B.2. Post-questionnaire

FZI

MIRROR

Questionnaire Live Interest Meter – LIM App

1. Your Participant Code

Please write down your Participant Code. Your code consists of the following 5 alphanumeric characters:

	The first letter of your place of birth	Your own day of birth (two digits)	The 1st letter of your father's first name	The 1st letter of your mother's first name
Your Code				

Example: A person born in **L**ondon on the **7**th of July, with parents named **J**ake and **S**ue would enter: "L" (for London) in the 1st blank, and "07" (for the birthday on the 7th) in the 2nd blank, "J" (for Jake) in the 3rd, and "S" (for Sue) in the 4th blank. So this person's code would be: L07JS.

2. Please write the current date (dd-mm-yyyy): ____________________

3. Please indicate your agreement with the following statements.

	strongly disagree	disagree	neutral	agree	strongly agree
I often reflect on my work in order to improve it.	O	O	O	O	O
We as a team often reflect on our work in order to improve it.	O	O	O	O	O
I think it is important to try to improve my presentation skills.	O	O	O	O	O
I frequently reflect on my lecture presentations.	O	O	O	O	O
Reflecting on held presentations helps me to improve my presentation skills in my lectures.	O	O	O	O	O
In team meetings we frequently talk about how we can improve our presentation skills.	O	O	O	O	O
Outside of meetings, I often talk with my colleagues about how to improve our presentation skills and hold a good presentation.	O	O	O	O	O
It is important to me to discuss frequently with others about how to improve our presentation skills and hold a good presentation.	O	O	O	O	O
Conversations with colleagues help me to improve my presentation skills.	O	O	O	O	O
Even a few days later, I can remember a certain lecture presentation well when I reflect on it by myself or with others.	O	O	O	O	O

4. Please evaluate the following sentences in relation to your lecture.

	strongly disagree	disagree	neutral	agree	strongly agree
I am in general satisfied with this lecture.	O	O	O	O	O
I am in general satisfied with my performance in my presentations.	O	O	O	O	O

Version 1.0 Page 1

FZI MIRROR

Questionnaire Live Interest Meter – LIM App

I am satisfied with the participation of the students in my lecture.	O	O	O	O	O
I am satisfied with the interaction between me and my students.	O	O	O	O	O
I am satisfied with the motivation of my students for the lecture.	O	O	O	O	O
I am satisfied with the general attitude of the students during my lecture.	O	O	O	O	O

5. How many questions do you usually get from your students during your lecture?

a. more than 3 in a session
b. 2-3 questions per session
c. 1 question every session
d. less than 1 question every session
e. 1 question during the whole semester
f. never

6. Do your students give you general feedback or comments on your lecture?

a. more than 3 in a session
b. 2-3 comments per session
c. once every session
d. sometimes (less than once every session)
e. once during the whole semester
f. never

7. Please answer the following questions regarding your presentation skills and refer therefore to your presentations during the past weeks of this semester.

	strongly disagree	**disagree**	**neutral**	**agree**	**strongly agree**
The speed/pace of my speech is always appropriate.	O	O	O	O	O
During my presentations and lectures I always speak clearly to my audience.	O	O	O	O	O
My vocal expressiveness (volume, pronunciation, tone) in my talks is adequate.	O	O	O	O	O
My speech is always fluent.	O	O	O	O	O
I always feel confident *before* my presentations and lectures.	O	O	O	O	O
I always feel confident *during* my presentations and lectures.	O	O	O	O	O
I always finish my presentations on time and achieve to present all the contents.	O	O	O	O	O
I always use clear examples in my presentations.	O	O	O	O	O

Version 1.0 Page 2

FZI MIRROR

Questionnaire Live Interest Meter – LIM App

	strongly disagree	disagree	neutral	agree	strongly agree
In my talks, I use a comprehensible/understandable speech.	O	O	O	O	O
My slides are always appropriate to my audience (format and style).	O	O	O	O	O
I always establish contact with my audience during the talk.	O	O	O	O	O
My audience is always motivated and interested in my talk.	O	O	O	O	O
My audience is always engaged and participates in my presentations.	O	O	O	O	O
I always establish eye-contact with my audience.	O	O	O	O	O
My presentations always have a very high quality and look professional.	O	O	O	O	O
I regularly collect feedback about my lectures and my performance.	O	O	O	O	O

8. Please indicate your agreement with the following statements about the use of the LIM App.

	strongly disagree	disagree	neutral	agree	strongly agree
The LIM App helped me to remember and reconstruct experiences from my held lectures.	O	O	O	O	O
The LIM App helped me to reflect on experiences from my held lectures.	O	O	O	O	O
The LIM App helped me to collect information that triggered reflection about my held lectures.	O	O	O	O	O
The LIM App guided me in capturing information about my work experiences.	O	O	O	O	O
The LIM App helped me to become aware of my presentation skills.	O	O	O	O	O
The LIM App helped me to identify significant topics worth reflecting.	O	O	O	O	O
The LIM App helped me to reserve a space for reflection.	O	O	O	O	O
The LIM App helped me to gain a better understanding of my audience.	O	O	O	O	O
Capturing feedback during my presentations is useful to reflect and think about my presentation skills.	O	O	O	O	O

Version 1.0 Page 3

Seeing the development of the feedback in the timeline of the lecture reports helps me to remember and restructure what happened during my work.	O	O	O	O	O
The lecture reports were very useful to recall the presentations/lectures.	O	O	O	O	O
The visualization of the feedback (average and percentiles) in the timelines of the lecture reports were very useful to reflect on my work.	O	O	O	O	O
The lecture reports helped me to review the data.	O	O	O	O	O
The topics of interest showed in the histogram helped me to recall my past experiences.	O	O	O	O	O
The topics of interest showed in the histogram helped me to better reflect about a certain situation during the lecture or presentation.	O	O	O	O	O

9. Please indicate your agreement with the following statements about the use of the LIM App.

	strongly disagree	disagree	neutral	agree	strongly agree
I made a conscious decision about how to behave in the future during my lectures and presentations.	O	O	O	O	O
I gained a deeper understanding of my lectures and presentations.	O	O	O	O	O
The LIM App helped me to improve my performance in my lectures and presentations.	O	O	O	O	O
I am satisfied with the LIM App.	O	O	O	O	O
I see the long-term advantage of using the LIM App in my lectures and presentations.	O	O	O	O	O
I would like to use the LIM App continuously as part of my lectures and presentations.	O	O	O	O	O
It is practical for me to continue using the LIM App in my lectures and presentations.	O	O	O	O	O
With the LIM App, I was more motivated to reflect on work in general.	O	O	O	O	O

10. The following questions refer to possible barriers for using the LIM App. Please answer them freely and honestly as this gives us very valuable feedback.

	strongly disagree	disagree	neutral	agree	strongly agree
I did not have the time to use the LIM App.	O	O	O	O	O
I did not have the physical space (e.g. necessary privacy) to use the LIM App.	O	O	O	O	O
I did not see an advantage in using the LIM App.	O	O	O	O	O
I was not motivated to use the LIM App.	O	O	O	O	O
I could find out how the LIM App worked myself.	O	O	O	O	O
I need more formal training with the LIM App.	O	O	O	O	O

11. Data gathering with the LIM App was...

	strongly disagree	disagree	neutral	agree	strongly agree
… accurate.	O	O	O	O	O
… effortless.	O	O	O	O	O
… relevant.	O	O	O	O	O
… timely.	O	O	O	O	O

12. How likely is it that you would recommend the LIM App to a friend or colleague?
(Please mark your score with a circle)

0	1	2	3	4	5	6	7	8	9	10
not at all likely					neutral					extremely likely

If you have any final comments, remarks or suggestions, please feel free to write them down in the box below.

Thanks for your participation!

Bibliography

M. B. Ada. MyFeedBack: An interactive mobile Web 2.0 system for formative assessment and feedback. In *Second International Conference on e-Learning and e-Technologies in Education (ICEEE), 2013*, pages 98–103, September 2013. doi: 10.1109/ICeLeTE.2013.6644355. (Cited on page 254)

M. Akbari, G. Böhm, and U. Schroeder. Enabling Communication and Feedback in Mass Lectures. In *IEEE 10th International Conference on Advanced Learning Technologies (ICALT), 2010*, pages 254–258, July 2010. doi: 10.1109/ICALT.2010.76. (Cited on page 254)

M. Andergassen, V. Guerra, K. Ledermüller, and G. Neumann. Browser-Based Mobile Clickers: Implementation and Challenges. In *IADIS International Mobile Learning Conference, 11-13 March 2012, Berlin, Germany*, Berlin, Germany, March 2012. (Cited on page 253)

M. Andergassen, V. Guerra, K. Ledermüller, and G. Neumann. Development of a Browser-Based Mobile Audience Response System for Large Classrooms. *International Journal of Mobile and Blended Learning (IJMBL)*, 5(1):58–76, 2013. doi: 10.4018/jmbl.2013010104. (Cited on page 255)

E. B. Andrade, T. Odean, and S. Lin. Bubbling with Excitement: An Experiment. Working paper, University of California-Berkeley, 2012. URL `http://ssrn.com/abstract=2024549`. (Cited on pages 164 and 182)

D. Andre, R. Pelletier, J. Farringdon, S. Safier, W. Talbott, R. Stone, N. Vyas, J. Trimble, D. Wolf, S. Vishnubhatla, S. Boehmke, J. Stivoric, and A. Teller. The development of the SenseWear armband, a revolutionary energy assessment device to assess physical activity and lifestyle. White Papers BodyMedia, BodyMedia, 2006. URL `www.bodymedia.com`. Pittsburgh. (Cited on page 20)

P. J. Astor, M. T. P. Adam, C. Jähnig, and S. Seifert. Measuring Regret: Emotional Aspects of Auctions. In M. Reimann and O. Schilke, editors, *2011 NeuroPsychoEconomics Conference Proceedings*, page 27, Munich, Germany, 2011. URL `http://neuroeconomics-journal.com/upload/pdf/2011_NeuroPsychoEconomics_Conference_Proceedings.pdf`. (Cited on pages 164 and 183)

P. J. Astor, M. T. P. Adam, C. Jähnig, and S. Seifert. The joy of winning and the frustration of losing: A psychophysiological analysis of emotions in first-price sealed-bid auctions. *Journal of Neuroscience, Psychology, and Economics*, 6 (1):14–30, 2013. doi: 10.1037/a0031406. URL http://psycnet.apa.org/journals/npe/6/1/14. (Cited on pages 164 and 183)

P. J. Astor, M. T. P. Adam, P. Jercic, K. Schaaff, and C. Weinhardt. Integrating Biosignals into Information Systems: A NeuroIS Tool for Improving Emotion Regulation. *Journal of Management Information Systems*, 30(3):247–278, 2014. URL http://www.jmis-web.org/articles/v30_n3_p247/index.html. (Cited on page 183)

M. Barber and D. Njus. Clicker Evolution: Seeking Intelligent Design. *CBE-Life Sciences Education*, 6(1):1, 2007. doi: 10.1187/cbe.06-12-0206. (Cited on page 253)

R. F. Baumeister, K. D. Vohs, C. N. DeWall, and L. Zhang. How emotion shapes behavior: feedback, anticipation, and reflection, rather than direct causation. *Personality and social psychology review an official journal of the Society for Personality and Social Psychology Inc*, 11(2):167–203, 2007. URL http://www.ncbi.nlm.nih.gov/pubmed/18453461. (Cited on page 156)

G. Bell and J. Gemmell. *Your Life, Uploaded.* Plume, October 2010. ISBN 0452296560, 9780452296565. URL http://totalrecallbook.com/. (Cited on page 20)

M. Beutner, D. Kundisch, J. Magenheim, and A. Zoyke. Support, Supervision, Feedback and Lecturers Role in the use of the Classroom Response Systems PINGO. In *Proceedings of the E-LEARN 2014 - World Conference on E-Learning*, New Orleans, USA, 2014. (Cited on page 255)

S. Bødker, P. Ehn, D. Sjögren, and Y. Sundblad. Co-operative design – perspectives on 20 years with 'the scandinavian it design model'. In *Proceedings of NordiCHI 2000, Stockholm, October 2000*, Stockholm, Sweden, 2000. URL http://cid.nada.kth.se/pdf/cid_104.pdf. (Cited on page 4)

M. Bonn, S. Dieter, and H. Schmeck. Kooperationstools der Notebook Universität Karlsruhe (TH). In *Mobiles Lernen und Forschen*, pages 63–71. Klaus David, Lutz Wegener (Hrsg.), November 2003. Beiträge der Fachtagung an der Universität Kassel. (Cited on page 255)

D. Boud, R. Keogh, and D. Walker. *Reflection: Turning Experience into Learning*, chapter Promoting Reflection in Learning: a Model., pages 18–40. Routledge Falmer, New York, 1985. (Cited on pages xi, 1, 15, 16, 17, 25, 39, 45, 156, and 271)

S. Brave and C. Nass. *The Human-Computer Interaction Handbook*, chapter Emotion in human-computer interaction, pages 81–96. L. Erlbaum Associates Inc., Hillsdale, NJ, USA, 2003. ISBN 0-8058-3838-4. URL http://dl.acm.org/citation.cfm?id=772072.772081. (Cited on page 156)

A. P. Brief and H. M. Weiss. Organizational behavior: affect in the workplace. *Annual Review of Psychology*, 53(1):279–307, 2002. (Cited on page 156)

A. Brockbank and I. McGill. *Facilitating Reflective Learning in Higher Education*. Society for Research Into Higher Education. McGraw-Hill, 2007. ISBN 9780335220915. URL http://books.google.com/books?id=SmZSEWPcreUC. (Cited on page 1)

J. Brophy-Warren. The New Examined Life, Dec. 2008. URL http://online.wsj.com/article/SB122852285532784401.html. [Accessed January, 2015]. (Cited on page 19)

D. M. Bunce, E. A. Flens, and K. Y. Neiles. How long can students pay attention in class? a study of student attention decline using clickers. *Journal of Chemical Education*, 87(12):1438–1443, 2010. doi: 10.1021/ed100409p. URL http://pubs.acs.org/doi/abs/10.1021/ed100409p. (Cited on page 253)

V. Bush. As We May Think. *Atlantic Monthly*, 176(1):641–649, 1945. URL http://www.theatlantic.com/magazine/archive/1945/07/as-we-may-think/3881/. (Cited on page 19)

B. Byun, A. Awasthi, P. A. Chou, A. Kapoor, B. Lee, and M. Czerwinski. Honest signals in video conferencing. In *Proceedings of the 2011 IEEE International Conference on Multimedia and Expo*, ICME '11, pages 1–6, Washington, DC, USA, 2011. IEEE Computer Society. ISBN 978-1-61284-348-3. doi: 10.1109/ICME.2011.6011855. (Cited on page 158)

J. T. Cacioppo, R. E. Petty, and C. Feng Kao. The Efficient Assessment of Need for Cognition. *Journal of Personality Assessment*, 48(3):306–307, 1984. doi: 10.1207/s15327752jpa4803_13. PMID: 16367530. (Cited on page 175)

G. Caginalp, D. Porter, and V. L. Smith. Financial Bubbles: Excess Cash, Momentum, and Incomplete Information. *The Journal of Psychology and Financial Markets*, 2(2):80–99, 2001. (Cited on page 175)

J. E. Caldwell. Clickers in the large classroom: Current research and Best-Practice tips. *CBE Life Sci Educ*, 6(1):9–20, Mar. 2007. doi: 10.1187/cbe.06-12-0205. URL http://www.lifescied.org/cgi/content/abstract/6/1/9. (Cited on page 253)

A. Carmichael. Get your mood on, September 2012. URL http://quantifiedself.com/2012/12/get-your-mood-on-part-1. [Accessed January, 2015]. (Cited on page 156)

K. K. Cetina and A. Preda, editors. *The Sociology of Financial Markets*. Oxford University Press, Oxford [u.a.], 2005. ISBN 0199275599. (Cited on page 164)

E. K. Choe, N. B. Lee, B. Lee, W. Pratt, and J. A. Kientz. Understanding quantified-selfers' practices in collecting and exploring personal data. In *Proceedings of the SIGCHI Conference on Human Factors in Computing Systems*, CHI '14, pages 1143–1152, 2014. ISBN 978-1-4503-2473-1. doi: 10.1145/2556288.2557372. (Cited on pages 2, 18, 19, 35, 135, and 156)

K. Church, E. Hoggan, and N. Oliver. A study of mobile mood awareness and communication through mobimood. In *Proceedings of the 6th Nordic Conference on Human-Computer Interaction: Extending Boundaries*, NordiCHI '10, pages 128–137, New York, NY, USA, 2010. ACM. ISBN 978-1-60558-934-3. doi: 10.1145/1868914.1868933. (Cited on pages 134, 156, and 157)

J. B. Cohen, M. T. Pham, and E. B. Andrade. The Nature and Role of Affect in Consumer Behavior. pages 297–348, 2008. URL http://ssrn.com/abstract=1115521. (Cited on pages 163 and 164)

T. Colombino, B. Hanrahan, and S. Castellani. Lessons learnt working with performance data in call centres. In C. Rossitto, L. Ciolfi, D. Martin, and B. Conein, editors, *COOP 2014 - Proceedings of the 11th International Conference on the Design of Cooperative Systems, 27-30 May 2014, Nice (France)*, pages 277–292. Springer International Publishing, 2014. ISBN 978-3-319-06497-0. doi: 10.1007/978-3-319-06498-7_17. (Cited on pages 13, 48, and 136)

S. Consolvo, J. A. Landay, and D. W. McDonald. Designing for behavior change in everyday life. *Computer*, 42:86–89, 2009a. ISSN 0018-9162. doi: http://doi.ieeecomputersociety.org/10.1109/MC.2009.185. (Cited on page 36)

S. Consolvo, D. McDonald, and J. Landay. Theory-driven design strategies for technologies that support behavior change in everyday life. In *CHI '09*, pages 405–414. ACM, 2009b. (Cited on page 268)

J. Cousins. Get your mood on, September 2010. URL http://quantifiedself.com/2010/11/jon-cousins-on-moodscope. [Accessed January, 2015]. (Cited on page 156)

S. L. Curran, M. A. Andykowski, and J. L. Studts. Short Form of Profile of Mood States (POMS-SF): Psychometric information. *Psychological Assessment*, 7(1): 80–8348, 1995. (Cited on page 158)

M. W. Daudelin. Learning from experience through reflection. *Organizational Dynamics*, 24(3):36–48, 1996. (Cited on pages 15, 16, and 135)

F. D. Davis. Perceived usefulness, perceived ease of use, and user acceptance of information technology. *MIS Q.*, 13(3):319–340, Sept. 1989. ISSN 0276-7783. doi: 10.2307/249008. (Cited on pages 236 and 240)

M. De Choudhury and S. Counts. Understanding affect in the workplace via social media. In *Proceedings of the 2013 Conference on Computer Supported Cooperative Work*, CSCW '13, pages 303–316, New York, NY, USA, 2013. ACM. ISBN 978-1-4503-1331-5. doi: 10.1145/2441776.2441812. (Cited on pages 135, 156, and 159)

G. A. Debourgh. Use of classroom "clickers" to promote acquisition of advanced reasoning skills. *Nurse Education in Practice*, 8(2):76–87, 2008. (Cited on page 253)

S. Deterding, D. Dixon, R. Khaled, and L. Nacke. From Game Design Elements to Gamefulness: Defining "Gamification". In *Proceedings of the 15th International Academic MindTrek Conference: Envisioning Future Media Environments*, MindTrek '11, pages 9–15, New York, NY, USA, 2011. ACM. ISBN 978-1-4503-0816-8. doi: 10.1145/2181037.2181040. URL `http://doi.acm.org/10.1145/2181037.2181040`. (Cited on page 252)

J. Dewey. *Experience and Education*. Macmillan, London & New York, 1938. (Cited on page 15)

A. K. Dey. Understanding and using context. *Personal and Ubiquitous Computing*, 5:4–7, 2001. (Cited on page 30)

A. K. Dey and G. D. Abowd. Towards a better understanding of context and context-awareness. In *In HUC 1999: Proceedings of the 1st international symposium on Handheld and Ubiquitous Computing*, pages 304–307. Springer-Verlag, 1999. (Cited on page 31)

J. M. DiMicco. *Changing Small Group Interaction Through Visual Reflections of Social Behavior*. Massachusetts Institute of Technology, School of Architecture and Planning, Program in Media Arts and Sciences, 2005. URL `http://books.google.de/books?id=1_sRtwAACAAJ`. (Cited on page 158)

M. Dufwenberg, T. Lindqvist, and E. Moore. Bubbles and experience: An experiment. *American Economic Review*, 95(5):1731–1737, 2005. doi: 10.1257/000282805775014362. URL `http://www.aeaweb.org/articles.php?doi=10.1257/000282805775014362`. (Cited on page 168)

K. Dullemond, B. v. Gameren, M.-A. Storey, and A. v. Deursen. Fixing the "out of Sight out of Mind" Problem: One year of mood-based microblogging in a distributed software team. In *Proceedings of the 10th Working Conference on Mining Software Repositories*, MSR '13, pages 267–276, 2013. ISBN 978-1-4673-2936-1. URL `http://dl.acm.org/citation.cfm?id=2487085.2487138`. (Cited on pages 135 and 159)

D. Duncan and E. Mazur. *Clickers in the Classroom: How to Enhance Science Teaching Using Classroom Response Systems*. Pearson Education, 2005. ISBN 9780805387285. URL `http://books.google.de/books?id=f5oYAAAACAAJ`. (Cited on pages 186 and 253)

M. Eraut and W. Hirsh. The significance of workplace learning for individuals, groups and organisations, Dec. 2007. URL `http://www.skope.ox.ac.uk/publications/significance-workplace-learning-individuals-groups-and-organisations`. (Cited on pages 1 and 13)

L. Feiten, K. Weber, and B. Becker. SMILE: Smartphones in der Lehre - ein Rck- und berblick. In *GI-Jahrestagung '13*, pages 255–269, 2013. (Cited on page 254)

M. Fenton-O'Creevy, E. Soane, N. Nicholson, and P. Willman. Thinking, feeling and deciding: the influence of emotions on the decision making and performance of traders. *Journal of Organizational Behavior*, 32(8):1044–1061, 2011. URL `http://eprints.lse.ac.uk/36157/`. (Cited on pages 163 and 164)

R. Ferguson. Learning Analytics: Drivers, Developments and Challenges. *International Journal of Technology Enhanced Learning*, 4(5/6):304–317, Jan. 2012. ISSN 1753-5255. doi: 10.1504/IJTEL.2012.051816. (Cited on page 37)

R. Ferguson, S. B. Shum, and R. D. Crick. EnquiryBlogger: using widgets to support awareness and reflection in a PLE Setting. In *ARPLE11, PLE Conference 2011, Southampton, UK, 11-13 July*, 2011. URL `http://oro.open.ac.uk/30598/`. (Cited on page 262)

A. Fessl, V. Rivera-Pelayo, L. Müller, V. Pammer, and S. Lindstaedt. Motivation and user acceptance of using physiological data to support individual reflection. In *2nd International Workshop on Motivational and Affective Aspects in Technology Enhanced Learning (MATEL '11)*, 2011. URL `http://ceur-ws.org/Vol-957/matel11_submission_5.pdf`. (Cited on page 87)

A. Fessl, V. Rivera-Pelayo, V. Pammer, and S. Braun. Mood Tracking in Virtual Meetings. In A. Ravenscroft, S. Lindstaedt, C. Delgado-Kloos, and D. Hernández-Leo, editors, *21st Century Learning for 21st Century Skills*, volume

7563 of *Lecture Notes in Computer Science*, pages 377–382. Springer Berlin Heidelberg, 2012. ISBN 978-3-642-33262-3. doi: 10.1007/978-3-642-33263-0_30. (Not cited.)

A. Fessl, G. Wesiak, V. Rivera-Pelayo, S. Feyertag, and V. Pammer. In-App Reflection Guidance for Workplace Learning. In *Design for Teaching and Learning in a networked World - Proceedings of the 10th European Conference on Technology Enhanced Learning (EC-TEL '15)*. September 2015. To appear. (Not cited.)

L. Festinger. *A theory of cognitive dissonance*. Stanford Univ. Press, 1957. (Cited on pages 17 and 268)

M. Fishbein and I. Ajzen. *Belief, Attitude, Intention, and Behavior: An Introduction to Theory and Research*. Addison-Wesley, Reading, MA, 1975. URL `http://people.umass.edu/aizen/f&a1975.html`. (Cited on pages 236 and 240)

R. Fleck. Supporting reflection on experience with SenseCam. In *CHI Workshop on Designing for Reflection on Experience*, 2009. URL `http://www.comp.lancs.ac.uk/~corina/CHI09Workshop/Papers/Fleck.pdf`. (Cited on page 1)

R. Fleck and G. Fitzpatrick. Teachers' and tutors' social reflection around sensecam images. *Int. J. Hum.-Comput. Stud.*, 67(12):1024–1036, Dec. 2009. ISSN 1071-5819. doi: 10.1016/j.ijhcs.2009.09.004. (Cited on page 39)

R. Fleck and G. Fitzpatrick. Reflecting on reflection: framing a design landscape. In *Proceedings of the 22nd Conference of the Computer-Human Interaction Special Interest Group of Australia on Computer-Human Interaction*, OZCHI '10, pages 216–223, New York, NY, USA, 2010. ACM. ISBN 978-1-4503-0502-0. doi: 10.1145/1952222.1952269. (Cited on page 37)

B. Fogg. *Persuasive technology: Using Computers to Change What We Think and Do*. Morgan Kaufmann Publishers, 2003. (Cited on page 39)

N. Frijda. Emotions and episodes. Moods and sentiments. In P. Ekman and R. J. Davidson, editors, *The nature of emotion*, pages 59–67. Oxford University Press, 1994. (Cited on page 156)

J. Froehlich, T. Dillahunt, P. Klasnja, J. Mankoff, S. Consolvo, B. Harrison, and J. A. Landay. Ubigreen: Investigating a mobile tool for tracking and supporting green transportation habits. In *Proceedings of the SIGCHI Conference on Human Factors in Computing Systems*, CHI '09, pages 1043–1052, 2009. ISBN 978-1-60558-246-7. doi: 10.1145/1518701.1518861. (Cited on page 36)

O. García, J. Favela, and R. Machorro. Emotional awareness in collaborative systems. In *Proceedings of the String Processing and Information Retrieval Symposium & International Workshop on Groupware*, SPIRE '99, 1999. ISBN 0-7695-0268-7. URL `http://dl.acm.org/citation.cfm?id=519452.830798`. (Cited on pages 45 and 136)

J. J. Garrett. Ajax: A New Approach to Web Applications, February 2005. URL `http://www.adaptivepath.com/ideas/ajax-new-approach-web-applications/`. [Accessed January, 2015]. (Cited on page 72)

G. K. Gay, J. P. Pollak, P. Adams, and J. P. Leonard. Pilot study of Aurora, a social, mobile-phone-based emotion sharing and recoring system. *Journal of Diabetes Science and Technology*, 5(2):325–332, March 2011. ISSN 1932-2968. (Cited on page 157)

J. Gemmell, G. Bell, and R. Lueder. MyLifeBits: a personal database for everything. *Communications of the ACM (CACM)*, 49(1):88–95, January 2006. URL `http://research.microsoft.com/apps/pubs/default.aspx?id=64157`. also as MSR-TR-2006-23. (Cited on pages 19 and 20)

H. Gimpel, M. Nissen, and R. A. Görlitz. Quantifying the Quantified Self: A Study on the Motivations of Patients to Track Their Own Health. In *ICIS 2013 Proceedings (International Conference on Information Systems)*, 2013. URL `http://aisel.aisnet.org/icis2013/proceedings/HealthcareIS/3/`. (Cited on pages 2, 35, and 133)

S. Govaerts, K. Verbert, E. Duval, and A. Pardo. The student activity meter for awareness and self-reflection. In *CHI '12 Extended Abstracts on Human Factors in Computing Systems*, CHI EA '12, pages 869–884, New York, NY, USA, 2012. ACM. ISBN 978-1-4503-1016-1. doi: 10.1145/2212776.2212860. (Cited on page 262)

J. J. Gross and R. W. Levenson. Emotion elicitation using films. *Cognition & Emotion*, 9(1):87–108, 1995. doi: 10.1080/02699939508408966. (Cited on pages 164 and 182)

J. Hadersberger, A. Pohl, and F. Bry. Discerning actuality in backstage - comprehensible contextual aging. In *EC-TEL*, pages 126–139, 2012. doi: 10.1007/978-3-642-33263-0_11. (Cited on pages 186 and 254)

A. Hariharan, F. Teschner, P. J. Astor, and M. T. P. Adam. Incorporating Emotional Information in Decision Systems. In *Emotion Representations and Modelling for HCI Systems, Lecture Notes in Computer Science*, Sydney, Australia, 2013. (Cited on pages 164 and 183)

S. G. Hart. NASA-Task Load Index (NASA-TLX); 20 Years Later. *Proceedings of the Human Factors and Ergonomics Society Annual Meeting*, 50(9):904–908, 2006. doi: 10.1177/154193120605000909. URL `http://pro.sagepub.com/content/50/9/904.abstract.` (Cited on page 213)

J. Healey, L. Nachman, S. Subramanian, J. Shahabdeen, and M. Morris. Out of the lab and into the fray: Towards modeling emotion in everyday life. In P. Floréen, A. Krüger, and M. Spasojevic, editors, *Pervasive Computing*, volume 6030 of *Lecture Notes in Computer Science*, pages 156–173. Springer Berlin Heidelberg, 2010. ISBN 978-3-642-12653-6. doi: 10.1007/978-3-642-12654-3_10. (Cited on page 157)

A. Hendriks. SoPHIE - Software Platform for Human Interaction Experiments. Working paper, University of Osnabrueck, 2012. (Cited on page 171)

S. Hodges, L. Williams, E. Berry, S. Izadi, J. Srinivasan, A. Butler, G. Smyth, N. Kapur, and K. Wood. SenseCam: A Retrospective Memory Aid. In *Proceedings of the 8th International Conference of Ubiquitous Computing (UbiComp 2006)*, pages 177–193. Springer Verlag, September 2006. URL `http://research.microsoft.com/apps/pubs/default.aspx?id=132537.` (Cited on pages 20 and 39)

R. Hogarth, M. Portell, A. Cuxart, and G. I. Kolev. Emotion and reason in everyday risk perception. Economics Working Papers 1108, Department of Economics and Business, Universitat Pompeu Fabra, Sept. 2008. URL `http://ideas.repec.org/p/upf/upfgen/1108.html.` (Cited on page 183)

T. Holocher-Ertl, C. Kunzmann, L. Müller, V. Rivera-Pelayo, and A. P. Schmidt. Motivational and Affective Aspects in Technology Enhanced Learning: Topics, Results and Research Route. In D. Hernández-Leo, T. Ley, R. Klamma, and A. Harrer, editors, *Scaling up Learning for Sustained Impact - Proceedings of the 8th European Conference on Technology Enhanced Learning (EC-TEL '13)*, volume 8095 of *Lecture Notes in Computer Science*, pages 460–465. Springer Berlin Heidelberg, 2013. ISBN 978-3-642-40813-7. doi: 10.1007/978-3-642-40814-4_39. (Not cited.)

A. C. Holzer, S. Govaerts, J. Ondrus, A. Vozniuk, D. Rigaud, and B. Garbinato. SpeakUp A Mobile App Facilitating Audience Interaction. In *The 12th International Conference on Web-based Learning*, 2013. (Cited on page 254)

S. Høyrup. Reflection as a core process in organisational learning. *Journal of Workplace Learning*, 16(8):442–454, 2004. ISSN 1366-5626. doi: 10.1108/13665620410566414. (Cited on page 13)

G. Huisman, M. van Hout, E. van Dijk, T. van der Geest, and D. Heylen. Lemtool: Measuring emotions in visual interfaces. In *Proceedings of the SIGCHI Conference on Human Factors in Computing Systems*, CHI '13, pages 351–360, New York, NY, USA, 2013. ACM. ISBN 978-1-4503-1899-0. doi: 10.1145/2470654.2470706. (Cited on page 156)

E. Isaacs, A. Konrad, A. Walendowski, T. Lennig, V. Hollis, and S. Whittaker. Echoes from the past: How technology mediated reflection improves well-being. In *Proceedings of the SIGCHI Conference on Human Factors in Computing Systems*, pages 1071–1080. ACM, 2013. (Cited on page 36)

A. Isen, T. Nygren, and A. F.G. The influence of positive affect on the subjective utility of gains and losses: It is just not worth the risk. *Journal of Personality and Social Psychology*, 55:710–717, 1988. (Cited on page 173)

J. Itten. *Kunst der Farbe*. Otto Maier Verlag, Ravensburg, Germany, 1 edition, 1971. (Cited on pages 51, 58, and 165)

D. V. Jaarsveld and W. R. Poster. Call centers : emotional labor over the phone. *Emotional labor in the 21st century : diverse perspectives on the psychology of emotion regulation at work.*, 2013. (Cited on pages 47 and 48)

D. Johnson and P. Joyce. Bubbles and crashes revisited. *Review of Economics & Finance*, 2:29–42, 2012. URL `http://EconPapers.repec.org/RePEc:bap:journl:120303`. (Cited on page 168)

R. Kaiser and K. Oertel. Emotions in hci: An affective e-learning system. In *Proceedings of the HCSNet Workshop on Use of Vision in Human-computer Interaction - Volume 56*, VisHCI '06, pages 105–106, Darlinghurst, Australia, Australia, 2006. Australian Computer Society, Inc. URL `http://dl.acm.org/citation.cfm?id=1273385.1273402`. (Cited on page 158)

D. L. Kirkpatrick and J. D. Kirkpatrick. *Evaluating trainings programs: The four levels. 3rd Edition*. Berrett-Koehler Publishers, Inc., 2006. (Cited on pages 114, 116, 140, 240, and 241)

J. Klerkx, K. Verbert, and E. Duval. Enhancing learning with visualization techniques. In J. M. Spector, M. D. Merrill, J. Elen, and M. J. Bishop, editors, *Handbook of Research on Educational Communications and Technology*, pages 791–807. Springer New York, 2014. ISBN 978-1-4614-3184-8. (Cited on page 269)

K. Knipfer, D. Wessel, and K. DeLeeuw. Specification of Evaluation Methodology and Research Tooling. FP7 IP MIRROR Deliverable D1.5, June 2012. (Cited on pages 114, 139, 175, 237, and 240)

D. A. Kolb. *Experiential Learning: Experience as the source of learning and development*. Englewood Cliffs, N.J.: Prentice Hall, 1984. (Cited on pages 1 and 15)

B. R. Krogstie. Using project wiki history to reflect on the project process. In *Proceedings of the 42nd Hawaii International Conference on Systems Science (HICSS '09), Waikoloa, Big Island, HI, USA*, pages 1–10. IEEE Computer Society, January 2009. doi: 10.1109/HICSS.2009.496. (Cited on page 37)

B. R. Krogstie. MIRROR Scenarios and Requirements. FP7 IP MIRROR Deliverable D1.3, October 2011. (Cited on page 46)

B. R. Krogstie, M. Prilla, D. Wessel, K. Knipfer, and V. Pammer. Computer support for reflective learning in the workplace: A model. In *Proceedings of the 2012 IEEE International Conference on Advanced Learning Technologies (ICALT '12)*, pages 151–153. IEEE, 2012. (Cited on pages 14 and 37)

B. R. Krogstie, M. Prilla, and V. Pammer. Understanding and Supporting Reflective Learning Processes in the Workplace: The CSRL Model. In D. Hernández-Leo, T. Ley, R. Klamma, and A. Harrer, editors, *Scaling up Learning for Sustained Impact - Proceedings of the 8th European Conference on Technology Enhanced Learning (EC-TEL '13)*, volume 8095 of *Lecture Notes in Computer Science*, pages 151–164. Springer Berlin Heidelberg, 2013. ISBN 978-3-642-40813-7. doi: 10.1007/978-3-642-40814-4_13. (Cited on pages xi, 1, 37, and 38)

C. M. Kuhnen and B. Knutson. The Neural Basis of Financial Risk Taking. *Neuron*, 47(5):763–770, 2005. doi: 10.1016/j.neuron.2005.08.008. URL `http://www.cell.com/neuron/abstract/S0896-6273(05)00657-4`. (Cited on page 183)

D. Kundisch, P. Herrmann, M. Whittaker, M. Beutner, G. Fels, J. Magenheim, W. Reinhardt, M. Sievers, and A. Zoyke. Designing a web-based application to support peer instruction for very large groups. In *International Conference of Information Systems, Reserach in Progress*, Orlando, USA, December 2012. (Cited on pages 186, 253, 254, and 255)

I. Li, A. Dey, and J. Forlizzi. A Stage-based Model of Personal Informatics Systems. In *Proceedings of the SIGCHI Conference on Human Factors in Computing Systems*, CHI '10, pages 557–566, New York, NY, USA, 2010. ACM. ISBN 978-1-60558-929-9. doi: 10.1145/1753326.1753409. (Cited on pages 18, 32, 36, and 133)

I. Li, A. K. Dey, and J. Forlizzi. Understanding my data, myself: supporting self-reflection with ubicomp technologies. In *Proceedings of the 13th International Conference on Ubiquitous Computing*, UbiComp '11, pages 405–414, New York, NY, USA, 2011. ACM. ISBN 978-1-4503-0630-0. doi: 10.1145/2030112.2030166. (Cited on pages 29 and 36)

S. Loucks-Horsley, K. E. Stiles, S. Mundry, N. Love, and P. W. Hewson. *Designing Professional Development for Teachers of Science and Mathematics*. Thousand Oaks, CA: Corwin, 1998. (Cited on pages xiii and 273)

J. Maitland, S. Sherwood, L. Barkhuus, I. Anderson, M. Hall, B. Brown, M. Chalmers, and H. Muller. *Increasing the Awareness of Daily Activity Levels with Pervasive Computing*. Institute of Electrical and Electronics Engineers (IEEE), 2006. (Cited on pages 36 and 271)

G. Mark, S. Iqbal, M. Czerwinski, and P. Johns. Capturing the Mood: Facebook and Face-to-face Encounters in the Workplace. In *Proceedings of the 17th ACM Conference on Computer Supported Cooperative Work & Social Computing*, CSCW '14, pages 1082–1094, 2014. ISBN 978-1-4503-2540-0. doi: 10.1145/2531602.2531673. (Cited on page 159)

A. Matic, A. Popleteev, S. Gabrielli, V. Osmani, and O. Mayora. Happy or Moody? Why so? Monitoring Daily Routines at Work and Inferring Their Influence on Mood. *5th UbiHealth Workshop in conjunction with UBICOMP 2010 Conference, Copenhagen, Denmark*, 2010. URL `http://www.create-net.org/ubint/ubihealth/papers/Matic_HappyOrMoody.pdf`. (Cited on page 158)

E. Mazur. *Peer Instruction: A User's Manual*. Series in Educational Innovation. Prentice Hall, 1997. URL `http://mazur-www.harvard.edu/publications.php?function=display&rowid=0`. (Cited on page 255)

J. McCarthy and P. Wright. *Technology As Experience*. The MIT Press, 2004. ISBN 0262134470. (Cited on page 135)

D. McDuff, A. Karlson, A. Kapoor, A. Roseway, and M. Czerwinski. AffectAura: an intelligent system for emotional memory. In *Proceedings of the 2012 ACM annual conference on Human Factors in Computing Systems*, CHI '12, pages 849–858, 2012. ISBN 978-1-4503-1015-4. doi: 10.1145/2207676.2208525. (Cited on pages 36, 135, and 156)

H. M. Mentis, M. Reddy, and M. B. Rosson. Concealment of emotion in an emergency room: Expanding design for emotion awareness. *Computer Supported Cooperative Work (CSCW)*, 22(1):33–63, 2013. ISSN 0925-9724. doi: 10.1007/s10606-012-9174-2. (Cited on page 48)

Moodscope. Moodscope, 2011. URL `http://www.moodscope.com`. (Cited on page 34)

J. A. Moon. *Reflection in Learning and Professional Development: Theory and Practice*. Routledge, 1999. ISBN 9780749428648. (Cited on pages 15 and 16)

S. Mora, V. Rivera-Pelayo, and L. Müller. Supporting Mood Awareness in Collaborative Settings. In *Proceedings of the 7th International Conference on Collaborative Computing: Networking, Applications and Worksharing (CollaborateCom '11)*, pages 268–277, October 2011. (Cited on page 78)

M. E. Morris, Q. Kathawala, T. K. Leen, E. E. Gorenstein, F. Guilak, M. Labhard, and W. Deleeuw. Mobile Therapy: Case Study Evaluations of a Cell Phone Application for Emotional Self-Awareness. *Journal of Medical Internet Research*, 12:10, 2010. (Cited on pages 36, 156, and 157)

B. S. Morschheuser, V. Rivera-Pelayo, A. Mazarakis, and V. Zacharias. Gamifying Quantified Self Approaches for Learning: an Experiment with the Live Interest Meter. In *Learning and Diversity in the Cities of the Future. Proceedings of the 4th International Conference on Personal Learning Environments, PLE Conference '13*, pages 66–78. Logos Verlag Berlin, 2014a. ISBN 978-3-8325-3811-8. URL `http://www.logos-verlag.de/cgi-bin/buch/isbn/3811`. (Cited on page 252)

B. S. Morschheuser, V. Rivera-Pelayo, A. Mazarakis, and V. Zacharias. Interaction and Reflection with Quantified Self and Gamification: an Experimental Study. *Journal of Literacy and Technology*, 15(2):136–156, 2014b. URL `http://www.literacyandtechnology.org/volume-15-number-2-june-2014.html`. (Cited on page 252)

L. Müller. Pervasive monitoring to support reflective learning. In *Proceedings of the 2013 ACM conference on Pervasive and ubiquitous computing adjunct publication*, pages 349–354. ACM, 2013. (Cited on page 39)

L. Müller. *From Context to Content: Designing Sensor Support for Reflective Learning*. PhD thesis, Karlsruhe Institute of Technology, November 2014. (Cited on pages 39 and 268)

L. Müller, B. Krogstie, and A. Schmidt. Towards capturing learning experiences. In *ConTEL: Theory, methodology and design, EC-TEL '11*, 2011a. (Cited on pages 31 and 32)

L. Müller, V. Rivera-Pelayo, C. Kunzmann, and A. Schmidt. From Stress Awareness to Coping Strategies of Medical Staff: Supporting Reflection on Physiological Data. In A. A. Salah and B. Lepri, editors, *Human Behavior Understanding*, volume 7065 of *Lecture Notes in Computer Science*, pages 93–103. Springer Berlin Heidelberg, 2011b. ISBN 978-3-642-25445-1. doi: 10.1007/978-3-642-25446-8_11. (Cited on pages 39 and 159)

L. Müller, V. Rivera-Pelayo, and A. Schmidt. User studies, requirements, and design studies for capturing learning experiences. FP7 IP MIRROR Deliverable D3.1, June 2011c. (Cited on pages 32 and 106)

L. Müller, V. Rivera-Pelayo, and S. Heuer. Persuasion and reflective learning: closing the feedback loop. In *Persuasive Technology. Design for Health and Safety*, pages 133–144. Springer, 2012. (Cited on page 39)

L. Müller, M. Divitini, S. Mora, V. Rivera-Pelayo, and W. Stork. Context Becomes Content: Sensor Data for Computer-Supported Reflective Learning. *IEEE Transactions on Learning Technologies*, 8(1):111–123, January 2015. ISSN 1939-1382. doi: 10.1109/TLT.2014.2377732. (Cited on page 275)

M. J. Muller, J. H. Haslwanter, and T. Dayton. Participatory practices in the software lifecycle. *Handbook of human-computer interaction*, 2:255–297, 1997. (Cited on page 4)

P. Munday. "GoSoapBox Classroom Response System Engages Students". *EDUCAUSE Review Online*, November 2012. URL `http://www.educause.edu/ero/article/gosoapbox-classroom-response-system-engages-students`. (Cited on pages 226 and 257)

V. Pammer and M. Bratic. Surprise, surprise: Activity log based time analytics for time management. In *CHI '13 Extended Abstracts on Human Factors in Computing Systems*, CHI EA '13, pages 211–216, New York, NY, USA, 2013. ACM. ISBN 978-1-4503-1952-2. doi: 10.1145/2468356.2468395. (Cited on page 38)

A. M. Passarelli and D. A. Kolb. The Learning Way: Learning from Experience as the Path to Lifelong Learning and Development. 2012. (Cited on page 1)

F. Pfeiffer-Bohnen, F. Kern, L. König, and H. Schmeck. nuKIT an Interactive Communication Tool via Smartphone Technologies. In J. Herrington, A. Couros, and V. Irvine, editors, *Proceedings of World Conference on Educational Multimedia, Hypermedia and Telecommunications 2013*, pages 339–349, Victoria, Canada, June 2013. AACE. URL `http://www.editlib.org/p/111978`. (Cited on page 256)

M. T. Pham. Representativeness, relevance, and the use of feelings in decision making. *Journal of Consumer Research*, 25(2):144–59, 1998. URL `http://EconPapers.repec.org/RePEc:ucp:jconrs:v:25:y:1998:i:2:p:144-59`. (Cited on page 182)

M. Prilla. User and group behavior in computer support for collaborative reflection in practice: An explorative data analysis. In C. Rossitto, L. Ciolfi, D. Martin, and B. Conein, editors, *COOP 2014 - Proceedings of the 11th International Conference on the Design of Cooperative Systems, 27-30 May 2014, Nice (France)*, pages 293–309. Springer International Publishing, 2014. ISBN 978-3-319-06497-0. doi: 10.1007/978-3-319-06498-7_18. (Cited on page 39)

M. Prilla and B. Renner. Supporting collaborative reflection at work: A comparative case analysis. In *Proceedings of ACM Conference on Group Work (GROUP '14)*. ACM, 2014. (Cited on pages 124 and 146)

M. Prilla, V. Pammer, and S. Balzert. The push and pull of reflection in workplace learning: Designing to support transitions between individual, collaborative and organisational learning. In *21st Century Learning for 21st Century Skills*, pages 278–291. Springer, 2012. (Cited on page 37)

M. Prilla, V. Pammer, and B. Krogstie. Fostering collaborative redesign of work practice: Challenges for tools supporting reflection at work. In O. W. Bertelsen, L. Ciolfi, M. A. Grasso, and G. A. Papadopoulos, editors, *ECSCW 2013: Proceedings of the 13th European Conference on Computer Supported Cooperative Work, 21-25 September 2013, Paphos, Cyprus*, pages 249–268. Springer London, 2013. ISBN 978-1-4471-5345-0. doi: 10.1007/978-1-4471-5346-7_13. (Cited on page 13)

K. Quibeldey-Cirkel, C. Thelen, P.-C. Volkmer, D. Gerhardt, D. Knapp, and J. Kammer. ARSnova: ein Audience Response System fr Inverted-Classroom-Szenarien mit Untersttzung von Just-in-Time Teaching und Peer Instruction 110. In A. Breiter and C. Rensing, editors, *DeLFI*, volume 218 of *LNI*, page 297. GI Gesellschaft für Informatik, 2013. ISBN 978-3-88579-612-1. URL `http://subs.emis.de/LNI/Proceedings/Proceedings218/article32.html`. (Cited on page 254)

K. K. Rachuri, C. Mascolo, P. J. Rentfrow, and C. Longworth. EmotionSense: A Mobile Phones based Adaptive Platform for Experimental Social Psychology Research. *International Studies*, pages 281–290, 2010. doi: 10.1145/1864349.1864393. (Cited on pages 36 and 157)

V. Rivera-Pelayo. Applying Quantified Self Approaches to Support Reflective Learning, September 2012. URL `https://www.academia.edu/7608381`. Doctoral Consortium Track at MobileHCI 2012, 21-24 Sept 2012, San Francisco, USA. (Not cited.)

V. Rivera-Pelayo and M. Kohaupt. Comparing Objective and Subjective Methods to Support Reflective Learning: an Experiment on the Influence on Affective Aspects. In T. Holocher-Ertl, C. Kunzmann, L. Müller, V. Rivera-Pelayo, A. P. Schmidt, and C. Wolf, editors, *Motivational and Affective Aspects in Technology Enhanced Learning (MATEL) : Proceedings of the MATEL Workshop 2013-2014*, volume 26. KIT, Karlsruhe, 2015. URL `http://nbn-resolving.org/urn:nbn:de:swb:90-480487`. (Not cited.)

V. Rivera-Pelayo, V. Zacharias, L. Müller, and S. Braun. Applying Quantified Self Approaches to Support Reflective Learning. In *Proceedings of the 2nd International Conference on Learning Analytics and Knowledge*, LAK '12, pages 111–114, New York, NY, USA, 2012a. ACM. ISBN 978-1-4503-1111-3. doi: 10.1145/2330601.2330631. (Cited on page 32)

V. Rivera-Pelayo, V. Zacharias, L. Müller, and S. Braun. A Framework for Applying Quantified Self Approaches to Support Reflective Learning. In I. Arnedillo Sánchez and P. Isaías, editors, *Proceedings of the IADIS International Conference Mobile Learning 2012, 11-13 March 2012, Berlin, Germany*, pages 123–131, 2012b. ISBN 978-972-8939-66-3. URL `http://www.iadisportal.org/digital-library/a-framework-for-applying-quantified-self-approaches-to-support-reflective-learning`. (Cited on page 32)

V. Rivera-Pelayo, J. Munk, V. Zacharias, and S. Braun. Live Interest Meter: Learning from Quantified Feedback in Mass Lectures. In *Proceedings of the Third International Conference on Learning Analytics and Knowledge*, LAK '13, pages 23–27, New York, NY, USA, April 2013a. ACM. ISBN 978-1-4503-1785-6. doi: 10.1145/2460296.2460302. (Cited on pages 213, 217, and 258)

V. Rivera-Pelayo, E. Lacić, V. Zacharias, and R. Studer. LIM App: Reflecting on Audience
T. Ley, R. Klamma, and A. Harrer, editors, *Scaling up Learning for Sustained Impact - Proceedings of the 8th European Conference on Technology Enhanced Learning (EC-TEL '13)*, volume 8095 of *Lecture Notes in Computer Science*, pages 514–519. Springer Berlin Heidelberg, September 2013b. ISBN 978-3-642-40813-7. doi: 10.1007/978-3-642-40814-4_48. (Cited on pages 227 and 258)

V. Rivera-Pelayo, P. J. Astor, A. Hendriks, and M. T. P. Adam. Investigating Reflective Learning in Trading: Mood Self-tracking in Financial Decision Making. Working paper, Karlsruhe Institute of Technology (KIT), 2015. (Cited on page 163)

V. Rivera-Pelayo, A. Fessl, L. Müller, and V. Pammer. Introducing Mood Self-Tracking at Work: Empirical Insights from Call Centers. Manuscript submitted for publication, in prep. (Cited on page 112)

J. Rooksby, M. Rost, A. Morrison, and M. Chalmers. Personal Tracking As Lived Informatics. In *Proceedings of the 32nd Annual ACM Conference on Human Factors in Computing Systems*, CHI '14, pages 1163–1172, New York, NY, USA, 2014. ACM. ISBN 978-1-4503-2473-1. doi: 10.1145/2556288.2557039. (Cited on pages 2, 35, 36, and 133)

G. Rubner. mbclick - an electronic voting system that returns individual feedback. In *IEEE Seventh International Conference on Wireless, Mobile and Ubiquitous Technology in Education (WMUTE), 2012*, pages 221–222, 2012. doi: 10.1109/WMUTE.2012.53. (Cited on pages 186 and 253)

J. A. Russell. A circumplex model of affect. *Journal of Personality and Social Psychology*, 39(6):1161–1178, 1980. ISSN 00223514. doi: 10.1037/h0077714.

URL http://content.apa.org/journals/psp/39/6/1161. (Cited on pages xi, 51, 52, 55, 58, 156, 157, 158, and 165)

J. A. Russell. Core affect and the psychological construction of emotion. *Psychological review*, 110(1):145–172, Jan. 2003. ISSN 0033-295X. URL http://view.ncbi.nlm.nih.gov/pubmed/12529060. (Cited on page 51)

T. Saari, K. Kallinen, M. Salminen, N. Ravaja, and K. Yanev. A Mobile System and Application for Facilitating Emotional Awareness in Knowledge Work Teams. In *Proceedings of the 41st Annual Hawaii International Conference on System Sciences (HICSS '08)*, pages 44–44. Ieee, January 2008. ISBN 0769530758. doi: 10.1109/HICSS.2008.31. URL http://ieeexplore.ieee.org/lpdocs/epic03/wrapper.htm?arnumber=4438748. (Cited on page 159)

J. L. Santos, S. Govaerts, K. Verbert, and E. Duval. Goal-oriented visualizations of activity tracking: a case study with engineering students. In *Proceedings of the 2nd International Conference on Learning Analytics and Knowledge*, LAK '12, pages 143–152, New York, NY, USA, 2012. ACM. ISBN 978-1-4503-1111-3. doi: 10.1145/2330601.2330639. (Cited on page 263)

N. Scheele, M. Mauve, W. Effelsberg, A. Wessels, H. Horz, and S. Fries. The Interactive Lecture - A new Teaching Paradigm Based on Ubiquitous Computing. In *Poster Proceeding of the CSCL 2003*, pages 135–137, 06 2003. (Cited on pages 254 and 256)

K. R. Scherer. What are emotions? And how can they be measured? *Social Science Information*, 44(4):695–729, 2005. ISSN 05390184. doi: 10.1177/0539018405058216. (Cited on page 156)

H. Schlosberg. Three dimensions of emotion. *Psychological Review,*, 61:81–88, 1954. (Cited on page 156)

A. Schmidt, C. Kunzmann, S. Braun, T. Holocher-Ertl, U. Cress, A. Mazarakis, L. Müller, and V. Rivera-Pelayo, editors. *Proceedings of the 2nd and 3rd International Workshops on Motivational and Affective Aspects*, volume 957 of *CEUR Workshop Proceedings*, MATEL 2011 and 2012, Palermo, Italy, Sep 20, 2011 and Saarbrücken, Germany, Sep 18, 2012, 2012. CEUR-WS.org. URL http://ceur-ws.org/Vol-957/. ISSN 1613-0073. (Not cited.)

E. J. Schoenberg and E. Haruvy. Relative performance information in asset markets: An experimental approach. *Journal of Economic Psychology*, 33(6):1143–1155, December 2012. URL http://ideas.repec.org/a/eee/joepsy/v33y2012i6p1143-1155.html. (Cited on pages 182 and 183)

D. A. Schön. *The Reflective Practitioner: How Professionals Think In Action.* Basic Books, 1 edition, 1984. (Cited on pages 59, 135, 226, and 263)

D. A. Schön. *Educating the Reflective Practitioner*. Jossey-Bass, San Fransisco, 1 edition, 1987. (Cited on pages 15 and 99)

A. J. Sellen and S. Whittaker. Beyond total capture: a constructive critique of lifelogging. *Communications of the ACM*, 53:70–77, May 2010. ISSN 0001-0782. doi: 10.1145/1735223.1735243. (Cited on page 28)

P. Sengers, K. Boehner, S. David, and J. J. Kaye. Reflective Design. In *Proceedings of the 4th Decennial Conference on Critical Computing: Between Sense and Sensibility*, CC '05, pages 49–58, New York, NY, USA, 2005. ACM. ISBN 1-59593-203-8. doi: 10.1145/1094562.1094569. (Cited on page 36)

S. B. Shum and R. Ferguson. Social learning analytics. *Journal of Educational Technology & Society*, 15(3), 2012. (Cited on page 37)

V. L. Smith, G. L. Suchanek, and A. W. Williams. Bubbles, Crashes, and Endogenous Expectations in Experimental Spot Asset Markets. *Econometrica*, 56(5):1119–51, September 1988. URL `http://ideas.repec.org/a/ecm/emetrp/v56y1988i5p1119-51.html`. (Cited on pages 163, 166, 167, and 168)

A. Ståhl, P. Sundström, and K. Höök. A foundation for emotional expressivity. In *Proceedings of the 2005 Conference on Designing for User eXperience*, DUX '05, New York, NY, USA, 2005. AIGA: American Institute of Graphic Arts. ISBN 1-59593-250-X. URL `http://dl.acm.org/citation.cfm?id=1138235.1138274`. (Cited on pages 51 and 58)

A. Ståhl, K. Höök, M. Svensson, A. S. Taylor, and M. Combetto. Experiencing the affective diary. *Personal Ubiquitous Comput.*, 13(5):365–378, June 2009. ISSN 1617-4909. doi: 10.1007/s00779-008-0202-7. (Cited on page 156)

K. Strampel and R. Oliver. Using technology to foster reflection in higher education. In R. Atkinson, C. McBeath, S. K. A. Soong, and C. Cheers, editors, *ICT: Providing choices for learners and learning. Proceedings ascilite Singapore 2007, Centre for Educational Development, Nanyang Technological University, Singapore*, pages 973–982, December 2007. URL `http://www.ascilite.org.au/conferences/singapore07/procs/strampel.pdf`. (Cited on pages 1 and 37)

D. A. Sugerman, K. L. Doherty, and D. E. Garvey. *Reflective learning: theory and practice*. Kendall/Hunt Pub. Co., 2000. ISBN 9780787265618. URL `http://books.google.com/books?id=lE-2vnmruGEC`. (Cited on page 1)

P. Sundström, A. Ståhl, and K. Höök. In Situ Informants Exploring an Emotional Mobile Messaging System in Their Everyday Practice. *International Journal of Human-Computer Studies*, 65(4):388–403, April 2007. ISSN 1071-5819. doi: 10.1016/j.ijhcs.2006.11.013. (Cited on page 157)

M. Swan. The Quantified Self: Fundamental Disruption in Big Data Science and Biological Discovery. *Big Data*, 1(2):85–89, June 2013. doi: 10.1089/big.2012.0002. (Cited on page 283)

J. Teevan, D. Liebling, A. Paradiso, C. Garcia Jurado Suarez, C. von Veh, and D. Gehring. Displaying mobile feedback during a presentation. In *Proceedings of the 14th International Conference on Human-computer Interaction with Mobile Devices and Services*, MobileHCI '12, pages 379–382, New York, NY, USA, 2012. ACM. ISBN 978-1-4503-1105-2. doi: 10.1145/2371574.2371633. (Cited on pages 186, 226, and 257)

E. R. Thompson. Development and Validation of an Internationally Reliable Short-Form of the Positive and Negative Affect Schedule (PANAS). *Journal of Cross-Cultural Psychology*, 38(2):227–242, Mar. 2007. ISSN 0022-0221. doi: 10.1177/0022022106297301. (Cited on page 158)

K. Tollmar, F. Bentley, and C. Viedma. Mobile Health Mashups: Making sense of multiple streams of wellbeing and contextual data for presentation on a mobile device. In *Pervasive Computing Technologies for Healthcare (PervasiveHealth), 2012 6th International Conference on*, pages 65–72, May 2012. (Cited on page 36)

V. Venkatesh and F. D. Davis. A theoretical extension of the technology acceptance model: Four longitudinal field studies. *Manage. Sci.*, 46(2):186–204, Feb. 2000. ISSN 0025-1909. doi: 10.1287/mnsc.46.2.186.11926. (Cited on pages 236 and 240)

F. Wang and M. J. Hannafin. Design-based research and technology-enhanced learning environments. *Educational Technology Research and Development*, 53(4): 5–23, 2005. ISSN 1042-1629. doi: 10.1007/BF02504682. (Cited on page 3)

D. Watson, L. A. Clark, and A. Tellegen. Development and validation of brief measures of positive and negative affect: the panas scales. *Journal of Personality and Social Psychology*, 54(6):1063–1070, 1988. URL http://www.ncbi.nlm.nih.gov/pubmed/3397865. (Cited on page 34)

A. Wessels, S. Fries, H. Horz, N. Scheele, and W. Effelsberg. Interactive lectures: Effective teaching and learning in lectures using wireless networks. *Comput. Hum. Behav.*, 23(5):2524–2537, Sept. 2007. ISSN 0747-5632. doi: 10.1016/j.chb.2006.05.001. (Cited on pages 254 and 256)

G. Wolf. Know Thyself: Tracking Every Facet of Life, from Sleep to Mood to Pain, 24/7/365. *Wired Magazine*, 2009. URL http://www.wired.com/medtech/health/magazine/17-07/lbnp_knowthyself?currentPage=all. (Cited on page 18)

G. Wolf. Our Three Prime Questions, September 2011. URL `http://quantifiedself.com/2011/09/our-three-prime-questions/`. [Accessed January, 2015]. (Cited on page 19)